A Technical Guide to
IPSec Virtual Private Networks

D1295415

OTHER AUERBACH PUBLICATIONS

A Standard for Auditing Computer Applications
Martin Krist
ISBN: 0-8493-9983-1

A Technical Guide to IPSec Virtual Private Networks
James S. Tiller
ISBN: 0-8493-0876-3

Analyzing Business Information Systems
Shouhong Wang
ISBN: 0-8493-9240-3

Broadband Networking
James Trulove, Editor
ISBN: 0-8493-9821-5

Communications Systems Management Handbook, 6th Edition
Anura Gurugé and
Lisa M. Lindgren, Editors
ISBN: 0-8493-9826-6

Computer Telephony Integration
William Yarberry, Jr.
ISBN: 0-8493-9995-5

Data Management Handbook 3rd Edition
Sanjiv Purba, Editor
ISBN: 0-8493-9832-0

Electronic Messaging
Nancy Cox, Editor
ISBN: 0-8493-9825-8

Enterprise Operations Management Handbook, 2nd Edition
Steve F. Blanding, Editor
ISBN: 0-8493-9824-X

Enterprise Systems Architectures
Andersen Consulting
ISBN: 0-8493-9836-3

Enterprise Systems Integration
John Wyzalek, Editor
ISBN: 0-8493-9837-1

Healthcare Information Systems
Phillip L. Davidson, Editor
ISBN: 0-8493-9963-7

Information Security Architecture
Jan Tudor Killmeyer
ISBN: 0-8493-9988-2

Information Security Management Handbook, 4th Edition, Volume 2
Harold F. Tipton and Micki Krause, Editors
ISBN: 0-8493-0800-3

IS Management Handbook, 7th Edition
Carol V. Brown, Editor
ISBN: 0-8493-9820-7

Information Technology Control and Audit
Frederick Gallegos, Sandra Allen-Senft,
and Daniel P. Manson
ISBN: 0-8493-9994-7

Internet Management
Jessica Keyes, Editor
ISBN: 0-8493-9987-4

Local Area Network Handbook, 6th Edition
John P. Slone, Editor
ISBN: 0-8493-9838-X

Multi-Operating System Networking: Living with UNIX, NetWare, and NT
Raj Rajagopal, Editor
ISBN: 0-8493-9831-2

The Network Manager's Handbook, 3rd Edition
John Lusa, Editor
ISBN: 0-8493-9841-X

Project Management
Paul C. Tinnirello, Editor
ISBN: 0-8493-9998-X

Effective Use of Teams in IT Audits,
Martin Krist
ISBN: 0-8493-9828-2

Systems Development Handbook, 4th Edition
Paul C. Tinnirello, Editor
ISBN: 0-8493-9822-3

AUERBACH PUBLICATIONS

www.auerbach-publications.com
TO Order: Call: 1-800-272-7737 • Fax: 1-800-374-3401
E-mail: orders@crcpress.com

A Technical Guide to
IPSec Virtual Private Networks

JAMES S. TILLER
CISSP, CCNA, CCDA, MCSE+I

AUERBACH

Boca Raton   London   New York   Washington, D.C.

Library of Congress Cataloging-in-Publication Data

Tiller, James S.
    A technical guide to IPSec virtual private networks / James S. Tiller.
        p.   cm.
    Includes bibliographical references and index.
    ISBN 0-8493-0876-3 (alk. paper)
    1. Extranets (Computer networks)--Security measures. 2. IPSec (Computer network
protocol) I. Title.

TK5105.875.E87 T55 2000
005.8--dc21

00-046759

Visit the Auerbach Web site at www.auerbach-publications.com

Dedication

To my loving wife Mary, daughter Rain, and son Phoenix. Without their support, sacrifice, and encouragement, I would have never realized my vision of writing this book.

Contents

Foreword

> If you reveal your secrets to the wind, you should not blame the wind for revealing them to the trees.

These are the words of the poet Kahlil Gibran, but they are relevant to any internetworking professional concerned about the unchecked influence of the Internet on data communications and security.

Do not blame the Internet for your problems. It is merely a meshed network that like the wind carries things, in this case bits and bytes of data, to isolated trees and islands of knowledge. How can you personally control the wind, or the Internet, or any public network? The answer is that you probably can not.

Here is another analogy. Back in the Wild West, bank robbing was pretty lucrative until real vaults came into being in the badlands. Then the heists usually resulted in a messy gunfight with five dollars grabbed out of the teller's drawer. Eventually, some enterprising Butch Cassidy-like rogue noticed that it would be much easier to grab the money while in transport, whether stagecoach or train, and that the ROI was much higher. The highwaymen of old and pirates of the Caribbean had caught on to the tactic centuries before.

Sure, you have secured your perimeter, built firewalls, created solid usage policies, good passwords, hardened your systems, dug a moat, whatever. Now what? Is it necessary to communicate with the rest of the world? You have probably been working on projects like E-commerce, Web access, remote salesforces, satellite offices, or looking for alternatives to expensive wide area networks. Uh-oh, you now have exposure to all kinds of scary scenarios.

Thank goodness there are options, tactics, tools, and methods for securing the integrity of the data you are transmitting. This is the best book to provide you with meaningful background, insight, and direction on one solution: the complex realm of IPSec and VPNs. I love this book for many reasons. One is that it is a technical guide but is written in plain old English. Hmmm, sounds simple, but there is an art to teaching a subject with the intricacies and granularity inherent in this book without spiking the reader's brainwaves. Jim is a gifted teacher and has done a great job of translating his topic to accommodate a wide range of audience skill sets.

Another reason I like the book is that you will not be skipping around trying to figure out what the author is talking about — a common occurrence in many technical books. Jim is a smart guy with a big brain; his Kung Fu is strong. Luckily for us, Jim is also a logical guy and the flow of this book reflects that trait. He starts out with a primer on the IP protocol suite, the "lingua franca" of the Internet. Jim taught me IP and subnetting a few years back, and believe me, if he could get through my thick skull, you will have no trouble understanding him.

The book then continues to "peel the onion" layer by layer through all the black magic and acronyms that your boss, client, CIO, friends, spouse, and dogcatcher expect you to know already. You will be introduced to security theory, cryptology, RAS, authentication, IKE, IPSec, encapsulation, keys, policies. Phew! Lots to learn, and it is all here. Do not worry; your loyal author will see you through it all.

That leads me to perhaps my favorite part of the book. Jim will not leave you hanging after giving you a brain dump of his vast knowledge. He wraps up his work with fantastic sections on implementation and product evaluation. Study these well and follow the methodologies. You have the advantage of his hands-on experience and expertise in designing and deploying these technologies in the real world for real companies.

I have known Jim Tiller for years as a good friend and fellow road warrior on the Information Highway. He is a widely respected engineer, consultant, solutions architect, and author. His love of his work and his subject shine through in this book. What is all the more impressive is the sheer amount of labor he shouldered during the writing. While it is true that all good professionals and consultants are born multi-taskers, Jim takes it to the next level and can actually multi-thread. His energy and drive would burn out a superconducting CPU. You are getting the result of this brainpower and energy without having to reinvent the wheel. I would urge you to seek out his other writings.

It is my sincere hope that you will enjoy this book as much as I have. Use it to make your life a little simpler while you are out fighting the good fight and protecting your data from evil-doers. Keep it with you, refer to it often, pack it to read on planes and trains (but not automobiles).

Joseph Patrick Schorr
jschorr@belenosinc.com

Joe Schorr is Manager of Delivery Services for Belenos, Inc., in Tampa, Florida. Belenos designs and builds next-generation voice/data networks for emerging service providers. Joe is a veteran of professional services consulting with a background in internetworking and remote access planning, design, and project management.

Acknowledgments

There are a few people who played an integral part in the creation of this book. First and foremost, my family, who put up with endless late nights in the office and the absence of a husband and father for an amazingly long time. Thank you once again, Mary, Rain, and Phoenix — to you I owe everything.

The editor, Rich O'Hanley, was the driving force who continually provided support and mentoring during the entire process. He was professional, supportive, and most of all understanding. It was an absolute pleasure to work with him and I thank him for the opportunity to allow me to share my thoughts with others. My technical reviewer, Bob Obreiter, was kind enough to read the manuscript and provide excellent comments and feedback that I immediately included into the final version. Bob is a CCIE at Netigy and is currently writing a book on Cisco network security.

There were several individuals who accepted my requests for help and spent their personal time in assisting me and ensuring that I did not make really bad technical mistakes. Jay Heiser is a Senior Consultant at NetworkCare, who provided incredibly valuable input. Jay writes articles for *Information Security* magazine, security-related whitepapers, a contributing author to the *Information Security Management Handbook,* and provides an endless stream of helpful information to his colleagues. Jay is a brilliant author and I urge you to seek out his work. Martin Rausche, CCIE, is a senior consultant for NetworkCare in Germany. We spent some time together in Germany working on a large VPN project and it was the beginning of a great friendship. Martin provided wonderful and valuable input throughout the writing of this book. His technical expertise was invaluable and his involvement was crucial. Clint Masters is a brilliant consultant and offered to take on the challenge of writing a packet decode for Etherpeek that allows the user to see the details of an IKE exchange explained in this book. Big thanks to Clint for taking this project on for me and providing added value to the reader. The decodes are available in the appendix.

There are some people who continually provided a sounding board for those days of writer block and moral support to keep me going. Bryan Fish, who co-authored a chapter with me for the *Information Security Management Handbook,* was a constant positive influence and is a great friend. Ted Baker, another close friend, constantly supported me and was a great pupil (he finally snatched the stone from my hand). His constant questions about IPSec assisted me in determining areas and directions of interest.

Finally, there are several people who continually provided moral support and simply egged me on with their enthusiasm and friendship. Joe Schorr is a longtime best friend and colleague who has given me endless streams of support and encouragement. He has consistently provided guidance and a cold beer on those hot summer days out on the boat, the "Rum Runner" as it is affectionately called. Todd Salmon, Laurie Bostic, and Morgan Stern were a constant presence of positive influences. Their total belief in my capabilities and the confidence they showed in me helped in ways they are completely unaware of. Thanks to all of you.

Introduction

VPNs have become analogous with the Internet. The ability to leverage a vast, global network to facilitate proprietary communications, and do it cheaply, has been the Internet's version of the search for the holy grail. Now, that distant, much anticipated capability has come within easy reach. Virtual private network (VPN) has become one of the most recognized terms in our industry, yet there continuously seem to be different impressions of what VPNs really are and can become. The concept is relatively simple: get data from point A to Z in a manner that is not necessarily native to the originating technology. The complicated part is B through Y.

It is unfortunate that the term has been so badly overloaded, but that is also a reflection of the pent-up demand for secure Internet connectivity. The term VPN can be used as an all-encompassing term that describes a technology, a business directive, a security methodology, or a process to enhance one of the previously mentioned aspects of communications. There are thousands of articles and whitepapers that describe VPNs in various forms and provide explanations of the nearly infinite applications. The recent, sudden increase in publications detailing the advantages and technical aspects of VPNs is a distinctive sign that this technology is not to be underestimated. It promises cost-effective communications, flexibility, and in some cases, robust security. As technology intensifies and communications are driven deeper into our everyday existence, VPNs, in some form or another, will surely be a part of the daily communication equation.

The explosive expansion of the Internet to every corner of the globe has eliminated time from everyday activities. Initially, the Web was used for virtual billboards, allowing organizations of any size to hang their shingle out for the world to see. Now, multimedia broadcasts and multi-player simulation games are taken for granted. The social implications, positive and negative, are evolving every minute. Commerce, intellectual property rights, business and personal interactions — all have radically changed through the capabilities the Internet has to offer. It is clear that the Internet is here to stay, and the race to exploit its new social and commercial possibilities is fueled by new security technologies.

The goal is to have all the functionality and access that we enjoy at the office over the Internet from home or on the road in some remote location; that is what we want from VPNs. The reality is that while much of what we want is plausible, the bliss that seems to permeate sales pamphlets and demo booths still eludes us in implementation.

The concept of VPNs is a relatively old one — at least in computer years — but as a well-defined technology, it remains an adolescent. This is certainly understandable given the environment. An ever-changing landscape of applications, circumstances, protocols, operating systems, and the ever-present legacy systems that must be addressed is a tough neighborhood in which to grow up. It is a virtual situation of two bits forward, one bit back. A vendor wanting to implement the latest technology runs the risk of drowning in a sea of yet-to-be-approved Request for Comments (RFC). The demand for technology forces vendors to produce solutions based on the unrefined standards that exist in that point of the standard's lifecycle. The result is much like that seem in the world of Asynchronous Transfer Mode (ATM) networks years ago: a new, very desirable technology that is not well-defined by a set of standards. To meet demand, vendors created solutions loosely based on the immature standards that were available at the time. The result was proprietary ATM networks that did not adhere to the finalized standards that followed. So, in the beginning, many of the promises were met and the excitement for the technology allowed acceptance of the limitations. As the standard grew, the relatively small margin of difference expanded and many vendors were forced to reorganize their product to meet the newer standards and customer demands.

VPN technology is experiencing the high demand–maturing standards point in its lifecycle. The standards are not well-defined and various points of details are being worked out. At the same time, dozens of vendors are producing larger and larger VPN solutions that are a hybrid of what is defined and what is in demand. A good example of this is IPSec remote access solutions. It is agreed throughout the industry that remote user access, within the realm of IPSec, is the most immature aspect, and current solutions simply reflect what works best for that vendor. In short, there are no solid standards that can be referenced when developing a remote access solution.

VPN users are experiencing a phenomenon common with new technologies — standards convergence. Much like the early railroads, using dozens of incompatible track gauges, the first commercial VPN products provided no cross-vendor interoperability. Just as the railroads converged, providing huge contiguous areas of compatible track, the VPN business is on track for compatibility. Unfortunately, the standardization process is not complete. This book is about how IPSec is making this compatibility a reality.

About This Book

A wide range of information is available on VPNs, including standards documentation, vendor manuals, and periodical commentary. This mass of information is not in the comprehensive and structured form that most readers expect for either a tutorial or reference of a new technology. This book is intended to fill this gap.

This book provides a brief history of IPSec and familiarizes the reader with some underlying technologies that are necessary to fully grasp how VPNs function. These early subjects include discussions about the basics of the TCP/IP protocol, the language of the Internet. Several scenarios will be introduced that reflect experiences with IPSec VPNs rather than detailing the RFCs and the availability of options defined within — which may not apply to foreseeable implementations. (History of Internet standards has demonstrated certain Darwinian tendencies. Those subsets of the standards that provide the most utility tend to be implemented, and those that do not provide any obvious immediate benefit rarely see life in commercial products. For this reason, IETF RFCs can be misleading.)

A critical aspect of IPSec, and one of the focuses of this book, is automatic key management currently being used to negotiate, on behalf of IPSec operations, keying material and security suite requirements defined in the VPN communication policy. IPSec encompasses several interesting technologies, many of which can be very complicated and open to interpretation, such as IKE (the automatic key management). However, IPSec-specific operations, such as the use of security protocols, are fairly straightforward and the implementation options, with regard to automatic key management, are what need to be conveyed carefully. The part that always seems to get attention in the realm of IPSec is the agreement of policy, authentication, and key material management. Face it, securing information is worthless unless great pains are taken in properly identifying the other party and ensuring that no one else has the key. Once the door is locked, the real issue is to whom the key was given — everyone can see the house.

Any discussion of IPSec would do a disservice by not making certain that the reader has an understanding of basic security concepts and their relationship to IPSec policy choices. Why are there VPNs? How has the Internet affected communications? These are fundamental questions that the reader needs to feel comfortable with to understand the impact of IPSec. An understanding of the Internet threat environment is crucial in fully appreciating the need for the robust security provided by IPSec. This book also investigates the overall security concerns with VPNs, regardless of the security of the transport itself. Being connected to the Internet and interacting with proprietary data, as if on the internal network, raises very interesting issues with regard to the level of realized enterprise security. As one dives into the security concerns surrounding VPNs as a whole, many assumptions will be conveyed and, quite frankly, represent the point of view of the author.

Security mechanisms, such as authentication concepts and applications, Public Key Infrastructure, and policies are discussed and their role in VPNs explained. Once a foundation is established, additional detail is provided in the realm of cryptography. Encryption and related processes, such as HASH algorithms and Message Authentication Codes, represent a strategic importance to IPSec and the creation of protection measures against several types of vulnerabilities. This book introduces the components of cryptography that relate to IPSec.

Implementation concepts, designs, and processes that reflect experiences with various products at different stages within the lifecycle of IPSec standards are then discussed. It will become very clear early in these discussions that what is available can be in stark contrast to what is provided by the IPSec standards. Examples, descriptions, and simple points of view regarding the various VPN solutions that are available are shared. By providing experiences, the hope is to shed some light on the details that seem to scurry into the darkness when problems occur.

There are many publications about VPNs that explain several other protocols, technologies, solutions, applications, configurations, and general commentary about VPNs. Knowing that many people have absorbed much of this information, and in general, many feel comfortable with VPN concepts, especially technical individuals, a collection of technical information seemed timely. In that light, many of the basics of VPNs, or standard concepts, are not discussed in great detail, but rather reviewed, allowing the reader to concentrate more on the technical underlying concepts.

The ultimate goal of this book is to peel away the layers from the general term of "VPN" and expose the relationships between encryption, authentication, protocols, and security and how they all conspire to function within IPSec. This book is about more than IPSec or VPN technology; it is about the components and their compilation into a complex set of protocols that result in perceivable simplicity. The book dives into the details to allow the reader to fully absorb the sheer intensity of the communication technology and the security that surrounds it.

How This Book Is Organized

The information about IPSec and the idiosyncrasies in implementation, operation, design, and security concepts exist at many levels of complexity. This book is designed to present the information in each of these levels, introducing aspects about the technology in early chapters and revisiting the subjects in increasing detail throughout the book. It is necessary to understand the flow of information and expectation of finer detail as the book evolves.

The author feels that this process of introducing preliminary technical aspects, building a foundation, not only allows the reader to absorb information, but also provides an opportunity to speak to specifics within each realm of discussion. Normally, the technological details would be simply covered with various explanations interspersed. However, there are many things about IPSec the author wants to share — some simple in nature while others require a full grasp of a certain concept. An example of this presentation is security associations. A fundamental part of IPSec, security associations are introduced early with some basic concepts. As more details about the inner operations of IPSec are introduced, security associations are included in the information fold and more particulars are exposed. Finally, as more complex characteristics of IPSec are covered, security associations become the tools to convey the details of greater elements of IPSec VPNs.

VPNs are incredibly interesting, and IPSec represents an extreme protocol that demands respect. Therefore, presenting the information in expanding portions provides a process that not only has great instructional value, but the entire book remains fresh. As one reads the book, rest assured that if the details one is searching for do not appear readily, they will appear in force shortly following.

The chapter "Getting Started" introduces the basic concepts of the Internet, information, and the security when the two are mixed. VPNs are discussed in general terms, including their effects on the communication landscape. Cost, scalability, security, and many other positive attributes of VPN technology are shared. Security policies and their role in the organization are discussed. Policies cannot be underestimated nor can their inclusion in a VPN be overlooked. Policies operate in many ways within an organization: as a security program to maintain security posture, or with IPSec, an operational application that defines traffic flow, control measures, and security levels. The intended audience is briefly discussed. This chapter lives up to its name and simply provides the basic components of VPN and where it is all going.

The following chapter, "Technical Primer," launches us into the technical realm — what this book is all about — covering the TCP/IP protocol, operational layers of communication, introducing other VPN technologies, and finally outlining cryptography. There is a great deal in this chapter that will have some impact on the remaining sections. The TCP/IP protocol is what IPSec was designed to operate for and within; knowing the structure, if only limited, can assist in understanding IPSec and internal functions intimately. Other VPN technologies are simply introduced and briefly described to allow the reader to get a feeling of other techniques. The chapter includes an introduction to cryptography, and introduces the basics of encryption, message authentication, and message hashing. It is simply a prelude to the chapter on cryptography that covers the technology's involvement in IPSec communications.

Chapter 3, "IP Security Primer" discusses in detail the history of IPSec and the various components that make it a reality. The standards and their structure are spoken to. The basic elements of the protocol are introduced, then, in greater detail, internal operations are covered. It is in this chapter that IKE is revealed and separated from IPSec. The term "IPSec" is not only a specific suite of protocols but acts as a "word" that encompasses several other technologies. These are dissected for further, separate analysis.

"Cryptography" is a great chapter that acquaints the reader with fundamental concepts and techniques in the realm of encryption and message authentication. It is in this chapter that concepts such as PKI, Diffie-Hellman, current and new encryption algorithms, and perfect forward secrecy are presented. These models are essential to IPSec and IKE operations for the creation of a VPN and understanding the rudimentary applications of encryption and message authentication; their use in IPSec will be easily absorbed.

The subsequent chapter, "Implementation Theory," comprises explanations and hypotheses about the use of VPN technology in the communication atmosphere. Standard communication designs and technologies are introduced and used as fodder for the argument for implementing VPNs as the communication medium.

The next chapter is "Authentication" and covers the different authentication methods supported by IPSec. The chapter also includes discussions on remote access IPSec solutions and the inherent problems that can occur. After establishing the problems, the solutions being developed are offered for review. Many concepts, such as protocols and cryptography, are revisited and greater details are exposed.

"IPSec Architecture" is a chapter that details the areas within IPSec and IKE that were presented earlier. Several technical details are covered and combined to display current solutions. It is in this chapter that vendor solutions are discussed, along with the implementation practices of those products with regard to the standards. There are many IPSec VPN products available; however, each provides the service slightly different from the next. Many of these differences are collected and offered to the reader.

The next chapter, "Security Protocols," covers in great detail the workhorse protocols of IPSec operations. A VPN is the application of these protocols and, therefore, a detailed representation is provided. In reality, the security protocols within IPSec are not very complicated. Implementation, structure, and operations of the protocols are relatively straightforward and their existence is the realized VPN. While not overly complicated, knowing the idiosyncrasies of the protocols is vital to becoming an expert.

The next chapter represents a great deal of information and intense technology. "Key Management" is where the complexities of IPSec rise to the surface. It is one thing to have a VPN, but setting it up — specifically, the negotiation — is powerful technology and can get amazingly complex. Each aspect of the IKE protocol is described in vast detail and built on for the next two chapters. The protocol and management of information into messages shared at exact points in the communication can be very involving and immensely interesting — when all the sight components are known. It is in this chapter that all the previous chapters will be needed to fully comprehend the internals of key management.

As promised, the following two chapters, "IKE in Action" and "Areas of Interest Within IKE," cover the details of the protocol. "IKE in Action" is the result of a lab with two routers; the configuration and establishment of a VPN are detailed. Finally, the logs of the communication are dissected line-by-line to show the reader each step in the IKE protocol that was covered in the previous chapter. "Areas of Interest Within

IKE" covers aspects about IKE that represent a weakness or issue in the protocol. It is interesting to note that the protocol, while very interesting and powerful, suffers from all things that are complex. Complexity can complicate the integration of security technology and practices, and some of this is seen in this chapter.

Policies are central to secure operations for any organization. However, policies are crucial to the operation of IPSec VPNs, not just defining the security around them but within them. "Security Policies and the Security of VPNs" is a chapter dedicated to the management and philosophy of VPN. The inherent security issues of IPSec, or any VPN for that matter, are discussed in this chapter. Many ideas are shared and the technology of VPN is compared to the security realized. Fundamental security concepts shutter when in proximity of a VPN, and knowing the issues will allow the adopter to mitigate the associated risk.

The following chapter, "Implementation Considerations," dives deeper into the implementation concepts and technology. It is in this chapter that routing issues within VPNs are revealed; client complexities, VPN policies, protocol mixtures, and Microsoft's solution are discussed. Routing and client operations and deployment are the focus of this chapter.

"Product Evaluation" provides some insight into selecting VPN products. The identification of requirements and wants are important and outlined in the chapter. Grading methodologies are detailed that allow the logical deduction of products into groups that can be scored against the defined requirements. Finally, lab testing concepts and procedures are shared to assist in the creation of a lab that will provide the greatest value.

The final chapter, "Report on IPSec," is a report on the technology by Counterpane Systems, Inc., that is augmented with comments from top engineers who helped develop the technology. This chapter catapults the reader into a stimulating debate over the validity of IPSec and the realized security. By this point in the book, the reader will have a detailed understanding of the protocol and will be in an excellent position to appreciate the conversation.

Why This Book Was Written

This book started several years ago, the direct product of a simple beginning. It began as the simple need for information about a technology that was growing faster than most people could keep pace. As the desire for VPNs grew, there began a wave of information attempting to convey the new concept of VPNs and the various underlying technologies. IPSec has quickly risen to the top as the VPN standard of choice and become the center of attention of vendors and consumers.

Many organizations began to inquire about using VPNs to accommodate remote user access requirements and reduce total cost of ownership. As a consultant, the author has worked with many of these organizations to assist them in properly testing, piloting, and implementing a VPN solution. The entire process required close interaction with vendors and the various product offerings. The author found himself inquiring about seemingly simple concepts that proved to be much more complicated than originally considered. In many cases, the author found himself assisting in the development of the product to accommodate issues discovered by careful system interrogation.

The author began writing notes that soon evolved into a set of drawings, commentary, points of interest, and details about VPNs that were nowhere to be found otherwise. It soon became evident that there must be others who were not satisfied with the clean explanations of VPNs that permeate the industry. It was felt that the bits and pieces that made up the nuances of VPN design, either on a large scale or small one, were worth building on and sharing with others who may be frustrated, as was the author, with the available technology.

Many available books are directed toward the general concepts of VPNs and contain very little detail about the inner working of the technology. There was a plethora of information that explained what was possible, based on what the standards detailed as achievable, but none really talked about implementation issues that affected the current state of the technology and the possibilities given the available tools and equipment.

Of the technical data that was available, it still seemed to glean over the details that interested this author. No one else seemed to tackle them in a clear and understandable fashion, and simply stated or reinforced the RFCs that defined the standard. It was felt that other individuals had a similar desire to know the fine points of IPSec and wanted a book that explained the technology. The goal was to allow the reader to have a single point of information that represents hundreds of resources and years of experience with IPSec VPN solutions.

IPSec is defined by several RFCs that build a group of documents that provide information about the different suites that make up the standard. Much of this book is the interpretation of those RFCs and, therefore, the information contained within this book is subject to change as the technology advances. Although the creation of this book is due, in part, to the RFCs, a great deal of it reflects real-world experiences and interaction with the technology on nearly every level. Knowing the RFCs is a definite advantage when dealing with IPSec, but the reader will learn, as the author did, that knowing the ins and outs of the RFCs can actually lengthen the learning curve when absorbing data about a new system, device, or VPN application and that system's involvement in VPN designs.

The author wanted to write a technical book that details the quirks of IPSec VPNs, the brutal caveats that can raise their ugly head, and the feeling of elation when it all works at the end of the day — the way one wanted it to.

Chapter 1

Getting Started

Communications are the fundamental driver of society and the value of the information being communicated has never been greater. The advent of several technologies and communication environments has fueled a storm of changes in the relatively recent evolution that is information technology.

The Internet, its speed, reliability, and the access to it have all expanded beyond every expectation set in the early years. The Internet has fueled the changes one sees in telecommunications, and the interaction between people, organizations, and countries has been affected.

During the explosive growth, many were asking how they could exploit the Internet and the timeless communication it provides. First, the baby steps were Web pages and e-mail. Then, as people gained interest in what was being sold through these virtual displays, it expanded into providing access to the commodity for the customer. The simple commerce soon expanded into sharing information for vendor interaction to provide virtual warehousing and reduced time to market for new merchandise.

To accomplish the development and dependency that organizations have on Internet communications, a new form of connectivity was required that could provide confidence in privacy, and remain inexpensive and scalable to accommodate the foreseeable future requirements.

Virtual private networks (VPNs) were developed to fill this gap and provide for secure communications over the Internet, or any untrusted network. The result was a process that required few system or communication modifications and promised to protect communication to anywhere in the world.

Information Age

The introduction of the computer into everyday activities was the turning point of the 20th century. Throughout history, there have been decisive milestones in the advancement of human society. The ability to create and use tools, then metallurgy and chemistry, and soon the industrial revolution solidified a working social environment.

The computer, at least the personal computer, opened a window of new opportunities to individuals to accomplish things never really considered before. By the time personal computers became a reality, computers were already being used for collective processing and huge number crunching. Only the guys with white jackets were allowed to watch all the lights. The PC made the computer accessible to people, and those people who were exposed included entrepreneurs that saw opportunity.

Nearly overnight, computers were at people's desks, instead of typewriters, using them to accomplish complicated tasks in a reduced amount of time and with increased accuracy. Tasks that seemed out of reach for small businesses just a short time earlier were now attainable. Soon, the data became increasingly more complex and large, requiring more computers and educated people to operate and manage them. As this expanded, the information became an integral part of the business success, and the protection of that data soon became a focal point for some organizations.

It was at this point, when assets veered away from machines, widgets, and warehouses to data, that the information age was born. Data is nearly everything. This seems logical — data is knowledge, and knowledge typically equates to money. Anything from a new drug formula, or the research that founded its production, to a set of architectural plans for a new house or a fighter wing, to the daily news or the stock value of a remote company in the China highlands — information has become the universal ether that surrounds us. People no longer simply work with it; they react to it and base nearly everything on it.

For society to operate and use the information, it must be communicated and controlled. The communication of information has advanced very rapidly over the last few years. Technological advancements, used to feed the desire to move information faster today than yesterday, matched with massive amounts of money to create larger and farther reaching information communications than ever before. However, during this same timeframe, but unfortunately not nearly as fast, the security of the communications was questioned. This is reminiscent of an old TV commercial where the formula for Coke passes the formula for Pepsi in a cloud of digital communications. The poetic truth is now realized, many years after the airing of that commercial: information can be very valuable.

The Internet

Since the first browser was used to provide a graphical interface for obtaining information from the Internet, the number of users and services has exploded. The Internet moved quickly and people and businesses realized the opportunities and potential of the Internet. Today, the Internet is firmly established as a basic requirement for business and social interaction; much like the telephone, it is expected almost anywhere one goes. Opportunities became very evident and opened an infinite variety of applications for business and personal endeavors.

The information coursing through the Internet evolved, seemingly overnight, from e-mail and basic Web browsing to much more sophisticated applications. Data that was being passed was becoming increasingly private and sensitive to the well-being of the original communication parties. Data that used to appear only on certain servers residing on internal networks was being accessed from across the country, moving through completely unknown territory.

As with any positive, there must be a negative. As technology increased and the use of the Internet for private interaction proliferated, criminals grew with the technology. Soon it was evident that deliberate abuse of the Internet could become a powerful weapon to cause disruption or increase personal wealth. A relationship developed between the development of technology to increase communication possibilities and the criminal's ability to take advantage of them. Criminals discovered vulnerabilities at an astounding rate. As processes and applications were implemented to mitigate the new threats, new ones would be discovered and those too would require steps to protect information from the new vulnerability. This process of find-and-fix-and-find-again has not stopped. The constant pushing toward ultimate communication and discoveries of new technologies will certainly breed a continuous flow of unforeseen weaknesses.

However, the vulnerabilities can be reduced with certain technologies that address one aspect of the communication. A well-defined set of protection measures can provide enough defense against theoretical types of attack to carry into the next form of technology. IPSec is a perfect example of protection measures that can remain applied at a certain level within the communication and allow other aspects of the communication to evolve. IPSec has become a robust foundation that appears to be applicable for many years to come.

Security Considerations

Communication technology has eliminated the basic level of interaction between individuals. For two people talking in a room, it can be assured — to a degree — that the information from one individual has not been altered prior to meeting the listener's ears. It can be also assumed that the person who is seen talking is the originator of the voice that is being heard. This example is basic, assumed, and never questioned — it is trusted. However, the same type of communication over alternate media must be closely scrutinized due to the massive numbers of vulnerabilities to which the session is exposed.

Computers have added several layers of complexity to the trusting process, and the Internet has introduced some very interesting vulnerabilities. With a theoretically unlimited number of people on a network, the options for attacks are similarly unlimited. As soon as a message takes advantage of the Internet for a communication medium without several layers of protection, all bets are off.

Authentication

Authentication is a service that allows a system to determine the identity of another entity that has presented its credentials. Authentication is the basis of many security mechanisms and some designs authenticate both parties in the communication.

Authentication is based on factors, such as 1, 2, or 3. The mantra of authentication is that it is based on something the user *knows,* something the user *has*, and something the user *is.* A good example of two-factor authentication is where users have something they know and something they have, such as a token. Users provide what they know, a username and password, combined with something they have, such as a number generated from a token. The number validates the possession of the token, which further validates the user with the name and password supplied.

The something the user knows is typically a password, pass phrase, or a Personal Identification Number (PIN) that only that person should know the value. Combine the personal knowledge of a private number or word with something the user has. This is typically associated with a token. Either one of these can be used in conjunction with something the user is. This is referred to as biometrics, the identification based on physical attributes. Biometrics can operate in many ways that range from entering a username or code in combination with a scan, or it can include something the user has, such as an access card.

There are several forms of authentication mechanisms used in nearly every aspect in system access. In the realm of IPSec and VPNs, the highest level currently being used is two-factor authentication. With most solutions, the protocol to include a token-generated number is nothing more than an extended use of CHAP or PAP, which are well-suited for remote access. However, in investigating IPSec remote access solutions more closely, one sees that there is absolutely no standard that provides for these extended authentication mechanisms. What is available today is simply what the vendor felt was the best technology that fit the proposed solution. In the absence of a standard, anything is fair game.

Access Controls

Access controls limit access to network and system resources based on communication attributes such as authentication data, traffic patterns or type, protocol, application, or any identifying characteristics of the communication that an administrator wishes to allow or stop.

Examples of simple access controls are ACLs, or access control lists, which are common among routers or access devices. An example might be:

```
permit ip 147.151.77.0 0.0.0.255 host 194.72.6.205
```

This ACL allows IP traffic from the network 147.151.77.0 to a specific host identified by its IP address, 194.71.6.205. To display the other characteristics that can be used in an ACL, more information can be provided:

```
permit tcp 147.151.77.0 0.0.0.255 host 194.72.6.205 eq 80
```

This ACL is very similar to the first; however, the protocol has been limited to TCP and only port 80. In these examples, one sees that restrictions can be applied to several differentiating factors in the communication. The first example simply isolated the network and system and the protocol being used to communicate. In the second version, the specific layer 4 protocols and the service port were isolated. (Many details of TCP/IP are covered in Chapter 2.)

There are solutions that integrate the authentication process with access controls. Kerberos is an example. In Kerberos authentication, the user authenticates to a central system, a Key Distribution Center (KDC), and is ultimately provided a ticket that can be presented to a resource for access. The level of access permitted can be directly related to the user, who is identified by an authenticated ticket. Therefore, the user's access controls are associated with his identity, which has been validated by a trusted KDC. It is easy to imagine a situation where access is controlled by the individual's identity, the protocol they are attempting to access with, and the application that is being run. It is this situation that is expounded upon in IPSec by the addition of varying levels of protection based on the same access control attributes. It is necessary to understand that limitations and access controls can be related to any attribute that has the ability of uniquely identifying a process, person, or activity. Within IPSec, there are properties called *selectors* that can be used to control communications in the VPN. Not only can the selectors be leveraged for applying access controls but they also allow the administrator to provide various protection levels to various communication patterns and flows. Much more of this is covered in detail in later chapters.

Data Integrity

Data integrity is the validity of the data at any given state. There are three basic states of data:

1. storage
2. processing
3. transmission

Typically, data in storage and being transmitted are the focal points of protection and integrity checking. When data is transmitted across an untrusted network, it is exposed to countless vulnerabilities and unwanted interaction. Data could possibly be modified while in transit and the valid participants could be completely unaware.

Data integrity is ensured by providing an authenticator, or an unchangeable representation of the data. Many protocols, including TCP/IP, provide a checksum process that produces a fingerprint that is transmitted with the original data. As the message and the checksum reach the destination, the recipient can verify that the data has not been altered in transit by verifying the checksum.

IPSec provides data integrity by employing message authentication processes (HASH algorithms) to produce a message fingerprint that can be used to verify data integrity. Message authentication is an essential process that IPSec provides. IPSec has two basic security protocols, one of which has the sole purpose of providing message authentication. The importance of knowing what is received is the same as what was sent is imperative. IPSec is constructed in a way that even if a key is obtained and used to modify the data, obtaining the necessary information to create an alternate authentication is highly complex. The details of message authentication and its application in IPSec are discussed in later chapters.

Confidentiality

Confidentiality is the ability to keep the data private and unexposed to unauthorized viewers. In the realm of communication security, confidentiality is synonymous with encryption technology. Encryption is the process of converting information into unintelligible data and, typically, back into the original information and format given a specific key, password, or any private data or device.

Non-repudiation

Non-repudiation is the inability to transmit information and then claim not having done so. In the nontechnical domain, papers can be signed, authorized, and witnessed to provide a legal binding between the person and the activity, document, or statement. In the digital world, this is a much more complicated process, but is based on a similar foundation as with signatures on documents. The inclusion of a third party and the use of multiple keys in the sharing of data provide an acceptable form of insurance that the information was signed by the claimed individual. To support this, several priorities must be met to ensure that the signing process is valid and unencumbered by unauthorized influence.

Policy

The term "policy" relates to an enormous amount of security implications for organizations. Policies are typically associated with company standards, guidelines, and procedures that ensure a secure working environment. Policies provide a means of stating a security posture and defining the associated requirements to accomplish its implementation. Policy is also a crucial aspect of IPSec with respect implementing a comprehensive VPN. IPSec policies are necessary to determine traffic flow and the protection it is to be provided, among other attributes. IPSec communications must not only be cognizant of the participants, data, and services allowed, but also the management of the connection with regard to maintaining security and communication integrity.

Network security — fundamentally what is being discussed here — is the synergy between required services and offerings, the protection of those services and data, and the operational conditions, or environment. Security policies exist to define the environment or it will be completely nebulous to the surrounding influences. In other words, without a defined posture, it would be nearly impossible to secure. IPSec influences the network security policy because it affects the very foundation of information security. Communication over untrusted networks is available through the use of IPSec VPNs, but the impact of data manipulation on those remote systems and networks represents a security concern for many organizations. Thus, policies exist to define network security posture, and VPN policies must be included in the provisioning of the service to remote users, organizations, offices, partners, and vendors. On the other hand, policies exist for the physical application of IPSec within the organization or enterprise. IPSec policies define the technical realization of the VPN. Ironically, while a technical representation of secure communications, IPSec polices reflect network security policies very closely. It is easy to envision a network policy being quickly interpreted into an IPSec VPN policy. However, the reverse is not necessarily true. One obvious reason is that a network security policy should exist before IPSec is implemented. Another is determining that security decisions based on a technology, especially a communication technology, will not result in a comprehensive security policy.

The following sections discuss properties of network security, the policies that accompany it, and the qualities of VPNs that affect policy; and finally, the technical aspects of VPN policies are introduced.

Network Security Considerations

The security-related decisions that are made, or fail to be made, largely determine how secure or insecure the network is, how much functionality the network offers, and how easy the network is to use. However, good decisions cannot be made about security without first determining what the security goals are. Until the security goals are determined, effective use of any collection of security tools and services cannot be properly utilized because no one will know what to check for and what restrictions to impose.

An organization's goals will be largely determined by the following key trade-offs.

Services Offered versus Security Provided. Each service offered to users carries its own security risks. For some services, the risk outweighs the benefit of the service and the organization may choose to eliminate the service rather than try to secure it. An example of this service-to-security relationship is File Transfer Protocol (FTP). There are several known security vulnerabilities with the protocol, and proper installation and maintenance can become time-consuming for the administrator. Unless there is a need to provide FTP service to users for collecting or providing files, the risk and overhead may outweigh its need.

To allow organizations to determine service use compared to the associated risk of providing the service, a risk analysis should be completed. For organizations that share files with many different types of clients and different operating systems, FTP may simply be necessary to allow business flow. An example is a software company that wants to provide updates and patches to the public over the Internet, where risks can be stated as "High" because of the exposure to the Internet and allowing public access. But the trade-off is to provide extended services to customers, which in turn can be quite valuable for customer retention and support. Therefore, the risk-to-value relationship can justify the overhead of administration and the exposure to multiple threats. For a company that produces a widget and is not tied to customer needs for data to maintain business core requirements, the thought of opening itself to various threats represents a risk that outweighs the benefits. This avenue typically results in not implementing services that are associated vulnerabilities or threats to business continuity.

Ease of Use versus Security. The easiest system to use would allow access to any user and require no passwords; that is, there would be no security. Requiring passwords makes the system a little less convenient, but more secure.

As security is applied, it takes on the form of layers, increasing the distance from the outside or unauthorized to the protected and controlled. As more layers are applied in the form of technology and procedures, the requirements for circumventing become too great and demand greater sophistication in the attack. However, for each layer of technology or procedure, there exist administration and maintenance in supporting and using that infrastructure.

There are many examples of usability versus security, and everyone has a story about an anti-virus program causing system problems, forgetting a password because one has seven to remember and each must be changed every 30 days — at different intervals. There are nearly an infinite number of examples because they directly relate to personality and the natural human resistance to "red tape."

Therefore, security that is mandated should attempt to enforce the necessary requirement to obtain the level of security, all the while maintaining awareness of the usability and interface. The more complicated the process, the less people will have a desire to cooperate and abide by the rules — possibly resulting in loss of security.

The simple fact in security is that ensuring a security posture requires work in of itself — above and beyond the normal data-to-data interactivity with the information one is trying to protect. Locking one's workstation if one steps away, and storing and locking all proprietary materials from one's desk before leaving, are very basic examples of overhead that some have difficulty in following. Nevertheless, there is a cost associated with increased security. Whether it is finite and measurable (as with door locks and special software) or intangible (as with proper system security etiquette), there is a usability-to-productivity ratio that must be maintained and is relative to the security posture desired.

Cost of Security versus Risk of Loss. There are many different costs to security: monetary (i.e., the cost of purchasing security hardware and software like a firewall), performance (i.e., encryption and decryption take time), and ease of use, as mentioned above. There are also many levels of risk: loss of privacy, loss of data, and the loss of service. Each type of cost must be weighed against each type of loss.

As the security process becomes engrained into information systems, the goals of the security structure must be communicated to all users, operations staff, and managers through a set of security rules and procedures.

An example of increased administration and costs can be represented by strong authentication requirements. Two-factor authentication is an example of something a user knows and something the user has that uniquely identifies that user. A normal username and password authentication process can have its own overhead in the maintenance of ensuring that passwords are a certain length and are changed regularly. However, two-factor authentication typically requires hardware in the form of a token or fob that provides a unique number every 30 or 60 seconds, or when a PIN is entered, that it is tied to a unique seed built into the device. The unique number generated with the seed is associated with a user, and sometimes a password, to provide final authentication. The hard costs are realized in the hardware and software requirements of the authentication server and, obviously, the tokens that must be distributed to the end users. The hidden costs can become extensive. Lost tokens, system hardware failures, client authentication software integration, and system support only scratch the surface. Because tokens are typically based on time synchronization with the server, as they become misaligned, the numbers generated will not work, ultimately resulting in false authentication failures. When authentication fails, the user calls the helpdesk or administrator, and the task of realigning the system and verifying the configuration consumes time and money. Finally, user education and training are necessary to ensure that the people holding the token know how to use it. Some people do not respond well when placed in a time-sensitive situation and have difficulty completing the necessary steps when unfamiliar with the process.

The more security implemented, the more the cost — on every level. Therefore, as security is implemented and used for more day-to-day activities, the greater the impact on business operations. The goal is to fit the level of desired security to the business operations to a point where they level out. By defining a virtual horizontal line of accepted security, risks can be weighed against it to determine if the desired security posture is being met. As new vulnerabilities are discovered, the exposure of the company can be calculated by comparing the existing security of the environment to the complexity and type of threat. In some cases, the threat requires various levels of information to be obtained by the attacker before representing a serious threat to business information or processes. If, in fact, completing the attack involved activities that could also be used for other less complicated attacks, then the mitigation of the original threat is out of bounds of the security posture. The concept of aligning known and expected threats to the risks for determining the security of a system is simply a risk analysis. However, knowing and understanding that there is a point where more money and security focused on a certain vulnerability can be a waste of resources. Acceptable security does not have to be overly expensive when implemented properly and security posture and expectations are established.

The Need for Security Policies

The overall objective of an information security program is to protect the integrity, confidentiality, the availability of information. Threats such as unauthorized access, denial of service, information dissemination, or data destruction all conspire to keep an organization from maintaining a secure environment.

Legal Reasons. Security polices provide several aspects to maintaining security in many forms. One of those forms is legal protection. In the even that an employee is released due to unauthorized activities that resulted in data loss, some form of document must be produced that states the punishment for such a violation. Typically, part of the hiring procedure is to require that applicants read, agree to, and sign a security policy to ensure that they are aware of the security posture of the organization. If an applicant does not agree, that applicant is typically not hired.

Business Requirements. To participate in business with certain organizations, such as the military or other government departments, a predefined level of security must be assured. A security policy is used as a foundation for any certification process to allow one organization to establish a level of trust with another.

A good example of the need for business-to-business security relationships is the third-party trust structure of Public Key Infrastructure (PKI) and the use of Certificates for identification. A business may have the need to interact with another to obtain services that are only available on the remote organization's network. A relationship may lead to the remote organization trusting Certificates issued by the business requiring the service. The establishment of a trusted relationship relieves the remote organization from having to manage user controls and managing them to accommodate access to the service. However, the organization must trust that the Certificates were issued with respect to the level of power they provide to the bearer. In this event, a security policy can be produced to convey how Certificates are administered within the trusted business.

General Control. Security policies typically define roles and responsibilities for groups, departments, or individuals that are required to perform certain tasks to ensure that the policy is enforced. The enforcement can include everything from proper management of data through the definition of data classification policies, to providing details on how to back up log files.

The Other Guys

The security mechanisms and processes introduced above are for a simple purpose: protection. Protection is needed from individuals or groups that can wreak havoc on personal, governmental, and business continuity.

For a long time, the security industry viewed hackers as high-tech geeks in dark rooms, driven by opportunity and greed. However, some industry leaders have exposed the fact that the assumed description is inaccurate and that cybercriminals cover the entire spectrum of character.

Donn Parker, the author of numerous books and articles on cybercrime, and the definitive expert on computer crime and the criminals who perform them, effectively identifies the fundamental characteristics of cybercriminals. Parker refers to these differentiating factors as SKRAM: skill, knowledge, resources, authority, and motives. The following sections briefly introduce Parker's definitions of SKRAM.

Skills come in many forms, including formal learning, experienced-based learning, and social skills. Of the three, social skills appear to have the least importance; however, the ability to manipulate people to obtain information is a desirable attribute. Combined with technical skills or the ability to learn from experience, social skills can assist in influencing people to reach the final goal.

Knowledge of tools and processes is essential in committing a cybercrime. Parker divides criminals into three categories: those who create the tools for the crime; those who have the necessary skills and knowledge and who plan to carryout the crime; and those who use others' knowledge and tools to perform the crime. The latter, in this author's opinion, covers the majority of cybercriminals on the Internet. It is common practice for a few misdirected and knowledgeable people to discover vulnerabilities and write scripts to automatically exploit them. Once the tools are made available to the public, anyone can exploit the vulnerability without having the knowledge to do so alone.

Resources represent the means to execute a crime. Obtaining resources, in most cases, is easy and many criminals will leverage their social and technical skills in doing so. However, uncommon systems or media can be more secure simply because less of it is available as a resource for the attacker to manipulate data and learn processes. Consequently, less popular operating systems or applications are more difficult to obtain resources for an attack because exposure is limited. A loose example of security relative to exposure is the proliferation of viruses in Microsoft operating systems. The shear volume of Microsoft ensures an effective result. The same holds true for cyber-crime. In the event a target system or network is a common environment, a criminal will have many more resources available than if the system or media is more atypical.

Authority refers to the assigned user rights or privileges that an attacker has or needs to execute the crime. The rights can range from the ability to run a certain application, manipulate files, or gain physical access to rooms or buildings. Obtaining the authority can be key to performing the attack, and therefore many criminals focus on passwords. Many tools and scripts that exploit various vulnerabilities are designed to retrieve data that will allow greater access at a later time. An example is vulnerabilities that may allow an attacker to obtain password files from a secure system. Once the necessary file has been obtained, an attacker can extract information from it offline, and use it to gain greater access to the system at a later date.

Motives are difficult to define, given the ever-changing environment and personalities of criminals. However, a motive must exist to provide the catalyst for the other characteristics of a criminal.

Once these attributes of a criminal are understood by a security professional, whose job it is to eliminate such an attacker from gaining access, various tools and technologies can be implemented to thwart criminal activities.

There are several elements in information systems that by their very nature are feared by attackers. Unpredictability and a layered infrastructure, or complexity, are two features that are very powerful against attackers. The term "complexity" in this subject area should not be confused with the technical complexity of a security mechanism, but rather the effective complexity of the attack path. An example is a door with two different kinds of locks. While simple in nature and implementation, it complicates the attack and preparation. Unpredictable environments increase the likelihood of being caught or discovered in some unanticipated manner. Obviously, the perfect crime requires ultimate anonymity; and in a known computing environment, anonymity can be attained through technique — unfortunately for the attacker, this is not true in a nebulous condition.

While IPSec VPNs cannot claim success in the area of unpredictability, nor can any protocol for that matter, a layered approached to security is certainly its forte. In discussing the security features of IPSec throughout the book, it will soon become clear that penetrating the security services will not be a trivial task. Knowing who the criminals are, what they need and their basic motivations, and each layer of security that IPSec provides, the reader will be able to successfully design comprehensive VPN solutions for any environment.

What Does VPN Mean?

VPN means several things, depending on where one is on any given day and the people one happens to talk to about VPNs. For many people, the term "VPN" encompasses several types and implementations of various technologies.

In a simple conceptual way, a VPN is much like a phone call. The caller knows a specific number to enter to communicate with someone. The next step involves an invisible maze of interconnections and call setup processes, in which many organizations interact to establish an association to allow the call to complete. From the caller's perspective, the other end rings and the conversation begins. The caller is completely unaware of the virtual sea of conversations that are happening over the same wire, or bouncing off the same satellites. At a very basic level, this is the same concept with VPNs. A private session is established over an open sea of alternate interactions and vulnerabilities. The differentiating factor that IPSec provides, which has been missing, is the suite of security services. These services operate not only to isolate private communication, but protect them as well, using a full arsenal of cryptographic and communication techniques.

Recently, there has been a direct association of VPNs and the Internet. This is completely understandable given that people want to use this technology to take advantage of an existing global network. However, the Internet is just another network. VPNs can be applied to any network, including internal local area networks (LANs) and wide area networks (WANs). While internal use is rare today, as security evolves and the realization that any unencrypted data — whether on a trusted or untrusted network — is vulnerable, VPNs on internal networks will soon become mainstream. An example of the trend in this direction is Windows 2000 and its support for IPSec at the host level. A user can configure a VPN to a certain server for a certain application, protecting the information from local threats (e.g., network sniffers). Through the use of group policies and leveraging Active Directory, administrators can identify certain systems and applications to be protected by VPN technology throughout the enterprise. Another unique aspect of IPSec is the ability to nest communications and establish various levels of security at different points in the communication path. Much of this will be covered in detail, but an immediate example is an Internet edge device that provides IPSec VPN services to a private network. Authenticated remote systems can establish a VPN with the edge device and then with an internal system. Depending on the characteristics of the communication and the VPN policy defined by an administrator, different levels of security can be applied to the VPN between the remote system and the edge device, and the internal resource to the remote system. VPNs today, at the time this book was written, simply do not operate at this level. However, Windows 2000 does introduce VPN technology for internal uses whereas typical scenarios revolve around the Internet.

For most, VPN is defined as an extension of an enterprise's private network across a public network, such as the Internet. The creation of a session through a public network to support operations on either side is typically referred to as a virtual network. The key point that separates the various definitions is security. While some VPN technologies provide a virtual connection between two hosts or networks, they are not necessarily secure. Some technologies tagged as VPNs simply provide a communication path from one private network to another. Some of these technologies simply absorb communication information from one network and transport it to another through a sea of technology that would not normally allow the original communication — without any protection. A good example is a tunneling protocol such as GRE (general routing encapsulation). A network that operates using IPX/SPX protocol can communicate over the Internet (TCP/IP protocol based) with other IPX/SPX networks by allowing the original protocol to be encapsulated and forwarded on a foreign network. There are several other examples, such as SNA and DLSW, all of which provide communication in a tunneled format, but without robust security for protection. These standards are properly referred to as tunneling protocols and should not be considered a secure VPN.

For the purposes of this book, a VPN is a network that provides authentication, confidentiality, and private communications over an untrusted medium.

Why are VPNs So Popular?

Open just about any trade magazine, book, or Web site and one can see some reference to VPN. Although technology has made substantial advances, people and business want more — and rightly so. As technology and the Internet have expanded at a break-neck pace, it has inadvertently trained the public in waiting for the next "big thing." How many times have people said they want a new computer but are waiting for the next processor they read about? It is in our blood and it is part of everyday activities in a technologically driven society.

VPNs offer a great deal to the business community. Why is the business community being isolated? The government maintains its own form of secure communications, and the cost of implementing a complex infrastructure is negligible compared to the information being shared. Also, the government is not concerned with ensuring income and keeping investors happy. If that were the case, IRS stock would be a poor investment. Personal VPN use is nearly nonexistent and personal activities are generally random and not typically the focus of attacks. In most cases, individuals who wish to have private communications use encryption for each message that they feel deserves the extra attention to confidentiality. Therefore, the focus here is on business, due to the limitless options available to them to confront the challenges forced upon them on a regular basis. It should also be noted that a very complicated issue arises when personal activities are married with business activities on home or personal systems on the Internet using VPN technology to access corporate private data. This aspect of VPNs equates to a direct threat to business information and continuity.

Cost Savings

Businesses are in business to make money; it is just that simple. VPN technology, in certain salutations and designs, can produce huge cost savings when compared to conventional communication technologies. The most obvious is remote access because business-operated phone lines do not need to be provided and the number of simultaneous connection is virtually unlimited. The ironic part is that IPSec is well-defined for remote access, specifically with regard to remote user authentication. Nevertheless, technology as a holistic solution is well-suited for remote capabilities. Before VPNs became easily available, remote access was supported by modem pools that became very expensive and were difficult to scale. The answer to having separate modems was virtual modems that operated as virtual ports that supplied signaling to remote users; however, this solution still required phone lines for each connection. It was not uncommon to see modem pools attached to access concentrators that ultimately fed into drones, or machines dedicated for remote users. Cubix and Citrix established a profitable business by providing consolidated systems. A remote user would dial in from a remote location, consuming a phone line, and use a remote control software package such as PCAnywhere to control the drone. Because the drone had direct connectivity to the internal network and all the necessary applications were loaded, the limited bandwidth of the dial-up connection was used simply for screen updates and keyboard input. Needless to say, this was an incredibly expensive solution, albeit popular.

VPN arrives on the market, promising huge numbers of remote access capabilities in a single box, although during the entire process, the essential driver was the advent of broadband Internet access. With high-speed, cheap Internet access, performance considerations were greatly reduced and the overhead of security protocols seemed acceptable. Ultimately, the fundamental popularity and cost savings realized by VPN technology was based on the ability to take advantage of expanded bandwidth to the Internet and move away from limited bandwidth provided by standard modems.

Network-to-network-based VPNs, as opposed to providing remote access for users, provide costs savings as well, but not nearly as dramatically as remote user access. The ability to save money by creating a WAN environment based completely on VPN is directly related to the design structure and communication's sensitivity to latency. In a point-to-point WAN, the same basic structure would be replicated by VPN; however, the cost of expanded Internet connectivity cancels basic WAN costs. On the other hand, in meshed networks where several sites are communicating with many others, the cost savings can be quickly realized. This is because each connection within a VPN incurs no added costs. Once the original physical connection to the Internet is established, virtual connection can be implemented instantly.

Scalability

The ability to scale a VPN solution is reliant on many factors, starting with the original design requirements and the product's overall performance history and capabilities. However, when VPN, as a technology, is compared to other forms of communication technology, the scalability options are tremendous.

In a remote VPN user support solution, a client package can simply be deployed to new users or groups as the service is required. When compared to conventional dial-up solutions, any substantial increase in the number of users to support would almost certainly mean the addition of equipment and possibly require an increase in the number of available phone lines. Of course, the VPN access device's ability to support multiple users is finite, but it is processor and memory based. Adding a user does increase Internet connection loads and VPN system loads; however, when properly designed for expected growth, these do not become operational issues. In contrast, the cost of a traditional remote access solution was so great that building scalability into the original solution was not cost-effective. It was very rare to see a remote access solution that had 100 modems when only 70 people could be on the system at any one time. The act of building 30 percent growth into modems, access systems, and phone lines into a solution was not typically considered. In nearly all cases, the components were added when required. The difference between traditional remote access solutions and VPN is that expandability can be harnessed immediately at the same entry cost, which ultimately reduces cost in the form of return on investment (ROI) and cost of ownership.

Enhanced Communication Security

Prior to VPN technology, communications were simply open to attack over conventional media. It was unusual to find encrypted information being shared on private networks. The differentiating factor was that data was traversing private networks and WANs that could be considered secure and protected from the general public. Frame Relay providers, such as Sprint, MCI, GTE, and AT&T, maintain physical and digital access standards, reducing the exposure of the data.

As the Internet grew and began to be used for conveying information, it soon became clear that anyone on the Internet could obtain that information. Simplified encryption was employed in e-mail programs and in basic application interfaces.

As VPNs were introduced, a shift in Internet communications followed: the protection control was removed from the application and user levels to the network levels. VPN technology allowed programs and operators to work normally without concern for data confidentiality. Security became inherent to the communication, virtually matching the level of security experienced with private networks. Now, with VPN technology, the Internet could be truly leveraged for private communications in a seamless network.

Intended Audience

This book can be used in several scenarios for a wide scope of people attempting to accomplish anything with IPSec VPNs. Everyone from network professionals and developers, to people who have the desire to learn more about popular technologies, have much to gain from reading this book.

Network Professionals

Several organizations have a desire to implement a VPN for many reasons. Some might want to conserve money, expand services, enhance performance, or provide new means of establishing communications to partnering businesses. Nonetheless, there are administrators who are tasked with determining and implementing a solution to meet whichever need has been directed. This book assists in exposing the inner workings and eccentricities that surround IPSec VPNs. By providing detailed examples of what can be typically seen in a VPN, network processionals and administrators are better prepared to confront issues in their environments.

Consultants

Many organizations look to an outside source to obtain a dedicated resource that fully comprehends the aspects of VPN technology. This is a typical scenario when internal resources do not know or have the time to invest in learning a new technology. Many organizations feel that employing a consultant allows them to benefit from the years of experience a consultant may have in other diverse situations attempting to deploy the same technology. Consultants who need to prepare for new engagements can use this book to draw from and learn more about IPSec and the issues that must be addressed when creating comprehensive designs. By knowing more about the technology as a whole, and not necessarily from a product perspective, pitfalls in selecting and determining the best solution can be avoided. Understanding the protocols, operations supported within IPSec, and the various design requirements will greatly enhance a consultant's ability to properly guide and support a client's needs.

Developers

While this book contains a great deal of detail and inner workings of the suite of IPSec protocols, the RFCs that define the standard are required to develop a compliant VPN solution. However, enough technical detail is available, which can be used to understand a system's role in a VPN from an operational perspective. When developing software or hardware, it is necessary to be aware of the proposed uses and expected functionalities. This book contains many points of interest — with regard to both deployment and use — that a developer can leverage to create a more inclusive solution.

Technical Individuals

There is a sea of individuals who have a desire to learn about interesting technologies that may not have a direct impact on their daily activities. Nevertheless, some people simply enjoy learning about new concepts. In reality, that is how people typically become experts in or knowledgeable about a certain technology. Individuals see something that interests them on many levels and then investigate it. The author has tried to create a collection of thoughts and experiences that not only provide valuable information but also stimulate the reader to think about the processes in-depth. IPSec is very interesting, specifically the key management aspects. The sharing of certain information at specific times in the communication can be incredibly fascinating. As novice readers become more involved, they can play with options of communication and formats using the building blocks of the communication standard to create communication scenarios. At first glance, this may sound odd, and a bit too geek-like, but many discussions in the IETF IPSec working groups are about variations on the theme to accomplish increased functionality. Therefore, everyone who knows a great deal about IPSec has entertained the idea of modified messages. The reader is encouraged to look deeply into the communication and ask questions. The options and information available never seem to stop changing.

What One Should Know

VPNs can be a complicated subject, depending on the depth of technical aspects being covered. VPNs touch on many aspects of computer communication technologies. Communication protocols, internetworking, security, architectures, and law represent some of the areas that require understanding.

To get the most out of this book, one should already be familiar with the operation of networking and how a typical system connects to the Internet. This book does cover some basic internetworking fundamentals and provides an overview of the TCP/IP protocol suite. This introductory process provides a common understanding of the aspects and definitions that will be leveraged and assumed to be understood later in the book.

The goal is to present the technical aspects of IPSec; therefore, an understanding of VPNs and the standard concepts and operations will certainly help in getting the most from this book. Albeit, not necessary because many of the concepts are discussed, but as more complicated theories and practices are discussed, the fundamentals will be required.

If one can understand the relationships that are maintained in a simple IP network, one will gain a great deal of insight into a technology that simply builds on those foundations. This book provides simple explanations and lays the groundwork to assist the reader in understanding every step of the process. If one is an experienced network or security professional and have worked heavily with VPNs, this book will shed some light on the inner workings of the IPSec suite. Also, one will benefit from experiences described for product selection processes, to lab testing, to pilot phase and rollout concepts.

Chapter 2

Technical Primer

This chapter addresses some of the underlying technology that makes up the communication that IPSec is part of. It also investigates other VPN standards and introduces the operations of cryptography.

The primary subject of this chapter is the TCP/IP protocol and where IPSec fits into the process. It is absolutely necessary to understand the basics of TCP/IP and the fundamental structure that allows IPSec to provide the security services.

To fully appreciate the IPSec protocol, it is necessary to not only be aware of, but to have a basic understanding of other VPN standards. There are several other standards and protocols that provide VPN connectivity at different levels within the operating environment to accomplish certain tasks. Each provides a specific service that relates to environmental demands that gave birth to the technology. In some cases, other tunneling protocol standards take advantage of IPSec and operate within an IPSec VPN.

Cryptography is the base of IPSec and provides the common process to create a secure VPN. Cryptography is a science and involves much more than encryption technologies that supply confidentiality. Cryptography includes authentication, integrity, digital signing concepts, and distinctive methods of merging these practices to accomplish a high degree of security.

TCP/IP Quickie

TCP/IP is the language of the Internet and it allows all different types of computers with very different operating systems to communicate seamlessly over an enormous network. This chapter defines the basics of TCP/IP and builds models that will be referenced throughout the book to illustrate the various aspects of VPNs. This chapter is not intended to teach or detail TCP/IP, but rather touch upon points of the protocol suite to provide a foundation for concepts to be detailed in later chapters.

Common TCP/IP Networks

The Internet is a vast network that utilizes the TCP/IP protocol for communications. Ironically, while the sheer size can be intimidating, the reality is that even the smallest of networks can emulate basic system interactions on the Internet. By providing the few required characteristics and components of a TCP/IP network, the fundamental properties of the Internet can be duplicated. Therefore, once the simple aspects of a TCP/IP network are understood, a great deal of that knowledge can be applied to the Internet and implementing VPNs for worldwide communications.

The effective simplicity of TCP/IP and the ability to duplicate massive networks in the smallest of labs are enormous advantages when testing IPSec VPNs. Name resolution, routing protocols, domains, services that are part of the real Internet — all can be eliminated without affecting IPSec operations. An example of a simplified lab can be a single router with two Ethernet interfaces configured with different network addresses. Connect a client system to one network and a target system to the other and configure them to play a part in the local network by assigning them a suitable IP address. The last step is configuring the gateway information so each system knows where to send packets that are not on the same network. In Exhibit 2-1, the example is displayed. The target and client system are both configured with an IP address that lets them participate on the same network as the router's interface. The client and target system's gateway is the router's interface on its immediate network. By having two networks defined and a gateway configured, the essential aspects of the Internet are met.

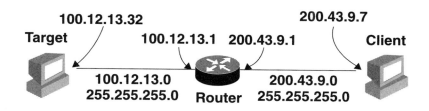

Exhibit 2-1.   Simplified Internet model.

Now, add one more component to represent a common Internet connection. A system is added between the router and the target host. The system can be a firewall or a VPN device; nevertheless, it fundamentally operates as another router on the network, providing access to the new internal network defined as 10.1.1.0 with a subnet mask of 255.255.255.0 (see Exhibit 2-2). The addition of the VPN device adds a slight complexity to the process of IP communications. If the client system wants to access the target host on the privately addressed network, it must traverse both routers. On the surface, this is a simple router modification where a static route can be added to allow communications to flow through both devices in either direction. However, one is trying to replicate the Internet and with that one must adhere to the same rules that govern basic Internet infrastructure.

One of the rules of the Internet is private addressing schemes, which are used by IP-based networks that do not wish to be routed throughout the Internet, and are not permitted to traverse the Internet. The allocation of private addresses allows organizations to have a set of IP address ranges that they can use without worry of contention with other networks. One of these ranges includes the 10.1.1.0 network in this example. Any Internet router will immediately drop a packet that has a private address for a destination. Therefore, to add a static route to the systems to allow open communications between the routers and host systems would violate this elemental property of the Internet.

The ramifications of misconfiguring an Internet representation in a lab scenario will be detrimental to the experiment. The author has seen examples where people have made this mistake and attempted to test the VPN solution. The result is that it seems to work correctly some of the time or communications were normal but not encrypted. What would happen is that the connection would simply route around the expected direction and not apply correctly within the VPN; it simply knew a better way to get to the target.

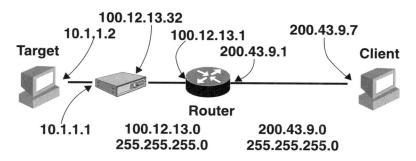

Exhibit 2-2.   Simplified Internet network with an added device.

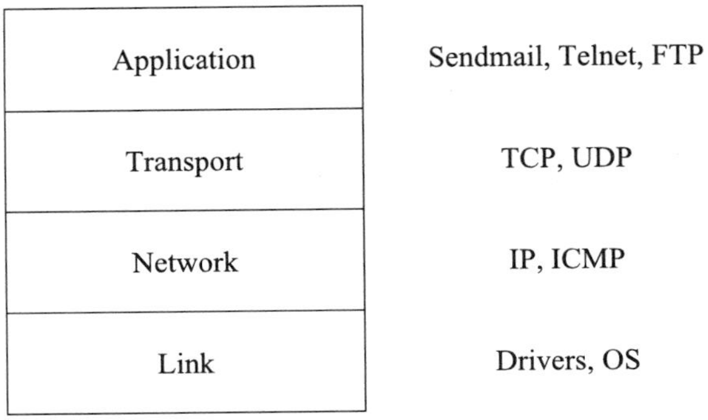

Application	Sendmail, Telnet, FTP
Transport	TCP, UDP
Network	IP, ICMP
Link	Drivers, OS

Exhibit 2-3. DOD reference model.

So, one may be wondering how the client system can access the target if there is no route to the 10.1.1.0 network and that IP address is not allowed to route through the primary router. This is where the details of IPSec become reality and provide the private connection through the Internet to the target. The seemingly simple task of data from the client to the target is an oversimplification of a very complex truth.

Reference Models

In the early 1960s, government-funded research projects that were tasked with developing a packet switching network for the Department of Defense (DOD) introduced a fundamental concept in networking technology. They could provide controlled communications by providing layers of protocols that addressed certain aspects of the communication. The result was the TCP/IP protocol suite, that is, the combination of several specifically assigned protocols that work in several layers.

The layers were made up of four levels, with the highest being the application layer, followed by the transport Layer, network Layer, and finally the link Layer, as shown in Exhibit 2-3.

The DOD reference model best represents a TCP/IP protocol stack. However, for overall computer operations, most processes are referenced against the Open Systems Interconnection (OSI) reference model. The OSI model is a seven-layered international standard developed under the guidance of the International Organization for Standardization (ISO). This model is used to explain the interactions of computer processes and how they relate to any set of protocols, applications, and networking technologies.

Note: In this book, the DOD model layers will be referenced by name (e.g., application, network, etc.) and the OSI model layers will be referenced by number (e.g., Layer 2, Layer 7, etc.). Unfortunately, both models must be consulted to express specific concepts and this will help eliminate any confusion.

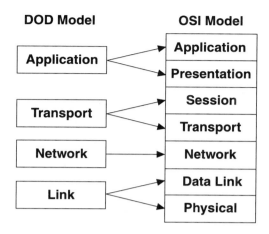

Exhibit 2-4. DOD to OSI reference map.

The OSI model is illustrated in Exhibit 2-4; a mapping between the OSI and DOD TCP/IP model is graphically displayed.

As described above, the DOD reference model best represents the TCP/IP protocol. To understand how TCP/IP operates and the roles of the different layers, the following gives a brief description of each layer.

Each layer, whether in a four-layered DOD model or a seven-layered ISO model, has a counterpart layer that is operating in the communication peer. One layer may allow TCP to communicate (over the transport layer), whereas the IP, or network layer, provides communication for the IP protocol. Each layer in the protocol stack is only aware of the communicating peer layer and relies on the other layers to provide their peer services to maintain the communications. The network layer that allows the IP protocol to operate is oblivious to the transport layer communications. The network layer simply accepts packaged data from the transport layer and communicates with its network layer peer. To do so, the network layer depends on the link layer to support its communication requirements.

The result is an internal hand-off of data up or down the protocol stack to accomplish paired layer communications between peer systems. This allows other specific operations to be added into, or between layers of operation to add functionality.

Application Layer. The application layer provides an interface for the applications wanting service from the IP protocol stack. E-mail, FTP, and Telnet are good examples of application layer interfaces with networking operations. The application layer handles the details of the particular application requiring network communications. It is concerned with the application requirements and not with the actual movement of data over the network. The application layer simply focuses on the details of the application and passes the necessary information to the lower layers to be transmitted to its peer application layer of the communicating partner. The lower layers are unaware of the application requirements or the activities of the application layer.

Transport Layer. The transport layer provides a controlled flow of data between the host's applications in the communication. In the TCP/IP protocol suite, there are two very distinctive transport layer protocols: TCP and UDP.

1. *Transmission Control Protocol (TCP):* provides a reliable flow of data in the communication; this is typically referred to as connection-oriented communications. TCP provides reliable flow of information between two peers. It is concerned with collecting and dividing the data it received from the application layer into predefined portions to be accepted by the network layer. It is required to acknowledge packets received and set time limits to wait for an acknowledgment from its peer that it received the transmission. Because TCP addresses the issue of the status of the communication, upper layer protocols are released from having to verify the communication.

2. *User Datagram Protocol (UDP):* provides simple forwarding of datagrams and is not concerned with the status of the communication once the datagram is sent. Because UDP is unaware of the status of the datagram and is unaware if the recipient received the data, it is referred to as connectionless-oriented communications. Given that UDP provides no guarantee that the datagram will reach the communication peer, upper layer protocols and applications must provide reliability if desired.

Network Layer. The network layer is concerned with taking the predefined datagrams from the transport layer and sending them in the appropriate direction to get to the defined destination. The network layer is typically referred to as the Internet layer because routing protocols that share physical connection information operate at the network layer. There are several protocols that provide services within the network layer. The Internet Protocol (IP), the workhorse of the network layer, is responsible for addressing connectivity. The Internet Control Message Protocol (ICMP) is considered part of the network layer. It communicates error messages and networking conditions that require some form of attention, either in the form of a modified configuration or automatic rectifications such as redirections. It is typical for the transport layer protocols to act upon the messages provided by ICMP, but upper layers as well can glean information and make adjustments based on the messages provided. Internet Group Management Protocol (IGMP) provides a service for multicast communications and messaging. All the hosts and routers on a physical network use IGMP to determine which systems currently belong to which multicast groups. This information is required by routers performing multicast functions so they know which multicast datagrams to forward to which interfaces. Like ICMP, IGMP is considered part of the network layer and uses IP to transmit its information through a network.

As stated previously, there are several protocols that exist at the transport and network layers that have not been introduced. Within the IP header, there is an 8-bit field, called the protocol identifier, which is used to identify the protocol that provided the information to the IP protocol. The protocol field will typically define the next header following the IP header. The maximum value is 8-bits, or 255 different values. Of the available values, there are 128 currently assigned; that is, 128 different protocols! (See the appendix for a complete list of protocols, their number, and associated RFCs.)

Link Layer. The link layer, also called the data-link layer and network interface layer, is tasked with managing the interface between the network layer and the operating system and the hardware providing the connectivity. The network layer may know an address to send a packet but has no idea how to put that packet on the wire. Network interface drivers installed on the operating system provide the link between the packet and the attribute required to send the data.

Included in the link layer are the physical attributes for communication. The wire, fiber, microwave, infrared, etc. are addressed in the link layer in the DOD model, and called the physical layer, or Layer 1, in the ISO model. In essence, the link layer is the combination of the first and second layers of the ISO model. It controls the data format, such as Ethernet, Token Ring, HDLC, PPP, Frame Relay, etc. to ensure that the communications matched not only the local physical requirements but also the communication topology. Once the topology has been configured and applied, getting the frames, cells, or transmission units onto the physical media is the next responsibility of the link layer (or Layer 1). All these tasks are realized by the marriage between operating system, hardware, application, and protocol to manage the task of low-level communications.

Communication Types

Many protocols have several formats they operate in to accomplish different tasks required by the applications and systems they support, or for self-management. In short, TCP/IP has three fundamental communication types that provide different services to the systems, applications, and network topology that it supports.

1. unicast
2. multicast
3. broadcast

Unicast is simply one host communicating directly with another. When using a Web browser to access a Web site, one is establishing a connection with that remote machine. In some cases, one may want to establish connections with other Web servers to obtain data to complete the final presentation; nevertheless, one has a peer communication with the other system.

Broadcast is nearly the opposite of unicast. In a broadcast, the originating system attempts to communicate with any system within reach that will answer. There are several protocols within TCP/IP that use broadcast messaging to obtain information about the environment. Even applications can demand the use of broadcasts for discovery purposes. An example is network neighborhood and the listing of other Microsoft-compliant systems on the network. If not supported by a naming infrastructure, like WINS (Windows Internet Naming Service), the client systems will broadcast in search of specific hosts that have a compiled list of other systems. And, of course, the system that maintains the list must broadcast to obtain the information and keep the list updated to share with the other systems. Unfortunately, for some networks, broadcasts from hosts can get out of control and the result is broadcast storms that can flood networks, rendering them useless. Many of the detrimental effects of broadcasts can be reduced by proper network design and operating system configuration. In a well-designed infrastructure, broadcasts can be helpful in communications and increase the usability of the network from the perspective of a user.

Somewhere in between broadcast and unicast is multicast. Multicast can become complicated, depending on the implementation, but there are rewards for doing it correctly. Multicast provides a messaging platform for the simultaneous delivery of data to multiple destinations. Unlike unicast where a connection must be established with each system — which can add up quickly — or broadcasts that seemingly have no direction whatsoever, multicast can communicate with certain groups of systems. There are several applications that can take full advantage of delivering information to multiple recipients. Conference calling, dissemination of information such as e-mail, or system operations such as remote booting all can rely on multicast to enhance communication. Multicast has a special address range, sometimes referred to as Class D; the IP addresses range from 224.0.0.0 to 239.255.255.255. A set of hosts that listens on a particular multicast IP address are called host groups, and they can span multiple networks. Some multicast addresses are assigned and operate much like the protocol or port numbers assigned to other IP communications. An example is 224.0.0.1, which is defaulted at all systems on the local subnet, and 244.0.0.2 isolates all the routers on a particular subnet. There are some addresses that are protocol specific, such as 244.0.1.1 for Network Time Protocol (NTP).

Packet Structure

As data is moved up and down the protocol stack, information that pertains to that layer is added or removed for processing. As illustrated in Exhibit 2-5, a simple explanation of this process considers an e-mail application sending a message. The application takes all the necessary steps to ensure that the mail server processes the message appropriately. This includes items such as a recipient e-mail address, sender identification, and attachment encoding that the server handling the message will require.

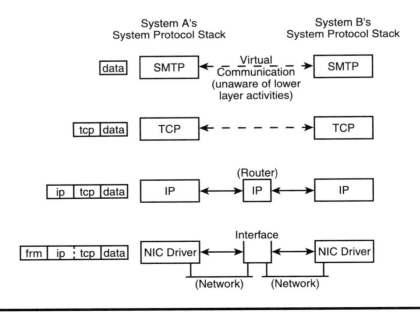

Exhibit 2-5. TCP/IP protocol stack.

The information is passed to the transport layer to be divided into appropriately sized packets and appended with transport layer-specific information. A header is appended to the beginning of the newly constructed packet. The header type will be TCP or UDP, depending on the application requirements or desire for flow control. In the example with sending mail, TCP is required to provide management of information as it is processed on either end of the communication. The information within the TCP header pertains to flow control and acknowledgment processes, among others. This includes information such as the source and destination service port number; in this example, port 25 is for sending mail (ports are described later in this chapter), flow control switches, and sequence numbers.

The completed packet is passed to the network layer where the packet is provided information required to get to the destination. Typically, the network layer is not concerned or aware of the upper layer information; it is simply concerned with providing the connection necessary to move the packet. As with the transport layer, a header is appended to the beginning of the packet to provide information to the destination and intermediate systems in the communication stream. The data in the IP header includes the source and destination IP address of the participating hosts, protocol type, checksum information, and various options that enhance the communication process.

Finally, the packets containing the data, flow control information, service information, and connection information are placed into a frame for transmission over a medium. The medium across the Internet can range from serial lines to fiber, running everything from Point to Point Protocol (PPP) to ATM.

As briefly described, the TCP/IP protocol suite provides several layers that are responsible for individual functions that work together to communicate data. One of the many advantages of providing a stack of predefined functions is the transparency provided to the next higher layer. An example: the network layer provides a completely unreliable service. It will obtain all the information necessary to get the packet on its way but there are no checking mechanisms to verify the communication. In contrast, TCP, which operates at the transmission control layer, provides the reliability in the form of sequence numbers, timeout values, and acknowledgments of receipt from both ends of the communication.

In the other direction from the network layer, the link layer hides the underlying physical technology. The upper layers are totally unaware of the idiosyncrasies of how the hosts are actually communicating. Communication can be provided by serial lines, Ethernet, Token Ring, fiber, ATM, microwave, radio, or just about any kind of communication platform or medium.

The combination of a layered protocol stack and the concept of transparency is one of the many reasons why the Internet has become such a success. The applications only need to be aware of some basic properties — service, IP address, and other locally significant data — to communicate with any other system in the world, regardless of much of the communication technology.

IPSec takes advantage of the layering and the aspect of transparency, limited application involvement, and the specifically assigned functions within a protocol stack. One will see the sheer inventiveness of IPSec and the simplicity in its basic operation.

Header. The headers, provided by the TCP/IP protocol suite, are based on 32-bit values that are transmitted in a specific order. Each 32-bit section, or *word*, represents 4 bytes of information sent in 8-bit groups. Bits 0 to 7 are sent, followed by 8 to 15,

16 to 23, and finally, 24 to 31, the last set to complete the 32-bit transmission. This is called the *network byte order* and represents how the 1s and 0s are transmitted.

The header length is the number of 32-bit words contained within the header. To explain further, the IP header length field allows 4 bits to convey the number of words contained in the IP header. If the value was F (in hex) or 1111 (in binary), the maximum number of bytes an IP header can be is 60. All 1s equals 15, which represents 15 words. Each word is 32 bits, or 4 bytes; therefore, 15 times the number of bytes (4) equals 60 bytes.

Internet Protocol

This section addresses the aspects of IP in greater detail. IP is the final layer that provides the last line of service to all the upper layer protocols in the TCP/IP protocol stack (see Exhibit 2-6). All the upper layer protocols, such as TCP and UDP, ultimately get transmitted as IP datagrams.

The intriguing aspect of IP (i.e., the focal point of TCP/IP communications) is that IP does not provide a guaranteed delivery mechanism. IP is unreliable and connectionless; that is, IP provides no direct means to verify delivery.

Unreliable is referred to as "best effort" when discussing IP. Each component in the communication path forwards the datagram based on the best option available to the system. However, in the event that there is an error in the processing of the IP datagram, there is little effective error handling available. IP provides a simple process that **may** work: if an IP datagram error occurs, the datagram is dropped and an ICMP error message is generated by the system that detected the error and sends it to the originator for notification. Unfortunately, ICMP relies on IP; thus, the error message is exposed to the same vulnerabilities as the original IP datagram.

The term "connectionless" means that IP provides no communication state information. As each IP datagram is received or sent, the process is localized and not affected by any previously received IP datagrams, or ones that might be awaiting transmission. Every IP datagram is handled independently, without regard to the communication of the upper layer protocols or the underlying network support. To illustrate the individuality of each datagram, if two messages are configured for the same destination, they may take completely different paths across the network and arrive in a different order than they were sent.

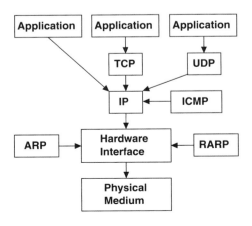

Exhibit 2-6. TCP/IP protocol hierarchy.

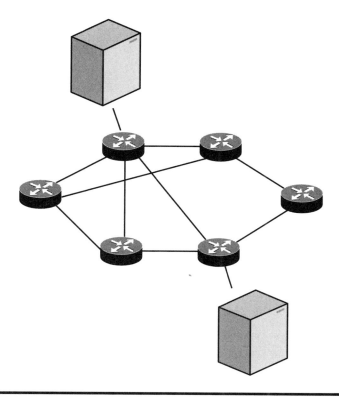

Exhibit 2-7. Redundant routed network.

Routing. The act of providing a best effort for data connectivity displays the assumption made by IP in that the network will ensure the delivery. This assumption places a great deal of responsibility on the infrastructure to efficiently forward datagrams with very low failure rates. To accommodate this requirement, many large IP networks have redundancy and many alternate paths to various destinations (see Exhibit 2-7).

An IP network is broken up into networks that represent a common addressing environment. For datagrams to travel from one network to another, a device that operates at Layer 3 is required to forward data based on the network layer attribute. Attributes can be source and destination addresses, type of service, and time to live. Routers perform this function and connect IP networks to provide internetworking. To provide the best effort, routers that have several connections to different networks may be able to provide an alternate route in the event one path is down or saturated.

Routing protocols are used to share information between routers so they can learn about the communication environment. Because IP assumes it will get to the destination, the routers will have to plan the communication to provide IP the service it requires. Routing protocol can be very simple or intensely complex. The routing protocols used throughout the Internet to ensure data reaches its destination can be extremely complicated. The inherent redundancy of alternate paths is one of the many reasons why IP datagrams can arrive at the destination out of order and at different intervals. Routing protocols are well beyond the scope of this book, but knowing they are there will provide an understanding of how network "A" can get to network "Z."

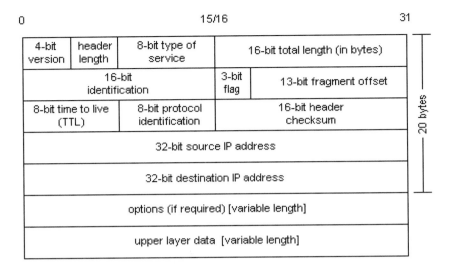

Exhibit 2-8. IP header.

Structure. The IP header (see Exhibit 2-8) contains information that pertains to the proper forwarding of the datagram. The header length is the number of words that the header uses. A typical IP header, without options, has a value of 5 (0101). Five words equates to 20 bytes of header data. This allows for 40 bytes of options because the maximum size of an IP header is 60 bytes.

Transmission Control Protocol (TCP)

This section addresses the aspects of the TCP in greater detail. TCP resides a layer above the operation of IP. Interestingly enough, UDP and TCP operate at the same level but the services provided are vastly different. TCP provides a connection-oriented process that provides a reliable communication service.

The term "connection-oriented" means that any participating systems must establish a connection with each other for a particular service prior to sharing any data.

TCP provides reliability by executing several activities. As data is passed down from the application, TCP packages the data based on network conditions that the application may be unaware of. By addressing the size of the data packages, TCP can send datagrams that will be transmitted more efficiently based on the network environment. The packages passed to the network layer are called segments.

As segments are transmitted, TCP provides a timer function that will resend the datagram if an acknowledgment is not received. In normal TCP communications, the recipient acknowledges each segment received. Because TCP segments are afforded communication by IP datagrams, the arrival of the TCP segment is not guaranteed. Therefore, acknowledgments are used to ensure the session is maintained. The process of timing that addresses the sending and resending of a segment is referred to as a TCP window. Each packet is provided a window of time that is allowed to wait for an acknowledgment prior to resending.

TCP also provides a checksum of the header data to provide a means of detecting any changes in the header during transit. If a segment arrives without a valid checksum, it is discarded. The recipient will not send an acknowledgment, and the TCP window of the initiator will timeout and resend the segment as if it was dropped in normal transit. The header checksum provided by TCP is completely worthless when discussing communication security. Any device that forwards the segment has the opportunity to change the header information and create a new checksum. As will be seen later, IPSec provides a more solid application of message authentication services.

Given that IP datagrams can take different paths to the destination, they may arrive at different times and out of order. TCP provides sequence numbers that are incremented for each segment. The sequence number restarts and returns to 0 after $2^{32} - 1$ is met. The sequence numbers provide identification to properly reassemble the data stream to be fed up to the application layers. This also allows TCP to discard duplicate packets in the event an IP datagram gets copied in transit.

Finally, TCP can provide limited flow control by the use of buffers. This allows a system to receive data that it has buffer space to accommodate. The sender can very quickly transmit data that falls within the TCP window.

TCP Application Ports. The TCP protocol supports the transmission of data on behalf of applications. To allow the protocol to address several applications with a single connection, service ports are identified. The size of the port number field is 16 bits, which allows the maximum of service ports to reach 65,535. The first 1023 are privileged ports that represent standard applications. The remaining ports are for the initial connection from the client of the service. Custom applications can, and are encouraged to, use the upper ports so as not to interfere with standard application ports.

An example of application ports is Simple Mail Transfer Protocol (SMTP), port 25. A client wishing to communicate with a server providing the SMTP service would create a TCP header with a destination port of 25 and a random source port over 1024.

Structure. The TCP header (see Exhibit 2-9) contains information that pertains to the proper handling of the datagram. It is concerned with services support, sequencing, session maintenance, and flow management.

The TCP header arrives directly after the IP header. The IP header contains a data portion that contains whatever data is being carried by the IP header. The TCP header and data reside within the data portion of the IP header.

User Datagram Protocol (UDP)

In complete contrast to TCP, UDP is a very simple datagram-oriented protocol that provides no reliability and is connectionless. UDP is typically relied upon for fast communications that are more time sensitive and can withstand the occasional delay of a retransmission.

UDP provides no reliability and is more aligned as a conduit to allow applications to send IP datagrams. The application is responsible for size and session management.

Structure. The UDP header (see Exhibit 2-10) contains very limited information. Basically, the header contains data that provides information about the origination and destination service points, length data, and a checksum to provide integrity checking.

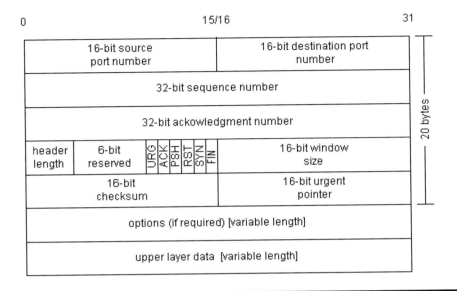

Exhibit 2-9. TCP header.

The UDP header arrives directly after the IP header. The IP header contains a data portion of whatever data is being carried by the IP header. The TCP header and data reside within the data portion of the IP header.

Pseudo Headers

One of the interesting, unpublicized aspects of TCP/IP is the inclusion of a pseudo header within TCP and UDP for the computation of the header's checksum. A checksum is a calculation, a hash, of the protocol header, options, and the payload (excluding IP) of the datagram. Therefore, a standard HTTP packet would have an IP header with its checksum spreading over the IP header, a TCP checksum covering the TCP header, and the http payload.

However, there is more to the story that will shed some light on IPSec VPN's role in certain IP networks and configurations.

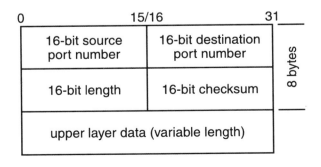

Exhibit 2-10. UDP header.

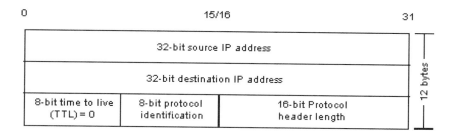

Exhibit 2-11. Pseudo header.

In Exhibit 2-11, the TCP header contains a checksum that covers the TCP header and payload. However, during the checksum computation, a 12-byte pseudo header is created and discarded once the checksum process is complete. The header contains the source and destination IP addresses from the IP header. The Time To Live (TTL) is set to 0 because TCP is transport layer and is not aware of hop count. The TTL sets an upper limit on the number of routers through which a datagram can pass, limiting the lifetime of the datagram. The originator of a packet can set the TTL to 32 or 64 and it is decremented by one for every router in the path. When the TTL reaches 0, the router discards the packet and sends an ICMP error message to the sender. By setting the TTL to 0 to create the pseudo header, the calculation of the checksum is free from knowing the number of hops from the destination.

Note: The manipulation of TTL values and the automatic error reply provided by ICMP allows such utilities as TRACERT (trace route) to operate.

The protocol field is directly from the IP header that identifies the protocol that passed data to the network layer for processing; this value should always be 6 (TCP) and 17 (UDP) because TCP and UDP are the only protocols that produce a pseudo header. Finally, the header contains the length of the protocol datagram. This is typically identical to what was previously calculated for the original header, not including the pseudo header. To include the pseudo header would be overly complicated, considering it is not included in the transmitted datagram.

The purpose of the pseudo header is to let TCP or UDP validate that the data has arrived at the correct destination and, in some cases, from the intended source. If the checksum is deemed invalid, the packet is silently discarded, as with IP checksum verifications.

Internet Control Message Protocol (ICMP)

Internet Control Message Protocol (ICMP) is typically considered part of the network layer. It communicates error messages and other conditions that require the attention of the commutation systems.

There are 15 different types of ICMP messages that contain variations identified by codes. Each type is basically an error message or a query performed by a system for discovery purposes; PING is a good example. One can use PING to determine the existence of another system.

For IPSec, one is concerned with code 3, destination unreachable. There are 15 codes that provide extended information about the actual problem. These are discussed in greater detail in subsequent chapters.

ARP and RARP

Address Resolution Protocol (ARP) and Reverse Address Resolution Protocol (RARP) are protocols that allow one layer to discover information about the other.

In the case of ARP, Layer 3 information is known; but to establish communications, Layer 2 must be provided information to allow data to flow between the two systems. ARP is used to determine who owns, or operates on behalf of, a certain IP address. Imagine two systems on the same physical network that have never communicated and only the IP address of the other is known. In the event one of the systems wishes to communicate, it will ultimately need to know the Layer 2 information to properly direct the frame containing the upper layer data. To accomplish this task, the system sends a message to everyone asking who owns the IP address that it wishes to communicate with. The system configured with the destination IP addresses responds with the Media Access Control (MAC) address of the interface connected to the network. Once the originator receives this information, it can establish Layer 2 connectivity to provide services for the upper layers.

However, there are occasions when the system may know the MAC address but is unaware of the Layer 3 IP address. The IP address is required to provide connectivity for upper layer protocols. Much like ARP, a request is sent out asking for the IP address that is configured for a particular MAC address. Once the system with an NIC configured with the defined MAC address receives the RARP request, it replies with the IP address configured.

Non-routable IP Addresses

With the worldwide explosion of TCP/IP technology, beyond the Internet itself, an escalating number of non-Internet connected organizations use TCP/IP for internal communications, without any intention of connecting to the Internet. Until RFC1918 was ratified, these various organizations using TCP/IP for internal communication addressing were using address space not assigned or owned by them. As organizations connected to the Internet, it quickly became clear that conflicts in addressing would complicate or stop communications through the Internet. To alleviate the use of non-assigned IP addresses, a group of IP addresses was slated as private and non-routable across the Internet. That is, if an ISP's router sees a private IP address, it is dropped immediately.

The Internet Assigned Numbers Authority (IANA) has reserved the following three blocks of IP address space for private internets:

- 10.0.0.0-10.255.255.255 (10/8 prefix)
- 172.16.0.0-172.31.255.255 (172.16/12 prefix)
- 192.168.0.0-192.168.255.255 (192.168/16 prefix)

An organization that decides to use these IP addresses can do so without any coordination with IANA or an Internet registry. The addresses can be used by many different organizations for internal communications. These private addresses will only be unique within an organization, or within a group of companies that chooses to agree on the IP addresses so they can communicate over their own private intranet.

Any organization that needs a globally unique address is required to obtain it from an Internet registry. An organization that requests IP addresses for its connectivity to the Internet will never be assigned the private addresses.

Network Address Translation (NAT)

The private range of IP addresses defined in RFC 1918 and allocated by the IANA discussed in the previous section is used for internal use, and ISPs will simply not forward traffic with those addresses. The first question that comes to mind is, what happens when one of the privately addressed private networks wishes to connect to the Internet?

As the Internet grew, many organizations simply connected their networks to the Internet using routable IP addresses assigned to them by the IANA or ISP. Unfortunately, this process was consuming IP addresses at an astounding rate. Therefore, a process was defined that allowed internal private IP addresses to be translated into valid Internet IP addresses. To reduce the numbers of used Internet routable IP addresses, several internal systems could communicate using only one external IP address.

Note: The translation process can work for any IP address and not just for the ranges defined in the RFC. The internal private addresses are consistently referred to, allowing simplicity and uniformity in the explanation.

Network Address Translation (NAT) is a method that allows the mapping of one network of IP addresses to another, differently addressed network. This is not routing — it is a translation process to get one network to communicate with another. NAT has been typically associated with providing access to the Internet for networks assigned with the private addressing scheme.

There are two aspects of IP communications that NAT attempts to answer. The first is allowing IP address to have valid communications to remote networks that may have the same IP address domain or would not normally allow communications from the assigned IP domain. Second, NAT provides anonymity by hiding the originating IP address from the external peer. The peer simply receives a datagram from the device performing the NAT for the hidden network.

Within NAT there are two basic states, each having a different name, depending on who one is talking to at the time; here, the two states are Hide and Static. Hide represents the state of the NAT device where any number of internal hosts assigned with private IP addresses can be allowed access to the Internet via a single valid address assigned to the NAT'ing device.

As shown in Exhibit 2-12, each internal system has its own private IP address. However, as the communication is forwarded to the Internet, the traffic assumes the IP address of the router's external IP address. Any remote system will see traffic originating from the router and not the internal systems. The router maintains a table of associations and state information to properly forward incoming packets to the appropriate internal system. The layers of operation within TCP/IP allow several

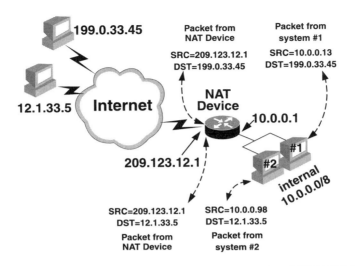

Exhibit 2-12. Hide network address translation.

instances communications. For example, if three internal users are accessing the same Web page at the same time, the remote Web server will establish three separate sessions with the same IP address — that of the router. The robustness of TCP/IP and the relationships between the layers of operations allow seemingly complicated transaction to happen nearly effortlessly.

The other state of NAT is Static. Static is a direct coloration of a single internal IP address to a single external IP address. This is simply a Hide NAT for a single box and nearly eliminates the need for a state table.

As shown in Exhibit 2-13, the communication is coming from the external system wishing to access services on System #1 on the internal network. In the example, the remote system is attempting to communicate with a virtual address. A virtual address is an IP address that is not necessarily associated with an interface or MAC address. However, the router has been configured to accept any packets for that IP address.

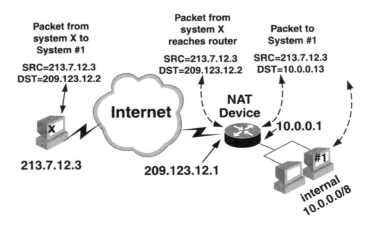

Exhibit 2-13. Static network address translation.

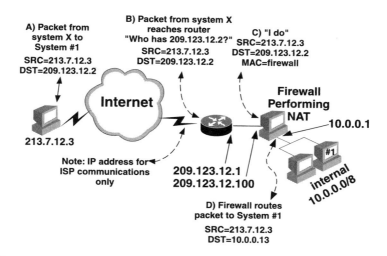

Exhibit 2-14. Static network address translation with proxy ARP.

In some configurations, especially with firewalls on a broadcast medium, the NAT'ing device (i.e., firewall) can be configured to answer ARP requests from external communication systems. In such a scenario, a router may be providing access to the Internet with a firewall behind the router, as shown in Exhibit 2-14. In any case, the IP address must be properly routed to the NAT'ing device, where a routing table resides that determines how to forward the packet. In the example, the router is forwarded to the virtual IP address because the ISP has assigned that range to the router. Once the packet is received, the router must determine who the IP address is assigned to forward it. If the router does not already have the MAC address of the owner, it will broadcast for it with an ARP request. Unfortunately, the system that needs the traffic is not only inside the internal network but does not have that IP address. To accommodate this process, the firewall is configured to answer any ARP requests for that IP address; this method is called an ARP proxy. The router obtains the firewall's MAC address and forwards the IP packet to the firewall. Because the firewall is the final destination for the data link layer, the protocol is removed from the frame and processed by the protocol stack. At that point, the firewall provides NAT service and forwards the datagram accordingly to System #1.

Note: It is possible to have Static and Hide NAT at the same time on the same device performing the NAT operations.

Network Address Translation is responsible for several operations and each depends on the protocols and communication being established.

1. changing the source IP address and destination IP address, depending on the communication direction and requirements
2. updating the checksum of the checksum of the protocol headers
3. updating IP addresses internal to the datagram payload
4. maintaining a communication state table to allow the multiplexing of internal communications to an external singularity

To accommodate these changes, the NAT device must change several aspects about the packet. Specifically, the checksums must be recalculated. In a simple scenario, only the IP header addresses and checksum must be changed. However, the TCP or UDP header checksum must also be updated, to allow for the pseudo header that was calculated during the creation of the datagram. This is true because some NAT provisioning systems modify the source service port to assist in keeping track of the NAT'ed communications. Therefore, because NAT operations modify all the way to the transport layer, the TCP or UDP checksums must be calculated.

IPSec and TCP/IP Layers

Of the layers of protocols, one is of concern for the purposes of IPSec — the network layer. IPSec operates at the network layer and has no impact on the upper layers by the services it provides. Furthermore, IPSec has no effect on the lower layers providing connectivity. The act of participating in a network connection at a certain level is one of the many aspects of IPSec that is so attractive. Simply put, IPSec can be applied to a communication stream without any modification to applications or intermediate systems providing the connectivity, like a router—that also works at the network layer.

IPSec goes one step further and interacts with the other processes that are being performed within the network layer. As data reaches the network layer, IPSec can be applied, or not, depending on the configuration of the VPN (see Exhibit 2-15). Communication information associated with the data is inspected by the IPSec process to determine if it should be provided IPSec services. If not, the data is then processed as if IPSec were absent. As will be seen later, there are several different applications of IPSec created by vendors that address the interaction within the layer differently. Some cases are best described as layers within the network layer.

As the details of the inner working of IPSec are revealed, the delineation between the layers and the overall operation becomes blurry. The simple fact is that application processes using a VPN are completely unaware of lower layer aspects, such as services and various security options. In addition, the VPN may need to operate according to the options demanded by the upper layer, just as any networking layer function would. In some cases, a VPN gateway may provide limited lower layer activities. An example is the virtual interface, introduced by Steve Bellovin of Bell Laboratories in the work "Pseudo-Network Drivers and Virtual Networks" at the Usenix Conference

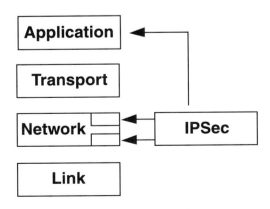

Exhibit 2-15.   IPSEC in the TCP/IP stack.

in January 1990. Virtual interfaces are used to associate a virtual connection over a common medium. The IPSec VPN implementation is provided as an intelligent network layer process that operates transparently for the applications but provides the necessary services for standard communications.

The integration of the IPSec processes into the network layer of an existing TCP/IP stack can range from a simple addition or modification to dramatic changes in the operation of the protocol stack. For dedicated VPN equipment, the protocol stack is refined to operate for the sole purpose of allowing only IPSec, disallowing all other traffic. In either case, the activities of IPSec within the network layer can be all-encompassing, providing much of the standard network layer functionality.

Other VPN Standards

This book focuses primarily on the IPSec suite of protocols and standards. However, there are other standards that provide VPN capabilities. Other technologies basically evolved from necessity and many work at several different layers to accomplish a variety of tasks.

Layer 2 Tunneling Protocol (L2TP)

Early in the evolution of communications, PPP was used to directly connect two systems to allow the flow of data. The protocol is designed for simple links that transport packets between two peers and are assumed to be delivered in the condition they were sent and in the proper sequence. PPP is not resistant to packet loss or line errors and does not handle inaccuracies efficiently. Frames that are passed along the connection provide for network layer protocols to operate. PPP has been used in many dial-up solutions and is typically used by ISPs to provide connectivity to the Internet. The problem with PPP is that the two systems must have a dedicated medium; a telephone line is an example that provides a direct serial link. Therefore, the PPP endpoint, the logical point of protocol establishment, was also the physical medium endpoint. An example is two modems connected by a phone line. The modem performs the same functions as a phone, provides PPP encapsulation, the endpoints of the communication, and the physical aspects are the same.

Layer 2 Tunneling Protocol (L2TP) was invented to eliminate the association of the communication technology — a phone line — with the communication topology — PPP encapsulation. L2TP allows the two to be on different systems connected by a packet-switched network, such as the Internet. Before L2TP, a roaming user would dial a number to a modem at the home office to establish a PPP session to provide protocol connectivity, such as IPX/SPX, to a Novell server. With the use of L2TP, that same user can dial a local service that encapsulates the PPP frame in a TCP/IP packet that gets forwarded over an IP network to the home office access device. The PPP session is terminated at the home office, and the IPX/SPX protocol session will operate as if connected by the original method.

The network layer is used to virtually connect two physical systems. In normal operations, the link layer PPP frame would have to be created and terminated in a point-to-point configuration. L2TP eliminates this requirement and encapsulates the original PPP frame in a TCP/IP network layer packet. For example, a roaming user dials into the home office remote access server's modem. The modems use PPP encapsulation for link layer operations and rightfully so, because each system provides the termination. The phone company provides the physical layer and the remaining

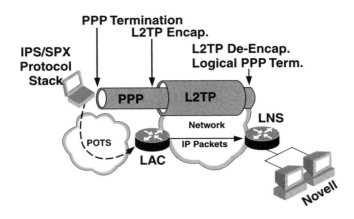

Exhibit 2-16. L2TP connection where the LAC is provided as a remote service by a provider.

upper layers are encapsulated in PPP frames. If the roaming user were to travel to a remote location and call the home office's RAS system, the cost could be overwhelming. If the roaming user dials an ISP, the connection still will not work. The PPP session to the ISP is terminated at the ISP and the network layer is used for communication throughout the Internet using an IP address assigned by the ISP, which is not valid for communications on the home office network that uses IPX/SPX. Ideally, the roaming user can call a local number that provides access to the home office.

In L2TP, there are two primary systems within the communication. The L2TP Access Concentrator (LAC) acts as an L2TP peer and provides PPP connectivity. The second participant is the L2TP Network Server (LNS), which provides the logical termination point for the PPP session and is the L2TP endpoint.

The LAC can operate in two modes: remote and local. As detailed in Exhibit 2-16, in a remote configuration, a client uses the phone system to dial an LAC and establish a PPP session. Through various authentication methods, either by the phone number used or simple authentication, the provider determines that that the client wishes to connect to the home office, which houses an LNS.

The LAC then encapsulates the PPP frames into IP packets and forwards them across an IP network to the corporate LNS. It is important to know that the IP network can be a Frame Relay cloud, ATM, wireless, Internet, or any IP-based network. The LNS acts as the new termination point for the PPP frames, allowing the remote client to interact with the LNS directly within Layer 2. The LNS de-encapsulates the PPP frames from the IP packet, and then simply operates as if the remote system had dialed directly into the home office. The PPP frames are processed and the IPX/SPX is injected into the network and operates as if the client were directly connected. In a local design, the LAC is a service or client package loaded on the laptop that encapsulates the PPP frames into IP packets prior to sending them across the Internet. Exhibit 2-17 reveals that in this case, the client establishes an IP session with an ISP, encapsulates the PPP frames in an IP packet with the source being the address assigned by the ISP and the destination is the Internet IP address of the home office's LNS. The LNS acts as the PPP termination point, allowing the communication to operate as if the user had dialed directly into the network.

Understanding the original goals for which L2TP was designed, it is easy to see how the encapsulation of information can be applied to many scenarios and not just PPP. L2TP can be used to transport Layer 3 protocols only over networks that the originating

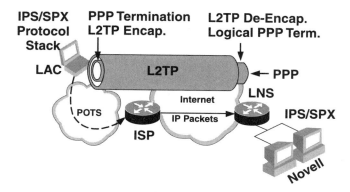

Exhibit 2-17 L2TP connection where the LAC is provided by client software loaded on the laptop.

technology could not communicate over under normal conditions. Simply forego the Layer 2 data, such as PPP, and encapsulate the protocol and forward it as normal.

However, there is one major aspect that is absent from the preceding description: security. L2TP provides no security services, and any communication that leverages L2TP over a public network is open to various forms of attack, not the least of which is a lack of confidentiality resulting in no privacy.

Layer 3

General Routing Encapsulation (GRE) is the process of encapsulating various protocols into a new protocol packet that can be sent over an environment not traversable by the originating protocol. A good example is IPX/SPX protocol; it cannot interact with the Internet, which is TCP/IP based. The answer is to encapsulate the IPX/SPX protocol into an IP packet and forward it to a destination that can de-capsulate the original protocol and forward it based on its attributes. This is much like an inter-office letter that may get placed in a new envelope to be sent by a public service to another office of the same company. Once the public envelope is removed, the internal office mail can be routed through to its final recipient via the private addressing scheme.

Layer 3 tunneling operates completely at Layer 3 and does not typically interact with Layer 2. There are some cases where Layer 2 functions are processed to enhance upper layer connectivity. IPSec is an example of a Layer 3 virtual network protocol.

Upper Layers

There are several existing security services that have been leveraged to provide a VPN-quality connection over public networks. These are referred to upper layer VPNs and typically operate at the application and session layers. There are several examples, including SSL, SSH, and SOCKS.

Secure Shell (SSH) is a derivative of the remote administration UNIX utility SH. SSH uses encryption to establish a private TCP/IP session from a host to a server to allow for secure administration. It soon became clear that any type of data could populate the data portion of the encrypted packet. Now, several VPN solutions leverage the SSH protocol to accommodate VPN connectivity.

Secure Sockets Layer (SSL) is, conceptually, very much like SSH. SSL is typically associated with application-based connectivity such as Internet browsing and the use of Certificates to authenticate clients and servers for encrypted communications. Recent history has changed the definition of SSL connectivity from application level encryption and relationships to network layer functionality. In its simplest form, an SSL VPN is an application that resides at the network layer processing the payloads with the appropriate attributes. Sound familiar? SSL, traditionally speaking, uses Certificates to authenticate the peers and uses the information to create symmetrical keys to encrypt the messages.

Aventail SSL VPN Solution. A good example of the new direction of SSL-based VPNs is Aventail. Aventail is a VPN product that is primarily designed for remote access and uses a sophisticated client to generate tunnels into the home network. The client operates low enough in the protocol stack to provide security services to upper layer applications without requiring changes to those application, exactly what IPSec accomplishes. However, many of the technical similarities stop cold at that point. The solution, at least from the client side, is based on a simple configuration file (.cfg) that can be generated by a configuration tool on the client and easily distributed via normal communication channels.

Following are some descriptions and exhibits that show how a VPN is configured using Aventail based on SSL. This book, of course, is about IPSec VPNs, and SSL represents the furthest from IPSec one can imagine, from a technical perspective. However, by including discussions about other solutions that are popular and successful in the VPN market, the reader is exposed to other options and can identify similarities in the aspects of VPNs regardless of the underlying support protocols. Simply stated, knowing more is good; understanding commonalities is better.

As with any VPN solution, one must configure servers and networks, the foundation of a VPN. What to encrypt and where to send it are the building blocks of secured communications.

First, one must create a secure server object that represents the final destination of encrypted packets — the security gateway. There can be several VPN gateways defined that reside on many networks and provide various services to internal networks, systems, and services — just like IPSec. Exhibit 2-18 depicts the creation of a server by giving it a common name that can be easily identified in the configuration tool. The actual identification is provided by an IP address or fully qualified domain name. The port number should look familiar — 443 is SSL. While other ports can be used, 443 is the most common, due to the nature of the VPN. There are different versions of proxy protocols that can be established with the remote VPN gateway by the client. SOCKS v.5 is the most robust of the available and provides a great deal of flexibility.

Note: Another primary technical difference between SSL-based and IPSec-based VPNs is that SSL is typically proxy driven. Remote clients make requests to the gateway and the gateway completes the transaction on behalf of the client. This is not network address translation, where the IP address changes to allow internal communications; an entirely new connection to the internal system is established. For many in the security industry, this represents the strongest form of security; however, it is only as strong as the implementation and the code being implemented to support the proxy services.

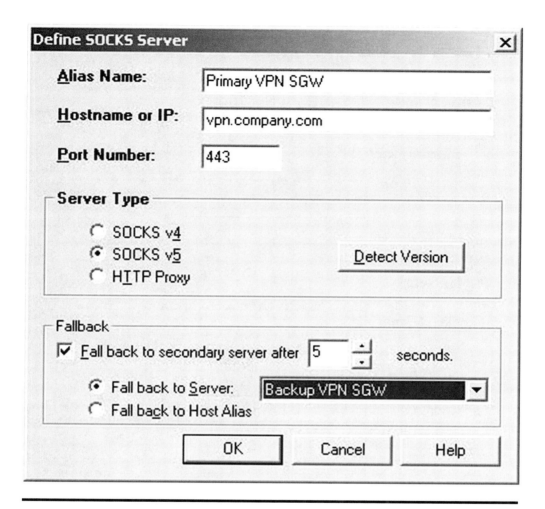

Exhibit 2-18. Creating a secure server object.

Finally, an option exists to provide another VPN gateway as a failover (see Exhibit 2-18). Many solutions provide this option, for example, Compatible, Altiga (both recently purchased by Cisco), Check Point, and VPNet, to name a few. In this section, one can see that a separate server object has been defined and is being used as a failover. Failover within the realm of VPNs represents a very interesting aspect not necessarily available in other data communications. For example, if the Internet connection goes down at the main office and 1000 remote users were accessing internal applications at the time of failure, a second VPN device on the same network that uses the same Internet connection will not be much help. However, many large organizations, ones that would have 1000 remote users, typically have more than one office that has an Internet connection. By placing the other VPN device on the remote Internet connection, the clients can resume communications over the Internet to the backup site and regain access via the wide area network — a communication backdoor so to speak. The other network can be half way around the world and will have little effect on the communications from the aspect of the client systems. Designs that take advantage of the Internet and natural redundancy are discussed later.

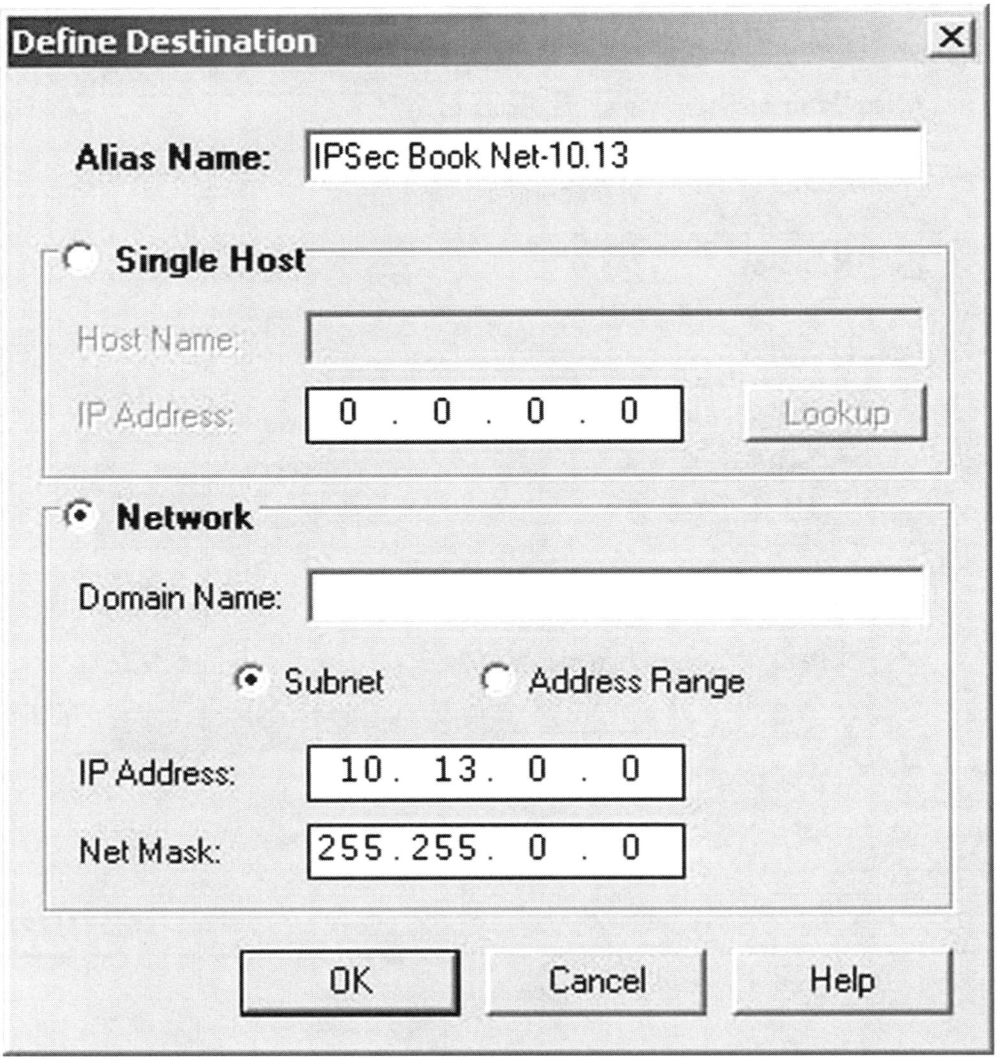

Exhibit 2-19.   Creating a network object.

Once the VPN device has been identified, configured, and is represented by an object, a network object can be created. When creating a network object, the VPN device is not identified. The goal is to define several servers and network objects and align them at a later point in the configuration. As mentioned before, everything so far is common among nearly every VPN solution with varying degrees of control and customization, as one would expect. However, the core components are identical.

As shown in Exhibit 2-19, there is not much to defining an object. This has been described as a network object because that is how it is used in the example, but a single host or a range of addresses can be defined to provide granularity. Remember this aspect of granularity in destination definition because later in the configuration one will be able to limit the services and ports. In the example, it will have the destination as networks, but one can configure it to the actual system's IP address.

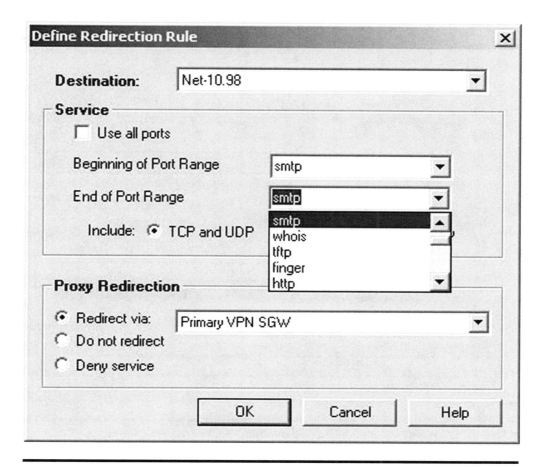

Exhibit 2-20. Creating a VPN rule.

The next major step it to associate the network, or system, object with permitted (or denied) services and the destination VPN system. At the top of Exhibit 2-20 there is a dropdown list of all the created objects that can be selected for this particular rule. Once the target is identified, one can define the applications to associate with the rule.

Once the application has been configured, or the option to protect all traffic is selected, the rule must have an action defined. The three states of action should look familiar — they are identical to IPSec. If traffic matches the rule, one can configure the rule to do one of the following: apply protection and forward it to the defined gateway, deny the packet, or simply pass the data to the Internet as normal.

Once the rule is defined, is can be combined with other rules and placed in a specific order to define a high state of granularity in the identification and control of traffic. Exhibit 2-21 provides a list of different rules with varying services being allowed. There is one added entry at the bottom that would not normally exist, but was added to convey a point. Of the bottom two entries, only one should exist to capture the remaining traffic.

The first of the two entries is a very typical addition for many currently installed implementations. By stating "everything else," representing all destinations other than

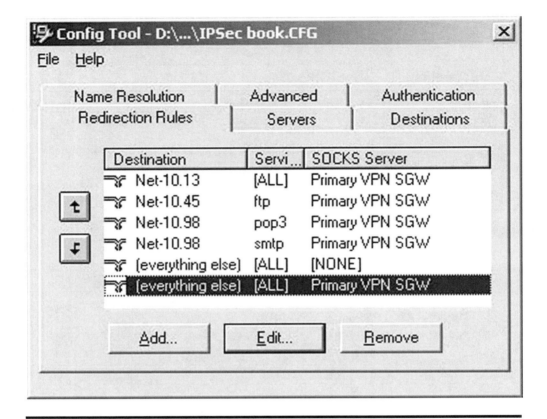

Exhibit 2-21. The list of rules to be applied to traffic.

the one defined in other rules, "ALL" represents the services to be identified, and finally the "NONE" is to specify the VPN gateway. In this case, there is no gateway defined, resulting in a split tunnel-like solution (which is detailed later).

The last rule states nearly the same thing; however the destination is the VPN gateway. In this scenario, all traffic will go to the VPN gateway, resulting in a single tunnel-like solution.

Aventail provides several different types of authentication for remote user access. A major aspect of SSL VPNs, when compared to IPSec, is that there is a lot more flexibility available in the authentication process (see Exhibit 2-22). However, it is important to know that IPSec is designed to be a global protocol that operates regardless of the implementation, and just as TCP/IP typically works between UNIX, Macintosh, Windows, among others, IPSec is vendor independent.

Exhibit 2-22 reveals a couple of interesting options. Available ciphers, a fancy word for encryption, allow the administrator to select DES or RC4 for encryption. Many people who like Aventail more than IPSec solutions typically forget that many more keys are used for IPSec, and DES is the lowest encryption supported. Therefore, performance can sometimes be better with SSL-based solutions, but most of the performance increase is due to the limited negotiation of policy, limited protection of the negotiation, and the size of the keys for the encryption. In short, it can be faster than IPSec due to the reduced communication requirements.

There are several levels of complexity and optional operations supported by IPSec that are not attainable when using modified upper layer security protocols. Many of

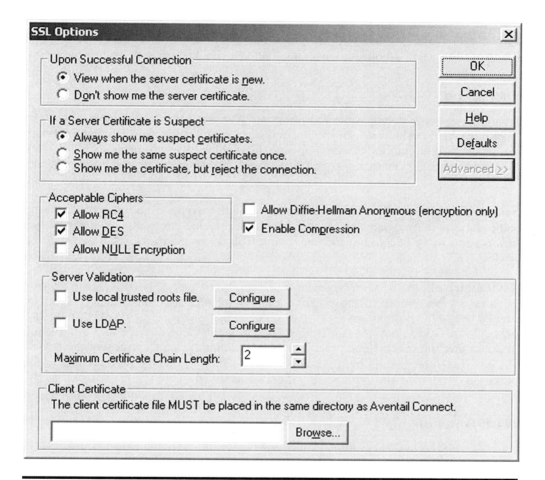

Exhibit 2-22. Configuring the SSL authentication details.

the similarities to IPSec revolve around tunneling and providing remote access solutions that terminate the connection destined for internal resources, much like L2TP. The differences begin when it is necessary to nest or combine communication options, or provide identity protection, message integrity, and security levels to various points along the VPN.

Cryptography

It is impossible to discuss IPSec VPNs without understanding the fundamental concepts of cryptography. IPSec standards currently define several types of encryption that can be used (DES, 3DES, RC5, IDEA, CAST, BlowFish, 3IDEA, and RC4) to protect information. However, in implementation, DES and 3DES are predominant, with very few solutions providing other encryption technology. TimeStep is one of the few available solutions that provides IDEA, Blowfish, CAST, and RC5.

IPSec also employs message authentication codes (MD5, SHA-1, and TIGER) to provide message integrity. To add to the several layers of complexity that this book delves into, IPSec supports several standards for authentication. There are three primary types of authentication within IPSec: shared secrets, public key cryptography (and a modified version of public key cryptography), and Certificates. Encryption, message authentication, and the authentication process are discussed in great detail in subsequent chapters; this section simply introduces the foundation behind each of these technologies.

Encryption

Encryption, simply stated, is the conversion of plaintext into unintelligible ciphertext. Typically, this is achieved using a key and an algorithm. The key is combined with the plaintext and computed with a specific algorithm.

There are two primary types of encryption keys: symmetrical and asymmetrical.

Symmetrical. Symmetrical keys are used for both encryption and decryption of the same data. It is necessary for all the communication participants to have the same key to perform the encryption and decryption. This is also referred to as a shared secret.

Asymmetrical. Public key cryptography is based on a pair of keys, typically referred to as private and public, that are mathematically related. Data can be encrypted with one of the keys, but can only be decrypted with the corresponding key. It is also necessary to know that the exposure of one key does not provide any information to determine the other. Hence, the terms "public" and "private" represent the role of the key pair. One of the keys is provided to anyone who needs or wants it, and the other is confidential and typically passphrase protected.

Hash Function

Hash functions are computational functions that take a variable-length input of data and produce a fixed-length result that can be used as a fingerprint to represent the original data. Therefore, if the hash of two messages are identical, it can be reasonably assumed that the messages are identical as well.

Message Authentication Code

Message authentication code (MAC) is the combination of encryption and hashing. As illustrated in Exhibit 2-23, as data is fed into a hashing algorithm, a key is introduced into the process.

MAC is very similar to encryption, but the MAC is designed to be irreversible, like a standard hash function. Due to the computational properties of the MAC process, and the inability to reverse the encryption designed into the process, MACs are much less vulnerable to attacks than encryption with the same key length.

MAC ensures data integrity like a message digest but the recipient must have the shared secret to produce the same MAC to validate the message.

Hash-Message Authentication Code

Hashed-based message authentication code (HMAC) is the process of combining existing cryptographic hashing functions with a key. The modularity of the allowable

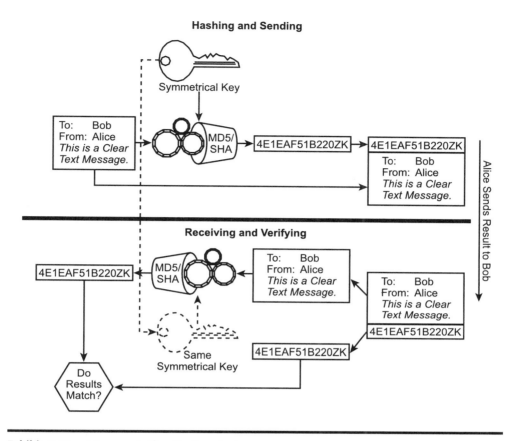

Exhibit 2-23. Message Authentication Code.

type of cryptographic function that can be used in the process is the reason that HMAC is so popular. The standard treats the hash function as a variable that can consist of any hash algorithm. The benefits are that legacy, or existing hash implementations can be used in the process, and the hash function can be easily replaced without affecting the overall functionality or solution. The latter example represents an enormous security advantage. In the event the hash algorithm is compromised, a new one can be immediately implemented, eliminating the threat.

Chapter 3

IP Security Primer

This chapter introduces IP Security (IPSec) and the base components that build the technology. The fundamental concepts of IPSec are detailed and their role in the protection of TCP/IP-based communications is established.

IP packets have no security associated with them. They are vulnerable to a plethora of attacks that include forging addresses, changing or replacing the contents, retransmittal of old packets, and they are completely modifiable in transit.

With IP, there is no guarantee that the packet is from the expected sender and the data contained is what was transmitted. Even if these two are not considered, there is no assurance that the contents have remained private and not been disseminated.

IPSec was created to thwart these vulnerabilities by a providing several layers of protection with authentication, encryption, message authentication, and the leveraging of existing security concepts applied in combination to the communication.

History

In October 1993, John Ioannidis of Columbia University and Matt Blaze of Bell Laboratories presented a case for IP layer security, appropriately entitled, "The Architecture and Implementation of Network Layer Security in UNIX." This paper represented a change in the application of security and communication, and was well ahead of its time. The paper discussed how to implement security features without altering the IP structure, and went on to discuss implementations of encapsulating IP datagrams in a new IP datagram. It also detailed the advantages of encapsulating protocols and authentication processes and the transparency that can be provided to upper layer activities.

Given the massive growth of the Internet, combined with the inherent security weaknesses of the TCP/IP protocol, the industry was in great need of a technology to provide security of data on the Internet. In 1994, the Internet Architecture Board (IAB) issued a report on "Security in the Internet Architecture" (Request for Comment [RFC] 1636). The report stated the general consensus that the Internet needed more and better security, and it identified key areas for security improvements. The IAB also mandated that the same security functions become an integral part of the next generation of the IP, IPv6.

Standards-based VPNs, as known today, started in 1995 with the AIAG (Automotive Industry Action Group), a nonprofit association of North American vehicle manufacturers and suppliers, and their creation of the ANX (Automotive Network eXchange) project. The project was spawned to fulfill a need for a TCP/IP network comprised of trading partners, certified service providers, and network exchange points. The requirement demanded efficient and secure electronic communications among participants, with only a single connection over unsecured channels. As this technology grew, it quickly became recognized as a solution for any organization wishing to provide secure communications with partners, clients, or any remote network.

Structure

IPSec is defined by several RFCs that detail the many layers of the technology. Some RFCs detail specific portions of the protocol, while others address the solution as a whole. The interrelationship and organization of the documents are necessary for understanding the development process of the overall standard.

Exhibit 3-1 illustrates the seven groups of documents that allow the separate aspects of the IPSec protocol suite to be developed independently while providing a functioning relationship that can be easily managed.

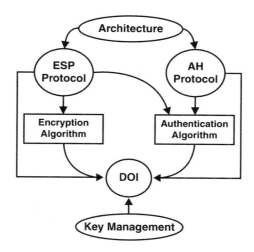

Exhibit 3-1. IPSec document roadmap.

1. The *architecture* is the main description document that covers the overall technology concepts and security considerations. It is a starting point for an initial understanding of the IPSec protocol suite and the RFCs that define the standard.

2/3. The *encapsulating security payload* (ESP) and the authentication header (AH) protocol documents detail the packet formats and the default standards for packet structure.

4. The encryption algorithm documents detail the use of various encryption techniques utilized for the ESP.

5. The authentication algorithm documents describe the processes and technologies used to provide an authentication mechanism for the AH and ESP protocols.

6. All of these documents specify attributes that require a value to be assigned and consolidated for proper interaction between the RFCs and other IETF-defined protocols. The domain of interpretation (DOI) specifies the numbers that identify certain aspects within each RFC. The DOI document is part of the IANA-assigned numbers mechanism and is constant throughout the standard. It provides the central repository for values, allowing other documents to relate to each other. The DOI contains parameters that are required for other portions of the protocol to ensure that the definitions are consistent.

7. The final group is key management, which details the standards defining key management protocols.

RFCs

Request for comments (RFCs) are documents that define an accepted technological form and suggest implementation details. RFCs must first be submitted as a draft to the Internet Engineering Task Force (IETF) for peer review. The IETF is segmented into groups that are responsible for certain projects. Although the final conversion of a draft to an RFC to become a standard is governed by the IETF, anyone can participate in the review process and provide points of view and comments.

Following is a list of IPSec-related RFCs and their corresponding descriptions:

- IP Authentication Using Keyed MD5 (RFC 1828)
- The ESP DES-CBC Transform (RFC 1829)
- HMAC: Keyed-Hashing for Message Authentication (RFC 2104)
- HMAC-MD5 IP Authentication with Replay Prevention (RFC 2085)
- Security Architecture for the Internet Protocol (RFC 2401)
- The NULL Encryption Algorithm and Its Use with IPsec (RFC 2410)
- IP Security Document Roadmap (RFC 2411)
- IP Authentication Header (RFC 2402)
- The OAKLEY Key Determination Protocol (RFC 2412)
- The ESP CBC-Mode Cipher Algorithms (RFC 2451)
- The Use of HMAC-MD5-96 Within ESP and AH (RFC 2403)
- The Use of HMAC-SHA-1-96 Within ESP and AH (RFC 2404)
- The ESP DES-CBC Cipher Algorithm with Explicit IV (RFC 2405)
- IP Encapsulating Security Payload (ESP) (RFC 2406)
- The Internet IP Security Domain of Interpretation for ISAKMP (RFC 2407)
- Internet Security Association and Key Management Protocol (ISAKMP) (RFC 2408)
- The Internet Key Exchange (IKE) (RFC 2409)

Clients and Networks

IPSec provides for three primary types of communication, each of which will be detailed throughout the entire book:

1. client to network
2. network to network
3. client to client

Client-to-network communication is typically associated with remote access solutions. A client is provided software that allows the remote systems to establish a VPN with a gateway connected to a private network. Typically, a client can establish a connection to the Internet through an ISP and use the VPN client to send data to the private network hosted by the VPN gateway.

Another type of VPN is network-to-network connectivity, which is becoming increasingly popular as people and businesses build confidence in the Internet. Unlike client-to-network VPNs, network-to-network VPNs provide security services to systems on either side, completely without their knowledge of the VPN. Internal systems simply send data destined for the remote network to a VPN gateway that appears to provide a standard routing service. However, the VPN gateways have an established security association that provides communication and protection services to data that is passed between them.

A more rare form of VPN is client-to-client VPNs. The IPSec standards provide for client-to-client VPNs on many levels — which are discussed in detail — but the vendor support is focused on client-to-network solutions. Vendors are providing remote access solutions due to huge market demand. However, as VPNs become more prevalent in normal organization communications, client-to-client VPNs will certainly be seen more frequently. These client-to-client VPNs will provide data protection over a public network to a VPN gateway and continued protection to the final destination inside the private network.

What Is an SA?

A security association (SA) is the foundation of an IPSec VPN. A security association is a set of communication properties that provides a relationship between two or more systems to build a unique connection. SAs are simplex in nature; two are required for bi-directional communications.

To properly interchange IPSec data between two systems, there must be a method of associating the security services and keys for use with the particular communication. The SA is the result of information on how to protect data, to whom it is going or coming from, the keys to use, and the data that affords the type of protection the SA is providing.

SAs are identified by a Security Parameter Index (SPI) number that exists in the security protocol headers, the destination IP address of the outer IP header, and the applied security protocol (AH or ESP). This allows the system to apply IPSec operations to a packet being sent or received according to the SA it is assigned. As a packet is received, the SPI is checked to determine which SA — or group of communication attributes — applies to the packet. The entire existence of SAs is to allow different data communications varying levels of protection through one interface.

An example is an organization with a remote office that has 200 users who access applications at the home office. However, 50 of those users access a very specific financial application, while the bulk of the other traffic is e-mail. As an example, one of those 50 users is accessing the financial application. As the request is received by the VPN security gateway, it can identify the traffic by the destination address (there are others, but this is for simplicity; the other methods are discussed in detail later). The destination IP address is used to identify the SA (level of encryption, which key to use, type of authentication, etc.) to apply to the data. Meanwhile, e-mail for this company is not considered nearly as secure as the financial data, and the SA associated with e-mail is afforded minimal authentication and protection.

It is important to understand the basic concepts of the process because there are several actions and aspects in the creation, collection, maintenance, selection, and deletion of SAs within IPSec. Each of these can sound much more complicated than they really are. To add to the confusion, much of what is defined in the standard is not being applied or worked around in the real world to accomplish much the same thing.

SAs are common among all IPSec implementations and must be supported to be IPSec compliant. SAs also exist in other security protocols, and much of the key management used with IPSec is existing technology allowing the key management to support other forms of VPN technology that use SAs. The set of security properties provided to the communication are dependant on the endpoints of the SA and the options selected during creation.

Authentication Header

The authentication header (AH) is used to provide data integrity and origin authentication for IP datagrams and optional protection against replay attacks. The AH provides authentication for much of the IP header and for upper level protocol data contained within the datagram. Not all of the IP header can be authenticated, due to the fact that some header fields might change in transit and the value when the packet arrives may not be the same as when sent.

ESP can be used to provide many of the same security services — plus confidentiality service. The primary difference between AH and ESP is the authentication provided. ESP does not protect any IP header fields unless those fields are encapsulated in tunnel mode.

Encapsulating Security Payload

The encapsulating security payload (ESP) is designed to provide a mix of security services within a VPN. ESP is used to provide confidentiality, data origin authentication, data integrity, and optional anti-replay. Confidentiality can be selected independent of all other services. All encryption algorithms used with ESP must operate in CBC mode. In addition, the authentication process must support HMAC-MD5 and HMAC-SHA.

Shims and Virtual Adapters

The installation process and how the VPN client interacts with the operating system are related to what the operating system can support. For example, Windows 98 is not as "service" oriented as Windows NT. Given the flexibility of a service in NT, most client installations tend to run as services on Windows NT platforms. The contrary to service-based install types is a new adapter in the network configuration seen on many Windows 98 installs. Both of these examples are methods used by the VPN client package to operate at the network layer while allowing upper layer operations to remain untouched for participating in a VPN.

Both of these types of client implementations are typically called shims. A shim is an added program that can implement a set of instructions based on configured parameters. The shim is slipped inside the network layer to allow normal operation of the upper layers. The shims are then typically associated with an application that is used to configure and determine IPSec functionality.

The VPN client package inserts intelligent code at a critical point within the IP stack that can identify crucial IP information for determining a course of action.

There are three primary actions that can be applied:

1. Do not apply IPSec and pass.
2. Apply IPSec and pass.
3. Do not apply IPSec and drop.

The first operation is to simply pass the packets unmodified by IPSec. The second action that can be performed is to apply IPSec to the data stream and forward the packets according to the IPSec policy configured for that data. Finally, the packets can be simply dropped. Dropping the packets allows the VPN device to perform minimal firewall capabilities and reduce vulnerabilities. In many cases, a VPN device will not accept any packet that is not properly constructed for a VPN.

Operating Systems Support

Operating systems can be a decisive factor in any VPN solution. Most IPSec implementations, at the time this book was written, typically only support the Microsoft line of operating systems, along with limited Macintosh support. However, there are vendors that provide Solaris and Linux clients in addition to Microsoft and Macintosh systems. The limited range of support is because of the obvious proliferation and market share among corporate users of Microsoft operating systems.

As IPSec implementations grow, the supported platforms will become increasingly diversified. Client support will expand as the use of alternate operating systems become more prevalent.

Operations Within the Standard

IPSec is layers upon layers of options and interactions of protocols and services. The IPSec suite provides two separate operations and two modes of communications.

The two operations represent a union to provide the final service: IPSec and IKE. The two modes are communication processes that can be manipulated and combined to support an enormous variety of configurations.

Two Distinct Operations

IPSec is a defined standard that is constantly growing, changing, and being modified to adapt to technological advances and implementation considerations. The establishment of SAs and the use of authentication protocols are typically associated with IPSec. However, IPSec is part of the entire process of establishing a VPN and is a suite of combined protocols that provide robust security and communication services. The suite of protocols and services require an entire undercurrent of key management operations that provide unique services to the final establishment of the VPN.

Ironically, key management produces the critical steps for the operation of IPSec SAs and authentication protocols. IKE is not addressed in the same context when IPSec is being discussed and it is rolled up into IPSec. This may be the due to the fact that key management can be extremely complicated and a fair amount of commitment is required to fully understand the process.

This section briefly introduces the two operations as being separate entities. This is done for two reasons: clarity and simplicity. The entire book revolves around the thought that the two systems are unique but operate in concert to create a VPN.

Internet Key Exchange. Internet Key Exchange (IKE) is the automatic key management protocol used for IPSec. IKE was created from several other key management protocols and is the default for IPSec, but other key management protocols can be used. In reality, no key management is required for IPSec functions and the keys can be manually managed. However, manual key management is not desirable for all implementations due to the administrative overhead and the fact that keys never expire. Having keys that never expire represents a plethora of security vulnerabilities.

Included in the group of IPSec RFCs is a document defining a key management process called Internet Security Association Key Management Protocol (ISAKMP). ISAKMP is not IPSec specific, but provides the framework for creating SAs for any protocol that can take advantage of them. ISAKMP provides the structure for authentication and key exchange but does not define the information for using ISAKMP. ISAKMP is designed to be information exchange independent, allowing support for many different key exchanges. ISAKMP is used as part of the IKE process, and along with other existing key management protocols, defines the keys to support automated key management.

This can be very confusing because many people use the terminology interchangeably. To simplify the definition, the automatic key management provided for IPSec is

IKE. IKE defines two other protocols — Oakley and SKEME — to provide key material to plug into the ISAKMP key management framework. When discussing key management in the context of IPSec, IKE is the proper terminology. However, if discussing headers and protocol interchange, ISAKMP messages will be shared.

There is several sections in this book dedicated to explaining the IKE technology and attempting to describe some problem areas. IKE can be incredibly complex, and in some people's eyes, too complex. IPSec, or more precisely the use of AH and ESP, is fairly straightforward and typically not questioned or argued. However, IKE is responsible for providing authentication and the creation of keys for IPSec. Therefore, it is constantly being scrutinized for security flaws. If IKE is insecure, there is no way IPSec can be secure. Admittedly, IKE does not map directly to IPSec operations as one would like. The creation of the keys and information management make some assumptions about the underling SAs. In some cases, one might argue that Null encryption for ESP is to facilitate interoperability between IKE and IPSec. IKE represents the most complicated portion of the IPSec VPN and consumes a large portion of this book.

IPSec Communication Suite. The IPSec communication operation is typically associated with standard IPSec functionality. This is where system SAs are managed by the use of the security protocols (AH and ESP).

The suite of communications is concerned with the application of IPSec. It encapsulates, encrypts, and hashes the datagrams and handles the packet processes. It is responsible for the management of data according to the available SAs and the security assigned to the data stream as defined in the policy and databases that govern SAs. However, IPSec is not included in the creation of keys or their management.

IKE and IPSec Relationship. The best way to think about IPSec and IKE is compare them to PKI and the use of Certificates. Certificates, by themselves, are quite simple and can be used for encryption, signing, authenticating, and a multitude of other services. IPSec is similar to the application that uses the Certificate to execute the desired actions, such as signing an e-mail message. Simply stated, the application is virtually unaware or concerned about the maze of trusts and policies governing the entire PKI from which the Certificate was created. IPSec is much like the application that uses the Certificate, and IKE is much like the PKI that creates and manages the Certificate. Inevitably, IKE is more complicated and subject to constant functionality and security concerns. IPSec is more concerned with properly implementing the security services and maintaining various forms of communication options.

Two Distinct Modes

To accommodate variations in communication designs and requirements, IPSec is unique in providing two forms of VPNs. Transport and tunnel modes can be used in combination or used alone for certain communication characteristics.

Transport mode is when the originating protocol is responsible for the entire communication path. IPSec simply provides encryption and message authentication. Transport mode is typically associated with services for systems acting as the endpoints of the VPN. To further explain, if two systems are participating in a VPN, the SA endpoints only exist at the two systems.

In contrast, *tunnel mode* provides encapsulation services, including encryption and message authentication. Tunnel mode also provides for the nesting of SAs and the creation of transport mode communications within the tunnel mode operation. Tunnel mode is typically associated with gateway activities and there can be various endpoint configurations. This mode represents the bulk of current IPSec VPNs and, therefore, has several variations of implementation.

VPNs and Policies

Any organization contemplating the implementation of a VPN must have some form of security policy to provide guidance in determining the services to provide and who gets them.

It is necessary to understand that a VPN that uses the Internet to extend an organization's network to reach around the entire planet. Firewalls gained great popularity in the mid-1990s and today they are a standard piece of equipment to protect the internal network from undesirable access from the Internet. It is well-accepted that a firewall is only one aspect of data security, but a necessary ingredient. Now imagine having thousands of firewalls. If one contemplates the true security aspects of VPNs, the number of firewalls is nearly infinite. Each system that is — or can be — on the Internet is a potential extension to an internal network.

This is a radical statement and may be quite difficult to fully understand or accept, but it is not entirely untrue. If a remote user establishes a VPN with a gateway on an internal network, that user now becomes part of that network. A more convenient way of looking at this situation is that the VPN gateway is, in effect, a firewall; and the remote users are systems requesting service, as would any Internet-based system.

As with most security aspects, it comes down to opinion and the level of security required relative to the application. For example, a standard remote access service that provides telephone numbers for access can implement several security features that are related to the isolated communication technology. Caller ID and call-back enforcement are two examples of security that cannot be applied in a VPN scenario. It will be necessary to evaluate the security options provided by a VPN solution to determine the level of control required

To determine the level of control that should be applied by a VPN solution, a security policy must address the aspects of extending the network to users that are operating in a possibly very insecure environment. This very aspect is discussed in detail in subsequent chapters.

Chapter 4

Cryptography

From the day someone deemed a piece of information valuable, people have been devising methods to protect information from unwanted access. This chapter introduces the basics of cryptography, and discusses the reasons and methods of cryptography and their use in IPSec for confidentiality, integrity, and authentication.

In this electronic civilization made up of hackers, viruses, electric fraud, and eavesdropping, there has been a heightened sense of security and protection of information. The need to protect data and resources from disclosure and attack has become a dependency and is no longer employed by choice. Cryptography is simple in nature but represents highly complex mathematical interactions with data to ensure ambiguity of the original data to provide protection in this volatile digital age.

History

Throughout history, communication methods have been coupled with developments in the science of cryptography. The evolution of cryptography is interesting to say the least. Some of the early versions of information confidentiality practices were the Caesar cipher, a process of substituting a letter in a message with another letter in the alphabet three places down.

plaintext: rain loves cookies

ciphertext: udlq oryhv frrnlhv

Here is an example of the code key.

ABCDEFGHIJKLMNOPQRSTUVWXYZ

DEFGHIJKLMNOPQRSTUVWXYZABC

Other early examples included the Roman stick, a strip of paper wrapped around a stick of certain diameter and the message written across the wrapping. Once the paper was unrolled, the letters and symbols were unintelligible. Secure battlefield communications during World War I were nearly nonexistent. The U.S. Army employed Choctaws to encrypt voice communications, using their native language, which itself is encoded. During World War II, the U.S. Marine Corps took the Army's work and refined it and only used Navajos to convey field communications. The Native Americans were referred to as Codetalkers and were an integral part of secure communications. Also in World War II, the German Enigma was a highly complex device that came in several forms. It was based on a code that defined the placement of three or five wheels, depending on the model. The operator would type in the message normally, but electrical circuits were formed, based on the position of the wheels, that produced an output of different character. Despite the sophistication of the German Enigma, equal accomplishments in cryptanalysis — the technique of determining the original message content when only the cipher text was supplied — provided the American and European forces with access to sensitive enemy information.

Symmetrical Encryption

Symmetrical key encryption occurs when the same key is used for the encryption of information into unintelligible data (or ciphertext) and the decryption of that ciphertext into the original information format. Symmetrical keys, as shown in Exhibit 4-1, can be cumbersome to implement and typically require extensive key management in the protection of the key. If the key used in symmetrical encryption is not carefully shared

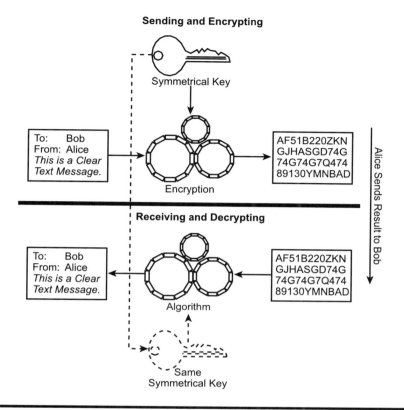

Exhibit 4-1. Symmetrical key encryption

with the participating individuals, an attacker can obtain the key, decrypt the data, view or alter the information, and encrypt the data with the stolen key and forward it to the final destination. This type of attack is defined as a man-in-the-middle attack and, if properly executed, can affect data cnfidentiality and integrity.

Typical Symmetrical Algorithms

There are several symmetrical algorithms available, each with its own key lengths and operations. Most symmetrical block ciphers (e.g., DES, RC5, CAST, and BlowFish) use the Feistel cipher, which is a round function. In the Feistel function, the data block is divided into two halves and repeatedly processed through a number of rounds using the key. The first half is used during the process to create the cipher for the second. Once complete, the compiled half is used to complete the process on the first half. Feistel is based on linear and nonlinear rounds and draws its strength from degree of diffusion.

To accomplish diffusion, some algorithms employ a process called substitution-box (S-box), such as DES and CAST, or bit-wise data-dependant rounds in which the data is used to drive diffusion. Bit-wise rounds can be seen in RC5. Other algorithms, such as IDEA, simply multiply their own rounds to accommodate diffusion in the entire process.

DES and 3DES. The most typical algorithms, at least in IPSec implementations, are DES and Triple DES (3DES). The Data Encryption Standard (DES) is the Federal Information Processing Standard (FIPS) 46-1 that details the data encryption algorithm (DEA), which is the ANSI Standard X9.32.

Originally developed in 1974 by IBM, NSA, and the National Bureau of Standards (NBS) (now called the National Institute of Standards and Technology [NIST]), and code named Lucifer, DEA is the foundation of the encryption process referred to as DES. DEA became an accepted standard in 1977 by the NBS.

DES is the most widely used encryption algorithm and was developed primarily for implementation in hardware. As previously mentioned, it utilizes a 16-round Feistel cipher that is easily computed by characteristics found in common processors.

NIST continually recertified DES every five years, ending in 1993. With the development of the Advance Encryption Standard (AES), DES will be phased out to accommodate a much faster algorithm.

DES is extremely popular in IPSec due to its performance capabilities, hardware support, and market exposure. DES is a fine-tuned, symmetrical algorithm capable of encrypting large amounts of data very quickly. There is a large quantity of hardware available that can accelerate the encryption and decryption processes. Therefore, IPSec is an excellent candidate for employing hardware-based encryption support.

AES. In January 1997, NIST announced the initiation of AES development and made a formal request for proposed algorithms in September of that year. The endeavor stated that AES would become an unclassified, publicly disclosed encryption algorithm, available free of charge worldwide. In addition, the algorithms for consideration must be based on symmetric key cryptography (e.g., DES) as a block cipher, and minimally support block sizes of 128 bits and key sizes of 128, 192, and 256 bits.

The goal is to develop a FIPS specification that defines an algorithm capable of protecting sensitive information for the foreseeable future. The algorithm is expected to be used by government as well as the private community.

In August 1998, NIST announced a group of 15 AES candidate algorithms at the First AES Candidate Conference (AES1). A Second AES Candidate Conference (AES2) was held in March 1999 to discuss the results of the analysis conducted by the cryptographic community on the proposed 15 algorithms. Once all the comments and suggestions were compiled, NIST identified five final qualifiers for the AES initiative. The AES finalists were MARS, RC6, Rijndael, Serpent, and Twofish. As the NIST hosts more candidate conferences, the final five will be reduced to one algorithm that will become AES. If all steps of the AES development process proceed as planned, it is anticipated that the standard will be completed by the summer of 2001.

Once AES is made available, the IPSec market will quickly shift to implement the new algorithm.* The sales aspects will be obvious: increased security and performance. AES is much faster than DES, and once applied to IPSec, communication issues such as latency and throughput will be greatly reduced.

MARS. MARS is a candidate developed by IBM and supports 128-bit blocks and variable key lengths up to 448 bits. As with all the AES candidates, it is designed to take advantage of current processor designs, whether integrated onto the processor itself or implemented via software operations.

---

* In October 2000, NIST selected the Rijndael data encryption algorithm as the new AES. Immediately, dozens of companies avowed their support for AES and announced products that implemented it.

MARS employs three core computations: S-box lookups, multiplications, and data-dependant rotations. It also uses a multi-phased approach to rounds, in that there are core cryptographic rounds supported by simpler mixing rounds. By employing many of the standard techniques into the algorithm, MARS obtains a great deal on diffusion and the result is a highly resistant output.

In early tests, the algorithm produced a throughput, on average, of 100 Mbits per second, and the developers expect a tenfold increase when implemented in hardware.

RC6. RC6 was developed by RSA (**R**ivest, **S**hamir, and **A**dleman) and is an evolutionary step from RC5. As with MARS, RC6 employs a second internal round, (or core round), which is similar to the half-round used in RC5. The AES block size requirement is 128 bits, and reorganizing RC5 to accommodate the enlarged blocks forces 64-bit registers because RC5 used two processing registers. The result was to develop a new algorithm based on RC5 that used four 32-bit registers to support the 128-bit block.

One of the primary factors taken from RC5 was the dependence on data-dependant rounds to create acceptable diffusion. An added process is integer multiplication used against the rounds to enhance the diffusion process creating a more robust ciphertext.

Rijndael. This algorithm was created by Joan Daemen and Vencent Rijmen, uses a 128-bit block, and supports keys of 128, 192, and 256 bits. Unfortunately, the algorithm is highly complex and it is difficult to provide a simple explanation of the foundation of the process because much of it is newly developed.

The algorithm obtains much of the diffusion from S-box manipulation in several instances of rounds performed. The process is primarily based on a process called iterated block cipher.

Serpent. Serpent was developed by Ross Anderson, Eli Biham, and Lars Knudsen, supports a 128-bit block cipher, and uses a 256-bit key. Serpent is directly based on DES and employs the well-known S-box process for diffusion.

The inventors decided to use well-tested and known technologies found in DES and then slightly modify the process to achieve enhanced performance. The greater security is obtained through a larger key size. The primary changes to DES were a modified S-box process and key schedule.

For the most part, Serpent is DES with a larger key refined to operate faster on current technology.

Twofish. Twofish is the next-generation encryption algorithm from the makers of Blowfish (i.e., Bruce Schneier and Counterpane Systems). Twofish is a 128-bit block cipher that employs a variable-length key up to 256 bits. As with other block ciphers, a 16-round Feistel function is used with four independent 8-bit S-boxes that are key dependant.

One of the processes that provides the algorithm its strength is the careful key schedule that is used during the encryption process, and its use with S-box processes.

Asymmetrical Encryption

Asymmetrical algorithms, referred to as public key cryptography, utilize a key pair that is mathematically related and generated by a complicated formula. The concept of asymmetrical derives from the fact that the encryption is one-way, in that either of the key pair and data that is encrypted with one key can only be decrypted with the other key of the pair. Asymmetrical key encryption is incredibly popular and can be used to enhance the process of symmetrical key sharing. Additionally, the use of two keys has provided digital signatures and Certificates.

Public key cryptography is the implementation of asymmetrical encryption techniques to provide a host of security options for communications and general data protection. Pretty Good Privacy (PGP) is a standard application, based on the RSA algorithm, that is an asymmetrical key implementation whereby one key is identified as private and the other as public. In reality, either key can perform the function of the other key; but for basic management issues, each must assume a given identity.

The most prevalent public key encryption algorithm is RSA, an acronym for its creators Ron **R**ivest, Adi **S**hamir, and Leonard **A**dleman. RSA is based on the difficulty of factoring two large prime numbers. For this very reason, some do not entirely trust the algorithm because any advancement in mathematical science that might result in a method for factoring prime numbers would quickly eliminate any protection currently afforded by public key cryptography — including authentication. Overnight digital signatures would mean nothing, and encrypted data would be available to anyone. Of course, the possibility of such a discovery is minute, albeit possible.

The use of two keys and sophisticated algorithms introduces two properties of asymmetrical encryption that complicate its implementation. Of the two, performance is a very serious issue, with respect to dynamic communications. IPSec uses asymmetrical encryption during some forms of authentication and symmetrical for encryption of upper layer data. Granted, the authentication of a VPN peer consumes very little time within itself, although each asymmetrical encryption process can be system intensive. Multiply the increased performance requirements by the number of connections being established and authenticated, and the result is a burdened system. In short, the process of information manipulation within asymmetrical algorithms is not designed for streaming data flow. The other complexity of asymmetrical encryption is that now one has to manage two keys. Not only does a key owner have to collect and distribute the public key, but that key owner must ensure that the exact opposite is true with the private key. There are public servers and other methods for sharing the public key, but it is far from automatic. Public key management can be highly complicated when certain services and requirements are placed on the use of those keys. Digital signatures, non-repudiation, authentication, and trust establishment are all examples of public key management issues. Many of these requirements have evolved into their own science or technology, depending on one's interaction, called Public Key Infrastructure (PKI) that incorporates methodologies and applications to accommodate the complexities of public key operations.

For now, RSA represents an incredibly strong encryption and authentication method that allows an entire half of the process (the public key) to be shared in the open without concern for the security of future communication utilizing that publicized key. Unfortunately, public key encryption is incredibly slow and requires substantial processor time to execute. One of the issues, as with symmetrical encryption, is that the key size in public key cryptography determines the block size to be encrypted. A key of 2048 bits can only be used on a block of data smaller. Therefore, a file of

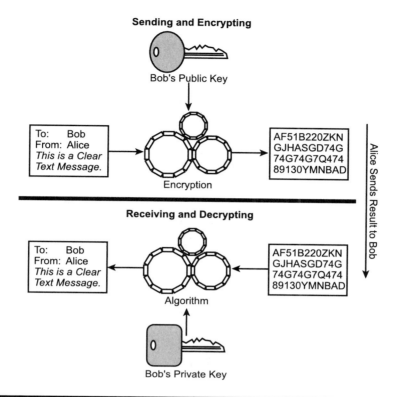

Sending and Encrypting

Bob's Public Key

To: Bob
From: Alice
*This is a Clear
Text Message.*

Encryption

AF51B220ZKN
GJHASGD74G
74G74G7Q474
89130YMNBAD

Receiving and Decrypting

To: Bob
From: Alice
*This is a Clear
Text Message.*

Algorithm

AF51B220ZKN
GJHASGD74G
74G74G7Q474
89130YMNBAD

Bob's Private Key

Alice Sends Result to Bob

Exhibit 4-2. Asymmetrical key encryption

4096 bits would require two instances of an encryption process, making public key inefficient for bulk data encryption. The advantages are so great with the use of a key pair that the authentication properties can be obtained while only processing small pieces of information, such as a hash.

An example of public key cryptography, as shown in Exhibit 4-2, is Alice could encrypt a message with Bob's public key and send the ciphertext to Bob. Because Bob is the only one with the matching private key, he would be the only recipient that could decrypt the message. However, this interaction only provides confidentiality — and not authentication — because anyone can use Bob's public key to encrypt a message and claim to be Alice.

To provide authentication, Alice can use her private key to encrypt a message digest generated from the original message, and then use Bob's public key to encrypt the original cleartext message and send it with the encrypted message digest. After receiving the message, Bob can use his private key to decrypt the message. The output can then be verified by using Alice's public key to decrypt the message authentication that Alice encrypted with her private key. The process of encrypting information with a private key to allow the recipient to authenticate the sender is called a digital signature. An example of this process is detailed in Exhibit 4-3.

A traditional signed document is difficult to repudiate due to several attributes the documents has, for example, the document is difficult to forge. However, the ability to change the verbiage of the document to modify the agreement without consent of the original person who signed the document is quite feasible. For this reason,

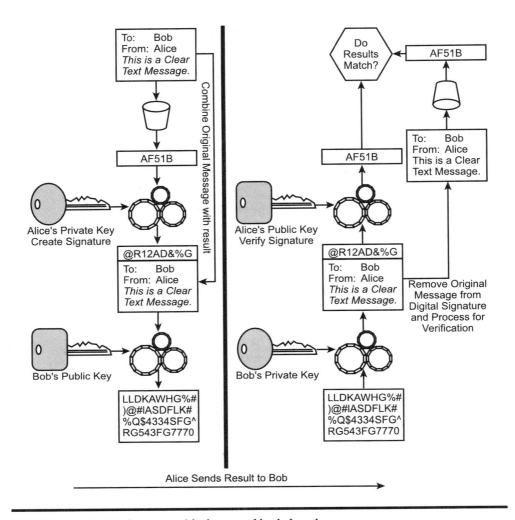

Exhibit 4-3. Digital signature with the use of hash functions

documents are typically copied a great deal and maintained in a secure location. Unfortunately, the Internet is a very public medium and the exposure to various forms of forgery, duplicity, and modification abound.

A digital signature must not only be difficult to repudiate, but it must also protect the integrity of the information being signed. If exposed to the Internet, it is necessary to protect against any test getting added, changed, or removed.

There are two primary types of digital signatures, one based on encryption and decryption (e.g., RSA) and the other based on a mathematical validation of generated information that can only be duplicated by the corresponding key. Digital Signature Algorithm (DSA) is very similar to RSA in that two keys are generated to allow the sharing of authenticated information without any preexisting relationship. RSA uses a private key to encrypt a block of specific data, such as a hash; and the authentication is solely based on the recipient's ability to decrypt that hash with the corresponding public key. The authentication is encryption and decryption based. On the other hand, DSA is designed just for digital signing of data and performs a mathematical operation that creates two 160-bit values that become the signature. The authentication is attained by demonstrating that the private key could have only created the two values presented as the signature. One might wonder as to the whereabouts of the data protection involved with this process. DSA's 160-bit numbers exist because the algorithm must employ a hash function for the signature (in this case, SHA, which creates a 160-bit digest).

Digital signatures are based on the management of public and private keys and their use in the communication. The process of key management and digital signatures has evolved into Certificates. Certificates, simply stated, are public keys digitally signed by a trusted Certificate Authority (CA). The CA provides a third-party trust relationship. This provides comfort in the knowledge that the public key being used to establish encrypted communications is owned by the proper person or organization based on a common trust of the CA. The collection of CAs, certificates, public and private keys, and the web of trusts established to provide the foundation are collectively known as PKI.

What Is PKI?

The purpose of Public Key Infrastructure (PKI) is to manage asymmetrical keys and their associated Certificates. PKI provides a variety of capabilities for use in electronic business and communications. By the use of encryption, PKI provides confidentiality and access control. By leveraging digital signatures, PKI provides trusted authentication, data integrity, and non-repudiation.

Trusted authentication is whereby users can securely identify themselves to other users or systems without sending private information over a network. Data integrity is provided by message authentication algorithms. This means that the verifier of a digital signature can easily determine if the data has changed in transit. Non-repudiation is when the user who signed the data cannot successfully deny signing the data.

PKI is the process of providing transparent security services based on trust and uses Certificates for secure communications. A Certificate is a public key signed by a third party, typically a Certificate Authority (CA). A CA maintains several aspects of PKI and signs an issued public key with its private key, permanently associating the Certificate and the public key pair to the CA.

Effective PKI

To maintain an effective PKI, there are a number of requirements that must be met to ensure proper implementation. The most important aspect of PKI is transparency. PKI users do not need to understand how PKI functions, but they must understand that the Certificates and keys are available and operate as expected. Other than this basic requirement, the following chapter sections provide some insight into PKI and Certificates.

Third-party Trust

Third party trust refers to a situation in which two individuals implicitly trust one another, even though they have not met or shared information. They trust each other because they each trust a common third party that vouches for the two participants. As illustrated in Exhibit 4-4, a CA can provide Certificates to two individuals who establish a trusting relationship based on the relationship they have individually with the CA.

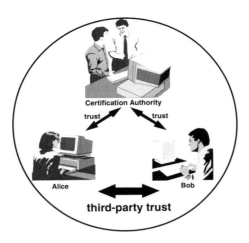

Exhibit 4-4.   Third-party trust

It is important to understand that the trust the users have in the CA is paramount. If a CA issues Certificates to anyone who asks, then a user provided with a Certificate from that CA trusts..., well, anybody. Because the CA is the only person who has access to the private key, the impersonation of a CA to issue bogus Certificates requires control over the CA or the private key. It is this very fact that CAs are well-protected physically, and in some cases taken offline for true protection (explained more later). The use of the CAs private key also inherently links the CA to the Certificate. Therefore, the issued Certificate provides non-repudiation of the CA. The CA cannot deny issuing the Certificate.

PKI Requirements

Certificates are associated with PKI, but Certificates are not the end of PKI. PKI is an enterprise service comprised of several layers of services that conspire to provide a coherent authentication and protection suite.

Public Key Certificates. Certificates ensure that the keys and identity of the bearer are valid by means of a third-party trust. CAs are people who and systems that create Certificates and bind them to the identified user. Certificates are a digitally signed collection of specific information. That information consists of the distinguished name of the user, the user's public key, the lifetime of the Certificate and associated keys, and what the supported operations of the Certificate are. Certificates can be used to encrypt data, digitally sign data, or provide both. Given the implementation and support for Certificates within an organization, nearly anything is possible with Certificates. An example is W2K PKI and the use of certificates or anything from Encrypted File System (EFS) control and recovery to authenticating clients, servers, and domain controllers. The ability to securely align an entity with specific information represents unlimited possibilities in the information age.

Certificate Repository. A Certificate repository is where the Certificate information is maintained and verified. The repository can be a database such as Micro Active

Directory by Microsoft or Novell's Directory Services. The repository is a combination of services, databases, and directories to provide a distributed authentication environment. The directory is typically LDAP compliant due to the various attributes of LDAP. LDAP is scalable, provides fast lookups and data retrieval, is an accepted standard, and works well with distributed environments.

Certificate Revocation (CRL). The most overlooked and underrated aspect of PKI is the Certificate revocation process. During the verification of a Certificate, there are several points of interest; of course, one of them is ensuring that the CA has not revoked the Certificate. If the Certificate has been revoked by the issuer, then trusting the Certificate should be avoided.

A Certificate revocation list is simply a list of the Certificates that the CA no longer supports or recognizes. As one can imagine, in the lifetime of a PKI solution, there will be many revoked Certificates. Managing the list and ensuring it is available for anyone attempting to validate a Certificate is paramount.

There are several reasons for revoking a Certificate: the validity time expired, the key was compromised, or employee dismissal.

Key Backup and Recovery. Certificate and key backup and recovery are necessary in the event the originals are lost or used and disposed. If a user loses a key or Certificate, and there is data encrypted with information, recovering the key can be very important. This is also important for a darker purpose. Information security is more than just fighting vulnerabilities; it includes ensuring the availability of data and ensuring its integrity. With the advent of encryption, there have been situations in which individuals have encrypted data and disposed of the keys. At that point, if there is no copy of the key for decryption, the data is lost. This is a reality that organizations must take into consideration; and therefore, a proper PKI solution must contain a key backup and recovery process.

Some people associate key backup with key escrow. A key escrow is where a third party, which was not involved with the creation of the Certificates or keys, is provided with a copy. Most people associate this process with the government and encryption laws and restrictions. A recovery and backup process on the issuing CA is necessary for proper enterprise security management. For that reason, the CA must maintain a backup. This is another reason for properly securing the CA system.

However, keys and Certificates used for signing purposes only are not backed up. The entire premise of digitally signing data is that no one else has a copy of the signing key. If the key is lost, a new one is simply issued and the user continues with the new keys. This has no effect on the availability of data, because signing keys cannot be used for encryption; as a result, there is no threat to the organization's data.

Non-repudiation. Non-repudiation is when the user who signed the data cannot successfully deny signing that data. Similarly, a CA cannot deny issuing the CA. Non-repudiation includes that someone cannot deny involvement in a transaction. The entire process is established by the privacy of the signing key.

Automatic Update of Certificates and Key Pairs. Keys should not be used for extended periods of time. The longer the key is in use, the greater the exposure to vulnerabilities. Periodic automatic update of keys and Certificates is the role of the PKI solution. Users should be unaware of the process and not be adversely affected by the process.

Key History. When keys are renewed, the keys that were replaced must be maintained for a period of time, due to the existence of data associated with the replaced keys. This is not the same as the backup and recovery of keys, which are geared toward the current keys being used. Key history is concerned with valid keys that have expired.

Cross-certification. Cross-certification extends certification domains beyond originating organization. This allows a trusted Certificate from another domain to be used. As shown in Exhibit 4-5, CAs can establish a trust that will extend the capabilities of the Certificate from either of the domains to the other.

The process requires specific steps. Basically, the trusting CA must provide a verification key to the trusted CA to be signed. Once the verification key is signed, the trust is established (one-way in this example; if two-way trust is desired, execute the process again in reverse).

There are examples in which trust can be established between two individuals from different domains. This is called a direct trust, as detailed in Exhibit 4-6. Two users can establish a relationship without the involvement of the trust domain's CAs.

Certificate Validation Process

As a system or user performs the activities that the certificate ultimately allows or permits, in some form or another, the certificate must be validated. The process exposes the interrelationships of PKI and the inherent complexities that can exist. The process, as seen in Exhibit 4-7, details the step-by-step procedure for validating the presentation of a Certificate.

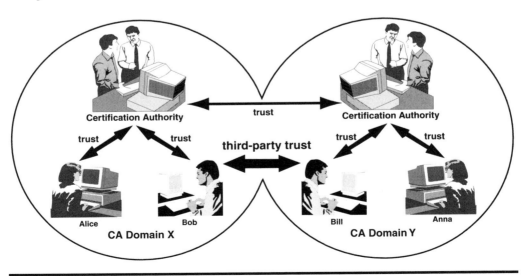

Exhibit 4-5.   Cross-certification

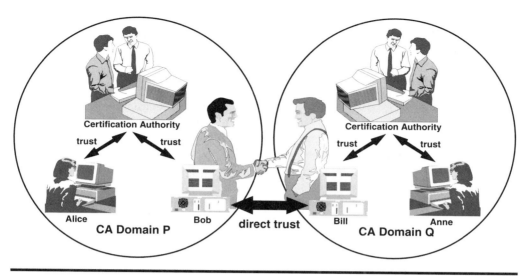

Exhibit 4-6. Direct trust certification

Message Authentication

As data is shared across untrusted networks, the opportunities for unauthorized interaction with the session are numerous. Of the many attacks that communications are vulnerable to, message authentication addresses a portion of the vulnerabilities. Message authentication is used as a tool to combine various communication-specific data that can be verified by the valid parties for each message received. Message authentication alone is not an appropriate countermeasure; but when combined with public key encryption, it can protect against various types of attacks.

Message authentication provides a means to enhance aspects of communication security. A message "fingerprint," called a digest, can be created in several ways, ranging from simple bit parity functions (hash), to utilization of encryption algorithms (DES-CBC-MAC), to complicated hybrids (HMAC). This fingerprint cannot only be used in to ensure message integrity, but given the inherent process of message reduction, it lends itself to signature processes.

Authentication Basis

To authenticate a message, an authenticator must be produced that can be used later by the recipient to validate the message. An authenticator is a primitive, reduction, or representation of the primary message to be authenticated. There are two primary types of authenticators:

- ciphertext
- message digest

Ciphertext. Encryption produces ciphertext, which becomes the authenticator for the original message. This is related to the trust relationship discussed earlier by assuming that the partner has the appropriate secret and has protected it accordingly.

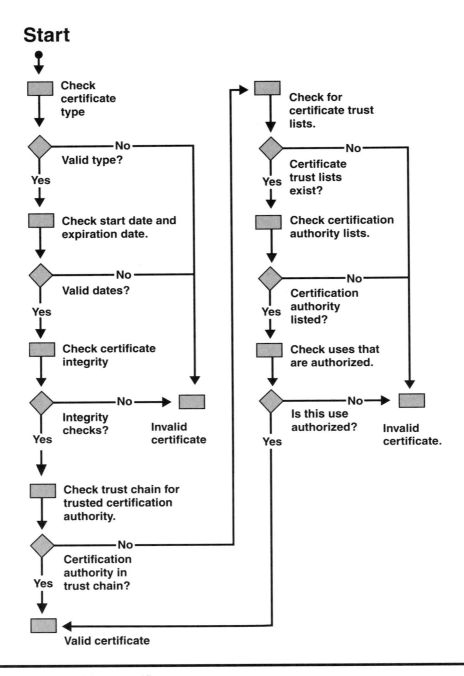

Exhibit 4-7.   Verifying a certificate

Consider a very basic encrypted communication example: a message sent from Alice to Bob encrypted with a shared secret. If the secret's integrity is maintained, confidentiality is ensured by the fact that no unauthorized entities have the shared secret. Bob can be reasonably assured that the message is valid because the key used is secret.

Message Digest. As briefly described earlier, hashing is a function that produces a unique, fixed-length value that serves as the authenticator for the communication. Hash functions are one-way, in that the creation of the hash is quite simple, but the reverse is computationally infeasible. A well-constructed hash function should be collision resistant. A collision is when two different messages produce the same result or digest. For a function to take a variable length of data and produce a much smaller fixed-length result, it is mathematically feasible to experience collisions. However, a well-defined algorithm with a large result should have high resistance to collisions.

Hash Functions

Hashing information to produce a digest will allow verification of the integrity of the transmitted data. To illustrate the process, Alice creates the message, "Mary runs every morning." Alice then hashes it to produce a smaller, fixed-length message digest, "AF43E7." Alice transmits the original message and the hash to Bob. Bob hashes the message from Alice and compares his result with the hash received with the original message. If the two hashes match, it can be assumed that the message was not altered in transit. If the message was changed after Alice sent it and before Bob received it, Bob's hash will not match, resulting in the loss of message integrity. This example is further detailed in Exhibit 4-8.

There are several caveats and layers of protection that have not been included. This simple representation is to explain the concepts of hash functions. It can be easily argued that an attacker could simply intercept the message, create a new one and corresponding digest, and forward it to the final destination. It is necessary to remember that hash is used as part of the overall process of message authentication and verifying data integrity. By no means can it provide robust security based solely on its own merit.

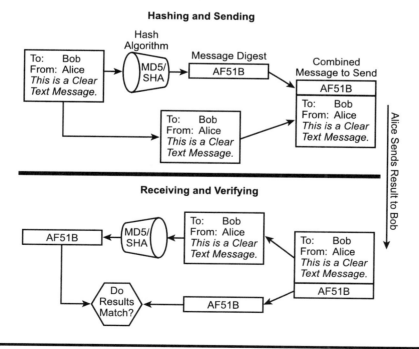

Exhibit 4-8. Hash function

Message Authentication Code (MAC)

Message Authentication Code (MAC) is an authentication process combined with a symmetrical key. MACs are created using a key so that the MAC can only be verified by the intended recipient who has the same symmetrical key. A plain hash function can be intercepted and replaced or brut-force attacked to determine collisions that can be of use to the attacker. With MACs, the addition of a key complicates the attack due to the secret key used in its computation.

Block Cipher-Based Message Authentication. Block cipher-based message authentication can be derived from block cipher algorithms. A commonly used version is DES-CBC-MAC, which, simply put, is DES encryption based on Cipher Block Chaining (CBC) mode of block cipher to create a MAC. A very common form of MAC is Data Authentication Algorithm (DAA), which is based on DES. The process uses the CBC mode of operation of DES with a zero initialization vector. As illustrated in Exhibit 4-9, the message is grouped into contiguous blocks of 64 bits; the last group is padded on the right with zeros to attain the 64-bit requirement. Each block is fed into the DES algorithm with a key to produce a 64-bit Data Authentication Code (DAC). The resulting DAC is XOR'ed with the next 64 bits of data and then again fed into the DES algorithm. This process continues until the last block, and returns the final MAC.

A block cipher is a type of symmetric key encryption algorithm that accepts a fixed block of plaintext to produce ciphertext of the same length. With Cipher Block Chaining (CBC) mode, each block result of ciphertext is exclusively OR'ed (XOR) with the previous calculated block, and then encrypted. Any patterns in the plaintext will not be transferred to the cipher due to the XOR process with the previous block. CBC is the minimum requirement for IPSec solutions.

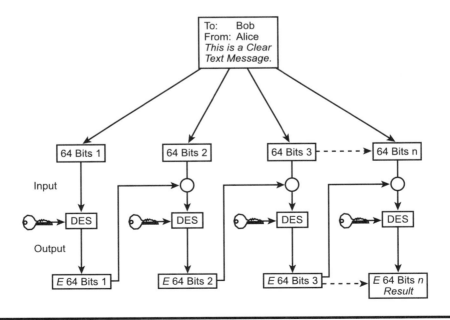

Exhibit 4-9. MAC based on DES CBC

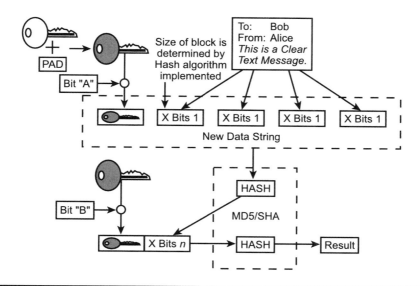

Exhibit 4-10. Simple HMAC example

Hash Function-based Message Authentication Code (HMAC). HMAC uses a key in combination with hash functions to produce a message digest. RFC 2104 defines that HMAC can be used with any iterative cryptographic hash function (e.g., MD5, SHA-1) in combination with a secret shared key. The cryptographic strength of HMAC depends on the properties of the underlying hash function.

The definition of HMAC requires a cryptographic hash function and a secret key. The hash function is where data is hashed by iterating a basic compression function on blocks of data, typically 64 bits in each block. The symmetrical key to be used can be any length up to the block size of the hash function. If the key is longer than the hash block size, the key is hashed and the smaller result is used as the final key.

As shown in Exhibit 4-10, the first step is to determine the key length requested and compare it to the block size of the hash being implemented. As described above, if the key is longer than the block size, it is hashed; the result will match the block size defined by the hash. In the event the key is smaller, it is padded with zeros to accommodate the required block size.

Once the key is defined, it is XOR'ed with a string of predefined bits "A" to create a new key that is combined with the message. The new message is hashed according to the function defined (see Exhibit 4-11). The hash function result is combined with the result of XOR'ing the key with another defined set of bits "B." The new combination of the second key instance and the hash results are hashed again to create the final result.

HMACs are heavily utilized for IPSec operations. This is a natural progression due to the available keys and the limited system resources required; as well, message integrity is a requirement for secure communications.

Digests over Encryption

The use of message authentication (e.g., hash functions) — and not encryption — to provide an authentication is based on several different concepts. Following are brief

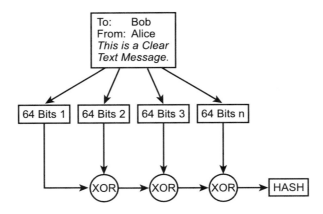

Exhibit 4-11. Simple hash function

examples that support the use of message digests, sometimes used in combination with public key cryptography, over the use of encryption.

Performance. Cryptographic hash functions, such as MD5 and SHA-1, execute much faster and use less system resources than typical encryption algorithms. In the event that a message only needs to be authenticated, the process of encrypting the entire message, such as a document or large file, is not entirely logical and consumes valuable system resources. By producing a message digest that is exponentially smaller than the original message and then encrypting the digest, time and effort are saved.

Application Considerations. There are applications in which the same message is broadcast to several destinations. One system may be elected as the communication monitor and verifies the message authentication on behalf of the other systems. If there is a violation, the monitoring system alerts the other systems. SNMP is an example in which command messages can be forged or modified in transit. A password can be implemented to act as a key for digest functions to allow a degree of authentication and message authentication. Each system in the community is configured with a password that can be combined with the data during the hash process and verified upon receipt.

System Performance. If a system is overburdened, the process of decryption would be overwhelming. Authentication can be executed in random intervals to ensure authentication with limited resources. Given that the hashing process is much less intensive than encryption, periodic hashing and comparisons will consume fewer system cycles.

Application Tampering. A program may be open to modification; therefore, a checksum can be included in the program that can be verified at runtime to ensure that the code is in the original format and should produce the expected results. Otherwise, an attacker might have constructed a malicious activity to surreptitiously operate while the original application was running.

Legacy Utilization. There is hardware designed for DES encryption processes. The use of DEC-CBC-MAC can take advantage of exiting technology to increase performance and support the requirements of the communication. As more advanced encryption becomes available and new standards evolve, the older hardware solutions can be utilized to enhance the message authentication process.

Legal Restrictions. No global export restrictions on cryptographic functions are defined. Currently, the laws enforcing import and export restrictions in the international community are complicated and constantly changing. Message authentication releases the communication participants from any export or import restrictions.

Diffie-Hellman

Symmetrical encryption, as explained earlier, is when the same key is used to encrypt and decrypt data. To establish communications with a remote system, the key must be made available to the participants for encryption and decryption purposes. Some interesting security issues include: how does one provide a key to the other systems without exposing it to unauthorized individuals? Better yet, what if there is no predefined relationship with desired communication peer? The answer to these questions and the hundreds that follow is that one can send a representation of the key that can be verified and used to create the final symmetric key. This action sounds much more simple than it is, but administrative interaction is limited and user interaction is nonexistent. The process is integrated into many applications and happens automatically. However, knowing the details will allow us to appreciate IPSec operations and the protection it provides by the intricate message content and timing.

In 1976, two mathematicians, Bailey W. Diffie from Berkeley and Martin E. Hellman from Stanford (California), defined the Diffie-Hellman Agreement Protocol (also known as exponential key agreement) and published it in a paper entitled, "New Directions in Cryptography." The protocol allows two autonomous systems to exchange a secret key over an untrusted network without any prior secrets. Diffie and Hellman postulated that the generation of a key could be accomplished by fundamental relationships between prime numbers. This allows communication of a symmetrical key without transmitting the actual key, but rather a mathematical portion or fingerprint.

An example of this process is system A and system B requires keying material for the DES encryption for the SA. Each system acquires the Diffie-Hellman parameters:

- a large prime number p
- a base number g, which is smaller than $p - 1$
- the host then generates the final number, X, which is less than $p - 2$

With these three numbers (p, g, X), a new value can be generated that is unique to the system. The numbers p and g must be hard-coded or retrieved from a remote system because large prime numbers are difficult to generate.

As shown in Exhibit 4-12, a new public value is generated with these numbers, $g^X \mod p$. The result Y, or fingerprint, is then shared between the systems over the untrusted network. The formula is then exercised again using the shared data from the other system and the Diffie-Hellman parameters. The results will be mathematically equivalent, regardless of the value of the Diffie-Hellmann parameters, and can be

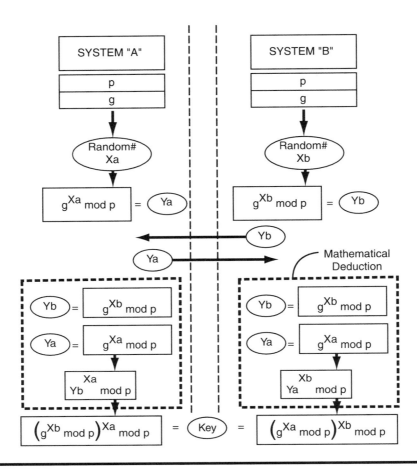

Exhibit 4-12.   Diffie-Hellman Exchange Protocol

used to generate a symmetrical key. If each system executes this process successfully, they will have matching symmetrical keys without transmitting the key itself. The Diffie-Hellman protocol was finally patented in 1980 (U.S. 4,200,770) and is such a strong protocol that there are currently 128 other patents that reference Diffie-Hellman.

An added feature of Diffie-Hellman is the Station to Station (STS) protocol that leverages asymmetrical encryption to further protect the Diffie-Hellman (DH) key. The Diffie-Hellman process has one primary weakness in the standard protocol: it is vulnerable to man-in-the-middle attacks.

Assume for a minute that an attacker knew that two individuals were going to establish communications using symmetrical encryption, and could intercept and control communications between the two peers. Once again, one can use the ever-present Alice and Bob to explain the relatively simple process. Alice creates the DH value and sends it to Bob so that Bob can create the necessary key for the following encrypted communications. Unfortunately, Alice's DH key is consumed by the attacker and denies it from Bob, but sends his own DH key to Bob in place of the one expected from Alice. Of course, as Bob sends his DH key, the attacker executes the same process in reverse. The result is that Alice and Bob have established keying material with the attacker but not with each other. The attacker has become the key proxy and all communications between Alice and Bob are open to the attacker. This is a very simplified example, as most attacker scenarios are, simply because the entire process is layers of complex interactions by the attacker, but these procedures are far from impossible.

The key point is that the public value should be protected. To do so, public key cryptography can be employed to enhance the underlying Diffie-Hellman protocol. As the DH key is created and prepared to be shared with the peer, it is encrypted with the peer's public key and then sent on its way. The simple addition of the encryption step eliminates the man-in-the-middle attack from the equation; but as with most increased security, the complexity is elevated as well. The inclusion of public key cryptography introduces all the administration required for implementing the technology. The added process is shown in Exhibit 4-13.

It is interesting to note that each property required to create a Diffie-Hellman public value can be different. In other words, the prime number and base number can be different on each peer; of course, the host-generated number will be unique as well. The actual mathematical properties of the Diffie-Hellman procedure are well beyond the scope of this book, but the basic components have been introduced and

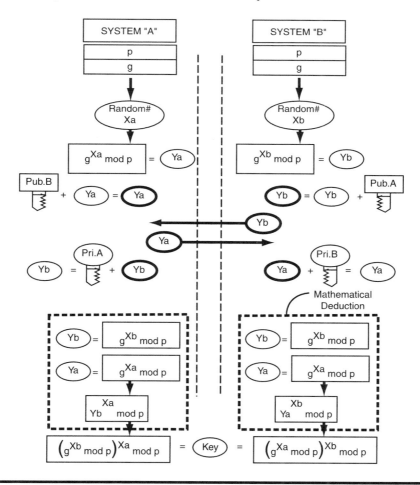

Exhibit 4-13. Diffie-Hellman Exchange Protocol with the use of public key cryptography

their role in IPSec will be continually revisited in remaining chapters. The use of Diffie-Hellman is crucial to IPSec operations because the vast majority of communication is encrypted with symmetrical encryption technology. As the advent of AES is integrated into the protocol to increase security and performance, Diffie-Hellman will remain as the utility to communicate key material.

Perfect Forward Secrecy

The material used to generate keys determines perfect forward secrecy. During the creation of keys, or the material to be used for key generation, any data used in the process from an existing key process does not provide forward secrecy. Symmetric encryption methods use keys with very short lifetimes when compared with asymmetrical algorithms. Part of this is due to the complexity of key management for asymmetrical key and the one-way properties of the asymmetrical algorithm.

In any event, data is shared between two systems, typically a Diffie-Hellman exchange, that provide for the creation of symmetrical keys. For security purposes, the time those keys are used is proportional to the overall security of the communication. The longer a key is used, the more opportunities for an attacker to obtain it, or determine it. At the end of the lifetime of the key, a new one is generated. If the key is thrown away and replaced by a new key that was derived from a new Diffe-Hellman exchange — that contains unique data — the two keys will have no relation to each other. If an attacker were to obtain the expired key, he or she would have access to the data that was encrypted with that particular key, but would not be able to use it to determine the value of the new key being utilized.

A system would not have perfect forward secrecy if there were a single set of data that was used to generate multiple keys. In the event a secret is used to create all the keys for the communication and the secret was available to the attacker, all the keys could be derived. Once the primary key has been broken, the attacker would have access to all the data protected by that key and all subsequent keys.

Chapter 5

Implementation Theory

There are several different types of IPSec VPN configurations. Some of the designs discussed in this chapter are currently attainable, while others only exist in the standards. The standards provide the means to create exquisite designs, but the equipment that is currently available does not support some of the concepts. This chapter discusses all the design possibilities, and the particular designs that are not yet available will become obvious very early.

This section discusses other communication technologies, specifically Frame Relay. It compares the basic operations of Frame Relay to the basic operations of VPNs. Several arguments are made in favor of VPN technology over conventional Frame Relay technology. Several design options are explained and compared to Frame Relay, and advantages over Frame Relay are explored at the expense of the Frame Relay technology. Many arguments can be made in defense of Frame Relay, but the reality is that Frame Relay provides enough similarity to VPNs to accommodate the explanation of new VPN concepts. Frame Relay is the communication of choice of millions of companies worldwide and accommodates the communication requirements. However, this presents an alternate view of communications and how they relate to business activities.

Moving to the Internet

The Internet is simply a network that everyone can participate in and use for communications with anyone or anything else on the Internet. In contrast, many companies use private networks to provide wide area communications, called wide area network (WAN). VPNs are conspiring to eliminate the need for the physical privacy present in typical WAN solutions.

Many organizations have several offices located throughout a region, country, or they have an international presence. As technology became more and more of an integral part of business, the computers needed to be connected to enhance the services and availability of data. To accomplish remote connectivity, many organizations purchase a communication line from a provider, such as MCI WorldCom, Sprint, AT&T, GTE, or any company that provides private wide area connectivity for each location. Once the line is "turned-up," equipment is introduced to provide the lower layers for the networking protocol.

For simplicity, assume a WAN is using TCP/IP and Frame Relay encapsulation (see Exhibit 5-1). Frame Relay is a packet-switching technology that encapsulates the protocols being used for communication into frames that can be transmitted. Frame Relay provides a subset of Layer 2 functionality and makes optimal use of bandwidth by statistically multiplexing traffic on a physical link.

By leveraging the bandwidth management of Frame Relay, organizations could implement inexpensive WANs compared to earlier technology of leased lines. A leased line is a dedicated point-to-point circuit that utilizes 100 perceent of the bandwidth even if very little data is traversing the line. The amount of bandwidth quickly equates to money; the more one uses, the more it will cost. Bandwidth consumes resources

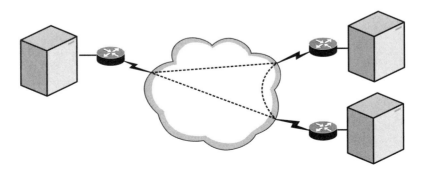

Exhibit 5-1.   Basic Frame Relay example.

of the provider, which limits the number of circuits that can be sold to other clients. Therefore, the provider will charge more. By using bandwidth efficiently, organizations can save money.

Frame Relay is based on committed information rate (CIR), how much bandwidth is guaranteed available. Also, committed burst provides a mechanism for extra bandwidth when required during heavy load. Of course, this is tracked and billed accordingly; however, it is still a fraction of the cost because the charge for extended bandwidth utilization is for brief periods of time. A similar situation is the public telephone service. Local calls are typically covered with a base charge and one can make as many locals as one wants. However, at certain intervals, one might call across the country and use more resources. Those resources that were used will increase the cost, but it would still be much less than if every call cost as much as the long-distance call.

Also, similar to the public telephone system, requests have to be routed. When dialing a telephone number, it provides the system with the information necessary to make the connection to the appropriate destination. Routing protocols in a network provide much the same service. As requests for an IP address are made, internal routing protocols forward that information based on knowledge about the network. In some cases, the knowledge about the network is learned, other times, information is provided by an administrator that determines the route of data. In either case, requests for a remote network, whether across a WAN or a VPN, must be forwarded to the appropriate systems that connect the networks.

Frame Relay (see Exhibit 5-2) provides a dedicated conduit through a cloud of switches and lines that route the information based on the data link control identifier (DLCI). The DLCI is a number that represents a virtual circuit that can provide an uninterrupted, permanent connection. The result is a permanent virtual circuit (PVC) that, in essence, a VPN emulates.

A VPN can be established between two or more sites to provide the same basic service that Frame Relay provides (see Exhibit 5-3). The fundamental technologies are completely different but the available communication remains the same. An office can connect a VPN gateway to the Internet to act as a router much like a router connected to a Frame Relay cloud. As application requests are made for a remote service, internal routing processes will forward the request to the VPN gateway. The VPN gateway will apply the protection services detailed by the policy and forward the information to the remote office's VPN gateway.

As illustrated in Exhibit 5-3, the communication is very similar to Frame Relay and provides seamless connectivity; however, the privacy is provided in the protocol and not the medium. As the discussion continues, the advantages of VPNs will become very evident.

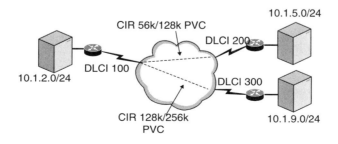

Exhibit 5-2. Frame Relay internals.

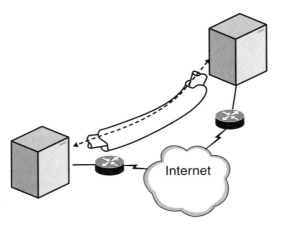

Exhibit 5-3.   Simple VPN example.

WAN Augmentation

In a typical WAN environment, data is routed to the final destination based on the attributes requested by the communication. If a service is provided in a remote location, the user application can simply request the service — by providing an IP address and service port — and the data will be routed across the WAN as if on the same network. From the point of view of the user, the connection is seamless. VPNs can duplicate this process and can be much more flexible and, in some cases, cost-effective.

Many organizations start augmenting their WAN environment with VPNs (see Exhibit 5-4) when the cost of a new PVC to a remote location is simply too expensive. A good example is a manufacturing company that has several small plants in sparsely populated, remote locations. To provide Frame Relay service to that location for simple

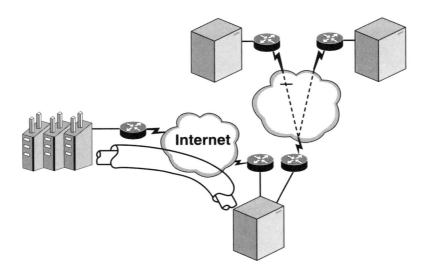

Exhibit 5-4.   VPN for remote office or plan.

e-mail or for a couple of office computers could become very expensive. A simple connection to the Internet can be provided by an available ISP. In this example, it will more than likely be a limited dial solution or some form of broadband solution such as a cable modem. Nevertheless, once the office is connected to the Internet, the communication capabilities are seemingly limitless.

Take, for example, four business offices and seven remote manufacturing plants. Each remote plant is connected to the Internet and is using VPNs for connectivity to the home office, which in turns provides connectivity to the other offices by a standard Frame Relay WAN. The home office has a VPN gateway that can communicate with VPN gateways at the remote plants. As the communication requirements increase and the plants need to share information, they can establish a connection with each other over the Internet, using existing equipment and their Internet connection. With a simple configuration change, a VPN can be established between two plants and have little or no impact on the remaining VPNs.

Providing Internet connectivity to another office can further expand the augmentation of the existing WAN. As the Internet is adopted, one office in an entire organization typically has the only Internet connectivity that provides services to the entire infrastructure. This is typically due to the management, cost, and security concerns of providing Internet connectivity. However, this process is changing as more companies are adding Internet connectivity to remote locations to relieve the WAN infrastructure of day-to-day Internet use, and the cost of providing Internet connectivity has become more affordable.

If, in this example organization, Internet connectivity is provided to one of the other offices, new connectivity options will become immediately available (see Exhibit 5-5). For example, suppose the plants that are already using VPNs to access the home office require the use of a service or need data from one of the other remote offices. Although the organization has taken advantage of the Internet for some resources, the WAN is still being saturated with traffic to the remote site's resources.

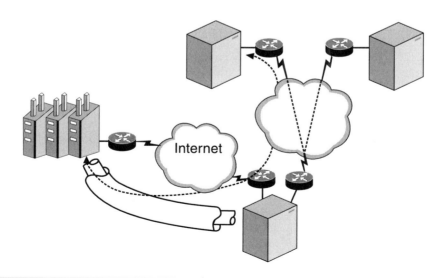

Exhibit 5-5. VPN providing access to WAN sites utilizing the WAN.

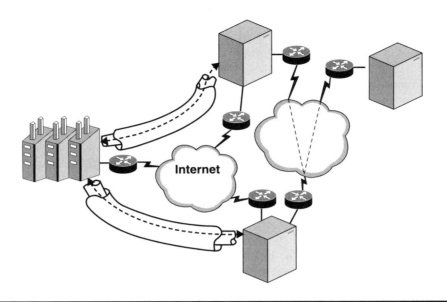

Exhibit 5-6.   VPN providing access to WAN sites utilizing the VPN.

The remote office provided with an Internet connection can be directly accessed via the VPN using existing services that are currently implemented (see Exhibit 5-6). Now, as requests from the plant are made for the service, the VPN can automatically route the data to the office that has the service and alleviate the load on the infrastructure.

WAN Replacement

The previous example represents one of the many attractive features of VPNs. The ability to provide new communications, nearly instantly, for no increased financial charge is an enormous leap over conventional WAN technology.

Compare the previous scenario with a Frame Relay-based topology. All the offices and the remote plants have Frame Relay connectivity that has some form of cost. Each plant has a PVC connecting it to the home office. The cost of the PVC is directly related to the CIR and total port speed allocation. Assume that these costs are equal to the Internet connection being provided at the sites.

However, a major difference is realized when connection from one plant to another is required. A new PVC must be purchased and allocated by the provider; this represents an additional annual cost. Not only are there monetary costs, but there are situations in which getting a PVC allocated can take excessive time; meanwhile, the existing PVC is providing a dual purpose by connecting the plants to the home office and communication between each other. Given the added communication, it can be assumed that the CIR is being surpassed and the charge of the existing PVC has increased.

For one PVC, this may seem overindulgent and unrealistic. The provisioning of new PVCs happens everyday for many organizations moving through changes, yet each scenario represents another PVC. In some organizations, it is necessary to allocate a PVC for each office connecting it to each of the others. When a PVC exists between

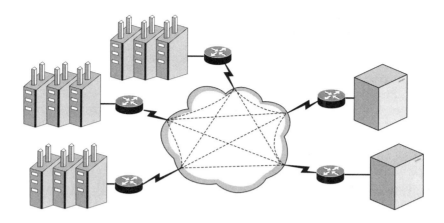

Exhibit 5-7. Fully meshed Frame Relay.

each site, it is called a fully meshed environment (see Exhibit 5-7). In this example, there are 11 sites that could be fully meshed. A simple formula can be applied to the number of sites to determine the number of PVCs, $n(n - 1)/2$, where n is the number of sites that will participate in the mesh. Therefore, $(11 \times 10)/2 = 110/2 = 55$ PVCs.

This is an extreme example and many organizations have learned how to accommodate communications while avoiding a fully meshed environment. However, there are still many situations in which a partially meshed WAN is necessary.

This example network can illustrate an example of a partially meshed network (see Exhibit 5-8). The four offices could have a meshed network that consists of six PVCs that provide connectivity and a form of limited redundancy, while the plants have a single PVC connecting them to the home office.

Redundancy Concepts. The offices are provided limited redundancy by the fact there is an alternate route to each of the offices if one were to become unavailable. In an earlier example, the remote offices maintained connectivity through a single PVC to the home office. If the home office were to go down, all communications

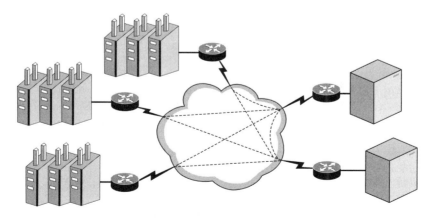

Exhibit 5-8. Partial mesh Frame Relay.

would stop enterprisewide. However, by having PVCs between each office, there is no single point of failure in the WAN structure.

Unfortunately, the redundancy is provided at Layer 2 and can become misleading. The connection to the WAN is typically provided by a single connection that all the virtual circuits operate. A portion of the redundancy applies to the connectivity being provided by the PVCs. If a physical connection were to fail, none of the PVCs would be accessible. Granted, this does not affect the entire enterprise and only has an impact on the local office, but the redundancy provided by the multiple PVCs is limited. This discussion has evolved over many arguments comparing VPN connectivity to PVC connectivity. The simple fact is that each typically relies on a single physical connection to provide access to a group of virtual connections that are multiplexed into that single connection.

The clear advantage that VPNs have over Frame Relay is the use of multiple connections to the Internet from completely different providers. Having different connections from different providers allows for continued connectivity in the event a wire is cut or a provider's system fails. It is possible to provide separate lines for Frame Relay networks to eliminate a single point of failure, but the configuration can become complex and expensive.

In the event that a Frame Relay circuit goes down and the alternate must take over, PVCs must be reallocated. This is sometimes referred to as "swinging a PVC" over to a new network. Depending on the technology, some PVCs can be created on demand; but typically, dormant PVCs must be allocated to act as a "hot standby" in the event of primary failure. As one might imagine, this can get very expensive.

On the other hand, IPSec VPNs operate at the network layer and are completely oblivious to the lower layer concerns. Unlike Frame Relay, which directly interacts and provides some Layer 2 functionality, IPSec is simply responsive to the overall path and not to the physical aspects of the communication. Routers can be implemented that handle the Layer 2 and 3 aspects of the communication failure. In an incredibly short period of time, all data can be routed through a secondary circuit. The VPN that was established will typically break and a new one will need to appear. However, this limitation is commonly associated with the product implementation of IPSec; it is feasible to realign the VPN after a short break in communications. As long as the endpoints of the VPN do not change and the Layer 3 configuration at the endpoints remains static, a VPN can continue over new circuitry. This should be apparent, given the connectionless aspects of the IP, but IPSec can be very sensitive to certain critical changes. If these are avoided, the VPN should continue to operate.

Reevaluating the WAN. In the above example, the support for a Frame Relay WAN must be questioned. The plants require very little bandwidth and the cost of providing a PVC to ten remote locations could become expensive compared to the service usage.

The fully meshed cloud between the offices is required for business information needs and continuity of service. However, once the Frame Relay PVCs are meshed, each additional PVC can be considered direct overhead when compared to a VPN. A single PVC implemented for each site is efficient and cost-effective. VPN connectivity cannot add much more in the arena of cost and, given the current Internet environment, VPN does not offer better performance. As the number of PVCs increases, the cost accrued for each is frivolous when compared to VPNs.

The commonalities between Frame Relay and VPNs are the connection cost and the ISP charge compared to the first PVC. The local loop, or the connection from the site to the service point, is common between the two technologies and the costs, for augmentation sake, can cancel out each other. The cost of a PVC to a remote location can be related to the cost of the ISP charges for access service. These are not absolutes and the cost can vary; but as the number of PVCs added to the aggregate of the single connection increases, the cost of VPN connectivity decreases.

Remote access

Prior to VPN technology, remote access services (RAS) were typically dial-up solutions that required dedicated equipment and telephones lines for each remotely connected system. One of the main reasons for the popularity of VPNs is the ability to eliminate the need to add circuits or equipment to support thousands of remote users.

Current Remote Access Technology

A typical RAS design would include a modem pool and a group of telephone circuits to provide connectivity. There are cases of RAS solutions operating with mountains of modems connected to a series of telephone switches and networking equipment. As technology increased, modems have became more streamlined and ultimately virtual interfaces on networking devices. However, the advanced technologies to modernize dial-up remote access are expensive and many organizations continue to use standard modems to provide access.

The scalability of standard RAS systems based on modems is limited and expensive. For example, if an organization has 150 sales personnel needing remote access, on average, 15 modems (a ratio of 10:1 or 8:1 is typical) would be required for a calculated connection rate. As remote users are added, the number of modems must increase. However, the number of remote users is increasing, and even when a reduction ratio is performed, the simultaneous connection requirements can be staggering. The addition of modems for expanded service is typically not a huge financial burden. The supporting issues, such as telephone equipment, telephone lines, and even space, can become concerns that must be considered when expanding an RAS implementation.

The most painful part in any upgrade is when the necessary requirements cannot be met by the implemented infrastructure. There have been many cases in which new phone lines needed to be added, but the telephone system could not support the number required or the type of technology that provided much-desired options. These situations typically force management and technical support teams to determine if it is in the best interest of the company to reinvest in the new technology.

VPN Revolution

Client-to-network VPNs have eliminated the need for dedicated equipment for each connection. Now, a single system can support an astounding number of simultaneous connections. With early VPN products the number of simultaneously supported users would range from 10 to 50. In a very short time frame, products were developed that could easily support thousands of connections. At the time this book was written, there were devices that could support over 100,000 simultaneous connections.

VPN technology had a direct impact on what constituted supported technology. With standard dial-in solutions, the access technology was typically limited. The most obvious are modems, which seem to have reached a maximum transmission rate of 56K. To allow for increased bandwidth, ISDN technology was implemented in many organizations to provide up to 128K of bandwidth. ISDN was very popular in other countries and acceptance was slow in the United States and the cost of ISDN reflected that. ISDN, to this day, is very expensive when compared to other communication technologies.

The primary commonality of these communication offerings is the ability to cheaply terminate the connection. Much like telephone communications, the phone itself is cheap; the service is relatively inexpensive; and the operation, from the point of view of the user, is simple. A person picks up the phone, dials a number, and someone answers at the other end. Each end is uncomplicated and inexpensive to terminate. In this example, the phone provides the termination for electrical signals into intelligible voice. Conversely, the underlying technology can be highly complex and expensive to implement. Therefore, ISDN modems and standard modems are based on the simple concept of leveraging existing infrastructure.

Today, there are several other communication technologies that provide connectivity at very high speeds. The most common are cable modems and xDSL technology — typically ADSL for home users. The first difference is that these technologies are usually associated with Internet access and not point-to-point services. These access technologies are designed for many people to gain access to a large network (i.e., the Internet). Cable and ADSL are typically not associated with standard RAS solutions, due to the complexity of the termination and underlying technologies.

VPNs eliminated the link layer from having to be supported in the communication. Therefore, communications could be established without regard to the communication technology. No matter what the technology being used to gain access to the Internet, once the connection is made, a VPN can be established. Once again, this relates back to the TCP/IP protocol stack and the close integration of IPSec into the network layer. TCP/IP can run on any operating system that supports it, and allows that system to participate on the Internet. Once IPSec is implemented into the operating system and the TCP/IP protocol stack, everything else about the communication is irrelevant to the security services provided.

LAN Security Augmentation

For much of IPSec's existence, it has been associated with the Internet and leveraging the global network for secure communications. Somewhere in between is the addition of the internal security provided by extending the tunnel into the network through the security gateway. A remote system can connect to the security gateway and establish another VPN nested inside the first with an internal system — ultimately providing protection from end to end.

However, any TCP/IP network can take advantage of IPSec. Even systems on the same network can establish an IPSec VPN. In short, if one can create an IP session, one can implement IPSec.

Various organizations have recognized the internal threat to information. In some cases, these insightful companies have implemented firewalls segmenting the proprietary traffic from areas of high vulnerability or uncontrolled access. However, certain trusts are created for the groups of computers or users provided access to a particular segment protected by a firewall. Many of the organizations that have implemented interdepartmental firewalls are struggling with internal controls of data within protected domains. The cost and administration of firewalls prohibit the granularity desired by the administrators or managers concerned with data privacy.

IPSec has become an interesting tool for applying security in a policy-based environment. A policy can be created for each security domain and provided to the workstations throughout the organization. Upon establishing a connection from a workstation to a server, the policy will go beyond standard authentication and ensure that only permissible data types traverse the network.

IPSec can verify and authenticate the individual systems through the use of certificates and determine traffic to be afforded to that workstation. Therefore, regardless of VLAN configurations or loopholes in network firewall implementations, a properly configured policy on participating systems will only allow data between a server and workstation that is defined in the policy.

Currently, there are very few products geared toward LAN security augmentation. It is the last frontier to be explored by vendors. Many are attempting to answer the cry for remote access solutions and securing those solutions, but very few have spent time developing LAN security based on the IPSec protocol suite. However, there has been one vendor that has pushed this quietly into the background of a greater noise of options and capabilities. Microsoft and the recent development of Windows 2000 has built in support for IPSec VPNs geared directly toward internal LAN security augmentation. Quite frankly, this was a brilliant move by Microsoft developers, whether they were aware of it or not. By integrating IPSec functions into the kernel of Windows 2000 and providing policy management through the existing infrastructure of Active Directory, the answer to internal security has begun to be answered.

Microsoft provided an interesting solution for IPSec communications; much more is available than meets the eye. Currently, there are three primary limitations that exist with today's solutions: end-to-end protection, kernel-based implementation, and centralized and integrated policy management.

There are many products that provide a client package that allows the operator to establish a VPN with a gateway. Access to internal systems is simply forwarded as normal traffic. There are very few solutions that provide software that can be loaded onto an internal system, allowing the remote client to establish a VPN with the gateway and have a nested VPN for internal communications. By Microsoft providing IPSec support in the operating system, end-to-end VPNs can be created and nested for extensive protection that simply does not exist that cleanly in any other solution. Of course, all of this is possible by leveraging Active Directory for management, distribution, and employment.

Even if Microsoft's solution only provides limited functionality under the best of conditions, it is still operating in a realm with little or no competition.

Performance Considerations

There are several discussions that can be waged against the concept of replacing an entire conventional-based WAN with an Internet-based VPN. Nearly all of them are based on performance concerns and the ability to support several sites and users through a single connection to an uncontrolled network.

The Internet

Of the compelling arguments against VPN, one stands out as the constant: the Internet. Simply put, the Internet has been labeled as an unreliable, high latency network that could come or go at anytime. This author can remember in recent history talking with managers from large organizations who felt that expenditures on a 256K connection to the Internet were ridiculous due to the uncertainty of the service. As the Internet has grown, we have become increasingly dependant on the services it provides, but the thought that the Internet has not grown physically remains.

This is a great irony because the Internet was primarily designed around a concept of creating a network that has no single point of failure. One can argue that the local connection to the Internet might fail or be severed, but the same holds true for many dedicated connections. It is common practice in today's communication industry to implement several backup systems or standby connections to provide service if the primary communication fails. Several organizations spend incredible amounts of money to simply bury a fiber cable or some form of connectivity on the other side of a building just to mitigate the risk of digging incidents. Given these two primary, standard practices and reasoning, why are the same concepts for Internet connections not accepted? For organizations that rely heavily on the Internet for business, such as ISPs, ASPs, and DotComs, multiple connections to the Internet are mandatory; but for the enterprise market, the focus on redundancy communications continues to reside in the WAN.

The reality is that the Internet has grown substantially in reliability and reduced latency. However, the connection from one ISP to another through many other ISPs begins to surface as the true straw that is breaking the VPN's back. The concept of connecting two sites through a network that is supported by several different vendors is not a new situation. In some Frame Relay networks, it is necessary for a primary provider to leverage another to accommodate connectivity to a remote location or a region not directly supported. This process is sometimes referred to as NNI (or network-to-network interface), which also represents the protocol for maintaining PVCs between networks.

Many of the early VPN implementers were not cognizant of the importance of Internet connections at specific points throughout the design. The result was high latency and packet loss, ultimately resulting in a major disappointment of VPN performance. The importance of selecting a well-designed and established ISP is absolutely crucial to the success of a VPN. For organizations based in developed countries, the options are many. Even international long hauls can be realized through Internet-based VPNs when the relationship between Tier 1 ISPs is properly investigated. Of course, problems begin to surface when remote locations are identified that do not have established connectivity to the Internet, and have limited Frame Relay services. Good examples are South America, Africa, and China, where the environment, economic status, and vast terrain complicate communications. Getting any form of connectivity can be challenging in these situations; and when limited bandwidth becomes available, many companies do not opt to add the complexities and latency associated with low-tier ISPs and rely on the guarantees of Frame Relay.

An example of the commitment required to fully investigate the Internet connections and relationships between ISPs can be seen in a client that this author consulted on an international VPN. The organization is huge; it firmly exists in over 130 different countries and maintains informational relationships with hundreds of partnering organizations — including competitors. The Frame Relay costs were unimaginable; a single, modest PVC across the Atlantic Ocean was costing over $10,000, and was only one of thousands of international PVCs.

The evolution of the VPN design was very interesting and was contrary to typical beliefs at the time. In that time, VPNs were considered "local," in that for long hauls over great distances, Internet latency and hops would become too excessive, thus resulting in poor performance. As the investigation of the ISP's networks continued, it became increasingly clear that the large ISPs had reputable international presence in the expected developed locations with very high bandwidth capabilities between locations. On one occasion, a shot from New York to London would run on SONET OC-48 (2488.32 Mbs) with peak time utilization of 60 percent, and plans were in place for implementing OC-96 (4976.64 Mbs). In contrast, a typical Frame Relay network was operating at OC-12 (622.08 Mbs) and realized utilization was greater due to the operation of Frame Relay technology.

As costs were compared between Frame Relay and ISP services, a trend contrary to normal belief became apparent. To purchase a T1 Frame Relay connection from New York to London, with a high CIR, quickly became expensive. The charge for a local loop, service, and CIR level all conspired to create a high reoccurring charge. However, Internet connection costs are not distance based, but merely bandwidth based: the more one needs, the more one pays. Once on the Internet, who cares where you go? There are, of course, cost overlaps, such as the local loop for the connection is typically canceled out when compared to Frame Relay. The real savings come from the ISP charges, which can be significantly less than the same bandwidth in Frame Relay.

The cost disparity is based on the fundamental differences in service. While Frame Relay is a guaranteed service and information rates can be closely monitored and controlled, the Internet simply offers a connection — after that, you are on your own — but is that always true? The answer is No. Take as an example the large ISP UUNet. UUNet operates many of the networks (equipment, cables, etc.) on which the Internet runs. The odds of UUNet routing a request for a remote portion of its network over someone else's network is quite low — actually, dramatically low. By combining the expansive service of an ISP to its primary locations and then overlaying the locations of the client sites, one can develop a comprehensive data flow over the Internet using VPNs instead of PVCs over a private network. Now, the client can spend a fraction of the money and receive two or three times the bandwidth to the Internet as opposed to Frame Relay.

The point where this concept does not necessarily compute well — cost versus performance — is in local communications in highly developed regions versus sparsely populated, limited technological regions. In technically evolved environments, the Frame Relay costs are very competitive and there is typically no NNI within a country. In technically limited countries, the available connectivity is usually low bandwidth and low on the priority list of the next-tier provider. In these scenarios, the cost of Frame Relay is either so competitive that it makes good business sense, or that the connectivity is so expensive that latency would destroy what little communications are being allowed.

In between these two realizations is interstate or European communications where the distances are not massive but the handing-off of data from one carrier to another becomes a point of interest. With Frame Relay, distance and exchanges have an impact on the final cost of the PVC. In contrast, an ISP may have support that extends out into the necessary regions, or the distance has little affect when data swaps ISP networks.

In each of these scenarios, one can see several typical designs, common directions and uses, and finally trends in technology implementations. Given the competitive costs and guaranteed service of Frame Relay, many organizations lean toward that with which they have become familiar. Also, the quickly realized savings tend to surround the remote access aspect of VPNs, which has resulted in many remote access VPN solutions, whereas network-to-network VPNs are more rare. However, with the advent of broadband Internet access, remote access VPNs are taking on a different look and affecting the definition of a remote user and network. With cable or xDSL, high-speed connections, normally only experienced at large organizations, can be obtained for home use.

The Internet's early reputation had been built on questionable foundations and limited bandwidth. Now, the Internet is maturing and high-speed access is the norm and not the exception. In the beginning, the concept of sending anything real-time over the Internet was affected by poor performance factors and latency of immature networks and relationships. Now that the Internet has evolved and technologies are being leveraged to enhance the service, selecting the proper ISP and understanding its data networks as well as its business ones, can greatly impact the performance impression of the VPN solution.

The Security

It is one thing to blame a network for poor overall performance, as with the Internet. However, add to the latency of basic communications the overhead of securing data, and it quickly becomes very clear that performance is impacted by the fundamentals of VPN. Encryption, authentication, data integrity, key management, and basic protocol maintenance all add up to create overhead that directly impacts the performance of a VPN solution.

Throughout this book, there is ongoing discussion of the details of IPSec and the various operations performed to protect information about the peers, as well as what information is being shared. Of all the services, encryption is typically the focal point of many vendors and implementers.

Message authentication usually leverages very fast one-way operations that have been optimized for performance and have a little overall impact on the VPN. Authentication and key management have significant associated costs, but operate at the beginning of the session and intermittently throughout the life of the VPN. It is agreed that encryption represents the bulk of the performance degradation within a VPN, and there are several factors that affect this determination and several situational remedies.

When in doubt, throw a processor at it. For many solutions, the addition of dedicated processors for the sole purpose of encrypting data provides enough cycles to reduce the load of the required overhead. In many circumstances, the system limitations become communication hardware and not the processing of data. A VPN gateway that has a 10/100 Ethernet card on one side and a T3 interface on the Internet side can be designed to handle 100 Mbs throughput, but one of the interfaces only supports half the system's capabilities.

The System

It is the details of hardware support for encryption that leads us into performance considerations for the three primary implementation types. There are dedicated hardware systems loaded with memory and processors that have no moving parts and whose sole purpose is to move VPN data. Much like a router, it is an appliance that can be dropped in an existing network to provide specific services. Another aspect is system or server-based VPN gateways. An example is Microsoft's PPTP solution that turns a server into a gateway that encrypts data. Server-based applications suffer from the obvious — not originally designed for VPN or routing, but rather a single tool for many different operations. The result is limited throughput capabilities because the processor(s) are not dedicated to just encryption operations. Finally, there are client systems that have an application that performs the necessary security tasks. However, unlike servers that use an application to perform much the same function, a client only needs to concern itself with that system, whereas a server may be responsible for hundreds of connections from remote users and networks.

The results from these determinations are two basic complements: hardware augmentation and technological advances in encryption. Hardware can be added in the form of an encryption card that can provide relief to the primary system processor for encryption functions. In various cases, this can come in the form of an expansion card that is installed in the system or a fob, a device that is connected to the system for offloading system processes. As this technology evolves, the encryption processes will move to the network interface card. As an example, 3COM has produced an IPSec-compliant NIC that provides the extra horsepower required topush data at acceptable rates. The greatest application for NIC-based IPSec support may best be experienced at the client system. Although the performance reduction of a client system is negligible without hardware support, as bandwidth increases and utilization increases, anything but a dedicated VPN gateway will suffer. The hardware augmentation can certainly help and assist the typical system-based gateway in nominal solutions, but supporting 5000 simultaneous connections from xDSL, cable, and dial-up users is extremely processor intensive.

Technological advances in encryption technology are providing much faster and safer encryption techniques that can greatly enhance the overall performance of a VPN. An example, discussed in detail later, is the Advance Encryption Standard (AES). AES is a new generation of encryption to replace DES and 3DES as the standard typical encryption algorithm. One of the primary goals of the designers of the various AES candidates is speed. Granted, increased security is always desirable, but increasing performance in the process is high on the list of accomplishments.

Implemented versus Required

Performance is fundamental and it is a near second to function. Previous sections discussed proper design from the perspective of ISP selection, relationship, and regional conditions and needs, the proper implementation of hardware, and advances in technology that can all combine to increase performance. Now the implementation of the services provided by IPSec VPNs must be addressed.

One of the most powerful aspects of IPSec is its ability to segment traffic and apply different policies based on various selectors, or identifiers, that the administrator can use to collect different types of traffic together that need similar protection suites. It is necessary to apply security at the appropriate level needed to complement the data. In other words, if sending or collecting financial data from a partnering organization through a VPN, more than likely it should have the highest level of supported protection applied. Conversely, if the information is publicly available or would have little impact if obtained by the competition, employees (past and future), partners, and investors, minimal encryption may be more than sufficient — or none at all.

There have been numerous consulting situations where the client simply installed a policy that forced all data to and from a remote location to have 3DES and SHA applied. In nearly all of these engagements, perhaps 20 percent might have required that level of protection. In some cases, data being shared through the VPN was accessible through normal Internet connections. E-mail is a good example. Microsoft's Outlook Web Access (OWA) is common among organizations with Exchange implemented. It allows a user to access, send, and receive e-mail from a browser. In one situation, an organization was allowing clear connectivity to the e-mail from the Internet, but forcing POP3 and SMTP traffic through the VPN...for protection. The result was that e-mail protection was directly related to the location, and the location that demanded an encrypted session was an internal office. Of course, both came through the same Internet connection, so an attacker only had to wait for an opportunity to capture data in the clear.

Simply stated, the level of encryption should be applied to the data stream that requires that level of protection. Some might argue that even the lowest of encryption still affects performance. In these situations where higher encryption levels are consuming the VPN, time management of keys can increase performance and security: shorter key lifetimes for sensitive information, while basic information that only needs limited protection can have long lifetimes on keys. This process will reduce the window of opportunity of the attacker for attacking the sensitive information, while still providing some protection for the other data.

Performance can be affected by many factors, but proper implementation and planning can sometimes produce the greatest advancements in performance enhancements.

Network Address Translation

Network Address Translation is widely deployed and is considered standard practice when connecting to the Internet. Therefore, there are situations where an IPSec VPN can be established from a system on a network that is obtaining access to the Internet via a NAT device. There are many examples where remote users are forced through a NAT device to access the Internet, possibly resulting in the failure of a VPN establishment. Some broadband providers are using private addresses for access into their network; and for a user to get to the Internet, NAT is applied to the datagram. For companies wishing to deploy VPN capabilities to users on broadband Internet access points, NAT could represent a problem to communications.

The problem arises when NAT applications change the IP address and checksums of an IPSec packet. The complications of NAT, with regard to IPSec, is by definition that NAT will change all or some of the address information in the IP packet. When end-to-end IPSec authentication is used, the IPSec integrity check will always fail.

In typical IPSec operations, ESP is employed to authenticate and encrypt the upper layer data, or the entire IP packet if implemented in tunnel mode. In doing so, NAT operations that only change the IP header's IP address and checksum will allow the packet to survive. Unfortunately, a NAT device must also change a TCP or UDP checksum as well, which are not only encrypted but contain the pseudo header. Therefore, if the packet were to survive a NAT process that only changed the IP header, the TCP or UDP checksum of a transport mode payload would fail upon arrival. There is a process being introduced that will modify the NAT RFCs to allow the recognition of IPSec traffic and modify the portions necessary for proper transport.

To complicate matters, if AH is employed, which will authenticate the entire packet, any modifications to the packet will result in a malformed authentication payload and ultimately be discarded upon arrival. This represents the unchangeable factor in the relationship between NAT and IPSec. AH is designed to detect any changes to the entire packet, where NAT is designed to change the data within the packet.

There have been several attempts to accommodate NAT in an IPSec VPN. In most cases, the NAT device must be IPSec aware — not only on a protocol level, but on a policy level as well.

It is necessary to know that tunnel mode IPSec implementations do not require NAT at all. The encapsulation of an IP transport payload into an entirely new packet eliminates the need for any translation. The issue at hand typically surrounds the remote access solutions where remote users have access to the Internet through a firewall that is typically employing NAT.

Current vendor solutions simply do not operate in this scenario, nor provide some form of non-IPSec data structure that can survive a NAT device. An example is the use of TCP/IP itself to encapsulate an IPSec packet into a TCP or UDP payload. One can then define the service port to masquerade the IPSec packet as an accepted service through most firewalls. In the case with TCP, port 80 for HTTP traffic, it is very common for firewalls to permit that are also performing NAT. When NAT is applied to the datagram, the original IP header and new TCP header will be modified according to the configured requirements. Once the modified packet reaches the security gateway, the temporary TCP header is stripped off, allowing IPSec to be processed as normal.

This process is a workaround that is susceptible to various forms of attack that IPSec attempts to mitigate. There are also implementation scenarios within IPSec that would be rendered useless, such as the AH security protocol. The war between AH and NAT still exists because the original IP header is used. In any event, for simple remote user support, encapsulation is certainly an option over non-communication.

Chapter 6

Authentication

Authentication as a model is very simple: prove your identity. In practice, the concept turns into complex protocols and processes designed to ensure that not only all the authentication information is valid, but protecting that information as well. This chapter details the available authentication mechanisms supported by IPSec and exposes the intense complexity of remote user authentication and the lack of a standard to build upon.

IKE, the automatic key management protocol that supports IPSec SAs, provides several different types of authentication for the systems that provide the termination points of the SA. There are four authentication methods within IKE that provide various options to the peers:

1. pre-shared secret
2. digital signature
3. public key encryption
4. revised public key encryption

Each authentication method provided by IKE has various advantages and disadvantages; but by making options available to the peers on the type of authentication, greater flexibility is obtained.

The authentication provided by IKE establishes a relationship between the two peer "systems." That is, in the case with remote users, there is no explicit option for the user to be authenticated via IKE — as of yet. Remote user support represents an enormous area of contention.Collaboration and general discussions have reached such a flurry that the VPN Consortium (VPNC) has established a separate discussion group to accommodate the conversations just about user authentication.

Note: The VPN Consortium (www.vpnc.org) established the IPSRA (IP Security Remote Access) mailing list in early 1999 and, as of March 2000, it was established as an official IETF workgroup. A similar story emanates from the extensive discussions about IPSec policy management. Once again, the VPNC created a mailing list to accommodate such discussions and now the IETF has recognized the group and created the IP Security Policy (IPSP) in February of 2000. The VPNC is dedicated to enhancing the standard and providing a sounding board for vendors to work together and promote interoperability. Much of remote access and policy management was considered smaller portions of the protocol and was not necessarily addressing the spirit of the IETF workgroup. Ironically, this is furthest from the truth and the IETF created the necessary official workgroups to accommodate the discussion threads. For a list of IETF workgroups, go to www.ietf.org/html.charters/wg-dir.html.

There are several topics regarding remote user authentication to be discussed — starting with introducing the authentication types supported by IKE in more detail.

Pre-Shared Secret

A pre-shared secret is nothing more than a password that each peer has configured and identified with the other. As the VPN is being created, IKE uses the pre-shared secret to create keying material that is used to build a key for encrypting the communications. The peers use the other's IP address to identify the associated secret to use for the creation of the key. As one system collects the necessary information from the other, a point in the communication is reached where both systems have enough information to create the necessary keys. The last attribute — the secret —

that is needed is not shared over the wire, for security reasons. The pre-shared secret is maintained and configured on each system prior to attempting to establish a VPN, by some out-of-band means, such as a phone call. Once the peer is identified by the IP address, and the preliminary key material attributes are collected, each system can look up the secret assigned to the communicating peer in a database. After the secret is identified, it is used to complete the key generation process. Each peer now has matching keys as long as the secrets that were configured were identical.

Pre-shared secret authentication is the most common form of authentication currently being used for VPNs. It requires very little configuration time and does not need a separate infrastructure to maintain. Authentication based on public key cryptography typically requires the use and management of some other technology at some point in the implementation.

Much of the authentication is based on the peer's ability to decrypt or properly encrypt a message or hash. If pre-shared secrets are employed, a key generated with an incorrect password will not allow the corresponding system to decrypt the data, halting them from further communications. For public key cryptography, the ability of each peer to validate a signature, or decrypt a message that was encrypted with a public key, will determine if the system is who he or she claims to be. Given that each method is loosely based on similar concepts, the overall security of the available authentication processes does not vary significantly. However, the selected authentication method does change the communication options, which may result, ultimately, in increased security of the entire negotiation and enhance the authentication process. Therefore, the many implementations that use pre-shared secrets are not necessarily less secure than their counterparts using other methods. The other methods are more sophisticated, require more management, and in many cases provide identity protection and increased flexibility of the IKE negotiation.

Digital Signatures

As described above, certificates are trusted ensembles of specific information that pertain only to the owner of the certificate and the issuer. Certificates can be used to authenticate the owner, based on a third-party trust. Furthermore, the certificate is typically the source of the issued user's public key. If the user's private key is employed to digitally sign a document, the certificate will provide authorization of the private key that was used by containing the public key and the associated trust with a third party. Certificates can be used to establish a trust relationship between VPN peers and participate in the assignment of security policies. Certificates are a refined implementation of public key cryptography and can be used for encryption, signing data, and authentication.

As for IKE authentication, various SA state information is hashed together with a key and the initiator signs the result. The initiator has the opportunity to send its certificate to the responder, along with the signed hash, allowing the responder to validate the signature. If the responder already has the initiator's certificate, it will not request it; however, the responder can request the certificate to be provided to verify the signature. When the responder uses a certificate, it must validate it by performing several steps to ensure that the certificate is valid.

1. Check the type of the certificate. If the certificate is not designed or authorized to be used for signing, then the process is invalid. There are certificates

specifically designed for signing data. To reduce processing overhead of the security gateway while performing authentication of a certificate, this first step will quickly eliminate improper certificates prior to further processing.

2. The dates associated with the certificate must be verified. If the certificate has expired, it is invalid and therefore cannot be used.

3. Once it is determined that the certificate has not expired and can be used for signing data, the integrity check must be performed. This is to verify that data contained within the certificate has not been altered, including the public key.

4. Next, the system must simply determine that the issuer of the certificate is a trusted entity. The first step is to check if the trust chain exists and if it is valid. If it is valid, the issuer must be checked to see if it is in the trust chain defined in the list. If the issuing CA is a member of the list, then the certificate is deemed valid and authorized for use.

As one can see, the validation process can be processor intensive and time-consuming. However, the administrator can typically mandate if certificates require validation. Of course, if this method is employed, only the originating Internet IP address can be used to verify authentication and association to the certificate. Otherwise, anyone can send a signed hash and provide any certificate to the responder to verify the signature.

Another aspect of using digital signatures for authentication concerns the certificate payload being sent to the responder encrypted. By encrypting the certificate payload, identity protection is obtained, which is a feature within IKE.

Public Key Encryption

Superficially, public key encryption that is used for authentication of a VPN may not seem very different from digital signature. Both are based on the ability to encrypt and decrypt (excluding signatures created with DSA) the data as the foundation of authentication. However, a digital signature is the encryption of a hash with a private key to be presented to the peer to prove its identity. In contrast, with public key encryption, the recipient uses the public key of the sender to confirm or deny the sender's claim.

In the event that public key encryption is used for authentication — and not digital signatures — the opposite process is used to accomplish authentication based on the same encryption and decryption procedure. With public key encryption, the public key of the receiver is used to encrypt certain data. The authentication is based on the ability of the receiver to decrypt the data with its private key. The receiver is being authenticated by its possession of the correct private key. With digital signatures, the initiator sends the authenticator (hash) to prove that they have the correct corresponding private key.

Of course, with IKE authentication processes, the roles are reversed within the communication to ensure that both parties are authenticated. The process of both parties being authenticated is referred to as bi-directional authentication.

Within IKE, there are two available forms of authentication based on public key encryption: standard and revised. Standard public key encryption requires several public key operations, which can consume an inordinate amount of time and processes. The revised mode of public key encryption only requires one public key encryption operation and uses the information contained within the encrypted data to create a symmetrical session key. The concept is simple in nature: use public key encryption to protect a specific piece of information that can be used to not only authenticate the session but also provide the missing link in creating a symmetrical key that can be used to decrypt other necessary data shared during the authentication process. Because symmetrical encryption is more efficient and requires fewer system resources, it makes sense to sustain the overhead of creating a key when compared to performing more public key encryption operations. An interesting aspect of the process is that most of the information encrypted with public key in standard mode is simply to protect it from prying eyes, while only one piece of data is used for authentication. In standard mode, because the public key encryption operation is so costly, only the authenticator and the data requiring confidentiality are encrypted. However, with revised mode, the cost of encryption is significantly reduced, thus allowing other data to be encrypted and enhancing the overall security and identity protection features.

This chapter section was intended to be an introduction to public key encryption authentication; the exact processes are detailed in Chapter 9 on key management.

Remote User Authentication

The authentication methods that have been discussed are the available mechanisms within IKE to authenticate peers of a VPN. The systems are configured with various information to allow the establishment of an authenticated SA. The information can be certificates, public keys, or passwords contained within the system that can be called upon to authenticate themselves to the other peer in the communication, and vice versa. However, these authentication mechanisms can be cumbersome and have limited scalability when utilized for remote access solutions.

History

Before VPNs were considered for remote access solutions, companies would invest in telephone lines, modems, access equipment, and an authentication infrastructure to allow remote users to dial into their network.

The authentication infrastructure consisted of protocols and applications designed specifically to authenticate a remote user wishing to gain access. Given that this type of remote access was the only available technology for many years, the authentication mechanisms became very robust and ingrained into the remote access solution.

Some examples of these technologies are RADIUS and TACACS, which may leverage other protocols such as CHAP and PAP. Protocols like CHAP and PAP are used as the workhorse that performs the authentication. RADIUS is a solution that consists of a protocol and application that can provide extended information to the client. In standard remote access solutions, a RADIUS system can provide an IP address, DNS IP address, or a wide range of information that may be needed by that particular remote user. In addition to being an authentication application and protocol for RADIUS operations, it can be used as a protocol to support an even greater range of authentication types. Security Dynamics (SDI) is a popular two-factor authentication platform that can use RADIUS to provide interoperability. In this scenario, RADIUS is used as the protocol from the remote user to the access device, which is acting as a client to the SDI system. RADIUS is used to employ its capability of providing several attributes within the communication. Therefore, if an IPSec remote access solution does not support RADIUS, it is effectively stripping the use of the SDI system. To take this one step further, SDI has a client that provides various information when dialing into an access device. The system may use RADIUS, which in turn can employ CHAP; or the system can use CHAP directly, without RADIUS, to provide the authentication. In either case, the absence of support for such protocol within IPSec is a hindrance.

The introduction of VPNs and their communication potions has all but eliminated the legacy remote access designs — all but authentication.

The available technologies for standard remote access authentication vary greatly, each providing different levels of security in the authentication process. Several examples exist, including (1) two-factor authentication, which requires that the user have a device that provides a number that can be linked to that user; or (2) challenge and response techniques used to enhance the standard username and password exchange. Each of these technologies has associated products and, obviously, cost. Any organization that has invested in a remote access solution authentication mechanism is not going to simply eliminate a well-defined and deeply integrated authentication process to accommodate a new communication technology. It is the responsibility of the technology to meet the demands of the proposed users — by popular demand; otherwise, the standard risks not getting adopted.

As previously mentioned, the legacy authentication mechanism represents the authentication database maintained by some form of software that can be managed by an administrator. However, one of the inherent advantages of some authentication mechanisms is to act as a gateway to larger, well-defined user databases. An example of this is the use of two-factor authentication by SDI. Although the authentication system might have its own user database, as with RADIUS, it can be configured to interact with several other forms of technologies that have a much larger user database. In some cases, the authentication is merely a shell that provides direct access to the centralized user database. A good example of this shell is BorderManager Authentication Services (BMAS), which is nothing more than RADIUS, as a protocol, wrapped around Novell's Directory Service (NDS). NDS is a directory of objects and their associated attributes that provides a single point of administration for an entire enterprise. As one would imagine, the fewer user databases employed, the simpler the administration and use. Another example of using RADIUS as a front end to a much larger, more complex administration facility is Internet Authentication Services (IAS) by Microsoft, which allows RADIUS authentication directly into Active Directory (AD), a feature implemented in Windows 2000. AD is based on the same foundation as NDS and is used to administer large enterprises with complex infrastructures. Directories are also used to provide various services (e.g., RADIUS support).

IPSec and Remote Authentication

Unfortunately, IPSec does not directly address the inclusion of existing, well-defined, and accepted authentication technologies for remote access solutions. The irony is that IPSec operates in such a way that it is being primarily used for remote access. As the standard grows, and workgroups within the IETF continue to expand, the production of a standard that encompasses legacy remote access authentication systems will soon evolve.

Currently, because IPSec does not address legacy authentication technologies associated with standard remote access solutions, vendors are forced to implement what is best at the time of development. There are several examples of vendor ingenuity in producing a solution that not only meets the requirements where IPSec left off, but sets the vendor apart from the others. While in some technologies vendors can implement different flavors and still operate in a heterogeneous environment, the same is not typically true for IPSec remote access solutions.

An example of one vendor's attempt to accommodate legacy authentication is its use of Secure Sockets Layer (SSL). SSL is a secure protocol that can be quickly established and provides an encrypted communication where authentication can take place normally. After an authenticated, secure connection is established, key material and configuration information can be provided to the client to be used in an IPSec connection. When the data is received and verified by the client, the SSL connection is dropped and an IPSec VPN is established.

Authentication Protocols

Authenticating protocols provide a mechanism to the partnering systems to share secret information while reducing the opportunity for unauthorized individuals to participate in the negotiation process. Passwords can be the Achilles' heel of security procedures. Without authentication protocols to protect the process of interchanging secret data, the secret can be discovered and utilized for illegal or unethical activities.

Authentication protocols of the type discussed here originated from a requirement set forth by the communication standard Point-to-Point Protocol (PPP). PPP provides a standard method of encapsulating network layer protocol information over point-to-point links. PPP also defines an extensible Link Control Protocol (LCP), allowing negotiation of an authentication protocol for identifying its peer prior to network layer protocol transmission.

The PPP communication standard has three main components:

1. method for encapsulating datagrams
2. LCP for establishing, configuring, and testing the connection
3. Network Control Protocols (NCPs) for establishing and configuring different network layer protocols

To establish communications over a point-to-point link, the two systems must first send LCP packets to configure the data link. After the link has been established, PPP provides for an optional authentication phase before proceeding to the network layer protocol phase. By default, authentication is not mandatory.

The concept of setting up the connection with a remote system based on its attributes, and then allowing an authentication protocol to determine the user prior to allowing data to flow, is being considered by some in the IPSRA.

Password Authentication Protocol (PAP). The least effective authentication protocol is Password Authentication Protocol (PAP). PAP negotiates all data as cleartext without hashing or encryption to conceal or protect the secret information being shared. In essence, if someone were to intercept the communication at the time of authentication, the username or identifier and password would be clearly readable and identifiable.

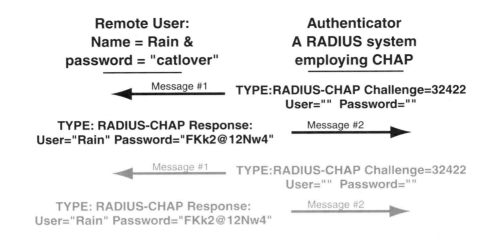

Exhibit 6-1.   Description of CHAP authentication.

Challenge Handshake Authentication Protocol (CHAP). The Challenge Hand-shake Authentication Protocol (CHAP) is used to systematically verify the identity of a remote user by means of a three-way handshake (see Exhibit 6-1). The handshake provides a layered authentication process that is difficult to repeat due, in part, to the authenticator sending a new challenge at random intervals. An example of a common application of CHAP is for use during authentication for a dial-in user. ISPs providing connectivity to the Internet require the remote user to authenticate to appropriately provide the desired access and bill accordingly. Typically, the user dials a phone number that allows his or her modem to establish a PPP session with a modem hosted by an ISP. The modems at an ISP can simply exist as a bank, or collection of modems tied to a router that provides access to the Internet. Once the PPP is established, a CHAP session can be initialized to request the username and password from the remote user. The information gathered under the protection of CHAP can be verified against an authentication database, such as a RADIUS system.

As shown in Exhibit 6-1, the authenticating device (or authenticator) sends a "challenge" to the system that wants to connect (a remote user). The challenge is a random value that is typically never repeated by the authenticator. The peer responds with a hashed result that the authenticator compares against its own calculated expected result. If the two results match, the connection is authenticated and data is forwarded based on the access control applied to that user or group. The authenticator sends a new challenge at random to the peer and repeats the authentication process from the beginning. In most implementations, the user is not prompted for a username and password every time the authenticator sends a CHAP challenge. Instead, the cache of the peer system provides the information.

The authenticator's challenge is a request for a username and password, and a randomly generated number that can be up to 16 bytes in length. The peer receives the challenge and generates a response value that is a hash calculated over a stream of bytes consisting of the challenge packet identifier, the secret, and the challenge. When the authenticator receives the response that contains the hash and the username, it retrieves the password from its database and hashes the same values and compares the results. If the two hashes are identical, the corresponding known values (ID, secret, and challenge) are validated.

One advantage of CHAP is that it can provide protection against playback attack by an unauthorized system by the use of an incrementally changing pac'<et identifier and a variable challenge value. To add further protection, the random challenges reduce the time the process is exposed to an attack. A disadvantage of CHAP is that it requires the secret be available in clear text in the database of the extended authentication system. If the system is compromised, all the secret data contained within the system will be available.

RADIUS. The Remote Authentication Dial-in User Service (RADIUS) was specifically designed to manage dispersed serial line and modem pools for large numbers of users. This relates to the origination of the PPP communication standard, in that common authentication systems provided authentication but did not address certain variables associated with remote access service. RADIUS has provided information critical to establishing communications and has become an intermediary for several types of authentication methods. RADIUS has support for the authentication protocols defined earlier, and it is utilized in many scenarios for extended authentication into larger databases.

One of the key features of RADIUS is the implementation of the client/server model. A network access system, such as a VPN device or router, operates as a client of RADIUS. The client is responsible for passing remote user information to its associated RADIUS server and acting accordingly, depending on the RADIUS server's response.

Another feature of RADIUS that sets it apart from other common authentication systems is its support for configuration information provisioning. During the time RADIUS was being developed, remote access was limited to serial lines and modems. RADIUS was developed to provide authentication and configuration information dependent on the user rights, times of the day, and access port, among other configurable attributes.

RADIUS servers receive the user connection requests, authenticate the user, and then return all configuration information necessary for the client to deliver service to the remote user. The relationship between the RADIUS server and client is established by the use of a shared secret, and all data communications are encrypted. That shared secret is typically a password that is entered by an administrator on the client and RADIUS server, and is subsequently used to establish trust and keying material for encryption purposes.

X.500 and LDAP. Extensibility of authentication processes is the key to obtaining a desired path to match the growth of technology. The capability to provide support for future technology requirements is paramount. Lightweight Directory Access Protocol (LDAP) is a protocol that provides the access to directories of user information, such as NDS and AD.

LDAP is an access protocol that allows reading and updating of X.500-compliant directory information. A directory maintains a hierarchical organized set of objects that can be arranged to best accommodate organizational needs. These needs include wide area network (WAN) considerations, organizational structure, application structure, and security policies. Within X.500 directories are layers of objects called *containers,* which essentially contain leaf objects that can represent servers, users, routers, or any object that warrants inclusion in the directory.

Each object can have scores of information associated with it. To further accentuate the relationship to VPNs, user objects can have remote access-specific information associated with them, which can allow an authentication process to include connection requirement data. Examples include keying material, IP allocation data, access control policies, routing information, and Internet service identification.

LDAP can be used to obtain detailed amounts of configuration-specific data to allow VPN implementations to reduce the complexity of the client. The client needs only enough information to get to the VPN gateway. After the gateway receives the request, LDAP is used to access a directory of information to push the approved and required configuration to the client.

Chapter 7

IPSec Architecture

This chapter examines the suite of protocols more closely and investigates various vendor implementations of the concepts covered. The IPSec protocols and concepts previously introduced are expounded upon, and various attributes of the communication will begin to surface.

IPSec is an all-encompassing term much like VPN; however, it represents a suite of protocols and technologies that interact to accomplish a common goal. The technology of IPSec and the structure of the multifaceted operations that makes it a reality are sophisticated technologies in their own right. Communication management, setup and negotiation, authentication, traffic control, and policy implementation are only a few components of the design that produce the final architecture that is IPSec.

Security Associations

Security associations are the result of the application of policies that define the encryption, keys, authentication, and all the services that are to be applied to the data. There are two basic forms of SAs in an IPSec VPN.

IKE Security Associations

IKE SAs are duplex, in that a single IKE SA can accommodate communications between two systems. As a VPN is established, IKE negotiates terms and conditions of the communication to authenticate and share connection properties. Once authentication is complete and the two systems are sure that they are connecting to whom they desired, an SA is established for continued communications. Once authentication is complete and the keys are created, the information being shared for key management can be encrypted, and therefore the creation of an SA. However, IKE does not use AH or ESP headers to maintain the SA, but rather a special header and SA identifiers called cookies.

IPSec Security Associations

IPSec SAs are simplex in nature, in that two SAs are required for authenticated, confidential, bi-directional communications between systems, as shown in Exhibit 7-1. IPSec SAs are created to accommodate transmission of data that requires a certain

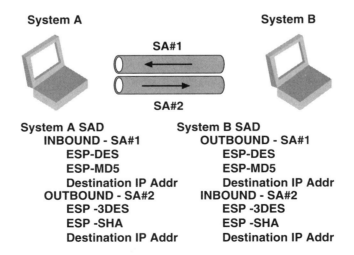

Exhibit 7-1.   Two SAs required for bi-directional communications.

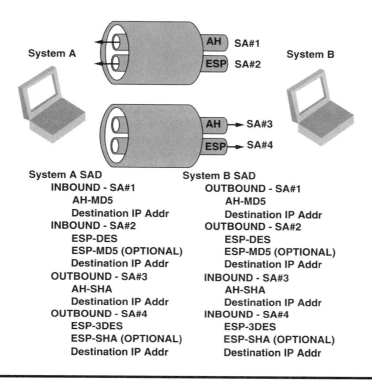

System A
AH SA#1
ESP SA#2
System B

AH SA#3
ESP SA#4

System A SAD
INBOUND - SA#1
 AH-MD5
  Destination IP Addr
INBOUND - SA#2
 ESP-DES
 ESP-MD5 (OPTIONAL)
 Destination IP Addr
OUTBOUND - SA#3
 AH-SHA
 Destination IP Addr
OUTBOUND - SA#4
 ESP-3DES
 ESP-SHA (OPTIONAL)
 Destination IP Addr

System B SAD
OUTBOUND - SA#1
 AH-MD5
 Destination IP Addr
OUTBOUND - SA#2
 ESP-DES
 ESP-MD5 (OPTIONAL)
 Destination IP Addr
INBOUND - SA#3
 AH-SHA
 Destination IP Addr
INBOUND - SA#4
 ESP-3DES
 ESP-SHA (OPTIONAL)
 Destination IP Addr

Exhibit 7-2. Multiple security protocols for bi-directional communications.

level of protection. SAs can be established that provide different levels of protection between peers for data with varying levels of sensitivity.

IPSec SAs can be defined by three components:

1. security parameter index (SPI)
2. destination IP address
3. security protocol identifier

The security protocol identifier is the security protocol being utilized for that SA. Note that only one security protocol can be used for communications provided by a single SA. In the event that the communication requires authentication and confidentiality by use of both the security protocols, as detailed in Exhibit 7-2, two or more SAs must be created for each direction and added to the traffic stream. Standard communications between two hosts require two SA, one for each direction of communication.

SAs are simplex, as described above, in that outgoing information has an associated SA that applies to it. In contrast, incoming packets are assigned an SA to understand how to handle the information being received. An example is two systems, each with an inbound and an outbound SA. The sender's outbound SA must match the properties defined in the receiver's inbound SA. These two SAs will share the same cryptographic information (i.e., keys, algorithm information, authentication information, and communication variables). Separate databases are maintained for inbound and outbound processing of information.

Security associations are groups of information handling the security of data; two primary management systems are employed to manage them: the Security Association

Database (SAD) and the Security Policy Database (SPD). SAD contains all the data pertaining to each SA being used, and SPD contains the policies that determine the character of the IP traffic coming into, or out of, the IP stack. The SPD uses selectors to map traffic to a policy, which ultimately maps to an SA that is maintained in the SAD.

Security Parameter Index (SPI)

A SPI is a 32-bit value used to distinguish among different SAs terminating at the same destination and using the same IPSec protocol. This data allows for the multiplexing of SAs to a single gateway.

The SPI is provided to map the incoming packet to an SA. Selectors are used to determine the SA, but they may be encrypted or unavailable. The SPI provides a mechanism for identifying the first SA that applies to that particular packet. Once the information for the SA is applied and the packet can be processed, the selectors are available for further identification and assignment to more SAs if applicable.

The SPI is a 32-bit random number generated by the sender to identify the SA to the recipient.

During security association negotiation within IKE, initiators present an offer, in the form of protection suites, to the responders. The SA payload within IKE is used to negotiate security associations in both Phase 1 and Phase 2 exchanges. This payload contains a field for an SPI; and in Phase 1, the SPI field is empty. However, during Phase 2 of IKE — where IPSec lives — the SPI values are negotiated. In either case, the SPI is from the IKE proposal payload that contained the transform payload that defines the SA.

A single SA negotiation results in two security associations: one for inbound data and one for outbound data. Different SPIs for each SA — one chosen by the initiator, the other by the responder — guarantee a different key for each direction. The SPI chosen by the destination of the SA is used to derive keying material for the associated SA. The responder, or recipient, must ensure that the SPI utilized remains unique in the SPD and SAD. The SPI is used as part of the ESP and AH headers to maintain the SA.

Given that the SPI is 32 bits and two unique numbers are required for basic communications, a single box could conceivably handle 30 million connections. Of course, that box would fill a barn and the Internet connection would be so large that the Internet would tilt, but it is fun to think about.

There are two crucial points with SPIs: (1) uniqueness at the SA endpoints, and (2) that they are properly mapped to the SAD and ultimately to the SPD.

Security Policy Database (SPD)

IPSec policies are maintained in the security policy database (SPD). Entries in the SPD define the traffic to be protected, how it is to be protected, and with whom the protection establishment can be made. As packets are created or received, the SPD is checked to determine the security of the packet and the handling of the information.

The SPD is responsible for determining the actions of the IPSec implementation. Either apply IPSec and forward to the appropriate destinations, or simply forward the data without intervention, or drop the packet altogether.

The SPD contains the information to determine what security services are to be offered to which data and how it is applied. As described, SAs are the incarnation of the information maintained within the SPD. The SA is the result of the security protocols enforcing what is defined in the SPD. The security provided to the SA is managed by the relationship between the SPD and the SAD.

The SPD contains a list of policies associated with session selectors — information that can be used to identify the communication. Selectors can be used to determine the level of control over the communication (i.e., IP address, name, or even the application TCP port being used). As traffic is processed, it is matched to a policy in the SPD by means of selectors. The SPD has entries of SA that can be used that are currently providing the protection services defined for that communication stream.

The order of information in the SPD can be important to the application of IPSec to the data transmission. There may be several policies that apply to a particular data stream; just as with firewall ACLs, more than one may apply. Therefore, the listing of policies and their selectors need to be parsed in order, and that order must be consistent.

As each packet is compared to the appropriate inbound or outbound SPD, SAs (or groups of SAs providing the same protection — SA bundle) are identified. There are situations where the SPD specifies protection requirements that must use multiple SAs in a specific order. To accommodate the interaction of the SPD to SAs, the SAD is linked to ensure consistent communications. For outbound communications, the policy is simply mapped to an existing SA or SA bundle. In the event the required SAs do not exist, the SPD requests are executed by the SAD for the creation of the necessary SAs or SA bundle. For inbound traffic, the SPI, the destination IP address (of the outer IP header), and the security protocol are used to map the traffic to an SA. It should also be noted that if the SA does not exist in the recipient's SPD or SAD, the packet is dropped.

Selectors

IP traffic is mapped to IPSec policies by selectors. A selector identifies an attribute of the communications to determine the alignment with an SA, or a group of SAs. Communications between two hosts can be afforded a single set of SAs for all traffic, or several SAs can be provided for various traffic attributes that are used to determine the level of security to be applied. The ability to forward data into specific SAs and make the appropriate identification association is provided by the information in the selector.

The selectors can be:

- destination IP address
- source IP address
- data sensitivity level (IPSO/CISPO mandatory access and data classification labels)
- fully qualified name
- upper layer protocols
- upper layer protocol service ports

Destination and source IP addresses are not that of the outer IP header. The destination IP address defined in the SA identifier (SPI, destination IP address, Security Protocol) is used to look up the SA in the SAD upon arrival to determine the security that was applied. Remember that the SA contains information about the authentication, encryption, and the associated keys. As the packet arrives, the destination IP address of the outer IP header is used to determine the SA. The destination and source IP address used as selectors are derived from the encapsulated data after decryption. Therefore, once the ESP has been processed based on the information in the SA, the inner IP header is used to obtain the Selector information. In the case with transport mode, there is no inner IP header information and the original SPD information is used.

As will be seen in more detail when discussing IKE, the destination IP address has an effect on much of the communication. Currently available VPN products place a great deal of trust in the IP addresses. In some scenarios, it is the only information available for processing. There are several reasons for the information not being available. Fragmentation and encryption are the two largest contributors. Therefore, certain information and decision processes rely on the available information. As a packet arrives, the selector information may not be available after the decryption process. The resulting data may not contain enough information to determine the next procedure. To avoid processing overhead, many vendors only use the destination IP address.

Security Association Database

The term SAD has been used throughout this chapter without much detailed explanation. While the SPD is policy driven and is concerned with system relationships, the SAD is responsible for each SA in the communications required by the SPD. Each SA has an entry in the SAD. The SA entries in the SAD are indexed by the three SA properties: destination IP address, IPSec protocol, and SPI. The SAD database contains nine parameters for processing IPSec protocols and the associated SA.

1. *Sequence number counter for outbound communications:* This is the 32-bit sequence number provided in the AH or ESP headers. Once again, the sequence number is always applied, but not necessarily used by the recipient. Therefore, this particular selector is only required for outbound traffic. Otherwise, the recipient not providing replay resistance would have to check the sequence number anyway.
2. *Sequence number overflow counter:* This sets an option flag to prevent further communications utilizing the specific SA. As discussed above, if replay resistance is applied, there must be a mechanism to delete the SA in the event the sequence number is near duplication.
3. *A 32-bit anti-replay window:* This is used to identify the packet for that point in time traversing the SA and provides the means to identify that packet for future reference. Given the nature of TCP/IP, packets can arrive out of order; therefore, if anti-replay is enabled, packets must be given time to make it to the destination. As each packet is received, the window is shifted. If a packet is not received by the time the window has shifted, it will be dropped when it does arrive.
4. *Lifetime of the SA:* This is determined by a byte count or time frame, or a combination of the two. Once the lifetime is met, the SA must be deleted and a new one created — or simply deleted. When both are implemented, the first to be met will take precedence.

   Of the two types of lifetimes, the SAD is also responsible for the management of the SA when the lifetime limit is met. There are two type of lifetime settings:

soft lifetime and **hard lifetime**. Soft lifetime determines a point when to initiate the process to create a replacement SA. This is typical for re-keying procedures. Hard lifetime is the point where the SA expires. If a replacement SA has not been established, the communications will discontinue.

5. *The algorithm used in the AH and the associated key.* By default, IPSec must support HMAC-MD5 or HMAC-SHA, both of which require a key.
6. *The algorithm used in the authenticating portion of the ESP header.* As with AH, ESP must support message authentication codes that utilize a key; therefore, the SAD will have references to the key.
7. *The algorithm used in the encryption of the ESP and its associated key information.*
8. *IPSec mode of operation — transport or tunnel mode:* This entry indicates the mode the AH or ESP is applied to the packet.
9. *Path MTU (PMTU).* This is data that is acquired from ICMP data over the SA.

Each of these parameters is referenced in the SPD for assignment to policies and applications.

SA Configurations

With the two basic modes of IPSec communication, there are several valid IPSec VPN configurations. Hosts must support both tunnel and transport modes of operations, while security gateways must only support tunnel mode. Depending on the environment, the combinations can become staggering.

Note: In the exhibits shown, there is one "tube" that represents an SA or SA bundle. At minimum, there are really two SAs (as shown before) for each SA in the following examples. To add another layer of complexity, if the SAs depicted are using AH and ESP for protection, then there are four pure tubes represented in the following exhibits.

Host-based VPN. Two hosts can establish an IPSec VPN in either tunnel mode or transport mode; both are supported. As shown in Exhibit 7-3, two hosts can establish a VPN between each other, regardless of what is in between. As long as a TCP/IP session can be maintained, a VPN can be created.

It can be argued that transport mode without the use of AH is not secure because the IP header is not authenticated if ESP is utilized. If AH is not desirable, then ESP tunnel mode would provide security to the original IP header. Transport mode is used

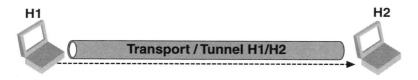

Exhibit 7-3. Host-to-host VPN using tunnel or transport mode.

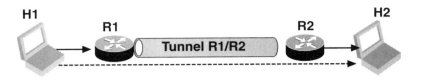

Exhibit 7-4.   Gateway-to-gateway VPN using tunnel mode only.

when end-to-end protection is desired and represents the endpoints of the SAs and the encryption. Host-based VPNs are not widely used; the reasoning and issues are discussed in the next section.

Gateway-based VPN.   As shown in Exhibit 7-4, two security gateways can establish a VPN between them to provide connectivity for their respective networks. This implementation represents the bulk — if not all — of the network-to-network solutions being utilized. Data created on one network destined for the other gets forwarded to the SGW to be tunneled to the IPSec partner. Once received by the other SGW, the data is decrypted and forwarded to the network based on its original properties.

Host to Gateway.   In Exhibit 7-5, host to gateway represents how remote access VPNs are being established. As shown in Exhibit 7-5, a remote system can establish a tunnel mode VPN to a SGW.

This example represents what is typical among VPN solutions. A remote host establishes an IP connection to the Internet. As the requirement for connectivity to the network hosted by the SGW, a tunnel mode VPN is established to allow the remote system to interact with the internal network.

Hosts and Gateways.   There are several configurations of SAs and combinations of tunnel modes and transport modes beyond the typical gateway-based and host-based. However, it is necessary to understand that these examples are simply not being leveraged. There are many implementations that can take advantage of the options, but very few do so.

Exhibit 7-6 shows an example of when a remote system uses tunnel mode for remote access, much like the previous example, but extends the security into the internal network to the final destination.

For many organizations, this is very desirable. It provides end-to-end protection of the information. Typically, this configuration would employ ESP tunnel mode from the host to the SGW and create an AH or ESP transport mode to the internal host.

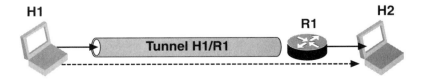

Exhibit 7-5.   Host-to-gateway VPN using tunnel mode: a typical remote access solution.

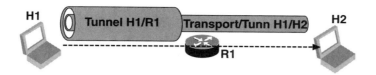

Exhibit 7-6. Host-to-gateway VPN using tunnel mode with transport or tunnel mode to internal host.

Tunnel mode can also be used. Establishing a VPN from a remote host to an SGW in tunnel mode is common, as discussed earlier. However, nesting a transport, or tunneling more SA within the tunnel to the SGW is not typical. This can be categorized as an extended remote access solution.

In Exhibit 7-7, a network-to-network VPN is augmented with extended protection, much like the extended remote access solution previously explained. In the event that two networks are connected via a tunnel mode VPN and two systems require end-to-end protection, a nested mode is needed. In the example, two SGWs are providing a tunnel mode for protection of data between the two networks. However, two hosts on the internal network require protection from prying eyes on the internal networks. For that reason, a nested transport or tunnel mode SA is established between the two hosts. In this environment, the internal networks are not entirely trusted.

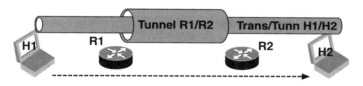

Exhibit 7-7. Gateway-to-gateway VPN using tunnel mode with transport or tunnel mode between internal hosts.

There are several cases in which the client may reside on an untrusted network and need a secured channel to a remote network that already has a VPN established with the remote network. Exhibit 7-8 details this scenario.

At first glance, this may seem odd; but there are many examples where this has been very desirable. The following example has presented itself to the author many times. An organization has established a limited access VPN with another organization — in a network-to-network configuration — possibly the competition, to share certain information for payment or the betterment of both organizations. Nonetheless, this exists in more environments than expected. Yet an employee from the

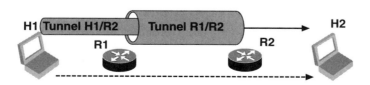

Exhibit 7-8. Host-to-gateway VPN using tunnel mode with tunnel mode between internal host and remote network.

primary organization is working from the competition's network. The user needs access to crucial information that could be devastating if discovered by the competition. To provide the necessary access and protection for the remote user on an untrusted network, a tunnel mode SA can be established to the remote network nested in the existing tunnel. The SA is not extended into the home network because it is trusted.

The remote user could establish a standard tunnel to the remote SGW without leveraging the existing tunnel between the networks, but that does not convey the available option.

Availability versus Standards

For the most part, however, there are two basic forms of IPSec VPNs being implemented at the time this book was written, and one more that the author feels will change the utilization of IPSec in most enterprises.

The two primary forms of IPSec VPNs are client-to-network and network-to-network; the third is client-to-client. Currently, most solutions are geared toward the first two. Specifically, remote access solutions utilizing IPSec equate to client-to-network with a security gateway providing tunnel termination. The money savings that can be realized from implementing a remote access solution using IPSec can have an immediate impact. However, there is another subliminal fact that is overlooked. Current dial-up access is not only limited by available technologies, but people have become accustomed to slow access from a remote location. It is an accepted fact when performance is extremely limited and the connection can be lost at anytime. Lack of performance for remote access solutions is acceptable, for the most part — but certainly not from the user's perspective, nor the developer, or provider — but expected nonetheless. Therefore, the performance concerns with IPSec VPNs over the Internet are miniscule compared to the added functionality, security, and cost savings. Thus, client-to-network gets a lot of attention.

As solutions are implemented, it becomes apparent that network-to-network solutions can have a positive impact on the cost of dedicated WAN implementations. This is especially true for international WANs or very long distances. WANs are typically implemented for very good reason and their continued operation and performace are expected. The thought of using VPNs over the Internet — and not traditional a WAN — bothers many companies. However, many organizations are moving to IPSec network-to-network in areas that are not delay sensitive or can operate with limited or fluctuating bandwidth.

Both of these options (client-to-network and network-to-network) take advantage of a single tunnel connection. For many products, providing nested operations is simply not in demand. This is not to say that it cannot be done. In fact, the RFCs define exactly how they can be accomplished and are worded in a manner that assumes nested operations.

It is necessary to fully understand where the standards start and the implementations begin. Much of what is available is not being implemented or supported, and much of this is due to incompatibility and the implementation of IPSec in hosts and gateways. Earlier discussion concerned the IPSec client; but if the IPSec operations were supported directly in the operating system, the options would begin to open up. For example, suppose one wants to establish a nested transport mode from host 1 to host 2 inside of a tunnel between two gateways providing access. This is a valid situation and easily supported by IPSec and IKE. However, when compared to the reality of what is possible and available, problems tend to rise to the top. For this example to work, IPSec-aware protocol stacks would have to exist on each host. But most of what is readily available for client installs is for remote access tunnel mode.

This limitation of IPSec support, tunnel versus transport support, and the integration of IPSec into the operating system brings us to the third aspect — client-to-client. At the writing of this book, there were two solutions that support the concept of end-to-end IPSec VPNS. Once end-to-end VPN is supported in the operating system, the options of functionality provided by IPSec can become reality.

Transport Mode

The concept behind a VPN solution is typically based on tunnels. A tunnel occurs when the original data is encapsulated into a new packet and forwarded based on the attributes of the new packet's protocol. The goal is to provide transparent connectivity for the underlying protocol. IPSec transport mode is unique in that there is no encapsulation in a new packet. The original IP header is maintained and the data is forwarded based on the original attributes set by the protocol.

As datagrams are passed down the TCP/IP protocol stack to the network layer, they are furnished with the appropriate header information from each layer. At the end of the network layer operations, IPSec removes the original IP header and encrypts the upper layer protocol header and data. Once the encryption is complete, IPSec adds the selected security protocol header before reapplying the original IP header.

As illustrated in Exhibit 7-9, the data is normally processed to the network layer, where it is ultimately handed to the IPSec operations. IPSec separates the original IP header from the remaining portions of the packet. The upper layer components are encrypted, and the authentication protocol header is calculated and added between the original IP header and the encrypted payloads of the original packet.

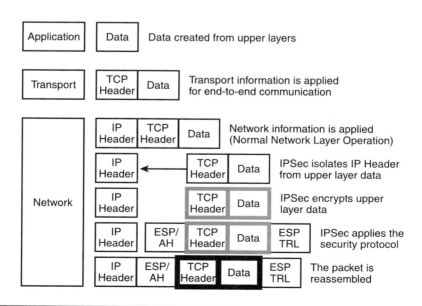

Exhibit 7-9.   IPSec operations within transport mode.

In transport mode, the original packet remains the same except for two critical changes: the data is encrypted and an authentication protocol is inserted into the packet. By inserting an authentication protocol, the packet is afforded integrity to ensure that the data was not modified during transit.

The primary limitation is that no gateway services can be provided within transport mode. If two systems are communicating in transport mode, the communication cannot be nested to provide communication beyond the endpoints of the VPN. Transport mode is reserved for point-to-point communications. If a transport mode VPN is established with a VPN gateway, the remote system is only afforded communications to the gateway itself and no data can traverse the internal network. As the receiving system de-encapsulates and decrypts the payload, there is only transport layer and application layer data. The original IP header from the initiator satisfies the network layer.

There are several examples in which transport mode is desirable. Transport mode VPN directly to the gateway can provide protected administration without concern for allowing access into the internal network. In situations where the VPN gateway is remotely managed by a third party, internal network access may not be desired.

The ability to nest transport mode SAs within a tunnel mode SA can provide extended protection beyond the gateway into the internal network.

Tunnel Mode

Tunnel mode is the most common of VPNs and is heavily used in IPSec implementations. The use of tunnel mode is typically reserved for gateway services because the encapsulation provides the ability to channel several sessions through a single point. This aspect lends itself to allowing the VPN gateway to de-encapsulate the data and forward it to the final internal destination.

Tunnel mode is encapsulating a packet designed to communicate on a network and encapsulating it in another packet for transmission to a counterpart on a remote network. The process allows for a protocol that is understood at the entry and exit points, to carry the passenger communication protocol that would normally not be forwarded across the network.

This process is relatively old technology and is apparent in many communications solutions. The concept of tunneling is what has now become "VPN." Many standards exist to take advantage of tunneling technology to provide extended connectivity, and therefore qualify as a VPN.

In tunnel mode operations, the entire original packet is encapsulated and encrypted, and a new IP header and authentication protocol header are added. The result is a new packet that contains two IP headers that are used for communication services on their respective networks:

- Inner Header
- Outer Header

The inner IP header applied to the original datagram as it is passed to the network layer is ultimately encapsulated in a new packet. The new packet gets an outer IP header that contains information imperative to the operation of the VPN.

As illustrated in Exhibit 7-10, the remote client makes a request to a server maintained on the internal network across the VPN. The packet is constructed as it moves down the protocol stack. At the network layer, a standard IP header is applied

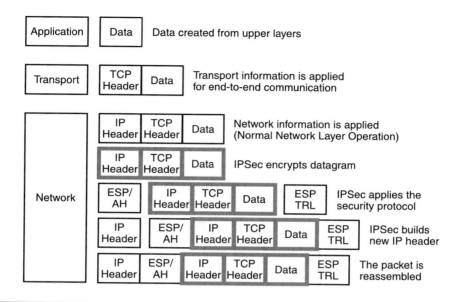

Exhibit 7-10. IPSec operations within tunnel mode.

with the source and requested destination; in the example the source is 199.16.84.3 and destination is 192.168.13.81. The IPSec function will see the address 192.168.13.81 as part of a VPN-defined network of 192.168.13.0 with the gateway destination of 202.47.193.7. The policies define the security to assign to the packet.

IPSec encapsulates and encrypts the entire original packet, and the authentication protocol defined will provide message integrity. The authentication protocol header will be created and appended to the encrypted data. A new IP header will be constructed to allow the remote client to send the data to the VPN gateway.

As the gateway receives the packet, the outer header is peeled away and the integrity is validated. The remaining data is decrypted to reveal the inner IP header that provides the final destination's IP address. The VPN gateway sends the packet to the internal server. As far as the client and server applications are concerned, they have a direct connection providing communications. As the server sends the response, it is forwarded to the VPN gateway to be encapsulated and forwarded to the remote system.

Remote Access, Routing, and Networks

Tunnel mode currently receives the most attention and consumes most of the IPSec install base. Remote access makes up a great deal of the VPNs in use today, and there exists an array of tunneling options to accommodate several different aspects of remote user communications that are not necessarily addressed by the standards. The result is vendor-specific remote access VPNs that leverage the basics to accomplish a desired design concept.

The issue that arises is the use of IP addresses. Because IPSec operations can manipulate the communication at the network layer, opportunities to enhance communication designs are available.

Network-to-network VPNs are relatively simple and, for the most part, static. Within network-to-network VPNs, there are two or more networks that are connected much like a normal routed network. A common tunnel mode implantation satisfies most operations. However, remote access is extremely dynamic and introduces a primary security risk: connects are established from anywhere.

In a network-to-network VPN, the networks participating can be predicted and assigned. An example is two networks, one with the IP address of 192.168.10.0, the other 192.168.30.0, and a VPN between them. One can construct routing protocols, policies, and access controls based on those IP addresses and not worry about the vast options of the Internet on which the VPN is built.

A remote access VPN washes the predictability away and various concerns can arise. To answer some of the operational and security needs, the inner and outer IP headers and addresses contained within are manipulated to provide levels of control and predictability. Control and predictability are two primary ingredients in creating a secure VPN environment.

IP Pools and Networks

Remote access VPN solutions can become quite convoluted, use several different aspects of communication, and perform different functions given the type of configuration. These different aspects can be introduced by the concepts of IP address pools and networks.

An IP addresses pool is a predefined group of sequential IP addresses that can be used for assignment to remote systems as they connect. A sequential set of IP addresses is a contiguous block of addresses, of which the following are examples:

192.168.17.1 to 192.168.17.254 provides 254 addresses

10.1.14.3 to   10.1.14.13 provides   11 addresses

As each system is authenticated and a data connection is established, the first available IP address is allocated to the connection. For each subsequent connection, an IP address is used from the available pool. Once the remote session is terminated, the address assigned for that system is released and reinserted into the pool of available IP addresses.

The issue that quickly becomes apparent is: what IP addresses to use? As one might guess, there are several valid answers to the question, and each is associated with a type of implementation concept.

Internally Available. There are several VPN solutions that require the pool of IP addresses to consist of available IP addresses from the internal network to which the VPN device is attached.

As shown in Exhibit 7-11, the internal network is addressed with an IP network of 192.168.13.0, with a subnet mask of 255.255.255.0. The internal network has 200 hosts, each with a unique IP address of that network. The VPN device's pool of addresses will need to be part of that network and consume the available address space for VPN users. If in the example the 200 internal systems were addressed from 192.168.13.1 to 192.168.13.200, the VPN device could be configured with a pool that ranged from 192.168.13.201 to 192.168.13.254. Given the amount of addresses allocated to VPN, the solution could support over 50 users.

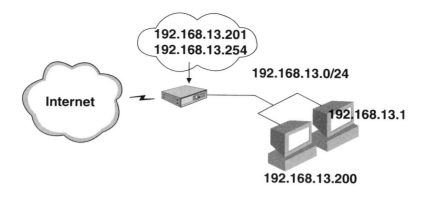

Exhibit 7-11.   Internally available IP addresses assigned to a pool.

As datagrams are received from the remote users and passed from the VPN gateway to an internal server, the server sees the source as if on the same network. Once the remote user's request is processed and the server needs to respond, it handles the packet as if the remote user were on the same network. Normally, this entails the use of ARP. The server's ARP request is replied to by the VPN device because it is hosting the remote user that is assigned with the IP address. As described earlier, this is a form of proxy ARP to convince the server that it is speaking directly with the remote user who appears to be on the same network.

Internally Networked. In the previous discussion about IP address pools that consist of existing IP addresses on the internal network, it became clear that the VPN solution would be limited by the available IP addresses. An example would be if the VPN device supported 1000 simultaneous connections. In that event, the internal IP addressing scheme would work even if there were no other hosts on the internal network. It is necessary to understand that even the smallest network can conceivably have thousands of remote users accessing services. Application service providers (ASPs) can place several services and clients on a small group of systems located on a dedicated segment. The clients that VPN into the network to access the offsite resources could number in the thousands. Meanwhile, the resources only consume a small network.

To provide for extended remote capabilities without the reassignment of IP addresses for an internal network, a router can be introduced.

Exhibit 7-12 displays a possible scenario when the VPN solution supports many more remote systems than the internal network is designed to address. The router can be used to create a bypass network that can be used to accommodate the vast number of remote systems, but only consuming a single IP address on the internal network.

The VPN device supports 10,000 simultaneous users that must have unique IP addresses provided as they attach. The IP pool consists of an IP address range from 172.16.0.0 to 172.16.254.253, which provides room for ample growth. The router will have an IP address of 172.16.254.254 on the VPN side and an IP address of 192.168.13.201 on the internal network side. As each user connects, they can access the internal network by having all the requests forwarded to the router to be sent to the internal systems. The internal systems can be configured to send all requests coming from the defined network to the router's internal interface to be forwarded to the VPN device, which in turn sends it to the remote user.

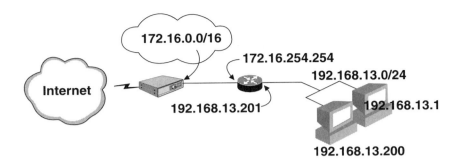

Exhibit 7-12. Isolated internal network supported by a router.

Virtually Networked. The two previous solutions described can be construed as clumsy, not necessarily scalable, and possibly difficult to implement in certain environments. Also, the VPN device was acting more as a bridge than a router.

The most desirable solution for remote access VPNs is the creation of a virtual network forcing router-based activities that afford flexibility and will fit into many environments without internal network IP address modifications.

As shown in Exhibit 7-13, the VPN device contains a pool of IP addresses that represents the remote VPN user community. The selection of IP addresses is subject to very few limitations or guidelines; for example,

- cannot duplicate any internal IP addresses
- cannot be Internetroutable IP addresses that are not owned by an organization
- should support the number of simultaneous users the VPN device supports

The address pool cannot duplicate any internal addresses or network throughout the enterprise that is accessible from the VPN community. If a network in a remote location is not accessible by VPN users, then it does not need to be aware of the VPN community network. Therefore, the remote network can have access to other networks that have the same IP address scheme as the VPN community. However,

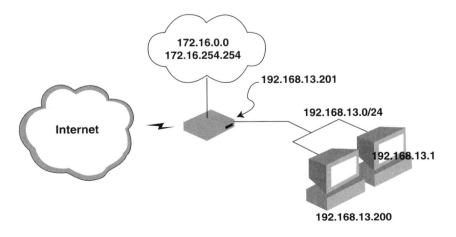

Exhibit 7-13. Security gateway acting as a router for a virtual network.

this should be avoided whenever possible, and the complexities involved are plenty and easily avoidable.

As with any implementation, the use of Internet-routable IP addresses not owned or directly managed by the organization that is implementing them is a recipe for disaster. If the Internet-routable IP addresses are available, their use is not recommended due to scalability, cost, and — quite frankly — there is no real advantage.

The pool of addresses represents a network, or group of systems. It is not necessarily a network in the true definition with a subnet mask, but it certainly should be contiguous. The pool must represent a collection of addresses that can support the incremental aspects of the connection assignment. Providing IP address pools that have gaps will simply not function in many cases in which vendors provide address pool configurations.

As technology has evolved, so has the number of support remote systems. As mentioned above, several solutions are in the tens of thousands of simultaneously support remote users. The IP address pool must take into consideration the number of simultaneous connections that will be supported. In several implementations, the pool will start small and quickly expand as the solution becomes more utilized. There is no real reason to limit the size of the pool in relation to the supported connections. If there is a lack of IP addresses that are desired for use within the solution, then the solution is oversized or the IP address range needs to be revisited. There have been instances in which the pool is reduced to limit the number of connections allowed at any one time to control access and not flood the device or connection. Most VPN solutions provide a maximum connection configuration that is not associated with the IP address pool.

In most scenarios, a pool is defined that will easily handle the number of system-supported connections and not be duplicated throughout the enterprise. Any connection controls are implemented in other available configuration modifications and not with ambiguous limitations that could lead to horrific troubleshooting issues.

Support for All. Each one of the previous examples typically represents a different product implementation. However, there are a few products that support different configurations, depending on the environment required.

Compatible Systems is a good candidate to explore one of the products that can be configured to accommodate varuous configurations.

As shown in Exhibit 7-14, this simple-looking dialog contains a plethora of options. There are two sections: the upper section has two radio buttons that allow one to configure a pool of addresses for a virtual network or extend an internal one; and on the bottom are the accessible networks or hosts provided to the VPN client to determine which destinations get IPSec applied.

In the example, the upper section has the value 192.168.13.201 (as shown in Exhibit 7-14) that configures the system to use the internal network, starting from the IP address 201, and going to the end of the defined network, identified by the mask value. The IP subnet mask will inherently identify the network number (in this example, 192.168.13.0 is the network number) and the IP address defined will be the starting point of the sequential assignment until the IP address prior to the broadcast address is assigned to a client system. The broadcast address in the example is 192.168.13.255, therefore leaving 54 available addresses for remote users. If one is wondering, the subnet mask is derived from the internal interface of the VPN system; because the addresses are considered local to the internal network, they must have the same mask. The result is that is no opportunity to enter a subnet mask due to possible conflicts.

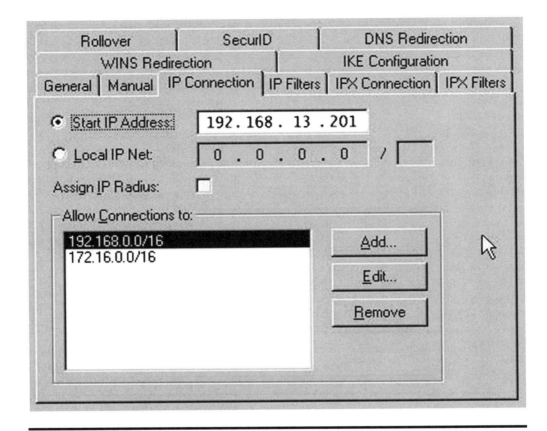

Exhibit 7-14. Compatible's address pool configuration based on internally available addresses.

However, if the lower of the two radio buttons is selected, the system provides the option of defining a virtual pool of addresses for use.

As illustrated in Exhibit 7-15, the new virtual network is 10.100.0.0/16, immediately resulting in an increase of remote users from 54 to more than 65,000 and the removal of a restrictive internal network addressing scheme. These addresses get assigned sequentially to the clients as they connect and the VPN device simply routes them into the internal network as if part of a remote network.

Thus far, the discussion has focused on the various options of the upper section of the dialog box and the effects each option has on the operation of the VPN device. The lower section of the dialog box provides the ability to define internal hosts and network.

As shown in the previous exhibits, the current internal networks are the 172.16.0.0 range of private addresses and 192.168.0.0/16, which encompasses various internal networks that use the addressing scheme. As an example, every remote office with less than 100 users gets a 192.168 address assigned to it. Of course, this assumes that there are less than 255 of these networks — but that is another issue. The first five networks installed under this design scheme receive 192.168.1.0, 192.168.2.0, etc., until 192.168.5.0. To allow for office additions without reconfiguring the VPN device each time, a network can be defined that includes all the possibilities. Therefore, as the network grows, the VPN device can provide access to them as they come online. This is nothing more than IP summarization techniques applied to a VPN

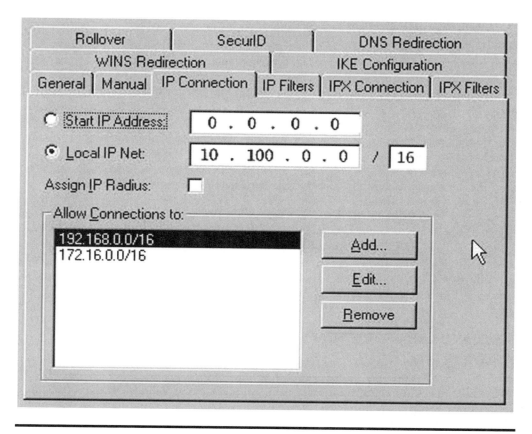

Exhibit 7-15. Compatible's address pool configuration based on virtual network.

configuration — another wonderful little detail about TCP/IP that can be leveraged to enhance the solution.

The result of this configuration is that the list is being provided to the client upon connection and instructs the client on how to handle requests to the defined values. Therefore, as the remote client makes a request for 172.16.23.44, it will have IPSec applied and forwarded to the security gateway.

Note: There are several considerations here. The process of providing policy information to a remote client, for many solutions, is leveraging a non-IPSec process or custom set of protocols within IKE. Currently, there is a great deal of work being done with regard to remote user access. However, there are some solutions that follow the IPSec RFCs closely and provide the detailed information in large proposal payloads. The concept of providing information to the client to define communication activities is a broad subject that falls under the heading of IPSec policies. There are several mechanisms and styles currently being implemented that are proprietary in many cases. Nevertheless, IPSec policies and their distribution are covered in detail in later chapters.

Acting As a Router versus a Bridge

In a virtually networked implementation, the VPN community is considered "remote" to other internal networks. The VPN device acts as a router supporting an attached network.

In the event that an internal system needs to communicate with a remote VPN system, as with replying to requests, the destination will be an IP address of the defined pool that represents the VPN community. To accommodate the communication, the packet must be routed to the VPN device acting as a router providing access to the remote network. Internal routers can use routing protocols or administrator-applied static routes that appropriately forward the request for the VPN network to the VPN device.

If the IP addresses of the VPN community are part of the internal network structure, the VPN device will act much like a bridge, forwarding traffic on behalf of the network it supports. An interesting aspect of this design was explained above (as internally networked). The addition of a router behind a VPN device acting as a bridge will interact in the environment as if it were a virtually networked implementation but bridging from the router to the VPN device. This is another reason why internally networked solutions are not desirable — overly complicated. However, this design is feasible and if a VPN solution is selected that outgrows an internal network infrastructure, this is a valid scalability direction.

Finding Gateways with Maps

Several aspects of VPN communication have already been discussed — from encryption, to authentication, to the introduction of the internal properties of an IPSec VPN. This section discusses the process of determining which data requires IPSec application and how to handle that data once IPSec is applied. As an example, Cisco uses ACLs within the IPSec communication configuration to identify interesting traffic to apply IPSec security services.

As detailed previously, IPSec operates in the network layer and uses an application to allow users and administrators to interface and configure how IPSec operates on the system. Client software typically supports a mechanism to instruct the network layer operations on how to manage data flowing to and from the system, based on desired policies. The incarnation of the administrative interface is sometimes referred to as a map and can exist in several formats, ranging from a simple text file located on the system's hard drive to a complicated set of parameters that exists only in memory.

A map associates requested destinations with a gateway that provides service to that destination. In the event that a request is made for a destination that is not part of the map, the request is forwarded based on the original attributes and IPSec is not applied. Maps are used to represent the administrative link between the SPD and SAD.

A remote user has connected to the Internet and the central office is also connected to the Internet by means of a VPN gateway. The user is assigned an IP address by the ISP providing the connection. The user makes a request for *www.yahoo.com* to browse the Web. *Yahoo.com* get resolved to an IP address, 204.71.202.160. As the request passes through the network layer, IPSec investigates the destination IP address and compares the result with the map. The map does not contain any attributes for the destination IP address and therefore forwards the request to the remaining network layer operations and a session is established to *www.yahoo.com*.

However, in the event the user makes a request for an IP address defined in the map, the operation of the communication is much different. Exhibit 7-16 displays an

Exhibit 7-16.   Checkpoint secure remote installation map.

```
(
    :options (
        :default_key_scheme (fwz)
        :active_resolver (true)
        :slan_enabled (true)
        :hide_binding_disorder (true)
        :no_policy (true)
        :use_cert (false)
        :policy (0)
        :policy_hash (abcdef21)
        :last_policy_server (0.0.0.0)
    )
    :fwrand_seed1 ("12345678 12345678 12345678")
    :fwrand_seed2 (123456789012345678901234567890012)
    :gws (
        : (CHKP.IP440
            :obj (
                : (199.199.199.2)
            )
            :keymanager (
                :type (refobj)
                :refname ("#_199.199.199.2")
            )
            :ifaddrs (
                : (199.199.199.2)
                : (10.1.2.10)
                : (192.168.1.0)
            )
            :topology (
                : (
                    :name (CHKP.IP440)
                    :type (gateway)
                    :ipaddr (199.199.199.2)
                    :ipmask (255.255.255.255)
                )
                : (
                    :name (CHKP.IP440)
                    :type (gateway)
                    :ipaddr (10.1.2.10)
                    :ipmask (255.255.255.255)
                )
                : (
                    :name (CHKP.IP440)
                    :type (gateway)
                    :ipaddr (192.168.1.10)
                    :ipmask (255.255.255.255)
                )
```

(continues)

Exhibit 7-16. Checkpoint secure remote installation map. (continued)

```
   :  (
      :name  (Net-10-1-2)
      :type  (network)
      :ipaddr  (10.1.2.0)
      :ipmask  (255.255.255.0)
   )
   :  (
      :name  (vpnftp)
      :type  (host)
      :ipaddr  (192.168.1.45
      :ipmask  (255.255.255.255)
   )
)
:fwver  (4.1)
:firewall  (installed)
:is_fwz  (true)
:is_subnet_support  (true)
:peers  ()
:key  (
   :public  (
      :value  (keykeykeykey)
   )
   :dhparams_id  ()
   :date  (12345678)
)
:disable  (true)
)
:managers  (
   :  (199.199.199.2
      :obj  (
         :type  (node)
         :  (199.199.199.2)
      )
      :dnsinfo  ()
      :last_auth_method  (none)
      :key  (
         :public  (
            :value  (keykeykeykey)
         )
         :modulus  (
            :value  (mod)
         )
         :date  (12345678)
      )
      :date  (12345678)
      :disable  (true)
      :to_expire  (false)
      :expire  (15)
```

Exhibit 7-16. Checkpoint secure remote installation map. (continued)

```
            :cache_passwords (false)
            :keyid (keyidkeyidkeyid)
        )
    )
    :policy_servers ()
)
```

example map from a Checkpoint Secure Remote installation. Secure Remote (SR) is Checkpoint's current VPN client solution that installs on a system to provide VPN services for accessing a VPN network hosted by a Checkpoint firewall. Prior to using SR the user must obtain specific information from the firewall to allow future communications and discover what networks and hosts are accessible via that particular gateway.

Typically, an administrator or help desk will provide the firewall's IP address or Fully Qualified Domain Name (FQDN) to initiate communications. Once this data is configured, the client software requests a configuration file, or map, that represents the properties of the firewall.

Map Example Internals. Several parts of this file provide a great deal of information about the structure of the VPN. However, for this particular exercise, the focus is on the information in bold.

The first thing in bold faced type is a section labeled ***gws;*** this simply defines the firewall and the necessary attributes that pertain to the VPN support of the gateway. The initial value is CHKP.IP440, which represents the firewall object defined in the firewall's database. This will be used throughout the file to represent the firewall's identification. Also, the suffix infers that the firewall is a Nokia IP-440 firewall appliance.

```
    :gws  (
        :  (CHKP.IP440
```

The next three entries define the firewall's object IP address, specify the key manager, and provide the IP addresses assigned to all the defined interfaces within the firewall. The type "refobj" allows the remainder of the configuration file to reference back to this object.

```
        :obj  (
            :  (199.199.199.2)
        )
        :keymanager  (
            :type (refobj)
            :refname ("#_199.199.199.2")
        )
        :ifaddrs  (
            :  (199.199.199.2)
            :  (10.1.2.10)
            :  (192.168.1.0)
        )
```

The section that directly relates to the concept of a map is topology. The topology section is a collection of predefined objects that can be reference to determine where to forward data.

```
: (
        :name   (CHKP.IP440)
        :type   (gateway)
        :ipaddr (199.199.199.2)
        :ipmask (255.255.255.255)
  )
```

The name references the original firewall object defined in the beginning statements. The type assists the client in determining the kind of system that is being defined and its role in the VPN. The `ipaddr` and `ipmask` are standard TCP/IP address identifications. The all 1s subnetmask signifies a single IP address and not a network. In this example, there are three gateways defined for each interface.

The next two sections (See Exhibit 7-16) relate directly to destinations that are supported by the gateway. The firewall has three interfaces, one connected to the Internet and two others for internal networks. The first entry is a network called "Net-10-1-2" that is defined with the IP address 10.1.2.0/24. When the client makes a request for any system that has an IP address of this network, IPSec will intercept the communication, apply the security defined in the policy, and forward it to the owner of the object, in this case CHKP.IP440.

```
: (
        :name   (Net-10-1-2)
        :type   (network)
        :ipaddr (10.1.2.0)
        :ipmask (255.255.255.0)
  )
: (
        :name   (vpnftp)
        :type   (host)
        :ipaddr (192.168.1.45
        :ipmask (255.255.255.255)
  )
```

However, in the second entry, a single system is allocated for the second internal network. If the remote user were to make a request to a system with the IP addresses of 192.168.1.45, the request will have IPSec applied and be properly forwarded to the gateway. If the user attempts to access any other system that may be on the 192.168.1.0 network, the request will be sent to the Internet.

The IP address of the destination can be private IP addresses or Internet routable addresses. This brings up an interesting scenario if a network is not using private IP addresses for internal use but rather Internet-routable IP addresses that are arbitrary. The use of Internet-routable IP addresses that are not owned by the operators of the internal network is becoming increasingly rare. However, of the cases that remain, a VPN solution will force the change of the internal IP addressing scheme to private

IP addresses. An example wherein this scenario causes a problem is if a request from a remote user is made to 202.12.3.24, which is part of the VPN, it will never be forwarded to the Internet. If the 202.12.3.24 IP address is assigned to a valid Internet resource, the users and networks of the VPN will not be able to access it. A single IP address does not pose much of a problem; however, if large ranges of IP networks are addressed, the problem can be crippling.

Vendor Modes and Remote Access

As with most standards, vendors tend to design solutions that follow the character of the standard rather the exact science. The results are several different products that have interpreted the standards and the client service requests in various ways.

An interesting aspect of VPNs is the type of communication that can be configured on the client. Tunnel mode is required when a VPN gateway is implemented and the remote user wants to establish connectivity with an internal system. Within tunnel mode, two types of communications have evolved: single and split. The product capabilities and solution design typically drive the type of operation utilized in tunnel mode. However, there are vendors that provide a means of selecting the type by way of configuration or a form of hybrid that enlists portions of each aspect of the two types.

The topic that seems to get the most activity is the handling of remote access and tunnel mode operations. The concern that some vendors and their clients have conveyed is the fact that each remote user represents a new access route into their network. The vulnerability is defined as when a user connects to the home office with a VPN an attacker can use the remote user's system as a router to gain access into the home office's network (see Exhibit 7-17).

To provide an answer to the vulnerability, many vendors have changed the way that remote access VPNs are implemented. In some cases, the VPN device acts as a router that supports a virtual network of remote users; others act as a bridge, connecting networks of the same IP addressing format. And some solutions are not even concerned with the remote user's IP address and simply de-encapsulate the session from the source IP address — after it has been properly authenticated, of course.

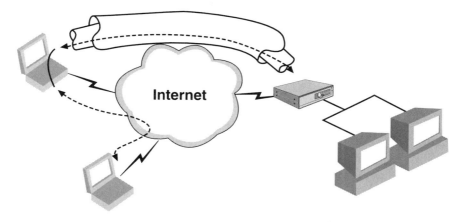

Exhibit 7-17.   VPN providing access to WAN sites utilizing the WAN.

Split Tunnel

Split tunnel is the tunnel mode of operations that closely reflect the RFCs. Split tunnel is when IPSec is applied to datagrams that match attributes defined by the communication policies.

In a split tunnel, the user requests are either handled by IPSec and sent to the appropriate gateway in tunnel mode, or simply processed without IPSec intervention. As illustrated in Exhibit 7-18, a remote user may have an established VPN with the home office while maintaining an HTTP browsing session with a Web server on the Internet.

In a typical split tunnel, the client simply receives an IP address from the ISP it connected to and the system communicates based on that Internet-routable IP address. As the remote client makes requests to an Internet-based resource, with an IP address not defined within the VPN policy, the packet is routed out onto the Internet as normal. In contrast, if a request is made by the client for an IP address defined in the SPD as private, or part of the internally defined network supported by the VPN gateway, IPSec is applied to the packet and forwarded to the VPN gateway. The VPN gateway connected to the Internet operates as a simple forwarding device. As the packet is received by the gateway, it is de-encapsulated and decrypted, if necessary, and sent to the internal destination defined in the inner-IP header. As the graphic displays (Exhibit 7-18) the crucial aspect is that the internal server responding to the remote client sends the response back through the VPN gateway to have IPSec properly applied.

This operation is called split tunnel because there appear to be two separate communication paths operating with a single connection from the client. One is open connectivity to the Internet; the other is a virtual connection to the internal network.

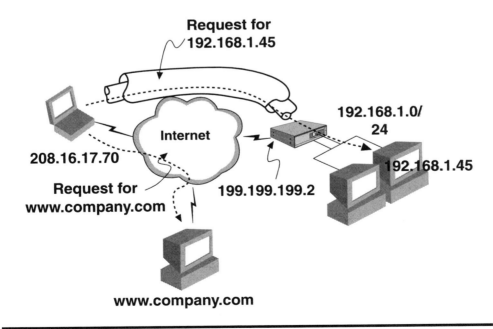

Exhibit 7-18.   VPN providing access to an internal network while allowing access to the Internet.

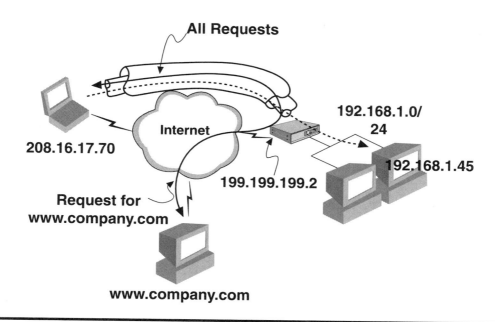

Exhibit 7-19. VPN providing access to the internal network and the Internet through only the VPN.

Single Tunnel

In contrast, single tunnel provides dedicated virtual connection to the VPN gateway, forcing all requests to the gateway regardless of the destination. Single tunnel does not directly follow the IPSec standard, and in some ways hinders its capabilities. Single tunnel was created to address certain security concerns and to enhance the administration over the VPN being provided.

As detailed in Exhibit 7-19, a remote user connects to the Internet and receives and IP address to allow communications over the Internet. When the user establishes a connection to the remote VPN gateway, a new private IP address is assigned the virtual adapter or shim operating in the network layer. Once the new IP address is assigned, all communications are sent to the VPN gateway.

As a remote VPN user makes a request for an internal service, the packet is passed to IPSec for encryption, regardless of final destination or policies, and is sent to the gateway. A map, a file, or a configuration providing the association between the destination network and the IPSec gateway is no longer required of the client for communication. All data passing out of the upper layers is stripped of the source IP address previously assigned by the ISP and replaced with the new one obtained from the pool of addresses configured on the VPN gateway. It is critical to understand that the IP address of the interface providing access to the Internet did not change. The shim or virtual adapter has the opportunity to manipulate the packets prior to passing them to the normal Layer 3 functions.

The process of modifying the address prior to passing it to the normal lower layer functions allows the system to operate normally and establish communications via a VPN without any changes to the operating system or applications beyond the VPN client package. As far as the IP stack is concerned, one has a single IP session with the VPN gateway.

Hybrid Tunnel Realization

Hybrids are implementations of tunnel mode types that are combined with the several available methods of IP pool addressing techniques discussed in the previous section. The options seem vast considering that there are two primary forms of tunnel modes and two primary forms of IP address pool configurations — with the addition of a combination of the two pool types by the introduction of a router.

Simply stated, hybrids can be implemented in two fundamental ways: (1) reverse static NAT, which can be related to split tunnel operations; and (2) map routing, which represents single tunnel operations.

Reverse VPN NAT

Reverse static NAT is not nearly as complicated as it sounds, but does promote interesting problems under certain conditions. Reverse static NAT is a standard split tunnel communication that utilizes a pool of internal addresses on the VPN gateway. Much like how the client modified the source address before sending the packet to the VPN gateway in a standard single tunnel mode, the VPN gateway must now perform those procedures.

The client exists as if operating in split tunnel. The requests are compared to the map and security policies, and forwarded accordingly. When the VPN gateway receives the session request, it de-encapsulates and decrypts the data and prepares to forward it, based on the original attributes. But before forwarding the packet to the internal destination, the VPN device assigns the SA an IP address from the pool of addresses that are part of the internal network. The source address of the packet — normally the ISP provided addresses — is changed to an address from the pool and sent to the original destination. The solution appears much like single tunnel because of the IP address pool on the VPN gateway. However, the total solution is a split tunnel that requires the VPN device to route communications to the remote system and perform bridging functionality for the internal network.

Whereas in a normal single tunnel, a client is given an internally available address to force all data into the VPN gateway, the client is forced to provide the translation and cannot communicate directly with Internet-available service. However, having internally available assigned IP addresses on the VPN device can assist various internal operations, which range from security policies to application requirements. Therefore, in the event internally available addresses are to be configured on the VPN device but the limitation of the client's Internet access is not desired, reverse NAT configurations will meet these needs.

Map-based Routing Table

In contrast to the reverse NAT hybrid, map routing allows the emulation of a single tunnel but using a virtually networked address pool on the VPN device. The map routing type of configuration allows the remote user systems to operate as if in single tunnel mode and the VPN device to provide routing capabilities. This type of configuration is not directly associated with a particular supported configuration, but rather the manipulation of a process to gain the desired results.

The concept is to take advantage of the map and its association with the shim in the IP stack and use it to force all data to the VPN gateway, when in essence, the configuration is split tunneled. In a normal split tunnel operation, the map is checked

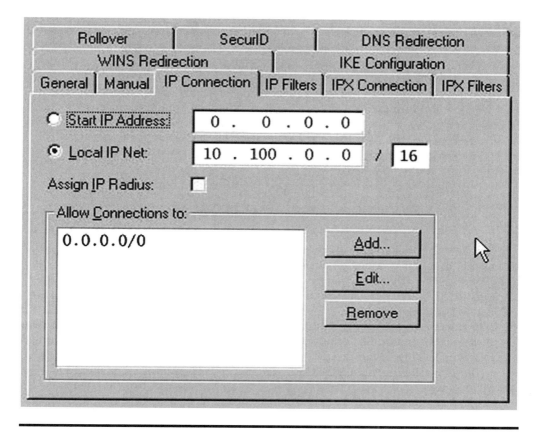

Exhibit 7-20.   Control of client access and split versus single tunnel.

for each packet to determine whether IPSec is applied and sent to the corresponding VPN gateway. The next step is to use the map as the routing table for the workstation. Thus, an entry at the top of the map will state that all traffic out of the stack gets IPSec applied.

As shown in Exhibit 7-20, the networks available to the remote VPN clients have been changed to 0.0.0.0/0. An all 0s IP address and subnet mask matches every possible address and network. What are the results of this configuration? Inherently, this is a single tunnel.

The first set of 0s will represent any IP address that is requested by the client. The next set of 0s will cover any network request by providing an empty subnet mask. Finally, the IP address of the VPN gateway is identified as the ultimate destination for all data. The simplicity of this hybrid gives the client its strength and flexibility. Now a single-client install can support either type of tunnel operation and can typically be dynamically configured based on the authentication from a central administrative location.

Arguments

Several discussions can arise concerning the various options made available by the different vendor approaches to remote access. Of the previous examples and types of configurations detailed above, single tunnel mode seems to be the focal point of arguments because of the direct relationship to vulnerability mitigation.

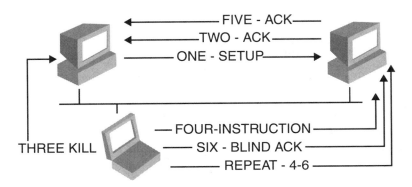

Exhibit 7-21. Spoof attack process.

As a remote user attaches to a home office through a VPN, that system can provide a routable loophole to an attacker. Single tunnel was devised to eliminate such vulnerability. The vulnerability is thwarted based on the fact that because all packets are forwarded to the VPN device, an attacker on the Internet would be able to send packets to the client, but not receive them.

The concept of one-way communication to alleviate the vulnerability is fuel to fire many debates. Some of the earliest computer hacking was based on a concept called "spoofing." Spoofing is the act of appearing as someone or something else to gain access, based on the previously defined relationship between the target and the system being emulated.

As depicted in Exhibit 7-21, a client system establishes an authenticated session with a server that identifies the session by the IP address. An attacker predicts the sequence of packets and, at the proper time, disables the client while injecting instructions into the server. The server is under the impression that the request is coming from the original client and sends the appropriate acknowledgments. However, the attacker will not receive the acknowledgments because they are destined for the original client. Therefore, the attacker must intimately understand the operations of the server to respond to acknowledgments that are not being received to complete the attack. Meanwhile, the client is helpless because the attacker has disabled it from participating in the communication.

This example of a spoofing attack proves that system communication interaction can be predicted. Therefore, the concept of single tunnel is questioned.

The primary argument for the use of single tunnel is against Trojan attacks that use some form of direct interaction with the attacker. Good examples of these types of Trojans are Back Orifice, NetCAT, and NetBus. Each of these has server utilities that operate surreptitiously on a system that allows a remote client to view and interact on various levels with the server system. If a single tunnel VPN were not being used on a system that had a Trojan of this type installed, an attacker would obtain the same access to the internal network through the VPN as the authenticated user.

Implementation Considerations of Tunnel Types

Beyond the considerations and arguments where security is concerned, there are several operational issues that arise when single tunnels are used. For a standard, single tunnel mode, the impact can become overwhelming on the infrastructure and routing requirements. It is necessary to understand that all requests are sent to the VPN device, regardless of the ultimate destination. Compared to earlier example, if the user opens a Web browser and goes to *www.internet-company.com,* it will be forwarded to the VPN gateway and back out to the Internet from that point. The response from the Web site will come back to the VPN gateway and then be routed out to the remote user. Single tunnel will basically double the bandwidth utilization on an Internet connection, or certainly consume bandwidth on an alternate connection that is being utilized for general Internet access.

By implementing split tunnel, the Internet connection is only used for required communications between the remote host and the services provided by the VPN. Other than specific data, the communication is allowed to communicate directly with the intended Internet host.

Another, less-often considered aspect of single tunnel is that requests to the Internet are being encrypted to protect them as they are transmitted over the Internet — only to be decrypted and forwarded back onto the Internet to the final destination. The performance of the client will certainly be affected, but the larger concern is for the VPN gateway. VPN performance will be derogated by performing irrelevant encryption processes.

Data Fragmentation

Fragmentation is the process of breaking a packet into multiple packets to accommodate transmission technologies/media. The process typically occurs on the host sending the packet, or the routers transmitting the packet from one environment to another. After fragmentation, each smaller packet is transmitted separately and reassembled at the destination.

The network topology being utilized places restrictions on the size of the frame that can be transmitted. The following are some examples of topologies and their maximum transmission unit (MTU):

- IEEE 802.5 (4 MB Token Ring) = 4464
- FDDI = 4352
- Ethernet = 1500
- IEEE 802.2 = 1492
- X.25 = 576
- PPP = 296

The requirements for fragmenting a packet are based on the inability of the network layer to control the size of the datagram. Fragmentation can cause some problems with performance. The simple act of transmitting more frames has an obvious derogation of performance. However, if a single fragment is lost or damaged during transmission, the entire original packet must be resubmitted.

When a packet is fragmented, the end of the packet payload is provided a new IP header with the same attributes of the previous IP header. Lets say that a UDP packet of 1473 bytes is transmitted over Ethernet. The IP header is 20 bytes, the UDP header is 8 bytes, and therefore the final packet is 1501, 1 byte larger than Ethernet can handle in the frame payload. The final byte of information (8 bits) is stripped off and given a new IP header. The original IP header is provided a fragmentation offset value (there is a 13-bit fragmentation offset field in the IP header) of 1480. This number is derived from the end of the original IP header and any options. Thus, it includes the UDP header of 8 bytes and the remaining user data of 1472 (minus the 1 byte for the second fragment). As the IP packets are received by the final destination, the IP headers are reordered and processed. When the IP protocol stack sees the offset value, it moves back through the collected data to the specified mark and finds the remaining byte of information. Once the network layer has assembled the UDP data, it is passed to the upper layers for continued processing.

Normally, IPSec is not affected by fragmentation because it operates at the network layer and fragmentation typically occurs after IP process. Therefore, fragmentation is executed on the datagrams to which IPSec has already been applied. Upon receipt of a fragmented packet, a system will reassemble the packet before providing it to the upper layers for processing; therefore, IPSec is only processed on whole datagrams.

In standard operations, as datagrams are generated by a host system it is aware of the local interface's MTU and the upper layer creates packages of the appropriate size given the local information. As the packet is processed and transmitted, it may encounter a router that supports the destination network. However, the other network's MTU is smaller than the originating network. If the Don't Fragment (DF) bit is set in the IP header, the router sends an ICMP message of type 3 and code 4 (fragmentation needed and DF set) that notifies the originating host that the MTU is too large. Otherwise, the router fragments the packet and forwards to the destination. In a perfect situation, the host will maintain a set of MTU statements with regard to the routes used. This allows the host to build datagrams of proper size to avoid fragmentation on the other end of the communication.

The IPSec process does have an effect on the underlying MTU; by the introduction of extra headers and extended data, the datagram created by a host's upper layer is enlarged. Typically, a host will maintain MTU information at the transport layer to create a stateful MTU agreement between communicating hosts. As IPSec is implemented between the two hosts, it will inform the upper layers, the transport layer, to reduce the datagram an amount to accommodate the information that is to be added by the IPSec operations. As MTU information is learned from the network layer (from ICMP messages), the IPSec implementation is checked to calculate the MTU that should be reflected to the transport layer. This is a necessary process because different networks and destinations may have different policies that dictate the use of the available security suites. In some cases, more options provided to the communication can increase the size of the IPSec payloads, resulting in further reduction of the datagram that must be generated by the upper layers. In fact, the IPSec SPD must be consulted to determine MTU information that is passed up to the transport layer.

As a packet is forwarded across a network and reaches a router that cannot forward it, due to fragmentation and the DF bit is set, the router sends the ICMP message with the first 64 bits (8 bytes) of the original message (excluding the original IP header — that would be redundant) to the originating system. However, IPSec communications represent an interesting situation.

Consider the scenario shown in Exhibit 7-22. There is a host at either end of a network (H1 and H2), that has various MTUs along the communications path. The network connection is provided by three routers (RA, RB, and RC) and a VPN is established between RA and RC. RA and RC have a policy that states that all traffic destined for either network where the hosts reside is to be tunneled in an ESP IPSec VPN.

A packet is generated by H1 that is 500 bytes destined to H2. As the packet arrives at RA, it has IPSec applied, resulting in a packet of 520 bytes, and forwarded onto the next hop router RB. Router RB receives what appears to be a standard IP packet (remember that RB is unaware of the VPN) and quickly determines that the exit

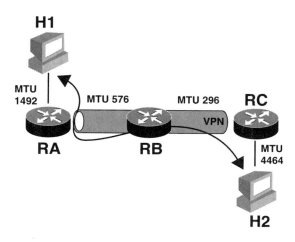

Exhibit 7-22. A network that may require fragmentation.

interface supports an MTU of only 296, which requires fragmentation. However, at some point, probably at the host, the DF bit was set, forcing RB to send an ICMP message with the first 64 bits of data to the originating IP address. The originating IP address in this example is RA, because RA tunneled the original packet and placed a new IP header on the IPSec payload. If ESP is employed, the resulting message returned to the originator is a new IP header, followed by the ICMP header, and the SPI and IPSec sequence number from the payload of the original IP packet. This is because the ICMP message only allowed for the first 64 bits. With AH as the security protocol, the SPI is returned along with the next payload and size of the original AH payload.

This situation creates some interesting issues. The first issue that immediately arises is that when the ICMP message reaches RA, it does not know the originating system. It simply receives a packet with an SPI, not an IP address, which simply represents the SA that is used to protect all traffic from the network H1 is on to the network H2 is on. Therefore, how does RA know which host, from the network it has an SA for, sent the original packet? Of course, we know because we can see that there is only one host n the example, but RA has no clue. There are two options to RA for handling this situation:

1. Send the ICMP MTU message to all the possible hosts that can be associated to the identified SPI. Depending on the SPD and SAD and the defined networks, this could include a single host, a range of IP addresses on a network, or every IP address on a specific network. In reality, there is an even worse scenario, wherein a wildcard is used to identify all traffic as interesting and to have IPSec applied, resulting in every possible host within shouting distance receiving an ICMP message — that could be bad.

2. Save the MTU and SPI information and wait for a host to make a request to the offending SA. As a packet from an internal host is received that is greater than the saved MTU associated with the offending SA, drop it, and generate an ICMP message based on the data collected from RB and the first 64 bits of information from the dropped packet, and then send it to the host. Basically, RA becomes an ICMP proxy for RB and notifies internal hosts using the SA — identified by the SPI that was returned in the original ICMP message — to reduce their MTU.

Of the two basic operations, the latter works in every situation, whereas the former can become problematic. Therefore, storing the SPI and SA MTU and providing it to the internal hosts as requests are made is a required feature for IPSec implementation.

An alternative that can be used to avoid some of these issues is for RA to not set the DF bit in the outer IP header although the inner header DF bit is set. The result is that the data will be immediately fragmented upon entry into RB, ultimately eliminating the entire ICMP process.

Discovery with ICMP

To avoid excessive fragmentation, IP layers perform an MTU discovery process called Path MTU (PMTU), typically using ICMP messages of Type 3 (destination unreachable), Code 4 (fragmentation needed).

ICMP messages are generated by routers and hosts that monitor the network to ensure efficient operation. ICMP can be used to convey many network environmental situations and issues.

IPSec does not produce fragmented packets. All fragmentation occurs after IPSec has processed the packet. Within transport mode, only whole datagrams are processed from the upper layers. Therefore, a transport IPSec packet that has AH or ESP applied could conceivably be huge. Once the AH or ESP is applied, the packet can be fragmented by the system transmitting the data or by a system en route. For tunnel mode operations, the AH or ESP can be applied to any IP packet that contains fragmented data. This may be very common where a security gateway is providing VPN services to an internal network — Ethernet, for the purposes of this example. A remote system somewhere in the vast internal network can be sitting on a remote Token Ring network. As the data makes its way to the VPN gateway, it becomes fragmented due to the changes in topologies. As the IPSec gateway receives the IP packet, it is not concerned with the size or the content, which can be a fragmented packet. If the size is greater than the network can handle on the outbound side of the gateway, it is up to the remaining network layer to fragment the IPSec packet and not IPSec operations.

Compression within IPSec

Compression is used in communications to reduce the size of data for increased performance and efficient use of bandwidth. By sending a smaller packet over the wire, less bandwidth is required, thus allowing more data over the same pipe. This is very common in voice networks where two conversations can be placed on a single DS0 normally designed for one conversation. Voice over IP (VoIP) is infamous for huge compression of data and limiting the little things that are often taken for granted — such as clarity in some cases.

Compression is designed to identify patterns and duplicated data within a file or package. Once found, the repetitions and patterns are indexed and associated with the data that is compressed to provide the necessary information for decompression. An interesting phenomenon can be experienced when encrypted data is compressed. Because well-encrypted data has little or no repetition or patterns in the data stream, the compression algorithm will actually increase the size of the data. Various communications that implement encryption techniques after the network layer, will experience performance issues and fragmentation.

The IP Payload Compression (IPComp) protocol was designed to allow IP communications to be compressed at the network layer. Because IPSec operates at the network layer, the encryption can be applied after the compression — eliminating the data expansion problem. Some compression algorithms utilize histories to reduce repetition in the processing of data for compression. This allows the algorithm to become more efficient over time. Unfortunately, this requires that the communicating systems maintain the state of the communication to align the compression information — referred to as stateful. Because IP is not a guaranteed service and packets can arrive out of order, the abilities provided by the history function of many compression protocols cannot be utilized.

PCP IP protocol, IANA protocol 108, includes a very simple 32-bit header. As with many headers, there is an 8-bit field to identify the next payload, an 8-bit field reserved for the IANA, and finally a 16-bit field for the CPI. The Compression Parameter Index (CPI) is an identifier that acts much like an SPI and defines the IPComp Association (IPCA) that can be automatically negotiated by ISAKMP. In the IPSec DOI, there are four types of IPSec security protocol identifiers. Two (AH and ESP) have been discussed in great detail. The others are ISAKMP and IPCOMP, allowing the key management protocol to negotiate on behalf of IKE itself, IPSec, and IPComp. As with transform sets in IKE to define the protection suite to be applied to data, such as ESP_DES, ESP_3DES, and AH_HMAC_MD5, among others, there are transform identifiers for IPComp that can be used to negotiate compression algorithms between the peers. Both systems must agree to establish an IPCA, as with IKE SAs and IPSec SAs. The values are as follows:

RESERVED	0
IPCOMP_OUI	1
IPCOMP_DEFLATE	2
IPCOMP_LZS	3

IPComp_OUI is a proprietary compression algorithm that can be agreed upon by the peers. This is usually accompanied by attribute fields to communicate the specifics of the algorithm. Typically, vendors will identify that they are communicating with a known device and implement a custom compression algorithm to increase performance.

IPComp_Deflate specifies the use of the zlib algorithm, and IPComp_LZS specifies the use of the Static Electronics algorithm.

As far as the IPCA is concerned, that is about all there is to it; no keys, cookies, or nonces to negotiate, just simply the algorithm and the identity of the association.

Processing IPComp, inbound and outbound, has some interesting aspects in that it does not always happen when configured to do so. In outbound processing, the compression is, of course, applied prior to encryption, or authentication; therefore, compression occurs before AH or ESP is applied. The type of information that is compressed can be upper layer information, as with transport mode, or an entire IP datagram, as with tunnel mode (see Exhibit 7-23). Once the compression is complete, an IPComp header is placed on the compressed data and the next header field is populated with the protocol that was compressed, such as 4, representing an IP header if tunnel mode is employed for IP traffic. Last, the header and compressed data are passed to IPSec for processing. IPSec applies a security protocol (e.g., ESP) and populates the next header field in the ESP header with 108 — IPComp. If the compression was unsuccessful, no IPComp header is applied and ESP is applied to the IP datagram and has the next header field populated with the value that represents the

AH in Transport Mode	IP Header	AH Header	AH Authentication Data	IPComp Header	TCP Header	DATA	

AH in Tunnel Mode	NEW IP Header	IP Header	AH Header	AH Authentication Data	IPComp Header	IP Header	TCP Header	DATA

ESP in Transport Mode	IP Header	ESP Header	IPComp Header	TCP Header	DATA	ESP Trailer	ESP Authentication

ESP in Tunnel Mode	NEW IP Header	ESP Header	IPComp Header	IP Header	TCP Header	DATA	ESP Trailer	ESP Authentication

Exhibit 7-23.   IPComp header placement.

original communication protocol. The elimination of the IPComp header in the event of an error simplifies the entire process. Rather than providing an error message that complicates the input of the peer, the recipient of the packet simply ignores the fact that it was not compressed and processes it as normal. Given that IPComp is a stateless protocol, because it operates within IP, there is no need to provide errors or acknowledgments, thus liberating the peer to operate in a local state — doing what is necessary on a packet-by-packet level at any particular moment in the communication.

As the peer receives an IPSec payload, which it identified because the protocol field in the IP header is AH, or ESP as with this example, it de-encrypts and de-encapsulates the datagram and inspects the next header field in the ESP header. If the value of 108 is discovered, the IPComp header is inspected to determine the IPCA and the next header to be expected once decompression is complete. After decompression is complete, the data is processed as normal and all compression information associated with that datagram is discarded. An interesting aspect of inbound processing, very similar to outbound, is the lack of errors in the event an IPComp header is not present in the payload. Of course, this means that the initiator did not perform compression for some reason — possibly an error — and applied ESP to the datagram normally. Although the recipient of the datagram has an established IPCA and expects an IPComp header for each packet, it does not really matter if it is absent.

There are many reasons that IPComp may not choose to compress the datagram. One aspect is that if the compressed data and the header combine to be equal to or greater than the original upper layer data, the datagram must not be compressed. Otherwise, the process will defeat the purpose of implementing compression and result in performance problems. It will affect performance in not only processor overhead and inefficient use of available bandwidth, but the expansion of the data causes fragmentation given that MTU discovery processes will not take into consideration an increased datagram. Small datagrams can fall victim to increased size post compression. The compression-specific data that must be associated with the original data can increase the size of the final payload. To accommodate this foreseeable event, thresholds can be implemented to simply ally compression to datagrams with a defined minimum size. Another example of when compression may not be applied is when the datagram has already been compressed by another process or application. The first question is: how can the IPComp tell what has been previously compressed? The IPComp compression protocol can make determinations about the outbound traffic with regard to the success rate of the compression algorithm. As a certain number of consecutive packets unsuccessfully compress, the system will not attempt to apply compression for a predefined number of following packets. Once the number of uncompressed packets has been met, compression is attempted again. If the compression fails for a number of times again, the cycle repeats. The number of failures and number of packets to not pass to the compression algorithm are implementation specific and can be some of the attributes negotiated during IKE. The concept of stopping the compression after failure is to accommodate certain data flows that may be mixed with other datagrams that need to be compressed. By flipping on and off, one hopes to avoid sections that cannot be compressed and compress the data streams that can benefit from compression.

Replay Protection

Anti-replay protection and, to a certain extent, origin authentication, are optional services provided by the ESP and AH security protocols. The ability to implement these services sits squarely on the shoulders of the recipient. A unique 32-bit sequence number that is incrementally increased with each packet is included within every security protocol header. However, the number is useless unless the recipient verifies the number. It may seem obvious to implement such protection by default, and most recipients do verify the sequence number, but it is necessary to understand that it is not mandatory. One of the reasons may be that when replay protection is implemented, in that the recipient verifies the sequence number, the number can never be duplicated for that SA. Each system sets the sequence number to zero when an SA is established. Because the sequence number is 32 bits, and each system must increment it by one for each packet, the maximum number of packets for an SA with replay protection is 2^{32}.

The sender is responsible for managing the sequence number. When replay protection is configured, the sender must ensure that the sequence number does not cycle. If the sequence number reaches a point where it must be cycled, the sender's and receiver's sequence numbers must be reinitiated and set to 0. To accomplish this, a new SA is typically created in place of the expired one. It is also the responsibility of the sender not to send a datagram with a sequence number that, when processed by the receiver, will result in a number that exceeds the cycle point. An example of this would be if the number is incremented by 3 and the sender transmits a datagram with a sequence value only 2 less than the maximum allowable value. The receiver would be unable to properly increment the sequence for the reply. The result would be the disintegration of the SA.

Replay protection is implemented by default and the sender assumes the receiver is processing the sequence numbers unless notified otherwise by the receiver. If the receiver does not monitor the sequence number and does not notify the sender, the sender will create a new SA when the sequence number needs to be cycled, which could cone as a surprise to the receiver.

In the event that replay protection is not implemented, by a notification from the receiver, the sender need only be concerned with the generation of the sequence number and not the monitoring of the numbers from the receiver. However, the sender still increments the sequence number; when it reaches the maximum value, the counter simply rolls over back to zero.

Wrap-around

What is wrap-around and how is it handled? When the sequence number is monitored by the sender and recipient for replay protection, the number is incremented to ensure that packets are received in the expected sequence (not in order). As each valid datagram is received or processed, the sequence window is advanced. When the sequence number reaches the maximum allowable value, the SA is replaced and communications commence.

However, at some point in the new SAs lifetime, the SA sequence number will be repeated. Under certain conditions, an attacker can take advantage of the repetition to inject datagrams or hijack the session. In either case, the attack could result in unauthorized access or the possible exposure of protected information. This attack is understandably complicated, but certainly plausible. Unfortunately, there is no solid answer to this condition other than that the complexity of the attack provides a form of protocol protection.

Chapter 8

Security Protocols

This chapter details the foundation of IPSec — the security protocols. IPSec leverages the se curity protocols to provide useful communication within the VPN. They are the workhorses that everything else is designed to support.

Security associations are established and maintained by the security protocol implemented. Security protocols are the heart of IPSec operations and their implementation determines transport or tunnel mode. Security protocols can be used in combination or nested to extend the VPN and its functionality.

There are two security protocols defined by IPSec — Authentication Header (AH) and Encapsulating Security Payload (ESP) — that are used to provide authentication, integrity, and, with ESP, confidentiality.

Encapsulating Security Payload (ESP)

ESP provides several security services, including data confidentiality, integrity, origin authentication, optional anti-replay services, and limited traffic flow confidentiality. The extent of confidentiality and integrity of the communication can, somewhat, be related to the mode of operation. In tunnel mode, the inner IP header is well-protected while the outer IP header is not. In transport mode, there is no inner IP header and, therefore, network layer protection is limited. The set of services provided depends on options selected at the time of Security Association (SA) establishment and on the placement of the implementation.

ESP provides confidentiality with encryption and data integrity with an authenticator. The algorithms used for the ESP are determined by the attributes used to create the SA. The ESP itself is not governed by specific algorithms and provides an open standard to the algorithms that can be used. This is much like the HMAC standard and the determination of the cryptographic hash functions. The standard defines the handling procedures and necessary actions for common encryption processes, but stops short of defining what can and cannot be used for the cryptographic service. The application of confidentiality is optional. However, if only authentication is desired, then AH should be employed.

Although authentication and confidentiality are the primary services provided by ESP, both are optional. However, one of the two must be implemented to apply ESP. In lab tests, there has been the desire to implement ESP with null encryption and no authentication, but this was more for "fun" rather than functionality. To avoid misunderstandings, the basic concept is to use ESP when one wants authentication and encryption, and to use AH when one wants extended authentication without encryption.

ESP Header Definition

The placement of the ESP header directly follows the IP header and options, regardless of the mode of operation of the VPN. Within the IP header, the protocol field will be 50 to represent that an ESP header will immediately follow.

As detailed in Exhibit 8-1, the ESP header contains several fields for the creation and maintenance of an SA.

In the IP header, the 8-bit protocol field will be 50. ESP is defined as protocol 50 by the IANA. That is, the next header following the outside IP header will be an ESP header.

The SPI field is the first 32-bit value in the header. Values from 1 to 255 are reserved, and zero is only used during the negotiations in ISAKMP of the SA. Following the SPI entry is an equally long value that is used for reply resistance and origin authentication. Once again, if replay protection is enabled, the Sequence Number must be unique for the life of the SA. If the number reaches the maximum number, the SA is deleted and a new one is established.

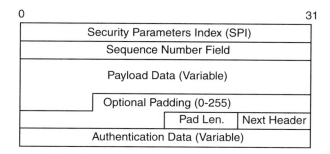

Exhibit 8-1. ESP header.

The Payload is a variable-length field that is directly related to the size of the data being transmitted from the upper layers. The process of controlling the size lies in the hands of the MTU process. Various encryption algorithms utilize a value to initialize the decryption process. The initialization vector (IV), if required by the encryption algorithm specified, is included in the beginning of the payload. While the payload is considered encrypted, the IV is a value related to the decryption process and appended to the ciphertext by the encryption process. Therefore, the encryption and decryption process is not a concern of IPSec, but rather the defined algorithm. The recipient simply injects the ciphertext into the algorithm directly, without regard to what is actually ciphertext and what portion is the IV.

Padding provides limited communication flow confidentiality, but this is more a by-product of other requirements. Padding is used to maintain encryption boundaries. Some encryption algorithms, as discussed above, require the original data to be a multiple of a certain number of bytes to equal the block size of the algorithm. Padding is also used to ensure that the pad length and next header fields are right-aligned to the 4-bit boundary. There are some issues with padding and with regard to attacks. Simply stated, if the padding value is not defined by the encryption algorithm, and it is needed to meet other requirements, the value should be checked by the recipient.

The Pad Length field (Pad Len. in Exhibit 8-1) is a value that notifies the recipient of the length, or amount of padding that was added to the ciphertext. Padding is a requirement to support but, of course, does not mean it has to be used. However, the length field must exist, even if the pad does not.

The Next Header field can be misleading by name. This value is to notify the recipient of the header type contained within the encrypted payload. This is required so that after processing of the payload — decryption — the material is handled properly.

An example would be a value of 6 for a transport mode VPN if the header that appears first in the decrypted payload were a TCP header. This is assuming a standard transport mode without nesting *and* assuming a TCP header is next and not ICMP, UDP, etc.). Transport mode populates the Next Header field using the original IP header that is applied to the datagram in the network layer prior to IPSec handling. It is necessary to read the protocol field of the IP header to properly determine the content. To do otherwise would cause excessive overhead. It also adds a layer of uncertainty in the outcome; it is best to assume that the original IP header knows what it is transporting. This is necessary because the next header could be another transport or tunnel mode packet, ICMP, UDP, etc.

With tunnel mode, the value could be 4, IP-in-IP specification — once again, assuming a standard tunnel without nested SAs. This represents the existence of the

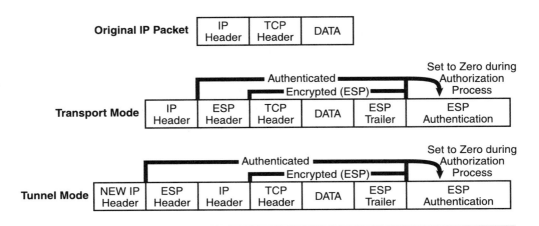

Exhibit 8-2.   ESP packet structure within tunnel mode and transport mode.

inner IP header. In tunnel mode, IPSec inspects the first header of the datagram to be encapsulated. For many implementations, this is usually IP, but given the vast options of IPSec VPNs, it could be almost anything.

These numbers are specific to IPv4 and defined by the IANA in RFC 791.

Finally, the authentication data contains the message digest computed against the ESP packet. The length is determined by the message authentication function employed. In the event that authentication is not specified or desired, this field is not included.

ESP Placement

As discussed, the placement of the header is dependent on the mode of communication. In transport mode, the header is inserted after the IP header and options and before any upper layer protocols, including other IPSec headers. In tunnel mode, the entire packet is encapsulated and the new IP header and options precede the ESP header; see Exhibit 8-2. From the perspective of the outer IP header, the ESP placement is the same as transport mode.

Process Execution

There is a sequence of steps required to properly apply the ESP. The procedures are directly related to the direction of the data: outbound or inbound.

Outbound Process. There are five general steps in processing the application of ESP. The steps described here assume that confidentiality and authentication are employed.

1. Encapsulate the upper layer data into the Payload field. If in transport mode, just the upper layer protocols are encapsulated. If the communication is in tunnel mode, the upper layer and the original IP header are encapsulated.
2. Add the necessary padding. Populate the Pad Length and Next Header fields.
3. Encrypt the payload, which includes the upper layer data, pad, pad length, and next header fields. If the encryption algorithm requires an IV, one is created and applied according to the encryption standard employed.

4. Once encryption is complete, authentication is applied to the ESP header information (SPI and Sequence Number) and Payload, which includes the upper layer data, padding information, and Next Header field. The resulting digest is appended to the end of the packet after the ciphertext.
5. Create the ESP header. The sequence number is inserted. A value of one is defined if this is the first packet.

Inbound Process. As described above, if fragmentation occurred in transit, the reassembly is performed prior to IPSec processing the ESP. Once the assembly is complete, there are several verification steps to complete. The association of the datagram to the appropriate SA must be executed to determine if the communication received for that SA is valid. The packet's data is checked. The verification steps include:

1. The SPI in the ESP header and the destination outer IP address are used to look up the SA in the SAD. If this process fails, the packet is dropped.
2. Verify the sequence number if anti-replay is enabled.
3. Use the SA determined in the previous step to authenticate and decrypt the ESP payload.
4. Once decrypted, use the inner IP header to map to a selector within the SA. The packet's inner source address is typically used to match the SA's selector for processing. *Note:* These steps are repeated until the protocol contained within the payload is not destined for the processing system. The steps must be repeated until the discovery of a next hop system due to the nesting capabilities within IPSec. As soon as data that is not for the gateway is discovered, the forwarding process can start.
5. Find the SPD entry that matches the inner packet data to determine that the packet is valid for the defined SA.
6. Forward the data to the final destination based on the inner IP header information in the packet.

ESP Authentication and Replay Protection

Within the IPSec protocol, there are mechanisms for protecting the communication from attacks based on collecting the communication data and replaying it at a later time. Sequence numbers in the security protocol headers are employed to accommodate replay protection.

There are several interesting aspects with regard to replay protection and ESP's role in the process.

Implementing replay protection requires the use of sequence numbers to be included in the security protocol header. The sender of the packet populates and manages the sequence number, and the receiver is responsible for checking them to complete the protection process.

In the ESP RFC (RFC2406), it states that replay protection can be selected only if data origin authentication is selected, and its election is solely at the discretion of the receiver. (Although the default calls for the sender to increment the Sequence Number used for anti-replay, the service is effective only if the receiver checks the Sequence Number.) If ESP is implemented without authentication and replay protection is applied, the Sequence Number is not authenticated. When origin authentication is employed in ESP, the Sequence Number is included in the authentication payload. If an attacker intercepts a packet and attempts to modify the Sequence Number when authentication is employed, the recipient will quickly discover the change and discard the datagram.

On the other hand, without authentication protection, the change can be made affecting the communication, sometimes dramatically. An example is when an attacker intercepts an IPSec datagram and modifies the sequence number to the maximum value, and forwards it to the intended recipient. For the purposes of this example, it is assumed that the original datagram is never received by the recipient nor by the originator, and the attacker has made the changes and sends the modified packet. Upon receipt of the datagram, the receiver checks the unauthenticated Sequence Number to find that it is set to maximum, forcing the SA to be deleted and a new one created in its place. Therefore, the attacker has the opportunity to inflict havoc on VPN communications and the option to force IKE negotiation at will. The advantage of this to the attacker beyond simple denial of service, it provides the opportunity to inspect the VPN establishment over and over to determine weaknesses or collect information for future attacks.

The ability to implement ESP without authentication is supported by nearly all solutions because it is suggested in the RFCs. Unfortunately, the elimination of authentication in ESP exposes several vulnerabilities. It is strongly suggested that one implement authentication when using ESP.

Note: It should be noted that the AH security protocol authenticates the Sequence Number by default. Therefore, a majority of security issues do not exist in AH applications.

Changes from Previous RFC

The original RFC that defined the ESP security protocol was RFC 1827. In many IPSec VPN solutions, the vendor may allow the older version of the security protocol to be used due to some of the leniencies in the previous standard. Some of the differences between the RFCs include options for replay protection, authentication, next protocol field definition, and encryption padding support.

Authentication Header (AH)

The AH provides data integrity, origin authentication, and optional replay resistance. The first aspect of AH that surfaces is that it does not provide any form of confidentiality. As a matter of fact, its primary function is to provide authentication services to the communication. Because AH does not provide confidentiality, there is no need for an encryption algorithm to be defined.

As detailed in Exhibit 8-3, the AH header contains several fields for the creation and maintenance of an SA.

In the IP header, the 8-bit protocol field will be 51. AH is defined as protocol 51 by the IANA. That is, the next header following the outside IP header will be an AH.

Much like ESP, the standard does not directly address the massage authentication code, but merely its utilization. Also, replay resistance is an option and requires the recipient to perform all the functions.

```
0                                                              31
┌─────────────┬──────────────┬─────────────────────────────┐
│ Next Header │ Payload Len. │          Reserved           │
├─────────────┴──────────────┴─────────────────────────────┤
│            Security Parameters Index (SPI)                │
├───────────────────────────────────────────────────────────┤
│               Sequence Number Field                       │
├───────────────────────────────────────────────────────────┤
│             Authentication Data (Variable)                │
│                                                           │
└───────────────────────────────────────────────────────────┘
```

Exhibit 8-3. AH header.

The similarities between ESP and AH tend to dissolve as the inner workings of the AH security protocol are investigated. AH provides authentication out to the outer IP header. It provides authentication services for the upper layer protocols, just like ESP, but ESP cannot authenticate the outer IP header. Once the packet is assembled, the AH process authenticates the entire packet and inserts itself into the packet.

The Next Header field is exactly like it sounds, unlike ESP. It defines the next header in the packet immediately following the authentication data. Of course, for nested operations, the Next Header could an IPSec security protocol.

The Payload Length defines the length, in 32-bit words, the amount of authentication data. The value is determined by subtracting 2 from the 32-bit words. As an example provided in the AH RFC, in the case of a 96-bit authentication value plus the 3 32-bit word fixed portion (equals "6"), this length field will be "4."

The reserved field is always set to zero. This is followed by the SPI for the SA in which the security protocol is participating. The next value is the 32-bin Sequence Number. The same issues that existed with the ESP Sequence Number and anti-replay protection exist with AH Sequence Numbers.

The authentication data is the message digest, or authenticator used to verify the entire packet. Once again, the size is partially controlled by the message authentication function selected. However, because the value must a multiple of 32 bits, padding may be required.

AH Placement

As discussed above with ESP, the placement of the AH header is dependant on the mode of communication. In transport mode, the header is inserted after the IP header and options, and before any upper layer protocols, including other IPSec headers. In tunnel mode, the original packet is placed behind the header, and the new IP header and options preceed the AH header (see Exhibit 8-4). From the perspective of the outer IP header, AH placement is the same as in transport mode.

Process Execution

There is a sequence of steps required to properly apply the AH. Much like ESP, the procedures are directly related to the direction of the data: outbound or inbound.

Outbound Process. There are four general steps to processing the application of AH to a packet:

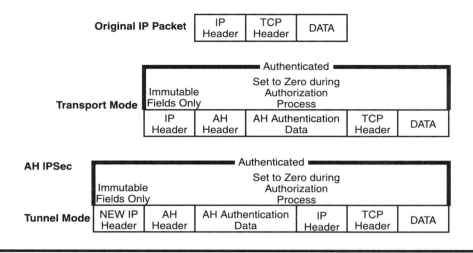

Exhibit 8-4. AH packet structure within tunnel mode and transport mode.

1. Determine the associated SA that calls for AH processing by the available information in the original packet; for example, IP address (source and destination).
2. Once the communication is determined to have AH applied, the header is inserted after the IP header and the SPI is implemented.
3. Generate a sequence number for application to the header.
4. Calculate and apply the message integrity, pad the digest, and apply to the end of the AH and before the upper layer protocols.

Because the AH is designed for authentication purposes, creating the authentication data that covers the entire packet requires some refined techniques when compared to ESP. During the authentication process, several aspects must be calculated, including:

■ Determine IP header fields that are immutable and mutable.
■ Set mutable fields to zero.
■ Collect AH header information; the authentication data is set to zero.
■ Collect the upper layer protocol information, assumed to be immutable.

An immutable field is predictable in that it will not change or be modified in transit. A mutable field is a value that may be changed in transit, and therefore invalidate the message digest that will be checked by the recipient. Mutable fields cannot be included in the authentication process. Therefore, once they are determined, they are set to zero prior to executing the authentication process. The fields are set to zero and not removed from the authentication process to allow proper alignment to be preserved. The following list defines the mutable and immutable fields of an IP header, also shown in Exhibit 8-5.

■ Immutable (to be included in the authentication process):
— version
— IP header length

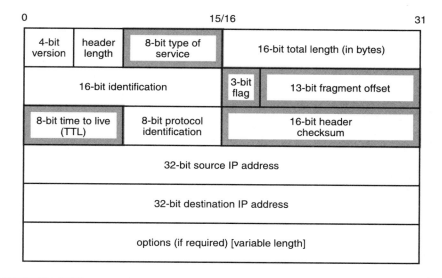

Exhibit 8-5. Mutable and immutable fields.

— total length
— identification
— protocol (will equal 51 for the AH)
— source address
— destination address
■ Mutable (to be set to zero prior to authentication calculation):
— type of service
— all flags
— fragment offset
— time to live (TTL)
— header checksum

Inbound Process. As with ESP, if fragmentation occurred in transit, the reassembly is performed prior to IPSec processing the AH. Once the assembly is complete, there are several verification steps to complete. The association of the datagram to the appropriate SA must be executed to determine if the communication received for that SA is valid. The packet's data is checked. The verification steps include:

1. The SPI in AH and the destination IP address are used to look up the SA in the SAD. If this process fails, the packet is dropped.
2. Verify the sequence number if anti-replay is enabled.
3. Use the SA determined in the previous step to authenticate the packet.
4. Forward the data to the final destination based on the IP header information.

The Purpose of AH

There have been many questions regarding the existence of two security protocols. In other words, authentication supported by AH can be implemented with ESP. The

ESP protocol could be modified to allow the implementation to provide a "switch" to permit the authentication of the outer header data. This would provide for a single protocol with multiple authentication options for various implementations.

Simply stated, and commonly agreed upon, there is little use of the AH protocol in light of a modified ESP protocol. Currently, the validity of AH employment is typically associated with protecting the integrity of the originating IP address. Unfortunately, in the world of the Internet and its associated vulnerabilities, the originating IP address is rarely trusted or used for security decisions. Other data within the IPSec datagram can be used for more controlled authentication; for example, tunnel mode has inner data that can be used without regard to the outer header data.

To fully understand the retention and existence of the AH protocol, the history of the creation of security protocols can be helpful. When the first RFCs were published to define the security protocols, RFCs 1826 and 1827 (AH and ESP, respectively), ESP did not provide authentication. Therefore, if message and origin authentication were desired, AH was required. Also, the AH protocol has different advantages in IPv6 as compared to IPv4. In addition, the IPSec solutions currently available support AH. Therefore, why remove it and widen the gap of interoperability?

Additionally, RFC 2401 discusses combining security associations (iterated tunneling) over several layers of IPSec communications. An example provided in the RFC details an end-to-end solution wherein ESP can be applied between two IPSec gateways and the communicating hosts using the VPN, provided one can employ AH SAs . The effective result would be a datagram that is encrypted and authenticated over untrusted networks and only authenticated while on internal networks. By not allowing encryption on internal networks, the data communications can be analyzed for intranet security violations while maintaining the integrity of the data. Nevertheless, the authentication is not being performed on the system providing the encapsulation that could expose ESP to some complex vulnerabilities with respect to authentication.

Note: For a highly detailed explanation of some vulnerabilities associated with ESP when authentication is not implemented, see Steve Bellovin's document at http://www.research.att.com/~smb/papers/badesp.pdf.

There are several arguments for and against keeping the AH protocol. It is expected that AH will remain because it is currently being implemented in most IPSec solutions, and IPv6 leverages the protocol in ways that are unique to IPv6 and not found in IPv4 standards. However, do not be surprised if a hybrid protocol is created.

Changes from Previous RFC

The original RFC that defined the AH security protocol was RFC 1826. In many IPSec VPN solutions, the vendor may allow use of the older version of the security protocol. The main difference between the RFCs is the inclusion of replay protection in the protocol. In the most recent RFC, replay protection is mandatory for the sender, as with ESP. Once again, it is the responsibility of the recipient to monitor the sequence number for replay protection to be effective.

Chapter 9

Key Management

Throughout this book, the discussion of keys and security associations has been the focus of IPSec and the creation of a secured, authenticated relationship between two or more systems. The creation of keys and the use of those keys to create a secure channel are the most critical steps in the creation of an IPSec VPN. This chapter details the negotiation, authentication, and management of keys within a VPN.

IKE (Internet Key Exchange) is responsible for the origin authentication, the creation and management of keys for subsequent communications. On the surface, the process of these three basic properties appears straightforward. However, the protocol must be prepared to accommodate several variations of each property. Furthermore, IKE is responsible for session establishment. The weakest point in any communication is the beginning: the point where each side is building a relationship and ensuring one another that they are who they claim. The beginning of the communication represents the creation of new session numbers and sequence identifiers that will be referenced throughout the communication. Any weakness in the process will open the initialization to denial-of-service attacks and could possibly render the service unavailable. IKE provides several layers and variation to protect the sharing of information and perform the necessary step to ensure that the communication is valid prior to committing to the communication.

It is necessary to understand that no matter the level of encryption provided, if the keys are not secured, the encryption is invalidated. The process of secure key management is an essential procedure in the overall security of the entire VPN.

Simply put, IKE is the IPSec VPN. The authentication, encryption selection, key creation, and key management directly result in SAs that are driven by the security protocols within IPSec. IPSec uses security protocols to create SAs; the way in which they are implemented are a direct result of IKE and the policies defined to create them.

This chapter explains the details of key management and the creation of the IKE standard, and examines the properties that make it the default key management protocol for IPSec. It will soon become apparent that the complexities of an IPSec VPN reside in the creation of the security association.

The Role of Key Management

Key management is implemented to accommodate the creation and maintenance of keys that are used in the encryption processes to provide the security services of IPSec. It is necessary for IKE to complete several layers of interaction to ensure that subsequent communications are afforded the proper security as defined in the policy.

IKE must authenticate the origin of the session. In IKE, the origination point is referred to as the *Initiator,* and the recipient of the request for session establishment is the *Responder.* Once authentication has been established and the systems are confident that the communication partner is who they claim to be, IKE negotiates the level of security to provide, based on the policy for that particular connection. During this operation, proposals for encryption and message authentication are either accepted or rejected. Once accepted, IKE can begin the process of creating the necessary key to service the negotiated services.

Once the level of security service is agreed upon, IKE is responsible for sharing the ingredients to create keys. The ingredients for the creation of keys embody an entire process of agreements and the generation of specific numbers to derive key material without actually sending the key to the corresponding partner. This is detailed in following sections.

Finally, IKE creates the keys by combining several components specific to the communication that conspire to further authenticate and protect the communication. Once the initial key is generated, more keys are created, depending on the encryption

algorithms specified, the application of the security protocols, and the overall requirements of the SAs.

Manual Key Management

Manual key management is the simplest form of key management. It requires an
administrator to manually enter the key information that is to be used for subsequent
key creation. Manual implementations are acceptable for very small, static environments that have limited processing power or bandwidth. By using manual key management, the systems involved in the VPN do not have the load of creating or updating
keys. There are several design and security considerations when manual key management is implemented. Design issues include scalability. Each association requires key
material for each level of protection demanded by a security policy. Also, each key
must be manually entered and changed accordingly at each site for communications.

In short, manual key management is tedious, requires administrative overhead,
and is less secure than automatic key management.

Automatic Key Management

The default key management should provide a means of creating key material and
the ability to update those keys without human intervention. This allows the VPN
solution to scale to accommodate an enterprise-level implementation

Creating IKE for IPSec

The Internet Key Exchange (IKE) protocol is a hybrid containing three primary, existing
protocols that are combined to provide specific key management for IPSec. The three
protocols are:

1. ISAKMP
2. Oakley
3. SKEME (Secure Key Exchange Mechanism)

Different portions of each protocol work in conjunction to securely provide keying
information specifically for the IETF IPSec DOI. The terms IKE and ISAKMP are used
interchangeably by various vendors, and many use ISAKMP to describe the keying
function. While this is correct, ISAKMP addresses the procedures and not the technical
operations as they pertain to IPSec. IKE is the default standard that best represents
the IPSec implementation of key management.

IKE is considerably complicated and several variations are available in the establishment of trust and providing keying material. Oakley and ISAKMP protocols, which
are included in IKE, each define separate methods to establish an authenticated key
exchange between systems. Oakley defines "modes" of operation to build a secure
relationship path, and ISAKMP defines "phases" to accomplish much the same process
in a hierarchical format. The relationship between these two is represented by IKE
with different exchanges as modes, which operate in one of two phases.

ISAKMP

ISAKMP defines the procedures for authenticating a communicating peer and key generation techniques. All of these are necessary to establish and maintain an SA in an Internet environment. ISAKMP defines payloads for exchanging key and authentication data. These formats provide a consistent framework, which is independent of the encryption algorithm, authentication mechanism being implemented, and security protocol, such as IPSec.

The majority of IKE is ISAKMP, and it is necessary to fully understand the phases of ISAKMP. Also, IKE's packet structure and payload framework are exclusively based on ISAKMP. ISAKMP provides negotiation in the first phase to identify one another and agree on the further protection of information. The second phase can be protected by the first and focuses on creating SAs for the underlying protocol suite.

There are several advantages to a phased approach in key management. The first phase session can be distributed between several second-phase operations to provide the construction of a new ISA without renegotiation. This allows for the creation of subsequent ISAs to be preempted via secured communications in the second phase.

Another benefit is that the first-phase process can provide security services for the second phase in the form of encryption keying material. However, no data can be used from the first phase if it does not meet the security protection requirements of the second phase.

In addition, the first phase is providing peer identification; therefore, the second phase provides the creation of the security protocol SAs without concern for authentication of the peer. If the first phase were not available, each new IPSec SA would need to authenticate the peer.

Oakley

Oakley provides examples and processes of an exchange protocol for supporting the underlying communication for ISAKMP. Developed by Hilarie Orman, a cryptographer from the University of Arizona, the protocol defines several aspects of authentication and key creation. It details the process of modes used to enhance the security between peers, based on the negotiation of those properties.

Within the Oakley protocol definition, there are also Diffie-Hellman groups. Diffie-Hellman groups define the strength supplied to the Diffie-Hellman calculation for the later creation of keys by the peers. Richard Schroeppel, of the University of Arizona, generated the groups and provided the calculations for display in the RFC. There are currently two primary forms of key groups. Three of the five available groups are generated from MODP calculations and the leveraging of very large prime numbers. The other two groups are based on elliptic curves. Each of these groups are EC2N processes with varying characteristics.

Groups 1 and 2 are MODP based and provide primes at 96 bytes and 128 bytes, respectively. Groups 3 and 4 are EC2N based and provide 155-byte and 185-byte Diffie-Hellman values. The last group, group 5, is based on MODP and provides a prime of 192 bytes (1536 bits). Groups 1 and 2 are the most common, for two reasons. The EC2N process is typically not supported on currently available VPN systems and the last group is a very large number, and performance is crucial. For example, if using group 5, the prime to use in several calculations looks like (a lot):

```
FFFFFFFF  FFFFFFFF  C90FDAA2  2168C234  C4C6628B  80DC1CD1
29024E08  8A67CC74  020BBEA6  3B139B22  514A0879  8E3404DD
EF9519B3  CD3A431B  302B0A6D  F25F1437  4FE1356D  6D51C245
E485B576  625E7EC6  F44C42E9  A637ED6B  0BFF5CB6  F406B7ED
EE386BFB  5A899FA5  AE9F2411  7C4B1FE6  49286651  ECE45B3D
C2007CB8  A163BF05  98DA4836  1C55D39A  69163FA8  FD24CF5F
83655D23  DCA3AD96  1C62F356  208552BB  9ED52907  7096966D
670C354E  4ABC9804  F1746C08  CA237327  FFFFFFFF  FFFFFFFF
```

IKE leverages the process of modes and groups from Oakley. IKE uses all the groups defined within Oakley, but only some of the modes that are available.

SKEME

In 1996, Hugo Krawczyk proposed a key management based on the use of Diffie-Hellman and public key cryptography. This allows the shared information to be authenticated. The process can be used to create random values that are shared using the public key of the peer. These values, once authenticated, can be used to create the keys. Therefore, the combination of SKEME sharing techniques and Diffie-Hellman provides for PFS.

IKE uses portions of SKEME for authentication with public keys and uses the sharing mechanisms for PFS.

Phases and Modes

Phase I takes place when two ISAKMP peers desire a secure, authenticated channel with which to communicate. Each system is verified and authenticated against its peer to allow for future communications. Phase II exists to provide keying information and material to assist in the establishment of SAs for an IPSec communication.

Within Phase I there are two modes of operation defined in IKE:

- Main Mode
- Aggressive Mode

Each of these modes accomplishes a Phase I secure exchange, and these two modes only exist in Phase I. Within Phase II there are two modes:

- Quick Mode
- New Group Mode

Quick Mode is used to establish SAs on behalf of the underlying security protocol. New Group Mode is designated as a Phase II mode, but the service provided by New Group Mode is to benefit Phase I operations. As described earlier, one of the advantages of a two-phased approach is that the second phase can be used to provide additional ISAs, which eliminates the reauthorization of the peers.

ISAKMP Framework

The framework provided by ISAKMP is very modular. This aspect is its greatest asset and conveys the commitment of the protocol to remain above the exact requirements of the underlying security protocol suite. The IPSec DOI and IKE exist to refine the ISAKMP to work specifically for IPSec. Of course, it is at the intersection of ISAKMP and IKE where things get complicated; however, ISAKMP alone as a support mechanism for SA creation is robust.

Simply stated, ISAKMP is a collection of headers and payloads that can be combined to create messages to provide communication-specific information for the establishment of an SA.

The following sections detail each aspect of ISAKMP and the individual modules that can be used to construct a dialogue between two systems wishing to establish IPSec SAs.

ISAKMP Header

All Phase I and II operations require an ISAKMP header that can be followed by a variable length of payloads. The constant existence of the ISAKMP header provides information required by the protocol to maintain association throughout the communication.

There are currently 13 defined payloads that can be distinctly identified in an ISAKMP header. Each one of these can be used to generate state information to create, manage, or delete an SA.

As seen in Exhibit 9-1, the ISAKMP header is 28 bytes and contains general required information for the relationship.

The initiator and responder cookies are 8 bytes of random numbers that are used to identify the ISA. The order of the cookies must be maintained, regardless of any changes in direction within the SA. An example would be a Quick Mode initiated by the responder of an earlier negotiation. The cookies are provided for the systems to quickly identify the validity of a particular communication. This reduces, slightly, the exposure to denial-of-service attacks by allowing the recipient to check a basic number shared in previous communications prior to processing the entire packet.

```
0                                                        31
+--------------------------------------------------------+
|                   Initiator Cookie                     |
+--------------------------------------------------------+
|                   Responder Cookie                     |
+-------------+-----------+------------+-----------------+
|  Next Pay   |  MJ Ver.  |  MN Ver.   |     Flags       |
+-------------+-----------+------------+-----------------+
|                     Message ID                         |
+--------------------------------------------------------+
|                      Length                            |
+--------------------------------------------------------+
```

Exhibit 9-1.   ISAKMP header.

The Next Payload is used in the ISAKMP header and the Generic header to identify the next payload contents. This is an 8-bit field that provides for 255 variations, once again, 13 of which are leveraged by ISAKMP/IKE.

NONE	0
Security Association (SA)	1
Proposal (P)	2
Transform (T)	3
Key Exchange (KE)	4
Identification (ID)	5
Certificate (CERT)	6
Certificate Request (CR)	7
Hash (HASH)	8
Signature (SIG)	9
Nonce (NONCE)	10
Notification (N)	11
Delete (D)	12
Vendor ID (VID)	13
RESERVED	14–127
Private USE	128–255

The Major and Minor versions (MJ Ver. and MN Ver., respectively, in Exhibit 9-1) are to determine the version of ISAKMP that is being employed by the peer. Peers will drop all communications when the major or minor of a peer is greater than the peer's.

The exchange type identifies the type of message being transmitted. There are several messages that can be used within ISAKMP, including:

NONE	0
Base	1
Identity Protection	2
Authentication Only	3
Aggressive	4
Informational	5
ISAKMP Future Use	6–31
DOI Specific Use	32–239
Private Use	240–255

The Flag field allows for the combination of three message states. The encryption bit is set to 1 if all the payloads following the ISAKMP header are encrypted. The next bit it the commit bit; this is used by ISAKMP to align key exchange processes. The use, support, and notification of this bit in implementation are scrutinized. The use of the commit bit, and other areas of IKE that are up for discussion, are covered in the following chapters. The authentication bit is intended for use when notify payloads are utilized.

The Message ID field is used to uniquely identify the protocol state in Phase II. The responder generates the message ID during the beginning of Phase II operations, as will be seen in the log files presented later in this section.

The Length field defines the length of the payloads and the ISAKMP header. It represents the length in bytes.

Generic Payload Header

The Generic header (see Exhibit 9-2) is provided to chain several payloads together in a single message. This is necessary in nearly every exchange of IKE and allows for the protocol to remain flexible. Each payload is assigned a generic header.

```
0                                                              31
 _____
|              |              |                              |
|  Next Pay    |  Reserved    |      Payload Length          |
|_____|_____|_____|
```

Exhibit 9-2.   Generic header.

The Next Payload and Length fields are identical to the ones found in the ISAKMP header. Exhibit 9-3 shows the use of this simple header and the chaining process it provides.

As one can see, the combination of the Next Payload value and the Length field allow for flexibility in the message creation and reduce the complexity of the ISAKMP header in having to support all the options.

Security Association Payload

The SA payload (see Exhibit 9-4) is used to convey the security attributes to be used in the establishment of an SA.

Included with the payload is the Domain of Interpretation (DOI) identification. This is a necessary identification because ISAKMP can be used for any protocol that utilizes SAs for secured communications and requires key management. For generic ISAKMP processes, the value is set to 0. However, so that the values included in the payloads reference the proper attributes for IPSec, 1 identifies the IPSec DOI. Once again, the DOI defines the attribute values for the underlying protocol.

The situation portion of the payload identifies the circumstances of the negotiation.

```
Sit_Identity_Only          0x01
Sit_Secrecy                0x02
Sit_Integrity              0x04
```

Sit_Identity_Only states that the SA will be identified based on the identity information provided by the peer. Sit_Secrecy identifies that the SA is being implemented with labeled information. Sit_Integrity specifies that the integrity requires labels for use in an MLS environment.

Proposal Payload

The proposal payload (see Exhibit 9-5) contains the bulk of the information associated with the creation of an SA. During the establishment of a secured relationship, each system must determine the level of authentication and confidentiality, and various information associated with the security relationship. A proposal payload is populated with transform payloads that contain the SA information. The initiator sends proposal

0   31

Initiator Cookie			
Responder Cookie			
Next Pay=1	MJ Ver.	MN Ver.	Flags
Message ID			
Length			

ISAKMP Header

Next Pay=2	0	Payload Length
1		
Situation		

SA Header

Next Pay=0	0	Payload Length	
Proposal #= 1	Proto ID=ESP	SPI Size	# of Trsfms= 2
SPI			

Proposal

Next Pay=3	0	Payload Length
Trsfrm #=1	Transform ID	0
SA Attributes (See Attribute Payload Configuration		

Transform

Next Pay=0	0	Payload Length
Trsfrm #=2	Transform ID	0
SA Attributes (See Attribute Payload Configuration		

Transform

Exhibit 9-3.   Using the generic header for chaining payloads.

payloads with one or more transform payloads within each that define the available security conditions for the particular communication defined in the SPD. The responder selects the proposal and associated transform set that best pertains to the communication, and sends the unchanged information to the initiator in a proposal payload with the original transform payloads.

The proposal number (Proposal #) represents the number of the proposal within the message. There can be several proposals for any given SA, and the numbers are used

0   31

Next Pay	Reserved	Payload Length
DOI		
Situation		

Exhibit 9-4.   Security association payload.

```
0                                                            31
┌──────────────┬──────────────┬─────────────────────────────┐
│  Next Pay    │   Reserved   │      Payload Length         │
├──────────────┼──────────────┼──────────────┬──────────────┤
│  Proposal #  │ Protocol ID  │   SPI Size   │ # of Trsfms  │
├──────────────┴──────────────┴──────────────┴──────────────┤
│                          SPI                               │
└────────────────────────────────────────────────────────────┘
```

Exhibit 9-5. Proposal payload.

to define logical operators. If the proposal numbers match, they are considered related and represent an AND logical operation; whereas if the numbers do not match, it simply represents another proposal for consideration, an OR logical operator. As an example, the SPD specifies that network 10.20.0.0/16 should use ESP with several optional combinations of encryption and authentication algorithms. However, there is the option of using AH with ESP, and the several combinations for those as well. The number of, and the assigned number of proposals are different; the assigned number simply represents relationships between the various number of proposals (see Exhibit 9-6).

Exhibit 9-6.   Proposal payload example.

Proposal 1:
   ESP
        DES and MD5
        DES and SHA
        3DES and SHA
Proposal 2:
   AH
        SHA
        MD5
Proposal 2:
   ESP
        DES and MD5
        DES and SHA
        3DES and SHA

Notice that there are three proposals and two classifications, 1 and 2. Proposal 1 is the first and defines that only ESP is to be used and offers three options for use within ESP. Proposal 2 has two related proposals: one for AH and the other for ESP. The second set of proposals has the same number and represents an AND logical operation; whereas the first proposal has a different number that represents an OR operation with the other proposals numbered 2. This collection states that ESP with any of the offered options is acceptable; OR AH and ESP must be used with the proposed security suites. This is a simple example and the proposal process can become extremely complicated.

The Next Payload field must be either a 2 or 0. The next payload following the proposal must be a transform payload (see Exhibit 9-7). Therefore, the Next Payload field is designed to notify the recipient that there is more than one proposal.

Protocol ID is the security protocol that the proposals are being negotiated on behalf of. This is an excellent example of the application of the IPSec DOI. The protocol ID for ESP is 50; however, the DOI that defines the ESP security protocol is 3.

RESERVED   0
PROTO_ISAKMP   1
PROTO_IPSEC_AH   2
PROTO_IPSEC_ESP   3
PROTO_IPCOMP   4

The SPI size allows for the integration of different underlying protocols other than IPSec. The SPI is included in the payload.

The number of transforms indicates how many transforms are provided for the proposal to create a transform set.

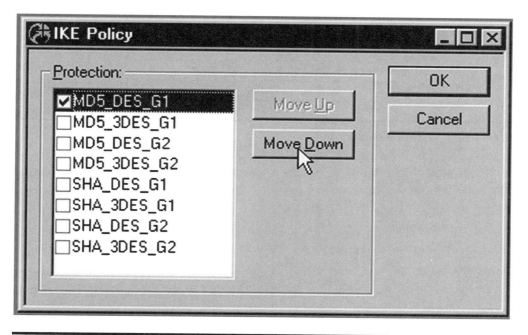

Exhibit 9-7. Multiple transform sets that can be prioritized into proposals.

Transform Payload

The Transform Payload (see Exhibit 9-8) contains a single attribute for the entire transform set. The transform number (Transform #) is required if the there is more than one transform provided within the proposal. It is very common to have more than one. If using ESP with DES encryption and MD5 authentication, one would have two transform payloads within the proposal.

0			31
Next Pay	Reserved	Payload Length	
Transform #	Transform ID	Reserved	
SA Attributes (See Attribute Payload Configuration)			

Exhibit 9-8. Transform payload.

The Transform ID specifies the protocol being considered for the transform.

The SA Attributes are contained within a special payload called Information Attributes. The details of the information format are covered in the following sections.

Identification Payload

Identification information is communicated between peers using the identification payload (see Exhibit 9-9). This information is used to determine the peers and the associated authentication information.

```
0                                               31
┌───────────┬───────────┬───────────────────────┐
│ Next Pay  │ Reserved  │    Payload Length     │
├───────────┼───────────┼───────────────────────┤
│ ID Type   │Protocol ID│         Port          │
├───────────┴───────────┴───────────────────────┤
│             Identification Data                │
└────────────────────────────────────────────────┘
```

Exhibit 9-9. Identification payload.

The identification types specify the associated information that can be used for authentication processes.

RESERVED	0
ID_IPV4_ADDR	1
ID_FQDN	2
ID_USER_FQDN	3
ID_IPV4_ADDR_SUBNET	4
ID_IPV6_ADDR	5
ID_IPV6_ADDR_SUBNET	6
ID_IPV4_ADDR_RANGE	7
ID_IPV6_ADDR_RANGE	8
ID_DER_ASN1_DN	9
ID_DER_ASN1_GN	10
ID_KEY_ID	11

This information should look familiar from the discussions on security associations. Each one of these is associated with selectors in the SPD and SAD alignment and can be used in the SA selection process for incoming and outbound communications.

The Protocol ID is used to identify the IP protocol represented by the collected information. This is required to work with the next field, Port. If the protocol is TCP, port 80 requires different handling than if the protocol is UDP.

Identification data is the collection of attributes defined in the previous portions of the payload.

Certificate Payload

The Certificate payload (see Exhibit 9-10) is used to provide certificate information to the peer for authentication.

```
0                                          31
┌──────────┬──────────┬──────────────────────┐
│ Next Pay │ Reserved │    Payload Length     │
├──────────┼──────────┴──────────────────────┤
│Cert Encode│                                 │
│          │      Certificate Data           │
└──────────┴─────────────────────────────────┘
```

Exhibit 9-10. Certificate payload.

The certificate encoding indicates the format of the following certificate information. There are several different types of encoding:

PKCS #7 wrapped X.509 certificate	1
PGP Certificate	2
DNS Signed Key	3
X.509 Certificate - Signature	4
X.509 Certificate - Key Exchange	5
Kerberos Tokens	6
Certificate Revocation List (CRL)	7
Authority Revocation List (ARL)	8
SPKI Certificate	9
X.509 Certificate - Attribute	10
RESERVED	11–255

The encoding allows for the certificate data, in the next portion, to be applied.

Certificate Request Payload

The certificate request allows a system to request the certificate of the communication peer (see Exhibit 9-11). Certificate requests are used when other, out-of-band requests are not utilized. The responder will send its certificate upon receipt of the certificate request, if the responder supports certificates. The interesting part concerns which certificate to send. Systems are capable of maintaining several certificates — some private, while others may be publicly assigned. If two systems attempt to establish a VPN and the certificate is the required authentication, then the certificate must be made available in some form or another.

Take, for example, two companies wanting to establish a short-term VPN and both are using private CAs for the distribution of system certificates. If certificate authentication is being used, the certificate for each system must be made available as well as the corresponding information, such as the CRL and trust chain — or root CA certificate. Nonetheless, this poses some very interesting situations that are discussed in section "Open Issues with IPSec and IKE."

```
0                                          31
┌──────────┬──────────┬──────────────────────┐
│ Next Pay │ Reserved │    Payload Length     │
├──────────┼──────────┴──────────────────────┤
│ Cert Type│                                 │
│          │     Certificate Authority        │
└──────────┴─────────────────────────────────┘
```

Exhibit 9-11. Certificate request payload.

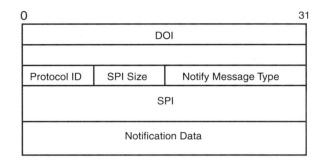

Exhibit 9-12.   Notification payload.

Notification Payload

The notification payload (see Exhibit 9-12) is used to convey informational and status information between peers. Its primary use is for error messages in the event a payload is bad, unaccepted, or malformed. It is also used for basic information exchange, such as lifetime notifications when the SA is coming to an end.

Notification payloads can be used during Phase I or II. Therefore, the information contained in the payload may vary. As an example, in Phase I, the cookies are used for ISA identification and not SPIs. Therefore, the ISA information is controlled by the cookies in the ISAKMP header and the SPI field is set to 0.

The Protocol ID specifies the following protocol based on the DOI versions. In Phase I, this is set to 1 for ISAKMP. This is followed by the SPI size that is provided for ISAKMP flexibility for underlying protocols.

The Notify Message Type is used to associate the message contents with the appropriate variable data (see Exhibit 9-13).

Delete Payload

The delete payload (see Exhibit 9-14) contains SA and protocol-specific information so that the recipient can remove the corresponding information from the SPD and SAD — deleting the SA.

As with other SA establishing payloads, the delete payload includes much of the same information. The DOI being used, the protocol ID specified in the DOI, and SPI size are familiar. The number of SPIs is a new field. This allows the identification of several SAs for deletion at the same time. The only caveat to using multiple SPIs is that only one protocol can be identified. Therefore, the SPIs included in the SPI payload must be for an ESP, AH, or ISAKMP SA.

Information Attributes

During ISAKMP Phase I and II messages, various information must be shared within the payloads (see Exhibit 9-15). For certain payloads, such as a Transform payload, the attributes are contained within an attribute payload that acts as the data portion of the carrier payload. An example is a Transform payload; it begins with the generic header and contains certain transform information, such as ID and number. The actual

Exhibit 9-13.　Message types.

INVALID-PAYLOAD-TYPE	1
DOI-NOT-SUPPORTED	2
SITUATION-NOT-SUPPORTED	3
INVALID-COOKIE	4
INVALID-MAJOR-VERSION	5
INVALID-MINOR-VERSION	6
INVALID-EXCHANGE-TYPE	7
INVALID-FLAGS	8
INVALID-MESSAGE-ID	9
INVALID-PROTOCOL-ID	10
INVALID-SPI	11
INVALID-TRANSFORM-ID	12
ATTRIBUTES-NOT-SUPPORTED	13
NO-PROPOSAL-CHOSEN	14
BAD-PROPOSAL-SYNTAX	15
PAYLOAD-MALFORMED	16
INVALID-KEY-INFORMATION	17
INVALID-ID-INFORMATION	18
INVALID-CERT-ENCODING	19
INVALID-CERTIFICATE	20
CERT-TYPE-UNSUPPORTED	21
INVALID-CERT-AUTHORITY	22
INVALID-HASH-INFORMATION	23
AUTHENTICATION-FAILED	24
INVALID-SIGNATURE	25
ADDRESS-NOTIFICATION	26
NOTIFY-SA-LIFETIME	27
CERTIFICATE-UNAVAILABLE	28
UNSUPPORTED-EXCHANGE-TYPE	29
UNEQUAL-PAYLOAD-LENGTHS	30
RESERVED (Future Use)	31–8191
Private Use	8192–16383
CONNECTED	16384
RESERVED (Future Use)	16385–24575
DOI-specific codes	24576–32767
Private Use	32768–40959
RESERVED (Future Use)	40960–65535

detailed transform information contained in the data portion of the payload is formatted into an attribute payload. Attribute payloads are based on a format that allows flexibility in the representation of information.

The attribute format (AF) bit is used to identify the following information contained within the payload. The data necessary to be shared among peers may require two of three fields to appropriately convey the attribute. The three attributes are:

1. Type
2. Length
3. Value

Next Pay	Reserved	Payload Length
DOI		
Next Pay	Reserved	Payload Length
Notification Data		

0   31

Exhibit 9-14. Delete payload.

Each requires a Type value to properly manage the data contained. The Length is used if the value has a variable length that needs to be identified. The Value is the information defined by one or both of the two previous attributes.

There are some types of information that have a fixed length and therefore do not need a length bit. If the length is known and the length bit is absent, the value can be contained where the length bit would normally reside. This is to reduce the length of the payload, and increase efficiency and performance.

If the AF bit is set to 0, the length is included and the value is transmitted in its own field. If the AF bit is 1, the length is not required and the Length field is populated with the value, reducing the payload by 4 bytes.

A F	Attribute Type	AF=0 Att. Length AF=1 Att. Value
AF=0 Attribute Value AF=1 Not Transmitted		

0   31

Exhibit 9-15. Attribute definitions.

Phase I Attributes. In IKE Phase I operations, there are specific transform attributes for defining the protection of IKE exchanges, as opposed to Phase II attributes that are used for the creation of IPSec SAs. IKE requires various information, ranging from the encryption algorithms to the type of authentication for the protection of IKE messages. The attributes are defined in the IKE RFC and not the IPSec DOI, or ISAKMP RFC, as one might expect. The following is a list of IKE attributes and their types.

Encryption Algorithm	1
Hash Algorithm	2
Authentication Method	3
Group Description	4
Group Type	5
Group Prime/Irreducible Polynomial	6
Group Generator One	7
Group Generator Two	8
Group Curve A	9
Group Curve B	10
Life Type	11

Life Duration	12
PRF	13
Key Length	14
Field Size	15
Group Order	16

Attribute type 1, encryption, has six defined values for use within IKE messages. The encryption algorithm defined will be used to protect various Phase I messages, Phase II (Quick Mode) messages, and any other messages within IKE requiring protection.

DES-CBC	1
IDEA-CBC	2
Blowfish-CBC	3
RC5-R16-B64-CBC	4
3DES-CBC	5
CAST-CBC	6

Values 7 to 65000 are reserved for IANA's use, and values 65001 to 65535 are for private use among mutually consenting parties.

Attribute type 2, hash algorithm, defines the message authentication algorithm to be utilized for all IKE exchanges.

MD5	1
SHA	2
Tiger	3

Values 4 to 65000 are reserved for IANA's use, and values 65001 to 65535 are for private use among mutually consenting parties.

Note: From this point on, the remaining values are typically reserved for IANA use and the last 534 are for private use.

Authentication, a type 3 attribute, is used to convey the authentication type to be used within IKE. This is extremely important in that it communicates to the peer in what format to respond and the structure of the messages to follow:

Pre-shared key	1
DSS signatures	2
RSA signatures	3
Encryption with RSA	4
Revised encryption with RSA	5

Group description, type 4, is to identify the Diffie-Hellman group to employ:

Default 768-bit MODP group	1
Alternate 1024-bit MODP group	2
EC2N group on GP[2^155]	3
EC2N group on GP[2^185]	4

The following types, 5 through 10, are available to convey extended Diffie-Hellman parameters, if desired. For example, group type can be defined in support of the group being used. Group types are:

MODP (modular exponentiation group)	1
ECP (elliptic curve group over GF[P])	2
EC2N (elliptic curve group over GF[2^N])	3

In many cases, if the peers wish to define specific parameters of the Diffie-Hellman group to be utilized, New Group Mode exchange can be used. The values shared can be conveyed in an attribute payload protected by the IKE SA created in Phase I, and not exposed in the clear as it would normally be in an SA proposal/transform chain.

Life type, type 11, provides two simple values; and type 12, life duration, is the amount that represents the valued specified in life type:

seconds	1
kilobytes	2

Type 13, pseudo random function, is currently not used. IPSec and ISAKMP do not have a defined PRF, and the HMAC portion of the message authentication process is used as a PRF for IPSec and ISAKMP operations.

Key length is used to define a key length for an encryption algorithm that supports variable keys. This option is not used for encryption algorithms that have predefined key lengths.

The field size is for the Diffie-Hellman group. The group order defines the order of the elliptical curve group.

Phase II Attributes. IKE Phase II messages, such as Quick Mode, are used to define IPSec SAs and therefore have specific attributes for their creation within IKE. Within Phase II operations, there are SA payloads that contain proposals and transform sets for the creation of IPSec SAs that require different identifiers than those available to IKE Phase I and the creation of an IKE SA. A proposal will exist for each security protocol configured, and have associated transform payloads. In the proposal payload, the IPSec security protocol will be identified, and in the transform payload, the transform type will be defined.

An example is ESP with DES encryption and MD5 authentication in an IPSec VPN. The proposal will have the protocol ID set to IPSEC-ESP, a transform ID of ESP-DES, and an attribute payload that can define the remaining details of the SA, such as the HMAC-MD5 for message authentication. There are nine values available for use in Phase II messages for the creation of an IPSec SA.

SA Life Type	1
SA Life Duration	2
Group Description	3
Encapsulation Mode	4
Authentication Algorithm	5
Key Length	6
Key Rounds	7
Compress Dictionary Size	8
Compress Private Algorithm	9

SA Life Type and Duration are identical to Phase I Life Type and Duration for ISAKMP messages. These attributes define the time allotted for the created SA. At the expiration of the SA, all data associated with the SA must be discarded.

Note: The creation of key material for IPSec SAs is based on the key material created during Phase I of IKE if PFS is not configured. If PFS is employed, a new Diffie-Hellman exchange is activated in Quick Mode (Phase II) and allows the peers to share new Diffie-Hellman public values, resulting in new key material without using material from Phase I (SKEYID_d and _a). Once the new key material is created (KEYMAT) for IPSec, the resulting keys used for operations within IPSec will be discarded when the SA expires. In the event a new SA is created for continuing communications, it is afforded new keys created from the material previously agreed upon. Therefore, subsequent IPSec SAs that do not require a Quick Mode exchange that includes a Diffie-Hellman public value, as in the case a new SA is created to replace one that will expire shortly, do not maintain PFS between them.

The group description is to provide an opportunity to Phase II for the creation of a new Diffie-Hellman relationship. Perfect forward secrecy can be obtained by sharing new Diffie-Hellman parameters.

Encapsulation mode is where the security protocol is configured to operate in transport mode or tunnel mode.

Tunnel	1
Transport	2

The authentication is to for defining the message authentication protocol:

HMAC-MD5	1
HMAC-SHA	2
DES-MAC	3
KPDK	4

The next three available types, 6, 7, and 8, do not currently have values associated with them and are always set to 0 for IPSec implementations.

Finally, compress private algorithm is a custom algorithm that can be agreed upon by the participants. The first three octets will be the IEEE-assigned company ID, followed by the vendor-specific data.

Other Payloads

In the beginning of this section, it was stated that there are 13 payload types. The other five payloads are simply data with the generic header applied. The remaining payloads are:

- Key Exchange Data
- Hash Data
- Signature Data
- Nonce Data
- Vendor ID Data

The selected encryption algorithm defines the key exchange. The contents are algorithm specific and are defined in the corresponding encryption RFC specified for IPSec use.

The remaining payloads contain information specific to the time and type of negotiation being executed. The use and contents of each are defined in the IKE phase sections.

Note: A nonce is a pseudo-random number that is shared between IPSec VPN peers. Nonces are heavily used and included in much of the key generation process. The inclusion of random numbers is to ensure liveliness to the communication and assist in the protection against replay attacks. The nonces are also included in the generation of some key material and authentication processes. The use of nonces in these mechanisms provides proof to both peers of the participation of the other in the exchange.

Phase One

The security associations that protect ISAKMP messages are negotiated and created during Phase I exchanges. The Phase I process is responsible for three steps to create an SA for further ISAKMP messages for the creation of IPSec SAs. Phase I must negotiate protection suites to be used throughout the communication between the two systems. Diffie-Hellman properties must be exchanged during Phase I to foster the creation of keys for encryption and data authentication for the protected communications in the latter part of Phase I and Phase II operations. Finally, Phase I must provide for authentication of the remote system or user.

Phase I can accomplish the three steps in Main Mode, Aggressive Mode, or — currently being developed — Base Mode. The most widely accepted modes are the Main and Aggressive Mode because they are defined in the IKE and ISAKMP RFCs, while Base Mode exists currently in draft format. Base Mode will be introduced because it appears to have a great deal of momentum and is suggested throughout the IETF as an acceptable mode of operation.

The primary difference between the modes is the number of exchanges it takes to establish an SA. In Main Mode, there are six exchanges, while Aggressive Mode only requires three; Base Mode falls in the middle with four messages. Other subtle differences exist as well, such as the ability to negotiate that certain parameters are nonexistent in Aggressive Mode. An example of this limitation with Aggressive Mode compared to Main Mode is that the Diffie-Hellman parameters must be exchanged in the first message from the initiator. Therefore, the responder does not have the opportunity to negotiate which Diffie-Hellman group to use for the SA. Other parameters are constrained as well, depending on the type of authentication mechanism being employed. In some cases, the perceived limitations of Aggressive Mode are used to enhance and accelerate the SA creation. This aspect is most obvious in remote access solutions.

Main Mode

Main Mode uses six messages in three exchanges to create an SA. The steps typically start with SA negotiations, followed by Diffie-Hellman and nonce exchanges, and then the authentication of the peer.

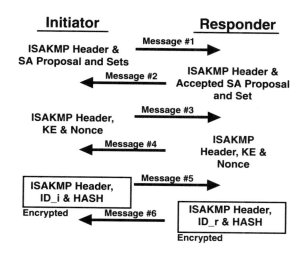

Exhibit 9-16. Main Mode with shared secret.

Pre-shared Keys/Secret. The use of a pre-shared secret for authentication requires that each system be configured with a password that is associated with the remote system's IP address being authenticated. The reader can step through each exchange detailed in Exhibit 9-16 to reveal the process.

First Exchange. The first exchange begins with a message from the initiator to the responder that contains an ISAKMP header and an SA header (see Exhibit 9-17). Contained within the SA header are the appropriate proposal and transform set payloads that present the security options to the responder. Included in the original message is a cookie from the initiator.

The second message is from the responder and contains an ISAKMP header and an SA header that contains a single proposal and transform set that will define the protection suite to be applied. Included is the responder's cookie.

At this point, each system has agreed upon the security suite that will be used to protect further communications and has exchanged cookies. The cookies reduce the ability for an attacker to introduce invalid packets into the negotiation of IKE.

Once the first exchange is complete, each system generates the public Diffie-Hellman values to be shared with the peer, based on the group defined in the agreed-upon proposal. After the first exchange, each system contains several pieces of information (see Exhibit 9-18), that can be used in the remaining exchanges, depending on the authentication type. Understanding the effect of the first exchange can be very

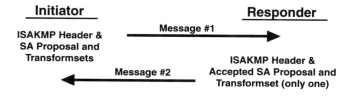

Exhibit 9-17. First exchange.

Exhibit 9-18.   What each system knows about the other after the first exchange.

Initiator/Responder
1 – Initiator's Cookie
2 – Responder's Cookie
3 – The proposed security suite
         (ESP-DES and ESP MD5-HMAC)

helpful because all Main Mode first exchanges, regardless of the authentication method, share the same information.

Second Exchange. The next portion of the communication allows the peers to share the Diffie-Hellman public values and a nonce, as shown in Exhibit 9-19. The nonce and cookies provide layers of protection and reassure that the peer in the communications is alive and actively participating, rather than just repeating previously collected messages or making bogus requests.

Once the public Diffie-Hellman values are shared and the second exchange is complete, each system processes the Diffie-Hellman value to create a primary key. Each system creates four keys:

1. SKEYID, the secret key upon which all subsequent keys are based. However, if PFS is enabled, this key is not used for the creation of future keys, and a new one is created for the generation of new Phase I and II keys.
2. SKEYID_d, used as keying material to create keys for SAs in Phase II operations (i.e., for IPSec)
3. SKEYID_a, the key used for data authentication and integrity
4. SKEYID_e, the key used to encrypt IKE messages

The root of the keys that are actually used in encryption and authentication are built from a primary key, SKEYID. The attributes used to create SKEYID are dependant on the authentication method being utilized. To build keying material, a pseudo-random function (prf) is employed with a key and various data that is combined to create a fixed value. This process should sound familiar from the cryptography chapter. A prf is a keyed hash function used to generate deterministic values that appear to be random, but are used for data validation. An example of the process is:

$$\text{Digest} = \text{prf (key/seed, data1 | data2 | data3)}$$

This section is detailing pre-shared secret authentication, and SKEYID is defined as:

$$\text{SKEYID} = \text{prf (pre-shared key, Nonce\_i | Nonce\_r)}$$

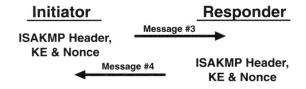

Exhibit 9-19.   Second exchange.

The HMAC function is used with the pre-shared secret as the key and the initiator's nonce combined with the responder's nonce to create the primary key. The HMAC is the pseudo-random function, unless a specific one is defined — currently, there are none for IPSec.

Note: The value followed by an _i or _r represents the initiator's or responder's value, respectively.

The SKEYID created for the other authentication processes will be introduced here to alleviate confusion, and re-introduced in the section that details the process for that particular key.

For digital signature-based authentication, the key is defined as follows:

$$\text{SKEYID = prf (Nonce\_i | Nonce\_r, DH\_key)}$$

For the SKEYID for digital signatures, the nonces are combined and used as the key in the message authentication process against the DH_key.

Note: The DH_key is the value derived from the Diffie-Hellman process and the result from sharing Diffie-Hellman public values. This value is not made public and is created independently by each peer using the public value provided by the other.

Next is the process to create the key for public key encryption authentication methods (standard and revised):

```
SKEYID = prf (HASH(Nonce_i | Nonce_r), Cookie_i | Cookie_r)
```

To create the primary keying material for public key encryption authentication, the nonces are combined and hashed, then used as the key for the message authentication function against the cookies.

The primary key is used in the creation of the three remaining keys as follows (same for all authentication types):

```
SKEYID_d = prf (SKEYID, DH_key | Cookie_i | Cookie_r | 0)
SKEYID_a = prf (SKEYID, SKEYID_d | DH_key | Cookie_i | Cookie_r | 1)
SKEYID_e = prf (SKEYID, SKEYID_a | DH_key | Cookie_i | Cookie_r | 2)
```

Note: The remaining three keys created with the use of the primary SKEYID are produced by the same method detailed, regardless of the authentication method selected or the exchange mode employed. That is, the keys SKEYID_x are created based on the SKEYID that may consist of different attributes, depending on the chosen authentication method.

At the completion of the second exchange, each system has enough information to begin encrypting communications (see Exhibit 9-20). It is necessary to realize that the keys to be used for encryption and authentication have been generated solely based on the peer's IP address. The Identification Payload provides options for authentication information exchange, such as IP address, mask, or fully qualified domain name. Unfortunately, the ID payload was not shared in the first or second exchange, which leaves only the IP address of the peer as a unique identifier. Some information about the peer must be used to align the peer to the shared secret in the database to include in the creation of the SKEYID.

Exhibit 9-20.   What each system knows about the other after the second exchange.

Initiator/Responder
1 – Initiator's cookie
2 – Responder's cookie
3 – The proposed security suite
        (ESP-DES and ESP MD5-HMAC)
**SKEYID, SKEYID_d,
SKEYID_a, SKEYID_e,
Nonce, and DH_Key**

What does this mean? Main Mode Phase I with pre-shared secret as the authentication process provides no identity protection and is completely based on the peer's IP address. This is an acknowledged limitation of Main Mode with pre-shared secrets, and for many situations it does not present a problem. However, in scenarios where the IP address is dynamic, the responder cannot maintain pre-shared secrets indexed by an IP address it does not know. Remote access solutions are an example where the initiator's IP address may be different for each connection. To accommodate these situations, Certificates can be used for remote access authentication. However, most remote access solutions available typically use Aggressive Mode because the ID payload is provided in the first exchange.

Third Exchange. The final exchange, as shown in Exhibit 9-21, consists of an ISAKMP header, ID payload, and a HASH payload to provide data origin authentication. The final exchange is encrypted with the SKEYID_e key.

The HASH combines several components that are already known by the peers and one that is provided in the fifth and sixth messages, the ID payload. The HASH consists of:

```
HASH = prf (SKEYID, Ya | Yb | Cookie_i | Cookie_r | SA offer | ID_i)
```

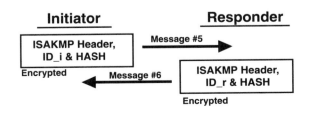

Exhibit 9-21.   Third exchange.

> *Note:* Yb and Ya are the public Diffie-Hellman values shared in the second exchange. The cookies and SA are from the first exchange. The ID payload included in the last exchange is included at the end. Also, the initiator's HASH (HASH_I) contains the initiator's cookie first and the ID payload created by the initiator (as shown). Whereas, the responder's HASH (HASH_r) creates a HASH with its cookie first and the ID payload it created for the third exchange. The attributes and their ordering are identical for other messages where noted.

Once the sixth message is received by the initiator, Phase II operations can commence.

Digital Signatures with Certificates. As described earlier, certificates are public keys typically signed by the issuer. Peers can be authenticated with public key signatures, either based on DSS or RSA standards. As shown in Exhibit 9-22, IKE provides a mechanism for sharing certificates between peers; however, the installation of the certificate in the client or SGW for use in the creation of a VPN is beyond the IPSec standards. The use of public key-based authentication, such as digital certificates and public key operations, requires that the system or user have the necessary keys used for the authentication. Ironically, this is exactly the same limitation that exists with shared secret authentication. The sharing or provisioning of the authentication properties (i.e., password, certificate, or key) is not part of the IPSec suite of protocols. In various communications within IKE, a certificate or public key can be communicated to the peer for authentication purposes, but the installation of that certificate in the system available for transmission is not considered within IPSec or IKE. In retrospect, this is viable and logical. There are other mechanisms being developed and available that provide for the implementation of public key operations — why complicate IPSec any further. PKI is a good example of certificate management and can be used to

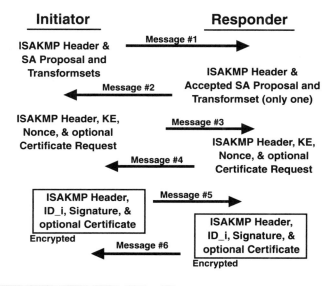

Exhibit 9-22. Main Mode with digital signature.

implement certificates into hosts, allowing those hosts to participate in a VPN authenticated with certificates.

For the purposes of IPSec and understanding the technology, it is best to assume the certificates and keys owned by the peers are installed and exist from pre-IPSec operations.

First Exchange. The first exchange begins with a message from the initiator to the responder that contains an ISAKMP header and an SA header. All Main Mode first and second messages are designed the same. The goal is to share cookie information and agree on a protection suite for the remainder of the IKE SA.

At this point, each system has agreed upon the security suite that will be used to protect further IKE communications and has exchanged cookies. Once the first exchange is complete, each system generates the public DH keys to be shared with the peer, based on the group defined in the agreed-upon proposal. Each system is aware of the security to be applied (see Exhibit 9-23).

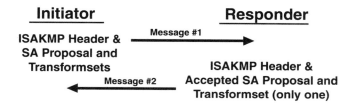

Exhibit 9-23.   First exchange.

Second Exchange. The next portion of the communication, shown in Exhibit 9-24, allows the peers to finally communicate the DH keys, a nonce, and optionally a certificate request can be included to obtain the peer's certificate.

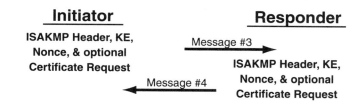

Exhibit 9-24.   Second exchange.

Once the DH keys are transmitted and the second exchange is complete, each system processes the Diffie-Hellman values to create the primary key and ultimately the three communication keys.

However, the root key for digital signature authentication utilizes different information:

$$\text{SKEYID} = \text{prf} \ (\text{Nonce\_i} \ | \ \text{Nonce\_r}, \ \text{DH\_Key})$$

Note: The initiator's nonce and the responder's nonce are combined and then used as the key in the pseudo-random function and applied to the Diffie-Hellman calculated key.

As with all other operations, the primary key is used to create the remaining three keys. The process for creating the three keys does not change and uses the same information regardless of the authentication or mode of the communication.

At the completion of the second exchange, each system has enough information to begin encrypting communications. One must realize that the keys to be used for encryption and message authentication have been generated solely based on the peer's nonce and Diffie-Hellman key value. For system authentication, a certificate request can be included to obtain the public key of the peer if the initiator does not already have it. The peer must have the other's public key to validate the signature and authenticate the peer in the third exchange.

Third Exchange. In Exhibit 9-25, the final exchange consists of several values that include an ISAKMP header, ID payload, a signed HASH payload to provide data origin authentication, and an optional certificate payload. The final exchange is encrypted with the SKEYID_e key.

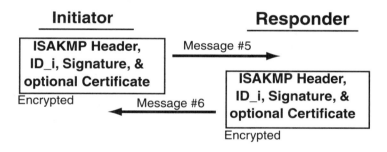

Exhibit 9-25. Third exchange.

The signed HASH combines several components that are the same for Main Mode with pre-shared secrets:

```
HASH = prf (SKEYID, Ya | Yb | Cookie_i | Cookie_r | SA offer | ID_i)
```

The HASH is then signed by the system with its private key and transmitted to the peer. If the peer had included a certificate request payload in the second exchange, the certificate would be included in the final exchange to allow the peer to validate the signature. Remember, the final exchange is encrypted and this provides for another level of protection in the exchange — identity protection.

The use of certificates provides for non-repudiation. If the two systems maintain the communication state during IKE Phase I operations, the peer would not be able to successfully deny that the communication took place.

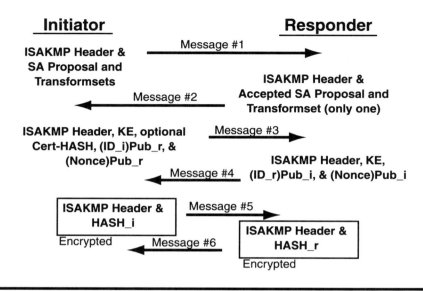

Exhibit 9-26. Main Mode with public key cryptography.

Public Key Encryption. Public key encryption authentication is a process whereby a system's public and private key are used to authenticate the communication. However, this process does not provide for non-repudiation. This limitation is due to not having a third-party trust, as with certificates, and is completely based on the possession of the private key. That is, anyone can obtain the peer's public key and encrypt the messages, resulting in that anyone can generate the messages with the publicly available key.

The nonces that are shared between the peers are encrypted using the other's public key. Upon receipt of the encrypted nonce, the peer can use its private key to decrypt the payload. The ability to decrypt the nonce with the private key provides proof that the peer has the necessary corresponding key, but does not provide irrefutable proof of the identity of the initiator because anyone can encrypt the data with the peer's public key. The authentication method is shown in Exhibit 9-26.

Within the exchange, the initiator has the option of sending a hash of the certificate from which the responder's public key was obtained. This certificate is provided to the responder to assist in the identification of the responder's private key.

There are actually two public key authentication processes that are defined in the RFCs. The original, which is being detailed here, requires two public key cryptic operations, whereas the "revised" edition only requires one, saving precious system cycles. Given that the standard method was defined some time ago, there are many systems in the field that employ it. Therefore, the replacement of the first public key authentication method with the revised edition was acceptable, so the revised process was simply added as another authentication option.

First Exchange. The first exchange begins with a message from the initiator to the responder that contains an ISAKMP header and an SA header. Once again, all Main Mode first and second messages are designed the same.

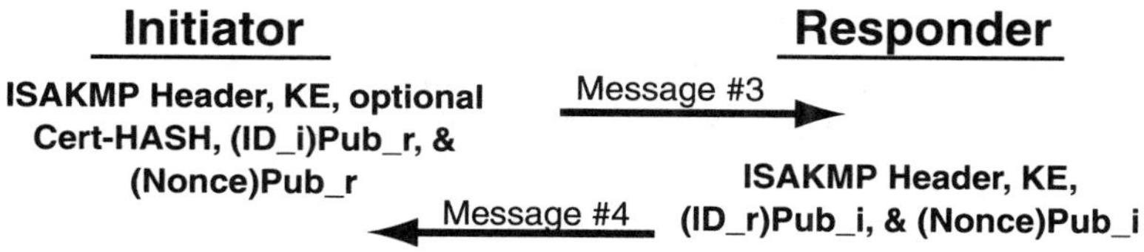

Initiator   ## Responder

ISAKMP Header, KE, optional   Message #3
Cert-HASH, (ID_i)Pub_r, &   ──────────▶
(Nonce)Pub_r   **ISAKMP Header, KE,**
                             Message #4   **(ID_r)Pub_i, & (Nonce)Pub_i**
                             ◀──────────

Exhibit 9-27. Second exchange

Second Exchange. The second exchange, in Exhibit 9-27, is where a great deal of information is processed and shared for authentication. Also, there are some optional payloads that can be included that depend on certain communication properties.

The third message uses the responder's public key to encrypt the initiator's ID payload and nonce. Of course, this can only be created if the initiator has the responder's public key, and vice versa. The method of obtaining the public key is not defined in the RFCs and must be provided by external means. This apparent limitation can be worked around in several methods. An example is remote access implementations where images or client packages are created that contain the responder's public key. Once installed, the client has the key necessary to complete the third message of the second exchange. The key that can be provided to the client can be in the form of a certificate, which can be hashed and provided by the initiator in the third message to allow further identification of the public key being used in the negotiation.

The encryption of the ID payload and the nonce represent the two-memory intensive encryption operations in dispute. These two areas, the inability of obtaining the public key of the peer within the negotiation and multiple encryption passes, are what were modified to create the revised version of public key encryption.

It is necessary to know that only the bodies of the ID and nonce payloads are encrypted. The generic headers remain in the clear to allow parsing of the data to properly decrypt.

As with the other two support authentication methods, the root key for public key cryptography authentication utilizes different information:

```
SKEYID = prf (HASH (Nonce_i | Nonce_r), Cookie_i | Cookie_r)
```

Note: The initiator's nonce and the responder's nonce are hashed, and the resulting digest is used as the key in the pseudo-random function that is applied to the cookies.

As with all other operations, the primary key is used to create the remaining three keys. Exhibit 9-28 shows that a great deal of information is available to each system after the second exchange.

The authentication process is primarily based on the peer's ability to decrypt the ID and nonce and includes the valid contents in the hash of the final exchange. This can be loosely compared to pre-shared secret authentication, in that pre-shared

Exhibit 9-28. What each system knows about the other after the second exchange.

Initiator/Responder

1 – Initiator's cookie

2 – Responder's cookie

3 – The proposed security suite
    (ESP-DES & ESP MD5-HMAC)

SKEYID, SKEYID_d,

SKEYID_a, SKEYID_e,

Nonce (after decryption),

ID payload (after decryption),

 and DH_Key

---

authentication is based on the ability of the peer to decrypt the data with a key generated with the correct password. Interestingly enough, with shared secret authentication, decryption is an issue with IKE and the inability to determine of the correct password until the data is being sent.

It is worth noting that the ID payload is encrypted and shared in the second exchange, allowing a great deal of control over whom the responder replies to. Various information contained within the ID payload can assist in further identifying the initiator prior to performing the two asymmetrical encryption processes.

Third Exchange. The final exchange contains an ISAKMP header and a HASH that is identical to the one used for the pre-shared secret authentication exchange. The final exchange, as shown in Exhibit 9-29, is encrypted with the SKEYID_e key.

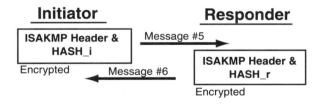

Exhibit 9-29. Third exchange.

Revised Public Key Encryption. The inability to share public keys or certificates in the original process and the multiple layers of encryption forced the production of a more efficient method of authentication using public key encryption, as shown in Exhibit 9-30.

The original process does not provide for the exchange of certificates or public keys. To exchange certificates without protection would eliminate the identity protection currently provided by IKE (in certain modes). Therefore, the initiator must know the identity of the responder prior to the initialization of the exchange. In many cases, this is not an issue; nevertheless, there is no provisioning for obtaining keying information within IKE. For a peer to obtain a key or certificate of a peer, some other

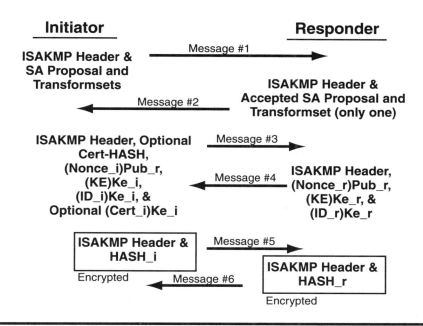

Exhibit 9-30. Main Mode with revised public key cryptography.

protocol must be supported, such as LDAP. However, in revised mode, the initiator has the option of sending its certificate to the responder, encrypted with the new symmetrical session key, which is new to the revised public key method.

The original process also requires two encryption steps: the ID and nonce payloads. Unfortunately, for the original method, there is no way around this limitation. Both must be encrypted and they cannot be combined in a single encryption process. To encrypt both the ID and nonce payload together, the generic header of the nonce would be unidentifiable, and therefore irreversible — remember, only the bodies are encrypted to allow parsing. To accommodate a single encryption process, several other properties would have to be calculated to determine and find the second generic header within the package, which would offset what cycles were saved by eliminating the load of the second encryption procedure in the first phase.

As mentioned, the revised version of public key encryption does not have the disadvantages of the original method. The revised method has half as many encryption processes and allows for the initiator to provide their certificate (public key). However, the initiator must still support some other protocol to obtain the responder's certificate. Once again, the ability of the initiator to obtain the responder's public key is beyond the scope of IPSec and IKE, but several other methods exist to accommodate the need. As mentioned before, with remote client access, the client system can be provided the responder's certificate at the install of the actual client software. This is an acceptable process for many companies because remote uses typically have their system brought in for maintenance and the installation of new packages.

First Exchange. The first exchange begins with a message from the initiator to the responder that contains an ISAKMP header and an SA header. Once again, all Main Mode first and second messages are designed the same.

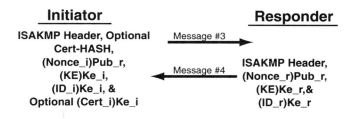

Exhibit 9-31.   Second exchange.

Second Exchange. The second exchange, as shown in Exhibit 9-31, can be a bit more complicated with various options. For starters, the nonce is encrypted with the peer's public key just as the original method.

However, the Diffie-Hellman calculated key value (KE) and the ID payload are encrypted with a newly created symmetrical key. Where did the symmetrical key come from? Much less, where did the algorithm become agreed? The algorithm used for the encryption is the one agreed upon in the SA proposal for IKE exchanges in the beginning of the negotiation. The symmetrical encryption process takes much less processing than the asymmetrical process; therefore, one can encrypt more data for authentication and protection by using a newly created symmetrical key based on the nonces. For the initiator, it uses data it has generated for the first exchange, the cookie and nonce.

$$Ne\_i = prf\ (\ Nonce\_i,\ Cookie\_i)$$

The responder creates a key in much the same way:

$$Ne\_r = prf\ (\ Nonce\_r,\ Cookie\_r)$$

When the responder uses its private key to decrypt the nonce it received from the initiator — which has been encrypted with the responder's public key — it can then use the initiator's nonce to derive the new revised mode key. In other words, the protection of the new key used to encrypt the ID, DH key, and optional certificate payloads rests on the shoulders of the public key encryption process that protects the nonce. Included in the responsibility of public key encryption is authentication; the fact that the peer can decrypt the message with the corresponding private key is proof of the system's identity. If an attacker obtained the nonce, which usually is in the clear along with the cookies, the creation of the key would be trivial and the authentication process would break down. Once the private key is used to obtain the nonce, the initiator's cookie is pulled from memory to create the Ke_x key, whichever is derived from Ne_x and required for the operation.

The Ke_x is created by employing a PRF against the Ne_x value as a seed with a hash value of 0. By using this method, if the Ne_x is not large enough to satisfy the encryption algorithm, several of these operations can be used to enlarge the key to satisfy the requirement of the selected algorithm.

For example, if the key is too small, the result of the primary hash is used with other hash functions to create a larger key by concatenating the results until the required size is achieved.

The following is used to create the Ke_x to be used in the encryption processes:

$$Ke\_x = prf\ (Ne\_x,\ 0)$$

In the event the key needs to be enlarged, the following process is implemented until the size key is met:

```
Ke_1 = prf (Ne_x, 0)
Ke_2 = prf (Ne_x, Ke_1)
Ke_3 = prf (Ne_x, Ke_2)
Ke_x = Ke_1 | Ke_2 | Ke_3 | Ke_n...
```

Note: The process is the same for the initiator as for the responder; therefore, the example does not expressly delineate between the two.

However, in the event that the Ke_x is too big for the selected algorithm, the most significant bits are taken from the Ne_x to create the KE_x of the desired length.

Another option available to the initiator is to provide its certificate to the responder in the third message, encrypted with the Ke_i key. By providing encryption services to the certificate, identity protection is realized. The inability of the initiator to send its certificate was another limitation of the original method. Even if the original method provided for the addition of a certificate payload, identity protection of the initiator would be lost.

Third Exchange. The final exchange contains an ISAKMP header and a HASH that is identical to the one used for the pre-shared secret authentication exchange. The final exchange is encrypted with the SKEYID_e key.

Aggressive Mode

The purpose of Aggressive Mode is the same as Main Mode; however, it completes the transaction in half the time taken by Main Mode. Although Aggressive Mode is a quicker process than Main Mode, the costs are in the inability to negotiate various options. Because more payloads are sent in the first two messages, each peer is committed to the contents and there is no mechanism for the selection or acknowledgment of certain parameters. As an example, the Diffie-Hellman public key is sent in the same message as the SA payload, which defines the DH group to be used — sort of the cart before the horse syndrome. However, once these limitations are known, the selection of Aggressive Mode versus Main Mode can be easier, for the most part.

Aggressive Mode was not designed for identity protection, which exists in Main Mode (except for Main mode shared secret) by the encryption of the ID payload. While the ID payload may be encrypted in Main Mode shared secret, the contents typically contain the data necessary to identify the shared secret — the IP address — that is known to the public. Aggressive Mode does not encrypt any ID payloads, and therefore the information is available to the public.

Although there appear to be several limitations to Aggressive Mode, there are many advantages as well. First, there are fewer message exchanges, resulting in less network overhead and quicker response. Given that half the messages are used for the negotiation of an IKE SA, forcing the ID payload into earlier messages unencrypted, the creation of the keying material can wait until the last authentication message is received. The final message can be encrypted because all the necessary information has been shared in the first two messages. Encrypting the last message is an optional execution; however, by waiting until the last message is sent, or received, prior to the creation of the keys, the peer can be fully identified, thus reducing the exposure to denial-of-service attacks.

Pre-shared Keys/Secret. Aggressive Mode sends much of the information required for the establishment of an IKE SA in the first messages, which include the ID payload (see Exhibit 9-32). By not providing identity protection, the ID payload can be sent in the clear, which can contain information to allow the responder to look up the password based on properties other than the initiator's IP address (e.g., username). For situations in which the initiator's IP address is not constant, such as remote user access, this provides a means for allowing identification. It is for this reason that Aggressive Mode is primarily used for remote access applications; Main Mode is rarely used for remote user support.

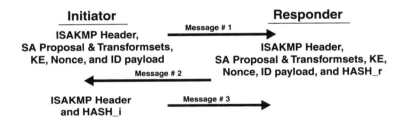

Exhibit 9-32.   Aggressive Mode with shared secret.

For some in the industry, the exposure of the ID payload represents insecurity to the protection of the session. The more information made available to an attacker, the more likely that individual will find enough of the remaining information to obtain unauthorized access. In Aggressive Mode, the ID payload can contain the fully qualified username, leaving only the password to be identified by an attacker. If the VPN gateway does not employ limited failed attempts, or an administrator has disabled it, it is only a matter of time before the attacker guesses the correct password.

To reduce the exposure of the user name in the ID payload — using the ID_USER_FQDN type, there is an identity type called ID_KEY_ID. The ID_KEY_ID, as defined by the IP Security Domain of Interpretation (RFC 2407) is an opaque byte stream that can be used to pass vendor-specific information necessary to identify which pre-shared secret should be used. This sounds a bit more complicated than it really is, and can best be explained, as with most things, with a picture (Exhibit 9-33).

A separate piece of information can be derived by the client package to further identify the individual or system requesting a VPN. Because this information is totally ambiguous, an attacker would have many more steps to derive information of any value.

Exhibit 9-33.   The use of ID_KEY_ID.

ID_KEY_ID	Real ID	Pre-shared Key
32srt33kutd234wqq	Phoenix Tiller	batman

The use of the ID_KEY_ID identifier can come in many forms because the RFC defines vendor specific information. The client package can ask for the username, HASH it, and forward it to the security gateway that performs the same function to identify the matching shared secret. Unfortunately, this requires that the security gateway hash every username, which not only consumes system resources, but many solutions use extended authentication resources, such as RADIUS and LDAP, removing the user database from the security gateway. In the event that RADIUS is being implemented, ID_KEY_ID can still be used to accommodate the overall authentication process. As the remote user connects, the client either asks for, or is configured with a group password or ID string that is passed to the security gateway. This allows the security gateway to determine the configuration associated with that group, a configuration that may include a RADIUS server. Subsequent messages may contain RADIUS challenges and responses to further authenticate the user. In practice, two activities are occurring simultaneously: an IKE SA is established by the use of the group ID to look up a shared secret, and as the IKE SA is being established, RADIUS information is exchanged to fully authenticate the user.

The use of Aggressive Mode is limited when compared to Main Mode, but can be very helpful in remote access solutions where the initiator's IP address is not known and pre-shared secrets are a desired form of authentication. Aggressive Mode is also helpful when the policy is known by the initiator before the communication is initiated; therefore, the power of Main Mode — the negotiation of policy — is not required.

Primary Exchange. As shown in Exhibit 9-34, the first two messages convey what is normally shared in a Main Mode exchange with four messages. At the end of the first exchange, each system has enough information to begin encrypting messages. As mentioned before, this is not required by the standards to reduce commitment of the peers in having to perform encryption and decryption prior to receiving the final hash from the initiator.

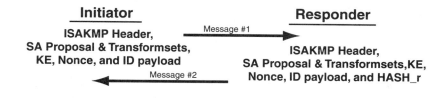

Exhibit 9-34.   Primary exchange.

Final Exchange. As shown in Exhibit 9-35, the final message completes the authentication with the inclusion of HASH_I from the initiator.

Exhibit 9-35.   Final exchange.

Digital Signatures with Certificates. As with Main Mode, Aggressive Mode provides a means of authentication with digital signatures (see Exhibit 9-36). However, with Aggressive Mode, the responder has the option of sending its certificate in the first reply message to the initiator. This technique assists in supporting early authentication.

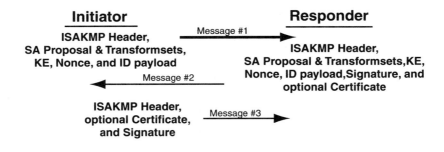

Exhibit 9-36. Aggressive Mode with digital signature.

Primary Exchange. As with the Main Mode, Aggressive Mode simply replaces the authenticator — a HASH — with a signature (see Exhibit 9-37).

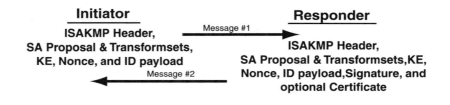

Exhibit 9-37. Primary exchange.

Final Exchange. The final exchange of Aggressive Mode is simply the header and the appropriate signature. Although the initiator has the option of sending its certificate, shown in Exhibit 9-38, the ISAKMP RFC 2408, upon which IKE is based, allows for the first message from the initiator to include the certificate payload as well.

Exhibit 9-38. Final exchange.

Public Key Encryption. As with Main Mode, Aggressive Mode provides a means of authentication with public key encryption (see Exhibit 9-39).

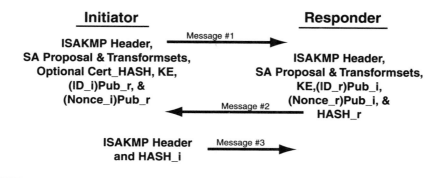

Exhibit 9-39.   Aggressive Mode with public key encryption.

Primary Exchange. The first two messages are nearly identical to Main Mode with public key encryption. However the first two Main Mode messages that contain the ISAKMP header and SA payload are included. As shown in Exhibit 9-40, the second message contains the HASH_r that is normally held to the last message of Main Mode.

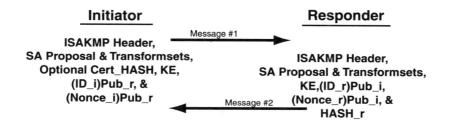

Exhibit 9-40.   Primary exchange.

Final Exchange. In the final message from the initiator (see Exhibit 9-41), the HASH_I is supplied to the responder.

Exhibit 9-41.   Final exchange.

Public Key Encryption Revised. As with Main Mode, Aggressive Mode provides a revised edition of public key encryption authentication (see Exhibit 9-42). The process of creating the new symmetrical keys in Aggressive Mode is identical to that in Main Mode. As with all Aggressive Mode messages, the ISAKMP header and SA payload are combined with messages that would typically be seen in the second exchange within Main Mode.

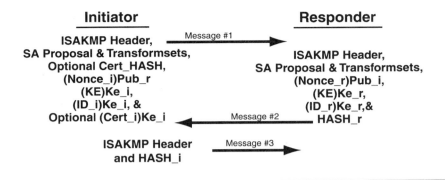

Exhibit 9-42. Aggressive Mode with revised public key encryption.

Base Mode

Base Mode is not an entirely new mode of operation within Phase I. The ISAKMP defines several exchanges that have been collected to create IKEs Main Mode and Aggressive Mode. Of the identified exchanges, there exist a Base Exchange designed to allow for the exchange of keying and authentication information to be transmitted together — sound familiar? The ISAKMP Base Exchange was slightly modified to allow several options to surface. By changing the HASH_i and HASH_r contents, depending on the authentication type being performed, the peers have the option of postponing the creation of the keys and the calculated Diffie-Hellman value. The reduction in processing requirements revolves around the responder because responders are the focal point for denial-of-service attacks. Base Mode provides a means of reducing the exposure to denial-of-service by limiting the processing of the responder until the final authentication message is received. Base Mode also provides another solution or remote access solutions because the ID payload is provided in the first message. However, unlike Aggressive Mode, many options are negotiable given the change to the HASH contents and what is included in the messages. In short, Base Mode attempts to provide protection against excessive processing, and reduce the number of messages while not losing negotiation capabilities.

The value HASH_I is redefined because the initiator must calculate it before receiving the Diffie-Hellman public value of the responder. HASH_I is calculated differently, depending on the selected authentication method.

For digital signatures:

```
HASH_I = prf ( hash (Nonce_i | Nonce_r), Ya | CKY-I | CKY-R |
  SA offer | ID_i | ID_r)
```

The nonces from each peer are hashed and used as the seed in the pseudo-random function employed to combine several attributes obtained during the exchanges. The Diffie-Hellman value from the initiator is represented by Ya, the cookies and ID payloads from each peer are included, and the SA offer is added to ensure SA alignment and identification.

A new HASH_I is defined for public key encryption and pre-shared keys:

```
HASH_I = prf ( SKEYID, Ya | CKY-I | CKY-R | SA offer | ID_i)
```

Notice that the SKEYID is used to create the HASH_I. This is desirable because the SKEYID for pre-shared secret and public key encryption authentication techniques does not include the calculated Diffie-Hellman value, reducing processing overhead. This is why the HASH_I had to be changed for digital signatures in Base Mode to eliminate the requirement of SKEYID — which includes the Diffie-Hellman calculated value. For this same reason, the HASH_R must be redefined for digital signatures to eliminate the use of SKEYID.

```
HASH_R = prf ( hash (Nonce_i | Nonce_r), Ya | Yb | CKY-R |
  CKY-I | SA offer | ID_r | ID_i)
```

With the changes to HASH_R for digital signatures, there is no need for the responder to calculate the Diffie-Hellman values, which also relieves the need to create the keys. The subsequent SKEYIDs (SKEYID_a, _d, and _e) can be created after the final authentication message is received from the initiator because none of the Phase I messages are encrypted.

Pre-shared Keys/Secret. As with all of Base Mode operations, the ID and nonce payloads are included in the first message. The sharing of the ID and nonce in the first exchange is much like Aggressive Mode; however, the option for negotiating the SA parameters is available (see Exhibit 9-43).

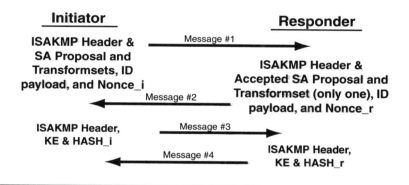

Exhibit 9-43. Base Mode with pre-shared secret.

The obvious advantage of Base Mode with pre-shared secrets over Main and Aggressive Modes is the ability to share identification information, such as ID_KEY_ID, while having the ability to negotiate the Diffie-Hellman group to be used. Given that the SKEYID and the new HASH_I do not include the calculated Diffie-Hellman parameters, the responder does not have to perform any costly operations prior to verifying the initiator's identity. Once the final packet is received from the initiator, the responder can confidently commit system resources in creating keying material.

Digital signature with Certificates. The digital signature (see Exhibit 9-44), as with the other modes of operation within Phase I, is the signing of the HASH payload. The removal of the Diffie-Hellman values from the creation of the HASH values relieves the responder from expensive processes.

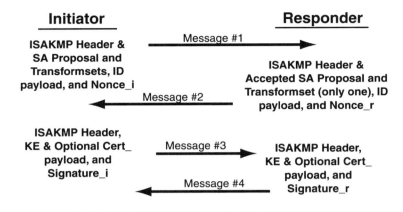

Exhibit 9-44.   Base Mode with digital signatures.

Public Key Encryption and Revised Public Key Encryption. Using public key authentication mechanisms (see Exhibit 9-45), the peer is authenticated by the ability to decrypt the nonce and produce the correct HASH value. As with other modes of operation, the public key encryption operation provides identity protection because the ID payload is encrypted. Once again, the peers are assumed to have the other's public key, which must be obtained through other protocols.

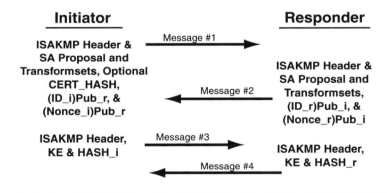

Exhibit 9-45.   Base Mode with public key encryption.

The use of only public keys does not provide for non-repudiation, and each part in the communication can successfully deny that the communication ever took place.

The standard mode of public key encryption uses two cycles of asymmetrical encryption with the peer's public key. As discussed previously, asymmetrical encryption is far more processor intensive than symmetrical encryption, such as DES. To reduce some of the overhead of the operation for the peers, especially the responder, the KE in the second exchange is not encrypted, as it is in the other two modes (see Exhibit 9-46).

In the revised mode of public key encryption, a new symmetrical key is created (identical process as in Main Mode) and used to encrypt the ID payload in the first exchange. Because both systems have reduced much of the public key encryption

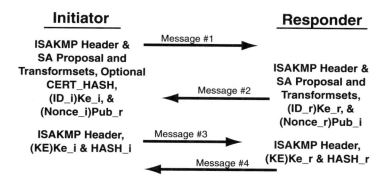

Exhibit 9-46. Base Mode with revised public key encryption.

process, the symmetrical key is used to protect the KE in the second exchange. This final operation comes at very small cost to performance, compared to public key computations, and the added security of protecting the KE is substantial. By protecting the Diffie-Hellman public value, there is a substantial reduction in man-in-the-middle attacks on the communication.

Phase Two

The security association created by Phase I operations is used to protect Phase II ISAKMP messages generated to create multiple SAs for a supported protocol — in this case, IPSec.

The second-phase operations are designed very similar to Phase I exchanges and modes. However, less emphasis is placed on authentication, given that the messages are being shared by way of an authenticated IKE SA. There are two primary types of modes used within Phase II operations to create SAs for IPSec. These SAs are constructed and implemented using the security protocols ESP and AH. How the security protocols are implemented, whether in tunnel or transport mode, combined or nested, is dependant on the VPN requirements and the policy defined by the administrator. During the first phase of IKE, ISAKMP was used as a message foundation to create exchanges to create a single security association, a relationship of policies and protection suites to allow further communications to exist in a protected state. Phase II of IKE employs the message structure of ISAKMP to provide keying material and characteristics for actual IPSec VPNs.

Quick Mode

Quick Mode is designed only for Phase II and does not exist in any Phase I operations because all data passed must be under the protection of an IKE SA. The SKEYID_a generated in the first phase — that is, linked to the primary SKEYID — is used to authenticate all Quick Mode messages, and SKEYID_e is used to encrypt them. It is this aspect of using keys created from material presented in the first phase that defines what is meant by the "protection" of the IKE SA created in Phase I. Phase II will be completely exposed to the attacker of the first phase, if successful in breaking the first phase.

Quick Mode is responsible of implementing the security suite defined in the first messages of Phase I — no matter the mode. The ISAKMP header and accompanying SA payload were used to agree on a set of protection details — a transformset. Those agreed-upon attributes were not only used in Phase I, but are also used for Quick Mode; therefore, the authentication and encryption algorithms selected will be used for Phase II. The Quick Mode messages are protected by key material and protection suites defined in Phase I, but are used to define keying material and protection suites for IPSec security protocols.

Quick Mode provides a mechanism of creating SAs for the protection of IPSec policy-specific information. As discussed earlier, an IPSec policy may state that traffic of a certain type must be protected with 3DES encryption and SHA authentication, while all other data is afforded only DES encryption. To accomplish this requirement, multiple SAs must be created; therefore, Quick Mode will negotiate new SAs on behalf of the IPSec policy. In the previous example, a minimum of four SAs will be created, and each SA must have an inbound SA and an outbound SA. To ensure that valid SAs are established and new keying material is protected, nonces are employed once again to make certain of communication liveliness and participation in the exchange.

Because multiple Quick Mode exchanges can be performed simultaneously, the message ID in the ISAKMP header is used to provide multiplexing of Quick Mode messages. Each ISAKMP header's ID is used to identify the associated Quick Mode negotiation, and the cookies of the header are used to identify the state of the messages. Several other aspects of Quick Mode rely on Phase I attributes. Another example is that the ID of the peer in Quick Mode is assumed to be the IP address of the Phase I peers; this is an obvious assumption because all Quick Mode messages are protected by keys created by these two peers. However, IKE is not that limited and offers client ID payloads, which are nothing more than ID payloads optionally passed between the peers. Interestingly enough, the ID payloads are not to provide extended authentication information, such FQDM, in Phase I. The client IDs are used to provide selector information used by the SPD and SAD within IPSec. This option can be used to enhance filtering capabilities and application of the security suites defined in the policy of the security gateways.

Selector information is passed in the form of the client ID payload in the same messages that contain the SA offer payloads. By combining the SA offers with the selector information, the assignment of the communication policy is achieved. The responder can look up the information in its own SPD and verify that the SA being negotiated is an appropriate and accepted form of communication based on the configured policy. If the SPD verification tests are successful, in that the communication request is valid when referenced to the policy, the message ID payloads and accepted proposal must be provided to the SAD. From that point forward, the SAD and SPD will ensure that the traffic identified by the message ID will flow only over the configured SA — and only allow specified traffic defined by the selectors identified in the ID payload.

Along with the optional use of client ID payloads, the peers have the option to employ PFS. If this is implemented due to a policy requirement, the Diffie-Hellman public values must be shared. While this is an optional negotiation, most systems support PFS because it is a stated requirement to support in the RFCs.

Primary Exchanges. A primary example of a Quick Mode exchange is shown in Exhibit 9-47. Remember that all the messages are encrypted and authenticated using SKEYID_e and SKEYID_a, respectively.

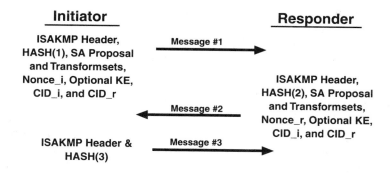

Exhibit 9-47. Quick Mode with optional KE payload and client ID payloads.

One may notice that there are some identifiers associated with the HASH payloads. Each message contains different properties to be included in the HASH that are dependant on what options are selected for use. An example of needing different HASH contents is the implementation PFS and the inclusion of the KE in the message. Also, if more than one SA must be created, an added SA payload can be included. Therefore, for each SA payload, two IPSec SAs will be created, based on the properties negotiated in the original SA payloads in Quick Mode.

Next is an explanation of the different HASH payloads; options are shown in "( )".

```
HASH(1)—prf ( SKEYID_a, M-ID | SA offer | Nonce_I | (KE) |
  (CID_I) | (CID_r))
```

The contents of HASH(1) are exactly as they appear in the message. Simply put, HASH(1) is the hash of the entire message.

```
HASH(2)—prf ( SKEYID_a, M-ID | Nonce_I | SA offer | Nonce_r |
  (KE) | (CID_I) | (CID_r))
```

Much like HASH(1), HASH(2) covers the entire contents of the message; however, the nonce of the initiator is included.

```
HASH(3)-prf ( SKEYID_a, 0 | M-ID | Nonce_I | Nonce_r)
```

The third type of HASH includes only the nonces and the message ID. This is to ensure liveliness of the communication prior to commencement of IPSec traffic. Without proof of participation by the peer, an attacker could use previously obtained packets identified as Quick Mode and replay them, consuming resources of the responder — ultimately a denial-of-service attack.

The "M-ID" is the message ID from the ISAKMP header that identifies the Quick mode exchange for that particular set of SAs. As with Phase I, the KE is the Diffie-Hellman public key used by the peers to create a symmetrical key for encryption in the security protocols of IPSec. The CID_I and CID_r are the client ID payloads, respectively. Notice the use of SKEYID_a as the seed in the HASH, as described earlier this key was designed for authentication of data.

Extended Exchanges. There is another option available to the peers in Quick Mode — the commit bit. The commit bit resides in the ISAKMP header and is to allow the responder to notify the initiator to extend the Quick Mode exchange by one message to postpone the ensuing transmittal of IPSec traffic by the initiator. If the commit bit is set, it is proper protocol that the initiator acknowledge the setting of the bit by reflecting it back to the responder in the form of setting the commit bit in the responder's ISAKMP header. Once the responder has been assured that the initiator is aware of a fourth message, it can compute the necessary keys and options — and then send the final messages stating it is ready for input from the initiator.

Once the initiator receives the first message from the responder, it has enough information to begin transmitting IPSec traffic. Although the initiator is bound by protocol to send the final third message containing the HASH payload, this does not necessarily mean that the third message will reach the responder before IPSec packets. A good example is that some systems are designed with quality of service and may place a higher priority on protocol 50 and 51 rather than on UDP 500; that is, IPSec traffic will get forwarded much faster than IKE traffic. This situation will result in the responder getting hit with IPSec traffic immediately after receiving the final message from the initiator or — a worse scenario — receive encrypted information before the final packet from the initiator. What if the responder is not ready for such traffic? The power of the communication is completely placed in the hands of the initiator — it can wait as long as it needs to in preparation of IPSec packets, whereas the responder is at the mercy of the initiator.

The use of the commit bit can seem peculiar at times; one would imagine that once the SA is established, data should commence. However, this is not always the case with many systems providing service. For example, it is Monday morning and 300 remote users are dialing in, attempting to create a VPN with the home office at 8:00 a.m. sharp. To reduce the amount of cache required to hold incoming IPSec packets, the responder can simply say, "Wait a second…OK, I'm ready, start sending." In times of heavy load or limited cache, the commit bit can be used to postpone the IPSec traffic that would normally follow the third message from the initiator. In any case, the responder may not have all the keys created or have the virtual interface up to accommodate the incoming traffic.

As shown in Exhibit 9-48, the commit bit forces another message to be sent to the initiator. In this example, the responder is setting the bit. The final notify payload is authenticated with another new HASH to accommodate the notification. The notification is type CONNECTED, which is the value of 16384. This notifies the initiator that IPSec transmissions can be sent.

As shown in Exhibit 9-48, there is a new authenticator, HASH(4), which is defined as:

$$\text{HASH(4)}-\text{prf (SKEYID\_a, M-ID | Notify)}$$

The CONNECT notification is included in the HASH so that it can be authenticated by the initiator. The inclusion of the message ID provides the initiator with the ability to identify which Quick Mode operation is going to be started.

Key Material. In Phase I, SKEYID_d was created to accommodate keys for non-IKE operations in Phase II. The creation of key material for the IPSec SAs is based on several components obtained in the first two phases. In Quick Mode, a single SA is negotiated and results in two SAs — one for each direction of communication — that have unique SPIs, which results in unique keys for each SA.

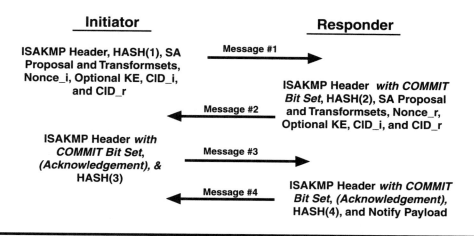

Exhibit 9-48. Quick Mode with the commit bit set.

The information used to create the IPSec keys is dependent on the options used in the original Quick Mode exchange, specifically PFS. If PFS is configured, the KE values must be shared between the two peers and included in the first two messages of Quick Mode. Therefore, the addition, or the lack of a Diffie-Hellman public key will determine the key created. Given that PFS is not required to be implemented, but is required to be supported, the default is to create a key without KE included, as follows:

```
KEY = prf (SKEYID_d, protocol | SPI | Nonce_i | Nonce_r)
```

Notice the use of SKEYID_d. This was created during Phase I to provide keying material for non-IKE protocols; hence, it is now used to build the key for IPSec SAs.

If PFS is configured, then the KE has been shared from one device to the other. It will now be necessary for each peer to calculate the Diffie-Hellman key specific to the Quick Mode operations (the second one, the first being created for IKE Phase I) and include it with the previous attributes for the IPSec KEY.

```
KEY = prf (SKEYID_d, DH_key(QM) | protocol | SPI | Nonce_i | Nonce_r)
```

Note: In phase I of IKE, the KE had to be shared to create the Diffie-Hellman calculated key to derive keying material for other operations. One of the keying materials created was SKEYID_d, the material used for the generation of IPSec keys. If PFS is not configured, then a second round of Diffie-Hellman will not be performed; hence, ALL IPSec keys created will be easily reproduced by an attacker of SKEYID_d were to be obtained. SKEYID_d will remain valid until the IKE SA is broken down and recreated; for most implementations, the lifespan can be as long as a week. And for manual key management, the key is valid until an administrator configures a new one. Implementing PFS breaks the link between the Phase I keying material and Phase II keying material.

The protocol and the SPI are from the negotiated ISAKMP SA proposals from the first two Quick Mode messages.

During ISAKMP, the initiator provides one or more proposals with accompanying transformsets. However, the responder must only select one of the proposals from the initiator. Therefore, each proposal is assigned a single SPI and protocol, allowing the key to be eternally linked to the SA for which it was created. As each SA is created (determined by when the key is calculated), each peer determines the SPI for its inbound SA, resulting in two negotiated SPIs and the ability of each peer to create the keys necessary for security operations for both SAs.

One last aspect of Quick Mode is that the initiator is not necessarily the initiator of the Phase I operation (i.e., Main Mode). As mentioned earlier, the IKE SA is bi-directional and a single SA will accommodate information flow in both directions. Therefore, either peer can initiate a Quick Mode exchange, regardless of which peer initiated the Main Mode (or Aggressive Mode) exchange. In the event that the responder of Main Mode becomes the initiator of a Quick Mode exchange, the roles are reversed during Phase II but the specific role information from Phase I remains. In Phase I, the IKE SA is identified by the cookies — in order from initiator to responder. To provide communications in Quick Mode the IKE SA is identified by the cookies in that order regardless of who is the Phase II initiator. Exhibit 9-49 details the use of cookies when the role of the system changes from Main Mode to Quick Mode, but the cookies from Main Mode remain unchanged to continue to identify the IKE SA.

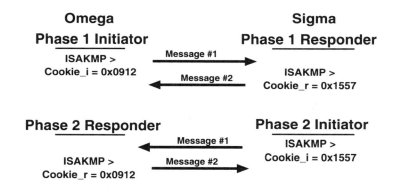

Exhibit 9-49.   Quick Mode with Main/Aggressive Mode cookies.

Initialization Vectors (IVs) in Quick Mode. As the number of keys increases and the protection of one phase is provided by another, the process of handling initialization vectors for the encryption and decryption processes becomes increasingly complicated. For IKE to accommodate the multiplexing of Quick Mode exchanges, each exchange maintains its own message ID. The message ID is also used to maintain coordination of IV while under the protection of a single IKE SA — hence, a single set of keys. The single set of keys created in Phase I is used to protect Quick Mode messages by encrypting them. As each message is encrypted and overlaid by other Quick Mode messages, the IV must be identified to ensure that the two peers remain synchronized to encrypt and decrypt messages associated with the same Quick Mode exchange.

Each Quick Mode exchange begins with an IV based on the final ciphertext block from the final Phase I message that was encrypted and the message ID of the Quick Mode exchange.

Note: If the messages from Phase I were not encrypted, as with Aggressive Mode, the IV calculated for Phase I operations is used for Phase II. Remember that the Phase I IV is calculated from the HASH of the initiator and responder's Diffie-Hellman public value — KE — obtained early in the Phase I exchange.

From this point forward, the IV is determined much like that of Phase I, each message's IV is the last block of cyphertext of the previous encrypted message. Once the Quick Mode exchange is complete, all the state information, such as the nonces, DH_key, KE, IV, can be discarded. The state information from Phase I must be maintained to protect future Quick Mode exchanges, until a re-keying process is started.

Other Phase Exchanges

All the modes and exchanges explained thus far have been concerned with identification, authentication, and the negotiation of security protocols for the protection of IKE messages and IPSec communications. However, once IPSec operations are functioning and Quick Mode operations have completed, the IKE SA is not utilized for transmitting any more data. During the writing of this book, Cisco routers were used to obtain interesting log information for various discussions. However, to get IKE debugging information (when wanted, read: no waiting) this author would reload the far-end router and watch the debug on the near router as the other came back online. Albeit inefficient, it was highly effective in getting the material. But it proved a point: once the IKE SA was established and Quick Mode was complete, very little traffic utilized the SA. To leverage the IKE SA, other exchanges were designed to accommodate messages that designed to support the SAs.

New Group Mode

New Group Mode was designed to allow IKE peers to renegotiate the Diffie-Hellman group established in Phase I. The exchange is based on a request and response process, much like other negotiations that use the SA payload. The initiator provides one or more requests to use a "new group" of Diffie-Hellman parameters, and the responder replies with the acceptable version.

Depending on the policy defined by the administrator, the responder will have to ensure the strength of the new request prior to agreement. If in fact the responder determines the request unacceptable, it must reply with a notification payload with the type of 13, ATTRIBUTE-NOT-SUPPORTED.

There are two examples of wanting to redefine the group to use. If Aggressive Mode was used, there was no opportunity to agree on a group to use and a New Group exchange can be used to re-establish the desired group. Another example is that the details and idiosyncrasies of the Diffie-Hellman can be passed protected and not in the clear as with Main and Aggressive Modes. In Phase I modes, the specifics of Diffie-Hellman can be conveyed in the SA proposal, such as generators, curve groups, and other details required; however, they are in the clear. If group specifics must be conveyed, they can be transmitted under the protection of the IKE SA, and only the identifier of the group need be communicated in the Phase I operations.

In Exhibit 9-50, the New Group exchange is comprised of the standard ISAKMP header, custom HASH, and an SA payload, containing details about the Diffie-Hellman group.

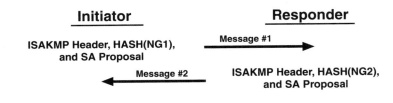

Exhibit 9-50.   New Group exchange within phase II.

The hashes included in the messages are nearly identical; a closer look may reveal that they basically exactly the same, when the rules of the protocol are applied. Essentially, the protocol states that a single proposal will be selected and returned. The hashes are constructed on the protocol concept; however, the initiator's HASH includes the entire SA (header, body, and proposal), whereas the responder's is simply the standard reply to an SA proposal.

```
HASH(NG1) = prf ( SKEYID_a, Message ID | Entire SA proposal,
   header and payload)
HASH(NG2) = prf ( SKEYID_a, Message ID | SA reply)
```

Notice the use of SKEYID_a, as described earlier. This key is generated in Phase I for the authentication of all IKE exchanges. SKEYID_e is used to encrypt all the messages, as with Quick Mode in Phase II. Although New Group is an exchange that can only happen after Phase I, an established IKE SA must exist between the peers, and it is not considered a Phase II exchange. Phase II is designed for the creation of further SAs for the underlying protocols, New Group is provided to augment the IKE process and not create SAs. The reasoning for employing the New Group Mode only after an IKE SA is established and can provide protection, is that the data can be very sensitive. An attacker can use the information within to learn more about the process and possibly employ a man-in-the-middle attack against the Diffie-Hellman process.

Notification Exchanges

As mentioned before, the IKE SA remains in place although IPSec may no longer be utilizing it, at least for a period of time. During this dormant time, IKE provides an "out-of-band"-like communication between the peers for various information exchange issues. The author uses the term "out-of-band" because the IPSec traffic is unaffected and is not aware of the exchanges. The messages shared are between the two primary IKE peers, which can be gateways supporting IPSec traffic between their respective networks.

Notification exchanges convey information between all the IKE peers regarding the status of the SA(s) or any errors that need to be addressed. To accommodate this, there are two exchange formats: unacknowledged and acknowledged. Unacknowledged is an unreliable message to the peer, whereas the second form of message must be acknowledged by the recipient.

These messages are very similar to other exchanges executed after Phase I and with an IKE SA. Each message is assigned a message ID to allow multiplexing of exchanges within on IKE SA. Also, the encryption is provided by SKEYID_e created in Phase I, and all authentication (i.e., HASH calculations) will be based on SKEYID_a. Once again, as with Quick Mode and other exchanges encrypted within the IKE SA, the IV is generated from the message ID and final block of the last encrypted Phase I message. If Phase I was not encrypted, the IV calculated for Phase I is used.

The unacknowledged informational exchange from the initiator contains an ISAKMP header, a HASH, and one or more notification payloads, which can be a notification payload or a delete payload. The HASH is calculated over the message ID and the payloads, using SKEYID_a as the key in the HMAC function.

An acknowledged exchange, of course, requires a message from the responder notifying the initiator of receipt of the message. The use of this type of message stems from the unreliability of ISAKMP. ISAKMP headers are marked as UDP 500 and all state information is only ensured by the peers. Therefore, if a critical message is sent, an acknowledgment exchange should be employed to allow verification of the message. An example is when an SA is deleted, a message is sent to the peer. Without an acknowledged exchange, the initiator would assume the responder received the message to delete, although the contrary is true and the responder continues to use the SA in vain.

As in Exhibit 9-51, the message from the initiator contains a nonce and a notification or delete payload. The responder's message contains a nonce and the original payload unmodified. Each message contains a special HASH that represents the information contained within the message and the state of the exchange. The initiator's HASH is as follows:

```
HASH(AK1) = prf ( SKEYID_a, Message ID | Nonce_i | Payload)
```

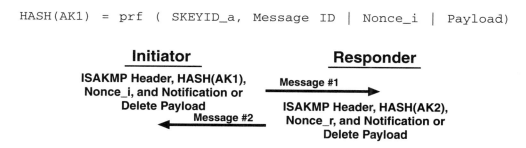

Exhibit 9-51. Acknowledged exchange.

The nonce is used to provide the responder with random information as fodder for a reflection to prove participation. The message ID is included to ensure that the proper exchange is being conveyed. This also allows for authentication of the ISAKMP header, which contains the ID field. Once again, SKEYID_a is being utilized for authentication processes.

```
HASH(AK2) = prf ( SKEYID_a, Nonce_i | Message ID | Nonce_r | Payload)
```

For the responder, the HASH is much the same, with the inclusion of their nonce in the attributes. The responder must not change the payloads sent by the initiator. To do so would disrupt the message authentication process, resulting in either an error exchange or a retransmission of the acknowledge notification. It is details such as these that have caused problems in interoperability. In the event the initiator and responder do not agree on the protocol concerning notification payloads, as an example, the entire communication will fail.

Chapter 10

IKE in Action

This chapter analyzes the interaction between two security gateways. Cisco's IPSec solution provides a good medium for dissecting the communication setup, process, and completion. Cisco has a debugging feature that one can take advantage of and watch some basic aspects of the VPN.

The setup is two routers, R1 and R2, connected via Ethernet cables and the employment of a simple hub. Each router has an Ethernet interface on the same network that the VPN is to be established.

In no way is this book endorsing Cisco or stating that the final VPN provided by a Cisco solution is superior to other products mentioned or available. However, the availability of the routers, the simplicity of the VPN, and the ease of setup compared to the detailed output provided was unattainable elsewhere.

Router 1 Configuration

Much of the configuration of the routers (see Exhibit 10-1) has been removed for simplicity's sake. However, much is left intact to understand placement within the configuration. Areas of interest are in **bold** and detailed at the end of the configuration.

Crypto is the Cisco command for interfacing with the IPSec subcommands. Just as IP can be used to configure many of the IP-related options within a Cisco router, Crypto is the IPSec interface (all the commands were entered in enable mode).

Explanation of the R1 Configuration

```
crypto isakmp policy 1

    authentication pre-share
```

The first line in this section defines a key management policy of "1." The only portion that one must define for the policy is the type of authentication for IKE. In this example, pre-shared secret is going to be used. Within this section, an administrator can define lifetime, DH groups, and other aspects; for our purposes, we'll use the defaults. It is possible to create several policies to accommodate different key management and authentication techniques, depending on the desired VPN.

```
crypto isakmp key MY-SHARED-SECRET address 10.1.1.1
```

Having stated that one wants to use a pre-shared secret for key management, one must define it and associate it with the proposed peer. Therefore, this command states that the **authentication** key is "MY-SHARED-SECRET" and the only remote system that can present this password is system 10.1.1.1 (R2). It is crucial to understand that the term "key" is misleading. This is not the key that will be used for encryption or data authentication processes. It will be used in the creation of the keys, but is not the key itself. The IP address used to associate the key to the peer must be the Internet routable IP address that is the final access point to the Internet of the peer. At first, this statement seems obvious; however, in some complicated configurations with the combination of IPSec and other tunneling protocols (i.e., L2TP) controlled by tunnel and loopback interfaces, the combination of addresses can become complex. When confronted with the question of which IP address to use to assign the shared secret, it must be the IP address that provides the Internet connectivity.

```
crypto ipsec transform-set SECURITY-SET esp-des esp-md5-hmac
```

This line is another addition to the system's SPD definition. As mentioned previously, the transform set defines the security protocols, encryption to be used (if ESP is

Exhibit 10-1. Router 1 configuration.

```
Current configuration:
!
version 12.0
!
hostname R1
!
!
ip subnet-zero
!
!
crypto isakmp policy 1
 authentication pre-share
crypto isakmp key MY-SHARED-SECRET address 10.1.1.1
!
!
crypto ipsec transform-set SECURITY-SET esp-des esp-md5-hmac
!
!
crypto map VPN-TO-R2 1 ipsec-isakmp
 set peer 10.1.1.1
 set transform-set SECURITY-SET
 match address 101
!
!
!
interface Ethernet0
 ip address 10.4.13.5 255.255.255.0
 no ip directed-broadcast
 media-type 10BaseT
!
!
interface Ethernet1
 ip address 10.1.1.2 255.255.255.0
 no ip directed-broadcast
 media-type 10BaseT
 crypto map VPN-TO-R2
!
!
!
no ip classless
no ip http server
!
access-list 101 permit ip 10.4.13.0 0.0.0.255 10.71.1.0 0.0.0.255
!
!
line con 0
 transport input none
```

(continues)

Exhibit 10-1.   Router 1 configuration. (continued)

```
line aux 0
line vty 0 4
 privilege level 15
 no login
!
end
```

utilized), and the authentication properties. What is not seen is the type command. The type of the VPN is tunnel mode, Cisco does not present this information because it is default. The transform set for the VPN is called "SECURITY-SET"; it is necessary to have several sets and associate them in various orders to different IKE policies.

```
crypto map VPN-TO-R2 1 ipsec-isakmp
     set peer 10.1.1.1
     set transform-set SECURITY-SET
     match address 101
```

This section is reminiscent of the mapping process discussed in previous sections. A map command is used as a linking process to associate the parts into a whole that can be used for a VPN. The map, called "VPN-TO-R2," will use policy "1" for use with IPSec and ISAKMP operations. Several policies can be defined and used in combination to accommodate various levels of protection for a single interface.

The "SET PEER" command completes the association with the regard to the map. It is necessary to provide a distinction between the map's peer and the ISAKMP shared secret association. With standard tunnels, such as GRE tunnels, the IP address that can be utilized is not necessarily the one that identifies the remote system, but rather a network or virtual address, such as a loopback address.

Of course, one must associate the transform set created, and finally the restrictions to the map. Access control lists (ACLs) are typically associated with limiting or controlling data flow. For Cisco IPSec policies, access control lists are not used within the VPN configuration to only define the permissible interaction between the gateways, but also provide a method for identifying interesting traffic. This allows the router to forward data based on information in the ACL. All the specifics of the VPN, IKE policy, IPSec operational attributes, and peer data are colledted into a map and finally associated with an interface that completes the mapping (location discovery) process.

```
access-list 101 permit ip 10.4.13.0 0.0.0.255 10.71.1.0 0.0.0.255
```

A number, in this example 101, identifies the ACL. However, in a real implementation, an administrator may want to consider the use of more flexible ***named*** ACLs. The ACL in the example is very simple; it allows all IP traffic between the two systems. In short, traffic that matches the ACL is identified to have IPSec applied. The ACL does not exist to restrict traffic and this can cause confusion. To restrict traffic, an ACL must be applied to the interface itself. An ACL associated with a map — that is, assigned to an interface — is only used to determine sessions that must be afforded the protection of IPSec. When implementing and testing the ACL to determine that the proper traffic is being matched to the ACL, the "show access-list" command will provide a "matched" column that will display the number of packets that the ACL has identified as interesting.

```
R1#sh access-lists
Extended IP access list 101
    permit ip 10.4.13.0 0.0.0.255 10.71.1.0 0.0.0.255
(64 matches)
```

In this example, it is worth noting that the IP address of the Ethernet 0 interface is entered in the ACL, forcing all IP traffic to have IPSec applied to data originating from the Ethernet 0. The flexibility of IPSec is most evident in this simple example. In the event there are several internal interfaces, not only can maps be constructed to provide various levels of encryption and authentication then assigned to interfaces, but ACLs can be constructed to identify specific information to have the different levels of protection applied. The ACL provides the culmination between the protection suite and the data that it is responsible for protecting.

In this example, much has been discussed using Cisco as a model, but there are many other solutions that accomplish the exact same functionality — in some cases, less complicated.

```
interface Ethernet1
    ip address 10.1.1.2 255.255.255.0
    no ip directed-broadcast
    media-type 10BaseT
    crypto map VPN-TO-R2
```

Finally, the configuration comes together at the interface level. In this example, Ethernet interface 1 is assigned the appropriate IP address and map. The assignment of the map not only provides an SGW discovery mechanism, but the map links back to all the independent desirable configurations. The map is the SPD for that interface. It is quite interesting to see the creation of the SPD so clearly and its relationship to an interface. The previously defined options (i.e., transform set and ISAKMP policy) come together at the interface by means of the map.

Router 2 Configuration

The configuration of the second router is nearly identical to the first (see Exhibit 10-2). However, seeing the configuration will assist in the understanding of what is actually happening. Once again, the interesting parts are in **bold** and much of the extraneous information has been removed.

Explanation of the R2 Configuration

```
crypto isakmp policy 1
    authentication pre-share
```

A policy of "1" is defined in the second router as well as in the first. The policy number is irrelevant to the VPN to be established. All that matters is that a policy

Exhibit 10-2. Router 2 configuration.

```
Current configuration:
!
version 12.0
!
hostname R2
!
ip subnet-zero
!
!
crypto isakmp policy 1
 authentication pre-share
crypto isakmp key MY-SHARED-SECRET address 10.1.1.2
!
!
crypto ipsec transform-set SECURITY-SET esp-des esp-md5-hmac
!
!
crypto map VPN-TO-R1 1 ipsec-isakmp
 set peer 10.1.1.2
 set transform-set SECURITY-SET
 match address 101
!
!
!
interface Ethernet0
 ip address 10.1.1.1 255.255.255.0
 no ip directed-broadcast
 crypto map VPN-TO-R1
!
!
interface Ethernet1
 ip address 10.71.1.89 255.255.255.0
 no ip directed-broadcast
 media-type 10BaseT
!
!
no ip classless
no ip http server
!
access-list 101 permit ip 10.71.1.0 0.0.0.255 10.4.13.0 0.0.0.255
!
!
line con 0
 transport input none
line aux 0
line vty 0 4
 privilege level 15
 no login
!
!
end
```

exists that defines the same properties to be utilized in Phase I of IKE. In the example, pre-shared secret authentication is selected.

```
crypto isakmp key MY-SHARED-SECRET address 10.1.1.2
```

The same password must be defined on both routers, and associated with the partnering router. In the example, the password is defined and aligned to the IP address of R1. This is a good example of out-of-band authentication configuration. IPSec protocols utilize authentication data preconfigured into the peers and does not concern itself with the manipulation of that data. In various situations, IPSec is not even aware of an incorrect password.

```
crypto ipsec transform-set SECURITY-SET esp-des esp-md5-hmac
```

A transform set is created that must be identical to the R1 transform set. If a transform set is defined that does not match, a VPN cannot be established. A router can have several transform sets that can contain one that matches. If the matching transform set is included in the map associated with the interface, it can be utilized for communication. In the example, the name of the transform set is the same as it was in R1, but this has no bearing on the communication whatsoever. Duplicate names of maps and transform sets are not allowed on the same system, but can certainly be duplicated on separate systems without any effect on the connection. Names of profiles and policies have only local significance. This allows the adminis-trator of the solution to develop policies and standards builds for router management for the entire solution. An example is the creation of standardized named transform sets. A transform set is a grouping of communication requirements, such as use ESP with DES and MD5 authentication. Given the available encryption algorithms and authentication codes — combined with being able to implement ESP or AH — the number of permutations is manageable. In a system that provides DES and 3DES for encryption and MD5 and SHA for authentication, the usable matrix can be easily standardized. An example may be:

> Normal = ESP DES
> Normal Authenticated = ESP DES, ESP MD5
> Standard Secure = ESP 3DES, ESP MD5
> Advanced Secure = ESP 3DES, ESP SHA
> Authenticated Adv. Secure = AH SHA, ESP 3DES, ESP SHA

These standard transform set identifiers can be shared among all the systems in the organization and provide configurable defaults that can be plugged into the policies as necessary. In reality, each one can be included in every policy created and the first matching set will be employed. The concept of matching an entry in a list that is parsed allows for more control in a diverse environment.

```
crypto map VPN-TO-R1 1 ipsec-isakmp
    set peer 10.1.1.2
    set transform-set SECURITY-SET
    match address 101
```

As with R1, a map is created that collects all the information configured thus far so that it can be associated with an interface. Also, an access list is provided in the map:

```
access-list 101 permit ip 10.71.1.0 0.0.0.255 10.4.13.0 0.0.0.255
```

The ACL used is nearly the same as in R1 and is used for the exact same purposes. Once again, the number 101, while identical to the one configured in R1, has only local significance.

```
interface Ethernet0
    ip address 10.1.1.1 255.255.255.0
    no ip directed-broadcast
    crypto map VPN-TO-R1
```

Finally, the map is associated with an interface to combine the information into a single point of application.

In Operation

Now that the routers have been configured, no SA is created until data is processed by the SPD. The SPD assigned to the interfaces must determine the appropriate action for each inbound and outbound packet. If an SA does not exist in the SAD, the SPD will request one for communications.

In Exhibit 10-3, router R1 sends an ICMP Echo Request to R2, using the ping command. Because any and all traffic between the routers falls within the map's ACL, a single ping will initiate the VPN. The result is the debug information from the two routers so that one can see IKE and IPSec in action based on the configuration outlined in the previous section.

Explanation of R1 Debug

The debug information collected from the router is very powerful in showing the actual process of the IKE protocol. It is one thing to discuss the attributes and messages; it is another to see the activities being performed. Interpreting log files is a crucial capability in the troubleshooting of a VPN. Each vendor provides different kinds of logs with their solution, and understanding the different types may take time. To add to the complexity of learning how to troubleshoot, many vendors do not follow the standards close enough for the reviewer to make certain determinations. A good example is when attempting to determine the problem with a VPN in a lab, the log was complaining about properties well into the communication. A quick determination was that communication was being established but somewhere at the beginning of Phase II, the operation was failing. After hours of work, the problem turned out to be the switch between the devices. The switch was replaced and the VPN began to operate. Given the results of the log files and knowledge of the IPSec standard, the final interpretation was wrong. Further investigation revealed that the log files were simply incorrect and the establishment of the VPN was not following the standards. The entire escapade was frustrating, but the lesson learned was that few systems provide logs that accurately reflect the operations. Much of this is due to the forced reduction of time to market for VPN products. Even early in Cisco's implementation, the debug information was very confusing and did not reflect the internal operations correctly. However, much of that has changed and Cisco now provides a good platform for sharing logging information about an IKE establishment and IPSec operations.

Exhibit 10-3.   ICMP echo request.

```
 1   R1#ping 10.1.1.1
 2
 3   Type escape sequence to abort.
 4   Sending 5, 100-byte ICMP Echos to 10.1.1.1, timeout is 2 seconds:
 5
 6   IPSEC(sa_request): ,
 7     (key eng. msg.) src = 10.1.1.2, dest = 10.1.1.1,
 8       src_proxy = 10.1.0.0/255.255.0.0/0/0 (type = 4),
 9       dest_proxy = 10.1.0.0/255.255.0.0/0/0 (type = 4),
10       protocol = ESP, transform = esp-des esp-md5-hmac,
11       lifedur = 3600s and 4608000kb,
12       spi = 0 x 0(0), conn_id = 0, keysize = 0, flags = 0 x 4004
13   ISAKMP (10): beginning Main Mode exchange
14   ISAKMP (10): sending packet to 10.1.1.1 (I) MM_NO_STATE
15   ISAKMP (10): received packet from 10.1.1.1 (I) MM_NO_STATE
16   ISAKMP (10): processing SA payload. message ID = 0
17   ISAKMP (10): Checking ISAKMP transform 1 against priority 1 policy
18   ISAKMP:       encryption DES-CBC
19   ISAKMP:       hash SHA
20   ISAKMP:       default group 1
21   ISAKMP:       auth pre-share
22   ISAKMP (10): atts are acceptable. Next payload is 0
23   ISAKMP (10): SA is doing pre-shared key authentication using id type ID_IPV4_ADDR
24   ISAKMP (10): sending packet to 10.1.1.1 (I) MM_SA_SETUP
25   ISAKMP (10): received packet from 10.1.1.1 (I) MM_SA_SETUP
26   ISAKMP (10): processing KE payload. message ID = 0
27   ISAKMP (10): processing NONCE payload. message ID = 0
28   ISAKMP (10): SKEYID state generated
29   ISAKMP (10): processing vendor id payload
30   ISAKMP (10): speaking to another IOS box!
31   ISAKMP (10): ID payload
32          next-payload            : 8
33          type                    : 1
34          protocol                : 17
35          port                    : 500
36          length                  : 8
37   ISAKMP (10): Total payload length: 12
38   ISAKMP (10): sending packet to 10.1.1.1 (I) MM_KEY_EXCH
39   ISAKMP (10): received packet from 10.1.1.1 (I) MM_KEY_EXCH
40   ISAKMP (10): processing ID payload. message ID = 0
41   ISAKMP (10): processing HASH payload. message ID = 0
42   ISAKMP (10): SA has been authenticated with 10.1.1.1
43   ISAKMP (10): beginning Quick Mode exchange, M-ID of 953616512
44   IPSEC(key_engine)  : got a queue event...
45   IPSEC(spi_response): getting spi 413467620 for SA
46          from 10.1.1.1      to 10.1.1.2      for prot 3
47   ISAKMP (10): sending packet to 10.1.1.1 (I) QM_IDLE
48   ISAKMP (10): received packet from 10.1.1.1 (I) QM_IDLE
```

(continues)

Exhibit 10-3.   ICMP echo request. (continued)

```
49  ISAKMP (10): processing SA payload. message ID = 953616512
50  ISAKMP (10): Checking IPSec proposal 1
51  ISAKMP: transform 1, ESP_DES
52  ISAKMP:    attributes in transform:
53  ISAKMP:       encaps is 1
54  ISAKMP:       SA life type in seconds
55  ISAKMP:       SA life duration (basic) of 3600
56  ISAKMP:       SA life type in kilobytes
57  ISAKMP:       SA life duration (VPI) of 0 x 0  0 x 46  0 x 50  0 x 0
58  ISAKMP:       authenticator is HMAC-MD5
59  ISAKMP (10): atts are acceptable.
60  ISAKMP (10): processing NONCE payload. message ID = 953616512
61  ISAKMP (10): processing ID payload. message ID = 953616512
62  ISAKMP (10): Creating IPSec SAs
63         inbound SA from 10.1.1.1 to 10.1.1.2 (proxy 10.1.0.0 to 10.1.0.0)
64         has spi 413467620 and conn_id 11 and flags 4
65         lifetime of 3600 seconds
66         lifetime of 4608000 kilobytes
67         outbound SA from 10.1.1.2 to 10.1.1.1 (proxy 10.1.0.0 to 10.1.0.0)
68         has spi 55772818 and conn_id 12 and flags 4
69         lifetime of 3600 seconds
70         lifetime of 4608000 kilobytes
71  IPSEC(key_engine): got a queue event...
72  IPSEC(initialize_sas): ,
73    (key eng. msg.) dest = 10.1.1.2, src = 10.1.1.1,
74      dest_proxy = 10.1.0.0/255.255.0.0/0/0 (type = 4),
75      src_proxy = 10.1.0.0/255.255.0.0/0/0 (type = 4),
76      protocol = ESP, transform = esp-des esp-md5-hmac,
77      lifedur = 3600s and 4608000kb,
78      spi = 0 x 18A503E4(413467620), conn_id = 11, keysize = 0, flags = 0 x 4
79  IPSEC(initialize_sas): ,
80    (key eng. msg.) src = 10.1.1.2, dest = 10.1.1.1,
81      src_proxy = 10.1.0.0/255.255.0.0/0/0 (type = 4),
82      dest_proxy= 10.1.0.0/255.255.0.0/0/0 (type = 4).!!!!
83  Success rate is 80 percent (4/5), round-trip min/avg/max = 4/5/8 ms
84  R1#,
85      protocol = ESP, transform= esp-des esp-md5-hmac,
86      lifedur = 3600s and 4608000kb,
87      spi = 0 x 3530692(55772818), conn_id = 12, keysize = 0, flags = 0 x 4
88  IPSEC(create_sa): sa created,
89    (sa) sa_dest = 10.1.1.2, sa_prot = 50,
90        sa_spi = 0 x 18A503E4(413467620),
91        sa_trans = esp-des esp-md5-hmac , sa_conn_id = 11
92  IPSEC(create_sa): sa created,
93    (sa) sa_dest = 10.1.1.1, sa_prot = 50,
94        sa_spi = 0 x 3530692(55772818),
95        sa_trans = esp-des esp-md5-hmac, sa_conn_id = 12
96  ISAKMP (10): sending packet to 10.1.1.1 (I) QM_IDLE
```

The following section addresses each section of the output and relates the information collected from the session back to the inner working of IKE defined by the RFCs.

```
R1#ping 10.1.1.1
Type escape sequence to abort.
Sending 5, 100-byte ICMP Echos to 10.1.1.1,
  timeout is 2 seconds:
```

The first lines show us the entry of the ping command and the message generated to the operator showing that the operation has been started.

```
IPSEC(sa_request): ,
   (key eng. msg.) src = 10.1.1.2, dest = 10.1.1.1,
      src_proxy = 10.1.0.0/255.255.0.0/0/0 (type = 4),
      dest_proxy = 10.1.0.0/255.255.0.0/0/0 (type = 4),
      protocol = ESP, transform = esp-des esp-md5-hmac,
      lifedur = 3600s and 4608000kb,
      spi = 0 x 0(0), conn_id = 0, keysize = 0, flags = 0 x 4004
```

The IPSec SA request portion details the SPD entries for the SA to be included in the SA payload as the proposal and associated transform sets. The first few lines of this section display the SPD's identification of the destination and source that allow it to define the security to be provided to the packets. Line 10 is informative in that it shows that a single protocol has been configured, resulting in one proposal that contains two transform sets —DES encryption and HAMC-MD5 authentication.

Although neither a lifetime limit nor a maximum data transmission was defined, they are defined by the default settings. Notice that the maximum amount of data is defaulted at over 4 GB of data. Because the configuration did not define a lifetime value or attribute, this is assumed as the maximum amount of data possible for the ISA; this value is realized by setting the 32-bit attribute in the SA transform set to 0×0 0×46 0×50 0×0. In addition, Phase I operations use cookies for IKE SA creation, and the SPI is set to zero. The connection ID is zero because this is the first packet being generated for the VPN. No keys are defined because DH has not transpired and the algorithms in the proposal have not been accepted.

The next section shows the Main Mode packet containing the ISAKMP header and SA payload information being sent to R2.

```
ISAKMP (10): Checking ISAKMP transform 1 against priority 1
               policy
ISAKMP:       encryption DES-CBC
ISAKMP:       hash SHA
ISAKMP:       default group 1
ISAKMP:       auth pre-share
ISAKMP (10): atts are acceptable. Next payload is 0
```

The responder replied with a single proposal that existed in the original proposal from R1. In the event that several proposals were provided to R2, only one can be selected and returned — unchanged. This section shows that the SA information has been received from R2. The first step is ensuring the data in the proposal has not been changed and that the accepted proposal is valid according to the policy maintained within the SPD. On line 22, one can see that the payload was processed and accepted. The next payload statement identifies that the generic header on the return proposal was the end of the chain of SA payload data.

```
ISAKMP (10): SA is doing pre-shared key authentication
                using id type ID_IPV4_ADDR
```

Line 23 shows that the router understands that the ISAKMP is a pre-shared key based on the peer's IP address and, therefore, makes the alignment for computation.

```
ISAKMP (10): sending packet to 10.1.1.1 (I) MM_SA_SETUP
ISAKMP (10): received packet from 10.1.1.1 (I) MM_SA_SETUP
ISAKMP (10): processing KE payload. message ID = 0
ISAKMP (10): processing NONCE payload. message ID = 0
ISAKMP (10): SKEYID state generated
```

Lines 24 thru 28 detail the exchange of the third and fourth IKE payloads that contain the nonces and public DH values. Once this information is obtained and verified, the keys can be created. The size and number of keys are known due to the proposal payload information agreed upon in the first two messages. Notice that the two systems have assumed that they have initiated a limited relationship, based solely on the peer's IP address and the associated policies. Line 28 states that the keys have been generated.

Another point worth noting is that the SKEYID is generated by the responder prior to sending its KE and nonce payloads to the initiator. By doing so, the responder is prepared for future exchanges; however, it has committed to the generation of the key prior to the initiator and prior to any solid authentication. Hence, this could be seen as a weakness and a possible denial-of-service against the router. Because the initiator can send only a few messages to the responder that can result in the creation of keys on the part of the responder, the initiator is free to flood the responder consuming system resources.

```
ISAKMP (10): processing vendor id payload
ISAKMP (10): speaking to another IOS box!
```

Next is Cisco taking advantage of the optional vendor ID payload entry to add one more attribute to the payload chain. It is almost humorous how excited the system gets when it realizes that it is talking to a cousin.

```
ISAKMP (10): ID payload
        next-payload              : 8
        type                      : 1
        protocol                  : 17
        port                      : 500
        length                    : 8
ISAKMP (10): Total payload length : 12
```

This section displays the creation of the ID payload to be presented to the responder. The next payload type of 8 signifies that the HASH_I is to follow. The type of 1 states that the ID payload will contain the IP address of the initiator. Interestingly enough, type 1 is assumed by the authentication process from payloads 1 and 2; but by providing the proper ID payload, there is no confusion, especially if NAT is involved. Protocol and port are defined by the IPSec DOI to be included. For ISAKMP, the protocol is UDP (17) and the port 500. The length statement and the total length statement can be confusing. The RFC states that the length represents the payload and the generic header. From the information gathered, it appears that the router is calculating the generic header length rather than assuming the entire payload and header.

```
ISAKMP (10): sending packet to 10.1.1.1 (I) MM_KEY_EXCH
ISAKMP (10): received packet from 10.1.1.1 (I) MM_KEY_EXCH
ISAKMP (10): processing ID payload. message ID = 0
ISAKMP (10): processing HASH payload. message ID = 0
ISAKMP (10): SA has been authenticated with 10.1.1.1
```

The last two exchanges — packets 5 and 6 — are performed and finalize the ISA. What is not detailed in the debug data from R1 is that this information is encrypted. The HASH that is included in the payloads is to authenticate the message and the information gathered to this point. Because the ID payload is included in the exchange, it is used as part of the HASH. Other information included in the HASH was exchanged previously. A good example is that cookies are included in the HASH, which were shared in the original ISAKMP header. Also included in the HASH are the DH public value created by the initiator and the one received by the responder. Using the HASH exchanged in the last few packets will validate all the peer information.

It is interesting to note that if the password is incorrect, the key generation will be based on bad information contained in desperate databases. The result is that the final exchange will be decrypted into gibberish and several vague errors will arise. Pre-shared key authentication is very popular, especially with remote access solutions, but there are several weaknesses to the process.

At this point, IKE Phase I is complete and Phase II can begin to create SAs for IPSec operations, as can be seen in line 43.

```
ISAKMP (10): beginning Quick Mode exchange, M-ID of 953616512
IPSEC(key_engine)  : got a queue event...
IPSEC(spi_response): getting spi 413467620 for SA
        from 10.1.1.1      to 10.1.1.2    for prot 3
ISAKMP (10): sending packet to 10.1.1.1 (I) QM_IDLE
```

This section reveals that R2 has followed through with VPN establishment and has initiated Quick Mode. Notice "for prot 3." Protocol 3 is the IPSec DOI identification for IPSec ESP. This can get confusing, knowing that the protocol ID for ESP is 50, but this is strictly the IPSec's DOI for the Phase II QM negotiation.

What is missing is the SA proposal from R2 that includes the transform sets. In the beginning of the original IKE exchange, one saw the identification of ESP, the encryption identification, and the authentication algorithm to utilize. It is necessary to know that the SA payload is defined, authenticated (HASH'ed), and included in the first QM packet. The creation of the transform set was not in the R2 debug. Of course, all of this is encrypted using the keys derived from Phase I.

```
ISAKMP (10): received packet from 10.1.1.1 (I) QM_IDLE
ISAKMP (10): processing SA payload. message ID = 953616512
ISAKMP (10): Checking IPSec proposal 1
ISAKMP: transform 1, ESP_DES
ISAKMP:   attributes in transform:
ISAKMP:       encaps is 1
ISAKMP:       SA life type in seconds
ISAKMP:       SA life duration (basic) of 3600
ISAKMP:       SA life type in kilobytes
ISAKMP:       SA life duration (VPI) of 0 x 0  0 x 46  0 x 50  0 x 0
ISAKMP:       authenticator is HMAC-MD5
ISAKMP (10): atts are acceptable.
```

In the next section, one sees that the QM packets get exchanged and R1 once again validates the proposal from R2 against the SPD. The line "encap 1" specifies that the SA will be using IP encapsulation; therefore, it is a tunnel mode ESP SA. Once again, the lifetime is in seconds and kilobytes — these should look familiar from Phase I. Finally, the authentication type to be used for the SA is derived.

```
ISAKMP (10): processing NONCE payload. message ID = 953616512
ISAKMP (10): processing ID payload. message ID = 953616512
```

After the proposals are validated against the SPD, the nonce and ID of the packets are processed.

```
    ISAKMP (10): Creating IPSec SAs
          inbound SA from 10.1.1.1 to 10.1.1.2
            (proxy 10.1.0.0 to 10.1.0.0)
          has spi 413467620 and conn_id 11 and flags 4
          lifetime of 3600 seconds
          lifetime of 4608000 kilobytes
          outbound SA from 10.1.1.2 to 10.1.1.1
            (proxy 10.1.0.0 to 10.1.0.0)
          has spi 55772818 and conn_id 12 and flags 4
          lifetime of 3600 seconds
          lifetime of 4608000 kilobytes
```

This section constitutes a prelude to the creation of the SAs by having the SPD reflect the policies in the log. It is necessary for the SPD and the SAD to communicate to ensure that what is required by the policy is created by the SAD. In essence, this is what we are seeing. Also, notice the two SAs for true communication.

```
IPSEC(key_engine): got a queue event...
IPSEC(initialize_sas): ,
  (key eng. msg.) dest = 10.1.1.2, src = 10.1.1.1,
    dest_proxy = 10.1.0.0/255.255.0.0/0/0 (type = 4),
    src_proxy = 10.1.0.0/255.255.0.0/0/0 (type = 4),
    protocol = ESP, transform = esp-des esp-md5-hmac,
    lifedur = 3600s and 4608000kb,
    spi = 0 x 18A503E4(413467620), conn_id = 11, keysize = 0, flags = 0 x 4
```

```
IPSEC(initialize_sas): ,
  (key eng. msg.) src = 10.1.1.2, dest = 10.1.1.1,
    src_proxy = 10.1.0.0/255.255.0.0/0/0 (type = 4),
    dest_proxy = 10.1.0.0/255.255.0.0/0/0 (type = 4).!!!!
Success rate is 80 percent (4/5), round-trip min/avg/max = 4/5/8 ms
R1#,
    protocol = ESP, transform = esp-des esp-md5-hmac,
    lifedur = 3600s and 4608000kb,
    spi = 0 x 3530692(55772818), conn_id = 12, keysize = 0, flags = 0 x 4
```

This section has a lot of interesting information to convey. At the top, one sees the "key_engine" receive an event to initialize an SA. The source and destinations are verified, and the SA proposals containing the necessary transform sets are compiled. This is simply words in a log that reflect the creation of the ISAKMP data to be handed off to the ESP header and associated operations.

One interesting aspect is as the process is completed and the VPN is established, the results of the original ping command are displayed. The ping used to initiate the VPN is displayed starting on line 82. The time it took to establish the VPN exceeded the time for the first ICMP echo request. Therefore, one sees ".!!!!," telling us that the first echo reply was not received. It is worth noting that the VPN being created in this lab experiment is being established on Ethernet, with no other processes running on the router — including no other data being routed. The routers in the test are simply establishing a simple VPN over a high-speed connection. Consequently, the establishment may seem very fast, only a 5-ms average round trip that includes the loss of 20 percent of the packets, but in reality the process was surprising slow. In some real-world implementations, only the second ping command showed any successful packets and even then the success rate was limited to the last few datagrams. This is an example showing that key creation and establishment of a VPN can have a significant impact on system resources.

```
    IPSEC(create_sa): sa created,
      (sa) sa_dest = 10.1.1.2, sa_prot = 50,
           sa_spi = 0 x 18A503E4(413467620),
           sa_trans = esp-des esp-md5-hmac , sa_conn_id = 11
    IPSEC(create_sa): sa created,
      (sa) sa_dest = 10.1.1.1, sa_prot = 50,
           sa_spi = 0 x 3530692(55772818),
           sa_trans = esp-des esp-md5-hmac, sa_conn_id = 12
```

Finally, the router displays the current SA's status. The SPIs relate to the two SAs and can be used to identify and track the activities of the respective SAs.

The following is the result of a command to display the ISAKMP SA status that allows one to verify the actions within the SAs. The command "show crypto isakmp sa" provides a detailed list of the security association attributes and statistics. It is interesting to see that the command output not only provides the IKE SA information, but also the IPSec SA data — for both protocols. This command is very valuable in troubleshooting and knowing what the system is doing with respect to the configuration. For some implementations, the result of this command can fill hundreds of pages.

```
R1#sh crypto isakmp sa
interface: Ethernet1
        Crypto map tag: VPN-TO-R2, local addr. 10.1.1.2
    local ident (addr/mask/prot/port):
    (10.1.0.0/255.255.0.0/0/0)
    remote ident (addr/mask/prot/port):
    (10.1.0.0/255.255.0.0/0/0)
    current_peer: 10.1.1.1
            PERMIT, flag = {origin_is_acl,}
        #pkts encaps: 7, #pkts encrypt: 7, #pkts digest 7
        #pkts decaps: 7, #pkts decrypt: 7, #pkts verify 7
        #send errors 2, #recv errors 0
            local crypto endpt.: 10.1.1.2, remote crypto
                endpt.: 10.1.1.1
        path mtu 1500, media mtu 1500
        current outbound spi: 188913E4
```

Within the command output, there are four sections that detail the existing inbound and outbound SAs. Included in the report are the sections to identify the two security protocols that can exist. However, in this example, there are no AH SAs because only the ESP security protocol was used .

```
    inbound esp sas:
       spi: 0 x 18A503E4(413467620)
            transform: esp-des esp-md5-hmac,
            in use settings ={Tunnel,}
            slot: 0, conn id: 11, crypto map: VPN-TO-R2
            sa timing: remaining key lifetime (k/sec):
              (4607999/3460)
            IV size: 8 bytes
            replay detection support: Y

    inbound ah sas:

    outbound esp sas:
       spi: 0 x 3530692(55772818)
            transform: esp-des esp-md5-hmac,
            in use settings = {Tunnel, }
            slot: 0, conn id: 12, crypto map: VPN-TO-R2
            sa timing: remaining key lifetime (k/sec):
              (4607999/3460)
            IV size: 8 bytes
            replay detection support: Y

    outbound ah sas:
```

It is interesting to note that Cisco supports replay protection by default, as defined by the RFCs. It is the author's opinion that this is realized by the identification of another Cisco device in the establishment of the VPN. Therefore, it is possible that Cisco implements replay protection when it is sure that the responder will properly track the SA. It is also possible that the Cisco implementation recognized the configuration of ESP authentication without AH, and assumed replay protection. Unfortunately, this assumption came long after the lab was available and the author was unable to test the theory. By simply applying ESP without authentication, would replay protection remain enabled? If the answer is no, then that would qualify as an excellent assumption and reflect the attention to detail by the vendor.

Chapter 11

Areas of Interest within IKE

As with any protocol, there are areas for improvement or enhancement. Given the complexity of the IPSec suite of protocols and the openness of the standardization process, many options have been suggested, added, and removed as the standard has grown. This chapter endeavors to expose areas of known weakness, introduce options presented to the IETF workgroup, show aspects of IKE not well-known, and generally shed light on the various intricacies that have labeled IPSec a maturing protocol.

Without a doubt, IKE represents the pinnacle of IPSec VPN complexity. Unarguably, it is intensely intricate and fraught with tangents that seem to come from every direction. IKE has come in and out of the center of attention, but will always remain questioned in its structure. There have consistently been suggestions and offers for modification of IKE exchanges to accommodate different perceived limitations in the protocol. Even IPSec operations, such as tunnel mode versus transport mode, are questioned on a regular basis. The security protocol AH is under constant scrutiny. The problem seems to arise when it is feasible to allow ESP to authenticate the outer IP header — technically eliminating the need for AH.

Some feel that the IETF's method of open development is the core reason for the complexity within the protocol. Some argue that because everyone, the public, has the opportunity to comment on the protocol specifics defined in the RFCs, the protocol will never evolve. Hence, the situation that currently exists: a protocol not quite mature and continually developing. At some point, many believe, a mediator must state what is to be defined in the RFC and put the proverbial foot down. However, this is contrary to the openness of the workgroup. Many of the authors of the primary RFCs that define IPSec and IKE spend a great deal of time in the IETF IPSec workgroup, supplying responses to various questions and suggestions. Some of these discussions are very detailed and some offer alternate methods of creating keys and exchanges, modifying the entire protocol. In various discussions, the modifications are to simply assist a local requirement or situation with which a particular individual must deal. However, in some cases, the presented solution is very well-thought out and presented, and represent real concerns with an underlying protocol problem.

This section touches upon various areas of IPSec and IKE that either expose a weakness or introduce an area under dispute. In some cases, the alternate options presented at different times in the life cycle will be shared to expose the reader to the alternative that surfaces on a regular basis.

Phase I with Shared Secret

One of the most debated IKE exchanges is Phase I with shared secret. With this type of authentication method, there is no identity protection and the ID payload is virtually worthless to the authentication process.

The limitations were outlined in earlier sections. In short, in Main Mode, the ID payload is not shared until the third exchange, which must be encrypted. Unfortunately, to generate the keys, the responder must know the password to create the key to allow it to decrypt the fifth message. The only way for the responder to determine the password is by the originating Internet IP address of the initiator. Unfortunately, anyone on the Internet can see the transaction revealing the identity of the initiator. The password is contained in a database and associated with the peer's IP address; therefore, when the messages arrive, the responder simply looks up the appropriate password and uses it to create the primary key, SKEYID.

For network-to-network VPNs, this is not a huge issue because the initiator's IP address typically does not change. This allows the responder to build a comprehensive table of IP addresses to passwords. Remote access solutions wherein the IP address is different for every connection cause the real problem. Aggressive Mode is used to accommodate this limitation. Although limitations exist with Aggressive Mode, it is not perfect; it allows the remote user to authenticate based on the ID payload rather than the IP address. But, unfortunately, it is unencrypted, resulting in the same lack of identity protection.

However, this section is dedicated to issues with the pre-shared secrets themselves being used in Phase I. If each peer is configured with the appropriate password associated with the other peer's IP address, what would happen if the password is wrong?

System A, with IP address 3.3.3.3 has a VPN pointing to its peer, system B with the IP address 7.7.7.7. System A says, to go to 7.7.7.7 use the password BOMB. System B should say, to go to system A use the password BOMB. As the VPN is established, each obtains the necessary nonce from the other and combines it with its own nonce and the pre-shared secret — BOMB — to create the primary key material SKEYID. In that case, what if the passwords do not match?

The keys will not be exactly the same, and as data is decrypted by the peer, it will assume that a valid key was used and attempt to parse the data as if correctly decrypted, while in reality, the data is nothing more than gibberish. At this point, some odd failure will occur somewhere in the SA setup, and the administrator will begin the arduous task of troubleshooting.

The troubleshooting will not be easy because there is an unclear error. How is the system supposed to know that the password is wrong? They never shared it. A perfect example, which the author has experienced, is setting up a quick VPN over the phone. "What should we make the password?", I asked the administrator on the other end of the phone line, in an attempt to allow him the opportunity to decide because it was his system and I was there to assist in the design and implementation of the VPN. "Last12Go," he replied. I followed up with the next obvious question, "What is the case?" Feeling I had it correct, I repeated it back to him, "LastonetoGo." "Yep," he replied. That was the beginning of the end. At the time, there was a great deal of unfamiliarity with the equipment and both of us felt confident that some other force was working against us. We ultimately found the mismatch.

The error was reproduced on two Cisco routers, first configuring them with the correct passwords to ensure the VPN operated correctly, then playfully changing the initiator's password, and finally reloading the router waiting to see the results in the debug of the responder router. Exhibit 11-1 displays the result.

In line 1, the responder is receiving the first message from the initiator. The initiator has come back online and wishes to establish the connection. In lines 2 through 10, the responder is processing the SA proposal and transformsets in normal operation. In line 11, the responder identifies the fact that pre-shared secrets will be used. At this point, the router looks up the appropriate password for the initiator's IP address.

In line 12, the responder replies with an ISAKMP header, and the selected SA proposal and associated transformset. Line 13, the third message in Main Mode is received from the initiator, and contains the Diffie-Hellman public value, the initiator's nonce, and a Cisco vendor payload. Once the KE and nonce of the initiator are received, the responder can calculate the SKEYID, and ultimately the SKEYID_e, because it has its own nonce, KE, and the password. Technically, the responder could begin encrypting messages; it has the IV and SKEYID_e — everything needed to build and use the keys. But, of course, the initiator needs that very same information from the responder to create the corresponding key to decrypt the information; therefore, the next message from the responder must be in the clear. Once again, by the responder creating the SKEYID state prior to the initiator even having the responder's KE or nonce, this can be seen as a vulnerability to a denial-of-service attack.

Nonetheless, after the router identifies the remote system as Cisco, the KE and nonce are prepared and placed in the fourth message to be sent to the initiator (line 19). Once the initiator receives the message, it can create the necessary keying material and determine the IV. Therefore, in keeping with the protocol, the initiator

Exhibit 11-1. Debug of responder router.

```
01  ISAKMP (0): received packet from 12.0.0.2 (N) NEW SA
02  ISAKMP (12): processing SA payload. message ID = 0
03  ISAKMP (12): Checking ISAKMP transform 1 against priority 1 policy
04  ISAKMP:        encryption DES-CBC
05  ISAKMP:        hash MD5
06  ISAKMP:        default group 2
07  ISAKMP:        auth pre-share
08  ISAKMP:        life type in seconds
09  ISAKMP:        life duration (basic) of 360
10  ISAKMP (12): atts are acceptable. Next payload is 0
11  ISAKMP (12): SA is doing pre-shared key authentication using id type ID_IPV4_ADDR
12  ISAKMP (12): sending packet to 12.0.0.2 (R) MM_SA_SETUP
13  ISAKMP (12): received packet from 12.0.0.2 (R) MM_SA_SETUP
14  ISAKMP (12): processing KE payload. message ID = 0
15  ISAKMP (12): processing NONCE payload. message ID = 0
16  ISAKMP (12): SKEYID state generated
17  ISAKMP (12): processing vendor id payload
18  ISAKMP (12): speaking to another IOS box!
19  ISAKMP (12): sending packet to 12.0.0.2 (R) MM_KEY_EXCH
20  ISAKMP (12): received packet from 12.0.0.2 (R) MM_KEY_EXCH
21  ISAKMP: reserved not zero on payload 5!
22  %CRYPTO-4-IKMP_BAD_MESSAGE: IKE message from 12.0.0.2 failed its sanity check or is malformed
23
24  ISAKMP (12): retransmitting phase 1...
25  ISAKMP (12): sending packet to 12.0.0.2 (R) MM_KEY_EXCH
26  ISAKMP (0): received packet from 12.0.0.2 (N) NEW SA
27  ISAKMP (13): processing SA payload. message ID = 0
28  ISAKMP (13): Checking ISAKMP transform 1 against priority 1 policy
29  ISAKMP:        encryption DES-CBC
30  ISAKMP:        hash MD5
31  ISAKMP:        default group 2
32  ISAKMP:        auth pre-share
33  ISAKMP:        life type in seconds
34  ISAKMP:        life duration (basic) of 360
35  ISAKMP (13): atts are acceptable. Next payload is 0
36  ISAKMP (13): SA is doing pre-shared key authentication using id type I
37  D_IPV4_ADDR
38  ISAKMP (13): sending packet to 12.0.0.2 (R) MM_SA_SETUP
39  ISAKMP (13): received packet from 12.0.0.2 (R) MM_SA_SETUP
40  ISAKMP (13): processing KE payload. message ID = 0
41  ISAKMP (13): processing NONCE payload. message ID = 0
42  ISAKMP (13): SKEYID state generated
43  ISAKMP (13): processing vendor id payload
44  ISAKMP (13): speaking to another IOS box!
```

Exhibit 11-1.   Debug of responder router. (continued)

```
45  ISAKMP (13): sending packet to 12.0.0.2 (R) MM_KEY_EXCH
46  ISAKMP (13): received packet from 12.0.0.2 (R) MM_KEY_EXCH
47  ISAKMP: reserved not zero on payload 5!
48  ISAKMP (13): sending packet to 12.0.0.2 (R) MM_KEY_EXCH
49  ISAKMP (13): retransmitting phase 1...
50  ISAKMP (13): sending packet to 12.0.0.2 (R) MM_KEY_EXCH
51  ISAKMP (12): deleting SA
52  ISAKMP (13): received packet from 12.0.0.2 (R) MM_KEY_EXCH
53  ISAKMP: reserved not zero on payload 5!
54
55  ISAKMP (13): retransmitting phase 1...
56  ISAKMP (13): deleting SA
57  ISAKMP (13): received packet from..
```

encrypts the fifth message and sends it to the responder. Unfortunately, the password is incorrect, resulting in a bad SKEYID_e. The responder receives the message and uses the symmetrical key created earlier to decrypt the message. The result is nothing more than a collection of characters and numbers that the responder must assume is correct. The responder starts to parse the data until the value of the ISAKMP header does not align, resulting in failure of what Cisco has logged as a sanity check.

Thus, IKE simply assumes the worst and starts the entire process from the beginning — going through Main Mode again from the first message. Based on the logs, it almost appears that the roles have reversed; regardless, the results are the same. To the author's surprise, this continues for several minutes, the boxes insisting they can speak to each other but a message keeps going bad.

There has been discussion that this issue represents a fundamental problem with certain areas of IKE. The SKEYID for pre-shared secrets is basically the password combined with the nonces from each system. It has been argued that the password should not be linked to the SKEYID because the authentication technically has little to do with the encryption process. The SKEYID can be created with valid material, such as the key for digital signatures, and use the password in the HASH to accommodate the authentication. See the following example.

$$SKEYID = prf (Nonce\_i \mid Nonce\_r, DH\_Key)$$

First create the primary key from the nonces as normal, but use the more powerful Diffie-Hellman calculated key instead of the password. This is the exact same process used to create the SKEYID for digital signatures. Of course, this material is used to create the SKEYID_e, which is used to encrypt and decrypt the actual messages.

The fifth Main Mode message, or the third Aggressive Mode message (if optionally encrypted), will contain a HASH that can be calculated with the password. This process will allow the encryption and decryption processes to remain sound if the password does not pass. For increased granularity, the password can be hashed on its own to allow the responder to know if the HASH error is the password or other attribute contained within the calculation.

This is simple commentary about a rare situation. Most situations in which pre-shared secrets are used in Main mode are for network-to-network implementations, and password misalignment is not all that common. For remote access, where the IP address is constantly changing, Aggressive Mode can be utilized. However, the password is still tested based on trial and error of the decryption process in Aggressive Mode as in Main Mode. Ironically, Aggressive Mode can be a worse situation if the final message is not encrypted. The error will not arise until the first Quick Mode exchange, making it exponentially more difficult to troubleshoot. But Aggressive Mode is flexible and RADIUS implementations can be included, allowing the PAP or CHAP within RADIUS to verify the password on behalf of IKE.

Nevertheless, the association of the secret to the key is continually being debated, and its inclusion in the primary key material is not necessarily required for operation.

Denial of Service

Denial of service (DoS) encompasses many aspects that can range from information destruction and unavailability to total system failure. Most people align the term DoS with brining a system down and forcing a reboot or re-initialization. The TearDrop DoS utility was used to upset the TCP/IP protocol stack that resulted in the system not accepting future datagrams. Systems that were vulnerable to this type of attack could easily be shut down and removed from service by sending a barrage of specially designed datagrams to the target system. This type of attack took advantage of a weakness in the implementation and was fixed in many systems once discovered. This attack also represents a situation in which the attacker must do very little to wreak havoc on another system.

Other types of DoS are not specifically designed to take advantage of a specific vulnerability, but rather to exploit a communication design flaw. By sending many valid packets, the target system must respond because there is no way to determine that the traffic is not a valid attempt to establish a connection. The SYN flood attack is a perfect example of this type of attack and is inherent in any system running TCP/IP as the protocol. Simply explained, a SYN flood is the result of an attacker sending many requests to communicate to a remote system. As the target system replies with SYN/ACK, acknowledgment to the request, the attacker simply ignores it and sends more requests to communicate — SYNs. The target system must assume that the lack of a response is due to network issues or some other problem and therefore waits and sends several follow-up SYN/ACKs for each received SYN. At this rate, the attacker can generate many more requests than the target can compute, ultimately resulting in that the buffer provided to the SYN/ACK history over runs and a system failure or overload is realized. In this example, the vulnerability exploited is in the design of the communication protocol. By using the communication setup process to make the target work more for each packet received, the attacker has to work to create and send them.

In some cases, the process can be amplified to reduce the load on the attacker and increase the load on the target. In the past, this was provided by utilities such as Smurf and PapaSmurf. These utilities took advantage of broadcast properties to amplify a single packet to thousands that could be directed at a single target. Smurf provides an excellent example of this process. A broadcast ICMP packet is transmitted from an attacker's system with the source address replaced by the address of the target system. A single broadcast packet could be received by hundreds of other systems that will answer the request, sending them to the system that appears to be the originator — in this case, the target system. This would be the equivalent of pinging a thousand computers at the same time. Within a very short period of time, the target system will be inundated with ICMP packets generated by a single packet from an attacker. Therefore, the attacker can create only a few packets that can be amplified into millions, ultimately rendering the target system too busy to handle valid requests.

IKE is a protocol that is used to provide first-level communication between peers. In other words, IKE is the first set of messages to initiate a relationship that will build into SAs, IKE SAs, and IPSec SAs — a VPN. As discussed in earlier chapters, IKE uses several messages with varying formats and content to build trust and share communication-specific data, such as keying material. During the negotiations, each peer is responsible for performing certain processes to advance the communication to the next phase. The creation of key material from the data provided by the peer can become overwhelming if several communication requests are made in a short time frame.

IKE provides a service by the implementation of several security features. By utilizing cookies, sequence numbers, and message authentication, IKE reduces the capability of an attacker to flood the target without becoming more involved in the communication. The ability to be "DoS resistant" is to reduce the CPU and memory load of the target while allowing the remote system to be authenticated. To accomplish this, the target must use as few resources as possible in identifying the remote system so that the remote system cannot continue to make invalid request and consume resources.

Commit Bit

The use of the commit bit in Quick Mode is to allow the responder to postpone the commencement of IPSec traffic. During IKE Phase II negotiations, the responder provides all the necessary data for the creation of the IPSec VPN to the initiator prior to having all the necessary information from the initiator. In the latter part of the messaging, the initiator receives attributes from the responder that allow it to create all the necessary keys and associated information to start sending IPSec protected communications. However, the initiator is bound by protocol to provide a final message that contains information that the responder requires to create the corresponding information to participate in the VPN and create the necessary SAs. Therefore, the initiator can send the final message to the responder, followed immediately by IPSec communication datagrams.

This communication practice can result in problems for the responder in two primary ways. The responder may be overburdened with other processes, or simply outperformed by the initiator, and cannot create the associated SA information before receiving IPSec communication data from the initiator. If this happens and the responder is unable to mirror the SA from the initiator, all the packets will be dropped or packed away in a buffer to provide a limited window of time for the responder to catch up. Another aspect that can affect the communication is when the packets from the initiator are received out of order. As an example, the final IKE Phase II message that contains the last attribute required by the responder is received after IPSec communication datagrams from the initiator. If the initiator transmits the final IKE message followed by IPSec communication data, there is an opportunity for the second datagrams to arrive ahead of the IKE message. This can cause obvious problems with the communication that will almost certainly result in VPN establishment failure.

The problem with the use of the commit bit stems from the RFC definition of when to use it and how to acknowledge the setting of the commit bit. The RFC states that the responder or the initiator has the option to set the bit anywhere in the communication — basically, the first or third message for the initiator. If the initiator sets the commit bit in the third message, the responder must reply to acknowledge the receipt of the commit bit and wait for a connect notification. However, this is complicated because the initiator is not supposed to be sending a connect notification. Also, if the initiator decides to set the commit bit in the first message, the responder does not have the opportunity to set the commit bit to relieve IPSec transmission because it will look like an acknowledgment to the initiator, basically shutting down that option to the responder.

Nevertheless, there are issues with the commit bit and how to use it. For many implementations, the initiator is not allowed to set the bit, while many other solutions do (IBM's AIX IPSec solution is an example). In short, the commit bit is mandatory to support; how one handles the bit if one is the responder or the initiator is what is up for grabs.

IKE, Algorithms, and the Creation of Keys

The generation of key material within IKE is primarily for IKE encryption and authentication, and is not directly responsible for the key material for the underlying protocol — IPSec. Nonetheless, IKE must create keys of proper length to accommodate the algorithms. During the creation of the keys for the various IKE Phase I authentication types (shared secret, digital signatures, and public key encryption), a pseudo-random function is used to assist in combining the material to create the keys. Because no pseudo-random functions are currently defined for use within IKE, the HMAC portion of the negotiated authentication algorithm is used — such as HMAC-MD5.

Each HMAC function is a message authentication code based on a keyed hash function. Hence, when the creation of the keys are defined, there is a key identified within the process itself (see the following example).

```
Result = prf (key, attribute1 | attribute2)
```

Because the HMAC functions are hashes, they are restricted to certain block sizes that will have an effect on the resulting key size. If a hash algorithm has a block size of 8 bytes, but the requirement of the final key is 30 bytes, the PRF has to be used four times into itself, combining the results and taking the most significant bits to produce the necessary key. The following is an example based on the creation of the pre-shared secret SKEYID, in which each Bx is one resulting block of 8 bytes.

```
B1 = prf (pre-shared-key, nonce_i | nonce_r)
```

This operation was previously defined as equaling the SKEYID. However, that would result in a key 4 times too small.

```
B2 = prf (pre-shared-key, B1 | nonce_i | nonce_r)
B3 = prf (pre-shared-key, B2 | nonce_i | nonce_r)
B4 = prf (pre-shared-key, B3 | nonce_i | nonce_r)
```

With four 8-byte keys, one can combine them and use the most significant number of bits necessary to create the final key. In this example, the final key is equal to 32 bytes; therefore, one takes the first 30 bytes of the result of combining the precalculated blocks of 8 bytes:

$$SKEYID = (!30 \ (B1 \ | \ B2 \ | \ B3 \ | \ B4))$$

The same process is applicable to other key generation operations. As the three constant keys are created (_a, _e, and _d), they must be increased to accommodate the encryption algorithm. For example, the creation of SKEYID_d, the first of the three to be computed:

```
B1 = prf ( SKEYID, DH_key | cookie_i | cookie_r | 0)
B2 = prf ( SKEYID, B1 | DH_key | cookie_i | cookie_r | 0)
B3 = prf ( SKEYID, B2 | DH_key | cookie_i | cookie_r | 0)
B4 = prf ( SKEYID, B3 | DH_key | cookie_i | cookie_r | 0)
```

Once the blocks are created, one can combine the results and take the first 30 bytes for a key.

$$SKEYID\_d = (!30 \ (B1 \ | \ B2 \ | \ B3 \ | \ B4))$$

Public Keys and Certificate Hashes

In the second exchange when using public key encryption, the initiator has the option to send a HASH of the responder's certificate. Why send the responder a hash of the certificate that represents the responder's public key? Does the responder not know its own key? At first glance, this seems like overkill and not entirely efficient. In many circumstances, the responder may have several certificates (or public keys) that are used for various system representations. In the event the responder maintains several public keys, the inclusion of the certificate in the message from the initiator allows the responder to look up the correct corresponding private key in its database.

Note: When the certificate is passed from the initiator to the responder, it is hashed. The first question that seems to quickly follow is, why hash a public certificate when certificates are designed to be shared in the open without risk to the integrity of the certificate? The answer is anonymity — identity protection of the peers. If someone were watching the communication, they may only get the Internet IP address and a collection of encrypted data. However, if the certificate is passed in the clear, the identity of the peer is exposed, ultimately adding to the knowledge of the attacker. Many aspects of IKE are designed around the protection of the identity of the peers. As the exchanges are examined more closely, one can see where the identity is open to the public for some exchanges (as with all of Aggressive Mode and pre-shared secret in Main Mode), and not with others.

One example of the need to know which public key the initiator is using is to accommodate access from multiple organizations or partners. In some scenarios, several organizations may provide a certificate to a central company's security gateway, such as a vendor common to many organizations. If a remote user or security gateway from one of the organizations requests a VPN, the responder of the vendor company can establish communications using the corresponding public key.

Another example is public keys that have expired could still be used by a remote peer. By sending a hash of the public key, or certificate, the responder can verify what key in its history is being used. This verification also provides the responder with the opportunity to accept the older key in the event it has recently expired and the initiator has not received the new certificate.

The inclusion of the of the HASH(1) in the third message is under fire with regard to whether or not to mandate the payload or let it remain as optional. If the payload is optional, there may be circumstances where one runs into the same problem seen with shared secret authentication. In shared secret authentication, the password is identified by the initiator's Internet IP address. In public key encryption, if the responder has 15 valid certificates that can be used by several different organizations, how is the responder going to know which private key to use when the third message is received from the initiator?

Currently, there is no answer. The initiator has the option of sending the hashed certificate, but is not required to do so. To add to the possible confusion, the public key used for the encryption does not necessarily have to come from a certificate. Therefore, the standard would have to be changed to state that the public key or certificate representing the public key used for the encryption must be hashed and provided to the responder.

Remote User Authentication Options

As stated before, IPSec currently has no accommodations for remote user authentication based on legacy authentication systems, such as RADIUS, CHAP, PAP, SDI, etc.

Several RFC drafts have been introduced to provide authentication services. Unfortunately, each required substantial changes to IKE, did not meet various requirements, or simply were not accepted by the majority. The names of some of the more popular are CRACK, XAUTH, and Hybrid.

CRACK

The RFC draft CRACK, IKE Challenge/Response for Authenticated Cryptographic Keys, was submitted as a new Phase I negotiation to provide for legacy authentication applications. One of the three authors was Dan Harkins, who was one of the authors of the IKE RFC, so CRACK was well-written and attempted to accommodate several scenarios.

CRACK defined several changes to various components of IKE and utilized currently accepted formats. An example of using existing formats is that CRACK uses keys that are based on the same creation techniques currently defined in IKE for digital signatures. In short, CRACK is a modified IKE Phase I exchange.

As shown in Exhibit 11-2, CRACK expounds on existing processes and introduces new ones to accommodate the new protocol.

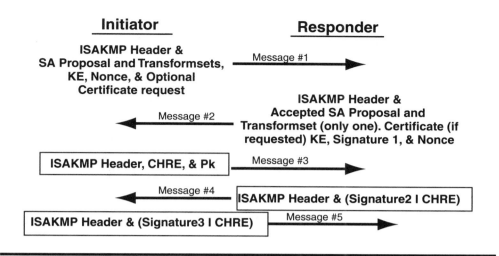

Exhibit 11-2. Replacement Phase I Exchange: CRACK.

The first message from the remote user contains an ISAKMP header, security association attributes, the Diffie-Hellman public key, and a nonce. An optional certificate request can be made to instruct the responder to include its certificate in the next message to allow the initiator to validate the signature accompanying the certificate. The signature provides system authentication, as with normal digital signature authentication methods.

The next message is very similar in nature. The ISAKMP header is included, as with all IKE negotiations, and an SA payload that contains the agreed-upon security association parameters. Next is the certificate payload that is included if the initiator provided a request. Also included is the Diffie-Hellman public key, signature, and nonce. The signature in the responder's message is provided to allow the initiator to authenticate the responder.

Once the initiator receives the second message, there is enough data available to create the necessary keying material, and therefore the remaining messages are encrypted.

In the third message, the CHRE represents a challenge/response payload that can be used by legacy authentication applications to authenticate the user of the system with which it now maintains a security association. The PK payload is the public key of the initiator. It is at this very point that the similarities to PPP and CHAP are evident. As with PPP, once a communication foundation is established, an authentication protocol can be injected prior to establishing network connectivity (NCP). CRACK represents much the same concept; it allows a security association to be created, and then the user authentication can commence. If the user authentication is successful, the VPN is authenticated and Phase II operations can begin creating IPSec SAs.

The fourth message is from the responder and contains a signature and CHRE payload. The CHRE payload may contain the challenge from the responder's internal RADIUS server. The final message is similar and contains the initiator's response to the challenge. Other messages can follow, allowing for several variations of authentication. By supporting a flexible message structure, the protocol allows for many different types of legacy authentication.

The following are some examples in which the number of messages can vary, depending on the authentication method.

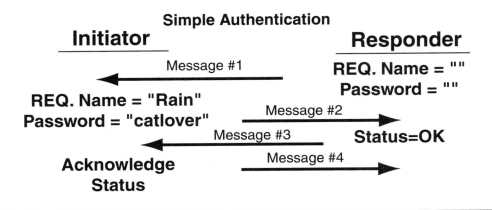

Exhibit 11-3.   Simple authentication.

In Exhibit 11-3, the responder simply asks for the user name and password. In a typical situation, this would be a PAP session. However, this exchange is under the protection of the keys previously created by the first two messages in CRACK.

Exhibit 11-4 is very similar to the CHAP exhibit presented earlier; however, this shows acknowledgments that can utilize messages added to the CRACK exchange.

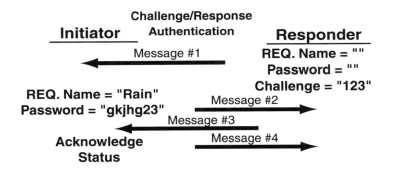

Exhibit 11-4.   A CHAP exchange.

As shown in Exhibit 11-5, the responder can simply ask for the PIN number to be included with the password. This does not necessarily enhance the communication; and in Exhibit 11-6 one sees that the responder can ask for the PIN separately.

Both of these examples are valid, and represent different flavors of obtaining the PIN. For some solutions that require PIN numbers to be calculated and shared, several messages are employed (as shown in Exhibit 11-7), to extend the authentication process. As with the other examples, there are several variations in the process of obtaining user credentials.

Using CRACK as an example, it has been shown that there is a way to accommodate legacy authentication systems into IPSec VPNs where there was none before. There are other examples of drafts that were not detailed but provide a very similar solution. The primary differences between proposals to the IETF is the phase in which the authentication takes place. Some provide new exchanges within IKE Phase I, such as CRACK, while others offer new exchanges to occur after normal Phase I operations but before Phase II operations that are designed to create IPSec security associations.

Challenge/Response
Authentication (two-factor)

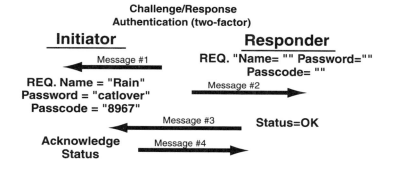

Exhibit 11-5.   Authentication with a PIN number.

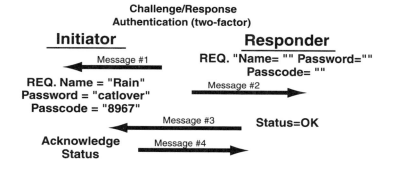

Exhibit 11-6.   Authentication with a PIN number Included in the challenge and not associated with the password.

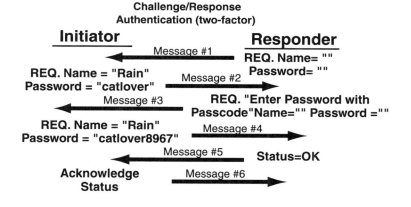

Exhibit 11-7.   Authentication with a PIN number provided in several messages.

Chapter 12

Security Policies and the Security of VPNs

Security policies are a fundamental part of security, and VPNs are no exception. However, VPNs represent an enormous change in the philosophy of information security due to the inherent relationship with the Internet. This chapter is dedicated to providing a perspective on some of the risks associated with the Internet and its use for remote access solutions.

Security policies were introduced earlier and the need for them outlined. However, the issue of security and how it relates to remote access security has never been faced with the massive number of vulnerabilities one sees today with the Internet.

Firewalls are becoming commonplace, and are a standard piece of equipment for any company connected to the Internet. Some of these firewalls provide VPN access capabilities, while others are augmented by VPN gateways operating in parallel, providing access to the internal network.

Security of Dial-in versus Continuous Internet Access

By allowing a remote user to connect to the internal network through the use of a modem dialed into an access device, several assumptions can be made about the security of the communication. It would be very difficult to hijack a modem session if the endpoints of the communication are not accessible to the attacker. When the remote user is connected, one can be fairly certain that there is no unwanted interactivity with the user's system or transmission. Although these are assumptions, most would agree that when compared to the Internet, dial-up solutions reduce the number of vulnerabilities to the user and home office. Finally, user interaction amounts to some types of vulnerabilities. As a user connects to a dedicated modem, that user is connecting for the sole purpose of accessing the internal network. If there is a desire to go to the Internet, and it is allowed, the user expects slower access times and limited resources if Internet service is allowed. In the past, prior to the explosion of the Internet and our increased need for it, the ability to prevent employees from using the Internet, at least with corporate equipment, was relatively simple. Access to the Internet was dial-up only and companies were not rushing to get employees their own Internet account. In short, the exposure to vulnerabilities to the user, the user's system, and traffic with remote dial-up access solutions is limited. Add to that the security associated with direct dial-up access into the home office, and the fact that some people were simply not sufficiently interested in the Internet to pay for a slow modem connection. Corporations also had the power to state in a security policy that no company equipment was to be used for Internet access — it was just that simple.

With the mad rush for VPNs, there has been an enormous counterstep in the implementation of security and the protection of corporate assets. Granted, the security industry has yet to see a publicized attack founded upon a VPN vulnerability. But as everyone knows, that does not mean it will not happen, nor that it has not already happened. The exposure to information is so great that many have overlooked the obvious. In some cases, people see that there is a fundamental issue with the security of information beyond the obvious communication provided by IPSec, but it is misplaced and limited in scope. An example is split tunnel mode versus single tunnel mode. Some feel that employing single tunnel mode will eliminate hijacking. Quite frankly, a hijacking session — especially IPSec — is a not trivial task and requires a substantial amount of sophistication. Ironically, when single tunnel is argued for, many forget that there still remains an IP connection with the Internet. If the level of sophistication required to hijack an IPSec VPN is available to an attacker, interacting with a system's IP connection is much less complicated in comparison. Another argument in the realm of hijacking is the use of an application or the ability of the attacker to route through the client into the internal network. In the case of routing, single tunnel does represent a greater challenge to the attacker than split tunnel. However, if routing through a remote system cannot be obtained, the installation of a Trojan is not far behind. A Trojan can perform many of the same tasks and frees the attacker to become involved only when necessary — reducing exposure and retaining anonymity. Simply put, there is a level of sophistication that is required to perform various attacks that can be compared against the level of acceptable risk — which ultimately equates to the mitigation of selected vulnerabilities.

The lack of security being spoken to has absolutely nothing to do with the security provided by IPSec or the authentication processes employed. Albeit, authentication is a point of weakness for any solution and with weak passwords, authentication is a focal point for many attacks. On the other hand, the sophistication required to crack an IPSec transmission is quite high, but doable given the proper resources. In any case, the security of the technology is not what is in question — the security of the concept is what has sneaked up on the technology.

As users connect to the Internet, they establish a TCP/IP connection with an ISP that provides access to every computer on the Internet, and vice versa. All the assumptions of the security of the connection that one had with dial-up connection have now vanished and the vulnerabilities have increased well beyond what many have considered.

VPNs offer a great deal: reduced costs, flexibility, consolidation of services, and extended reach of those services. To accomplish many of these added-value attributes of VPNs, the Internet is employed as the communication medium, and ISPs are used to get to that medium. As soon as remote users connect to the Internet, they are "in the open" and a valid target. When remote users leverage the Internet for VPNs, a pattern of insecurities surfaces that can have a direct impact on organizational security — in some cases, reducing the effectiveness of implemented security measures at the central office.

What is on the Box

Previously, the possibility of proprietary data on the remote system was briefly discussed. In many cases, VPNs are used to access files that are normally protected by firewalls and robust network security at the central office. VPNs are also used to access application information, where standard client packages access internal databases or middleware to accomplish a task.

In either case, information can exist, with regard to the end-user system, in three states:

1. *On the hard drive.* Typically from being copied over by the user in an attempt to increase performance while editing the file. However, data that is cached to the hard drive is vulnerable as well.
2. *In memory or in process.* As information is accessed, much of it is maintained in memory, or virtual memory, that can be exposed to certain types of vulnerabilities. In some cases, information is completely in the clear, but when on disk or transmitted, it is not.
3. *In transit.* When data moves from one system to another, it is vulnerable to a myriad of risks and influences.

As for VPN security, the transit state is what has primarily been addressed. The security of IPSec and IKE is impressive and when IPSec is employed correctly, the transmission of data should be the last concern when analyzing the security of the VPN. It is the other two states that this section addresses.

Of the remaining two states, physical representation on a hard drive represents the greatest risk, especially on an operating system that does not provide file access restrictions, such as Windows 95 or 98. The concept of data residing on a machine physically attached to the Internet represents an issue that security practitioners fought so hard to put a stop to as firewalls were pushed as a necessary technology.

For example, Bob has a computer on the internal network that has acceptable levels of risk to data, given the limited threat exposure attained through several security controls. These internal security controls can range from physical security, host security, application security, firewalls, to simply the overall environmental security posture. As Bob works on data, it can reside on his workstation or on a server — each protected and associated with logical levels of security provided by technology and policy: technology being the systems, firewalls, authentication mechanisms, access cards, etc., and policy being the yardstick to which all the systems and process are to be measured against to ensure that the desired level of security is maintained.

Bob goes home and connects to the Internet to gain access to the same files on the same systems using the same credentials. Bob uses the VPN, understanding that the authentication is sound and the data is protected in transit, but the proprietary file is opened for editing over the VPN, or is copied to his local machine, and it is now beyond the security provided earlier. Now that data resides beyond the confines of a controlled and validated security infrastructure that has had a form of risk analysis performed to provide acceptable protection of that data.

Connected All the Time

With the advent of broadband, the attraction of VPNs has increased tenfold. Now, users can connect at extremely high speeds that in the past were only available to universities and large organizations. Users can have a high-speed connection to the Internet and leverage that bandwidth to gain access to the corporate network and work with files and applications that would be absolutely impossible with dial-up accounts. In nearly all cases, broadband is provided by a special modem or router connected with various forms of technology based on the location of the home (or small office) and the services being offered. There are the cable modem providers, such as Time Warner and @Home, which use the cable infrastructure to provide a signal, and xDSL technology that uses the existing telephone infrastructure.

Note: xDSL represents several technology types based on a common foundation called Digital Subscriber Line; ADLS, IDSL, and SDSL are some of the variations of the communication medium that are typically driven by the type of local telephone loop and the distance the termination point is from the point of presence. The point of presence is typically a co-location where many technologies and providers place access equipment to provide services to end users. In the case of xDSL, a DSLAM is used to terminate the broadband signal and pass it off to a high-speed backbone, typically ATM.

Broadband typically terminates into a modem that converts the signal into Ethernet and allows a home computer to remain on the Internet as if connected to a LAN. This represents an enormous change in Internet philosophy. In the past, one had to pay per-minute for access; now, one can easily have a computer sit on the Internet and simply do anything one wants with little concern of dropping a connection and waiting for that 10-MB file — those days are gone. However, this represents an enormous risk. Most people simply have an Ethernet card installed in the home computer and are instantly connected to the Internet. Very few ask themselves what risks have just been introduced to them. Some believe that the ambiguity that existed with dial-up access to the Internet remains; that is, each time they connected, they would get a new IP address and the time connected was limited — a moving target. As everyone knows, that cannot be farther from the truth; and now that people are connected for extended periods of time, the odds of having the same IP address are very high. Some people go to great lengths to not disconnect their computer in hopes of keeping the same IP address to accommodate providing services such as e-mail and Web pages.

There are several advantages to the attacker when a constant connection is established with the Internet. However, many of the attacks introduced in this section apply to dial-up in exactly the same way, but a constant connection provides a greater window of opportunity.

Common Operating System and Increased Vulnerabilities

Typical end-user operating systems, such as Windows 95 or 98, are the focal point for many attackers and, therefore, result in more than their fair share of attack tools and utilities. To add fuel to the fire, many home users do not implement available security features and available software packages to mitigate the risks. For some, the attitude is, why should they? They have only basic applications and not much data of any value to an attacker. Obviously, this may not be true in various scenarios where personal finance information is maintained, but in the case with VPNs, there is a real chance that company proprietary data may reside on that personal computer in some format. In short, the more popular the operating system, the more attention to finding holes is paid by the attacker — market share does have its downside.

More Time on the Internet, More Time for Attackers

A consistent connection allows the attacker to complete a task without too much concern about the connection being terminated. The more something is predictable and consistent, the more the vulnerability becomes a greater risk. The more time the machine is on the network (i.e., the Internet), the more time the attacker has to find the system and make some determinations about that system. If the attacker deems the system of some value — whether it is for fun, a sense of accomplishment, or to see what can be found — that attacker can begin the process of establishing a hidden relationship with the target system.

It is critical to know your adversary and its capabilities; do not assume it cannot be done. A very popular attack, when dial-up was prominent, is to implement a program that collected keyboard activities and, at the next connection, e-mail that data to the attacker at some untraceable account. This is an extremely effective technique. The ability of an attacker to surreptitiously implement a program to collect information about your system and operate as a slave when the system comes online is a common reality.

Identification and Location

It is easy to locate an individual when certain environmental elements are met, such as using a cable modem. If the target system's IP address is discovered, the attacker can start the next attack by trying that IP address first. If that does not work because the IP address of the target was updated, the attacker can make some determinations. Some broadband technologies are based on networks, LAN segments, and, therefore, the attacker can take the original IP address and deduce the number of alternative IP addresses the target system may be configured with. Once the range is determined, a simple scan for a system signature or a Trojan call sign will produce the new IP address and the attack can commence.

Note: To add to the ability of an attacker to locate someone, the IANA (in July of 1995) allocated 24.0.0.0/8 to the cable industry for use with cable modems. At first glance, this range is fairly encompassing, containing over 16 million different IP addresses. However, these IP addresses must be divided between the providers and each location is segmented, allowing the attacker to make determinations on an IP address by simply knowing the network one may have been on before or the area one is living in. The fact that the IP address can be associated with a limited region has to be the one of the most interesting aspects of Internet access. If I know you live between 3rd Street and 9th Street, I can begin to focus on your system if I know you may have valuable information on that system. (To see the allocation of other IP addresses, go to www.isi.edu/in-notes/iana/assignments/ipv4-address-space to get a list of prime ownership and assignment.)

Connected to the Internet and the VPN

Up to this point, the discussion has focused on the vulnerabilities associated with connecting to the Internet, and the increased exposure when the connection is consistent and "LAN-like." Also introduced was the concept of Trojans, which can be used to interact with the system when isolated and to convey collected information back to the attacker when a path is provided. To further accentuate this attack type, the Trojan can perform various tasks while being controlled by the attacker when the system is online. When one combines the various avenues available to an attacker to the system, they typically get extended to the internal network by way of a VPN.

The ability to use the remote system as a router while in split tunnel is very feasible. However, the use of single tunnel does not entirely negate the vulnerability, but simply raises the bar on the complexity of the attack.

In Summary

The above discussion encompassed several different aspects of information security relative to the security of remote systems and their connection to the Internet. As systems connect to the Internet, they pose a risk to data that resides on that system that would normally not have been if a VPN was not available to that user. As those same systems connect to the Internet and establish a connection with the internal network, they are providing a looking glass into the network. The VPN stretches the internal network out to the remote host, where it becomes exposed to nearly limitless vulnerabilities. Finally, there is a combination of the two threats. As users ignore system security, their systems may have Trojans installed that can gather information on the system itself and from the internal network. If properly developed, they can turn the valid client system into an active attacker. This concept echoes the dynamic denial of service that plagued the Internet for a time. It was based on a slave/master concept where remote applications, slaves, are provided information from masters that are ultimately controlled by a single attacker. When properly developed and planned, a very sophisticated application can be constructed to anything the target system has rights to do within the network.

The Next Step

All the details conveyed in this section are currently haunting organizations that have leapt to the VPN as a solution and have not determined a policy to manage the security and the associated risks. As mentioned previously, administrators and implementers know there is something fundamentally insecure about having a remote user totally exposed to the Internet and connected to the corporate office simultaneously. However, the bigger problem cannot be seen — the proverbial "can't see the forest for the trees." Developers of VPN systems have begun to answer portions of the issue with the advent of single tunnel technology; however, this does not help the fact that a user can simply disengage the VPN client, and the data on that remote system then becomes available to attackers.

The answer is currently in its infancy: host-based firewalls and intrusion detection. BlackIce has answered a need that has existed for some time and is the next evolutionary step in the implementation of system security. From the introduction of a mainstream solution, such as BlackIce, others are beginning to surface that offer different options and defensive techniques. As this technology expands, various operations will become available. Some organizations are implementing these types of products for their remote users to reduce some of the risks involved with remote VPN support.

The most recent example of the "empower the host" concept can be seen in prototype products. The concept is a client package that not only acts a VPN client, but also includes inspection code that can be leveraged to enforce communication security policies. At first, it appears not much more than what BlackIce offers; however, the policy is not only controlled and implemented by the corporate management system, but the inspection code can remain loaded even if the VPN has been eliminated. Once the remote user connects to the VPN, the policy is uploaded to the client to implement the administrator's defined policy on permitted Internet activities.

This thought process represents the obvious next step in VPN and host security. The capability of centralized policy management for VPN communications and the protection of the remote system beyond the control of the end user are going to become mainstream. As more and more users work from home on personal or company-provided systems connected to the Internet by continuous dedicated service, the desire of the organization to control the security of that remote system will become paramount. It is obvious that proprietary data will exist on the remote systems and any protection implemented at the central office will be completely insignificant if the data it was designed to protect exists beyond the confines of the protected environment.

In essence, the goal that will soon be realized is a firewall-like implementation on client systems that not only provides VPN connectivity, but allows the selective processing of information flow in and out of the client system. Many people's first reaction typically revolves around performance. However, the system is only respon- sible for inspecting local traffic and that requires limited processing compared to inspecting several communication streams and providing other services, such as NAT. Of course, there are performance considerations with respect to the VPN operations, but those are accepted levels of system impact and the advent of AES encryption will reduce that accepted load. A central remote access gateway solution can provide user profiles and access control lists, or rule sets that can be collected into templates, groups, or applied to individual accounts for uploading to the connected client. On the client system, the software will load on boot and use the default firewall rule set or the last one used from the previous connection. If a connection to the Internet is detected, the client will collect the updated policy for that user, which is identified by a certificate that was initialized and associated to the user at logon. At this point, the client system becomes an extension of the perimeter protection policies adhered to at the central office.

At first glance, this has obvious advantages, but many more begin to surface. Not only have the VPN policies been shared with the initiation process upon connection to the Internet — satisfying a huge IPSec gap in current implementations — but the information flow can be optimized. As an example, access to the Internet is only outbound HTTP, SMTP, and POP3 protocols, while the Citrix or Terminal services used to access several backend applications are the only application allowed through the VPN. Meanwhile, no communications other than IPSec-related protocols — from the defined gateway only — are allowed into the system (of course, stateful inspection will accommodate the higher port assignments for Internet return communications).

This is the author's impression of the next obvious step in the evolution of VPN security. Currently, there is absolutely no real protection of the data that can reside on employee home systems or the portable systems they work on from home. With the addition of continuous Internet service into the home, the options for attackers to obtain private information or corporate proprietary data appear limitless. When closely examined and compared to the breakneck pace of VPN adoption, the security implications rival that of the early Internet years when shell accounts were the norm.

It is imperative that organizations fully understand the implications of remote systems access to private information while connected to the Internet. It is equally important to realize that this has absolutely nothing to do with the underlying communication technology. IPSec accomplishes much of what it promises when implemented properly — communication protection. As far as the security of the systems the information resides on, that is far beyond the scope of IPSec. The IPSec suite of protection protocols, combined with the massive explosion of high-speed Internet access, provides the foundation for extensive information sharing and remote access to that information like never before. It is much like blaming a highly tuned sports car for injuring the driver when he drove head-on into a tree. The car is not responsible for the actions of the driver nor the existence of the tree; it simply did what it was designed to do — carry the passenger. As a society, we are wielding a new weapon that appears as the new, cool toy. In reality, we are opening ourselves to unforeseen vulnerabilities. Unfortunately, there is no real technological answer. The ideas shared herein do not exist and the author is unaware of any product development that even slightly reflects the concepts shared. The only solution that can be implemented to mitigate the vulnerabilities to information security that have been introduced is properly designed and managed security policies. Information and organizational security policies that define standards, guidelines, and procedures are essential to information security. Also, IPSec policies are a critical component in defining the allowable data and communications attributes within the VPN. Once these are defined and properly implemented, at least the risks to corporate information are defined and categorized.

Chapter 13

Implementation Considerations

As organizations pursue VPN technology, they must be aware of the inherent complexities and nuances within the technology. As with any communication modification, IPSec has an effect on several aspects of accepted processes that may be changed, fundamentally, ultimately influencing the final design. This chapter is dedicated to introducing areas such as routing protocols, IPSec policy considerations and examples, client issues, helpdesk and support, and hybrid VPNs made of IPSec and L2TP technologies.

The installation of a VPN device is only the beginning of the long process of utilizing VPNs. Depending on the selected technology and the requirements of the solution, several problems may arise if not properly planned for and mitigated. There are extenuating circumstances that accompany a VPN implementation that do not normally exist in other communication standards. The absence of collateral complexities in other communication platforms and technology is because IPSec employs so many levels of communication — like no other. It operates at the network layer interacting with existing processes; it employs encryption, authentication, and integrity processes that within themselves are complicated; and finally, it is responsible for communicating data. The data can be upper layer application information, or other protocols that attempt to leverage IPSec for its security, or the actual connection it provides, such as routing protocols.

As IPSec attempts to accommodate all the features it inherently provides, other issues tend to surface in support of those features and must be addressed. Because IPSec was designed to operate seamlessly in the protocol stack, releasing applications and network infrastructure from the responsibilities of protecting data, typical operations may not function as expected.

L2TP over IPSec Considerations

The L2TP protocol functions at Layer 2 and can be configured to tunnel nearly any protocol over TCP/IP; unfortunately, it does not provide any protection to the accompanying data. Although L2TP lacks security features, it releases the constraint of only supporting TCP/IP protocol traffic for VPN communications. IPSec operates at Layer 3 and is deeply ingrained into the protocol it supports. L2TP will simply encapsulate nearly anything that is presented to its interface, but without security.

To allow L2TP to provide security and permit IPSec communications for non-TCP/IP protocols, each protocol can be used to leverage the other's advantages. In this scenario, IPSec and L2TP complement each other in fulfilling requirements foreign to the other. L2TP does not contain any security services whatsoever. All communications that utilize L2TP are vulnerable to a plethora of attacks. Despite its security shortcomings, L2TP operates on behalf of the link layer, which is not concerned with the Layer 3 protocols; as a result, L2TP can be used to tunnel nearly any protocol.

IPSec provides several security services, to which this book is dedicated in describing. In contrast to L2TP, IPSec operates at the network layer and therefore is associated with a certain network layer protocol — obviously TCP/IP. In a situation where a different protocol is required, the use of IPSec alone will not suffice.

By combining L2TP capabilities of encapsulating at the link layer and IPSec security features, some vendors have migrated to the L2TP over IPSec solution. With L2TP over IPSec, the IP packet used to house the L2TP header and the encapsulated foreign protocol is protected by IPSec, as in any other TCP/IP communication. Because L2TP is providing the tunneling properties and the LAC and LNS are the termination points, IPSec transport mode can be used as the protection suite. Exhibit 13-1 shows what a transport IPSec packet would look like using ESP, and Exhibit 13-2 shows a similar example using AH as the security protocol.

Thus, the process is for the original protocol to be encapsulated into an IP packet and adorned with a new UDP header that contains an L2TP header and the associated data. The IP packet then has IPSec applied with the security protocol in transport mode. The result is a point-to-point IPSec-secured VPN that can support multiple protocols.

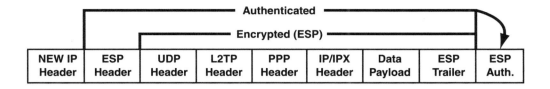

Exhibit 13-1. L2TP over IPSec ESP Transport Mode.

L2TP is an example of Layer 2 functionality being enhanced by Layer 3 operations, and providing a means to leverage a public network. Also, this represents the simplest form of VPN, because it simply provides a communication tunnel. The obvious lack of security features does not necessarily qualify it to be called a VPN by today's standards, and can add to the confusion when VPNs are being discussed or debated.

		Authenticated					
Immutable Fields Only		Set to Zero during Authorization Process					
NEW IP Header	AH Header	AH Authentication Data	UDP Header	L2TP Header	PPP Header	IP/IPX Header	Data Payload

Exhibit 13-2. L2TP over IPSec in AH Transport Mode.

IPSec and L2TP Limitations

There are some operational implications when employing L2TP functionality with the protection of IPSec. The information normally made available to IPSec operations for policy determinations is not provided by way of the L2TP encapsulation. As data is encapsulated into an L2TP payload, IPSec is only aware of the UDP header of the L2TP datagram, thus limiting the decision-making penetration of IPSec into the tunneled data. In other words, in normal IPSec implementations, the original network and transport layer protocol are available after decryption to make necessary decisions for properly routing the communication. Unfortunately, after decryption, IPSec is presented with L2TP information — not the original data that the policy is configured to manage.

A good example is the inner IP header information. In the event tunnel mode is used for operations, there is no inner IP header to make several security operation determinations. For many solutions, the inner IP header is typically "trusted" when compared to the outer IP header. Unless AH is employed, the outer IP header could have been manipulated; therefore, the inner header is typically used to make policy determinations. As a standard IPSec tunnel mode packet is received, the inner header is used to determine filtering policies and SA selection for inbound and outbound packets.

There are several discussions within the IETF and with vendors about eliminating tunnel-mode IPSec and utilize transport mode allowing the implementations to select their own tunneling protocol (i.e., L2TP and GRE). The primary argument against L2TP replacing tunnel mode IPSec is the elimination of various security services, authentication, and proper SA management with regard to the information being routed. For example, IPSec over L2TP loses many of the access control features because the receiver no longer examines the inner IP header to see if it matches the selectors for the SA for which the packet arrived. Because the SA binding is lost as soon as the packet arrives, no filtering can be provided later in the process, and nesting of tunnels is non-existent.

The argument that supports L2TP over IPSec provides that a link can be provided to associate the user authentication and data alignment is provided by normal protocol operations, to which L2TP automatically supplies. The goal is to align authentication to L2TP tunneling points that can be associated to IPSec SAs. L2TP tunnel interfaces can be defined that use protocol encapsulation, and then the application of IPSec can provide the security. Filtering controls can then be applied to the tunnel interface and used to manage communications after IPSec is applied. Other arguments for L2TP include the direct relation to PPP. Remote access solutions that use PPP for encapsulation can allow extensive services and options to the solution. Authentication, protocol manipulation, and attribute sharing — to name a few — have made remote access solutions based on PPP very flexible and robust. L2TP can be used to provide many of the services once only found in PPP. Therefore, as L2TP is utilized and aligned to IPSec communications, IPSec can be used as a robust remote access solution — where none currently exists.

However, without an inner IP header to accommodate the SA association to the data by means of a selector, various attribute controls will be lost and IPSec will not have control. In other words, if FTP and HTTP require different levels of encryption and authentication, a selector is used to provide that determination. If a foreign tunneling operation is used, that data would not be available until that tunneling process is executed, which would come long after IPSec operations are complete. Another loss in the IPSec operations and integrity of the solution is the inability to control the protocols being tunneled. Traffic would nearly be completely processed before certain decisions could be made about the forwarding of the data under the protection of IPSec. Providing tunneling with IPSec, a single policy can be implemented to provide the several layers of protection typically desired by most IPSec implementations, whereas once combined with L2TP IPSec policies lose their effectiveness. Because IPSec is the first operation when receiving and the last when transmitting data, it is ultimately unaware of the traffic it is furnishing services to — inherently breaking the advantages of IPSec security. Granted, the communication — the actual datagram — is protected, but the overall solution is weakened.

The L2TP protocol is a well-defined, mature communication protocol that enjoys a large install base. However, simply combining two dissimilar protocols does not provide the best of both worlds.

Routing protocols introduce another issue and the use of IPSec tunnel mode. If IPSec provides the tunnel operations, the IPSec-enabled interface must understand the requirements set forth by a broadcast routing protocol (e.g., RIP) or multi-cast protocols (e.g., OSPF). Current tunneling interfaces, such as GRE and L2TP, support routing protocol requirements. By applying IPSec to the final interface, routing protocols are provided the security, while the interaction with the interface does not change. This is also an argument for backward compatibility and interoperability.

As drawn from this discussion, there are arguments for and against the elimination of IPSec tunnel mode and the adoption of L2TP to provide that service. The simple fact is that by using L2TP, the intrinsic security services that are provided by IPSec are lost. To recoup the features lost, L2TP will need to be controlled and some form of association from L2TP will need to be supported to align them with IPSec SAs — the ultimate carrier of the data. The immediate advantage of the complicated marriage between IPSec and L2TP is the support for various routing protocols without modification and the ability to provide IPSec communication security features for non-IP protocols.

It has been argued at some point that the combination may evolve into an integrated solution rather than exist as two protocols creating one operation. Unfortunately, the two protocols are so different from each other, and operate at different layers within the OSI model, that the odds of creating a combined protocol are slim. Nevertheless, the argument over tunnel mode and transport mode, and the use of other tunneling protocols to support various aspects that IPSec does not, will remain for some time.

Information Security

Information can exist at varying levels of sensitivity. Typically, this is controlled and managed by a data classification policy that defines the organization, handling, and identification of various data. Information labels can be employed to identify the data's sensitivity as it traverses a network. This process is designed to prevent the unauthorized transmission of data from a secured network to an unsecured network or between unauthorized systems. Because the data itself is identified on the network, it is irrelevant who or what is attempting to violate policy.

The ability to support data classification and the application of labels is referred to as multi-level security (MLS). MLS requires access controls that prevent unprivileged users and systems from transmitting sensitive data. IPSec can be used to facilitate MLS environments. By operating at the network layer, IPSec has the opportunity to label data and validate other labels as they traverse the system.

The security protocols provided by IPSec can be leveraged to accommodate many aspects of employing MLS. An example is the AH security protocol; it can be used to tie the IP header to the data label through the authentication process. In standard IP-based networks, data labels are available for implementation; however, there is no form of authentication associated with the label. The label can be removed, forged, or modified without discovery. IPSec can be applied to eliminate the vulnerability.

The ESP security protocol can be used to encrypt information exchanges between systems. When combined with the appropriate key management and algorithms, MLS can be implemented to accommodate several levels of security. Key management can use classification labels to accommodate access controls based on several different attributes. By providing distinction in the key management process, data is only forwarded to authenticated systems and users. Once IPSec and IKE policies are merged with MLS policies, the two can be leveraged in many ways to accommodate controlled, secured communications with several transform sets for layered communications.

SA Provisioning

IPSec is based on the application of security protocols that are implemented in a VPN based on the policy of the network and defined within the system. The combination of the security protocols with well-designed policies in the SPD will facilitate MLS.

Normally, an SA is established to provide a secure communication relationship based on various attributes shared in the creation process. A good example is Main Mode with pre-shared keys. The VPN is entirely based on the peer's IP address. Once the VPN is established, only then does the responder know the provided details of initiator. However, the application of data labels will allow an SA to be created based entirely on the data itself. An example is a tunnel VPN between two SGWs providing connectivity over the Internet for two autonomous networks. As data is shared from one network to the other, data labels are used to identify predefined security controls for that data stream. New SAs can be created to accommodate only that communication stream. The communication can be between two systems that are already communicating using differently labeled data. Once information of a different label is discovered, an SA or SA Bundle must be identified or created for private operations.

Much of this is accomplished by the inclusion of sensitivity information as one of the available selectors for SA alignment and creation. This allows the SPD and SAD relationship to accommodate the information with the desired security protection suite.

For the process to be successful, IPSec must maintain the association of the data to the assigned label during processing. This includes the actions taken after IPSec is applied. IPSec must determine if the requested operation of forwarding or sending up to the upper layers is allowed by the policy of the data classification. During the processing of datagrams, the IPSec policy is queried to determine if the policy allows the tagged data to be passed from IPSec operations to the upper layer functions and application. The result is robust communication security and information flow control, united with the ability to inspect the labeled data for application management.

IPSec Communication Policies

Throughout this book, discussion has focused on transform sets, security suites, SAs, IKE SAs, IPCA, granularity, bundles, SPD, SAD, and countless other aspects of IPSec and its implementation. The management and application of data protection to any given situation is an IPSec policy. Included were discussions about the SPD and the SAD that maintain the critical information for identifying and protecting specific traffic with various security suites.

It is clear that organizations need a security policy, especially if implementing a VPN solution. However, there is another definition of security policy and how it pertains to IPSec. An IPSec policy is the buffer between the SPD and SAD and the administrator's desires. The goal is to provide the administrator with a method for converting the natural assumptions into computer-recognized information used to execute the ultimate policy. As one might imagine, the process is very important to make certain that the interpretation is correct and applicable.

In addition, the IPSec policy is much more than a user interface into the management of VPNs — it is a mediator between the various components of IPSec and IKE. As an example, the policy must know the various valid proposals to offer when faced with certain types of traffic going to predetermined destinations. A more in-depth example is fragmentation. As the upper layers produce data, the policy must be consulted to determine the final packet size so as not to interfere with controllable transmission issues. Once the final values are determined based on the policy for that particular traffic, the value is presented to the upper layer.

The IPSec policy is a VPN management tool that is common among all VPN implementations; without it, how could one configure IPSec? Thus, if all implementations have some form of policy management, what is the standard? The answer is, there is none. As previously mentioned, the IETF (in February 2000) created an IPSec policy workgroup determined to define a standard on the control of policies from a functional point — an agreement and distribution of policy standards. Because no standard exists, every vendor implements some form of management at some level. Every IPSec solution must have some form of distribution of policy; whether it is manual, automatic, centralized, or distributed, the policy must be provided to each system involved in the enterprise's VPN network. The result is vendor solutions that use everything from nothing to the employment of other security communication protocols. An example of "nothing" is the early Cisco solution. In the IOS, a policy is defined that is purely local and must be duplicated on other routers that wish to communicate. Of course, an administrator can use other IOS configuration deployment utilities, but that does not result in an IPSec policy management tool; rather, a configuration coping process. On the other extreme is VPNet's use of SSL. As a remote system wishes to communicate, it establishes an SSL connection that will allow encrypted communication between the peers protecting the policy information that is passed. Once the policy is received, the SSL connection is discarded and an IPSec VPN is established. This example represents the ingenuity of vendors when faced with having no foundation or anything to compare to. For all intents and purposes, the solution meets the requirements and protects the information during distribution.

Network security can be very complex, even in the smallest of networks. Distribution of information represents areas of complexity within itself. Examples can include items as simple as logon scripts. Without proper distribution in various authentication environments, the logon script may become out of date and cause various issues. A similar example can be shared with regard to IPSec. The inability to synchronize IPSec policy among all the devices would result in loss of function. A policy modification on one system may conflict with others in the VPN, which could result in IKE negotiations failing to agree on a communication policy. Even small networks that may have only a few devices will still feel the impact of policy misalignment and modification. Because synchronization problems can exist on even the smallest of implementations, any true policy solution would have to address this closely to avoid scalability problems. An example of poor implementations is after a policy is updated, many products need to be restarted. Compatible, TimeStep, and Altiga, to mention a few, require a restart when certain policy configurations are changed. At first glance, this seems to be an oversimplification. However, if one has ten VPN devices providing network-to-network communications and one needs to add one more to the mesh, 11 devices need to be configured and 10 — more than likely — will need to be restarted. The result is that the VPN/WAN will be brought down periodically and then take a short time to come back online. In the normal WAN world, where routers are implemented, this concept is ludicrous and interfaces can be configured online — it is very rare to reload a router for a configuration change. However, even Cisco is not immune to reloads where VPNs are considered. If a policy is changed, the tunnels will have to be cleared to implement the new policy. While the system itself is not restarted, the VPN is — which results in the same conclusion — brief stoppage of communications.

IPSec Policy Implementation Requirements

An IPSec policy defines the inner workings of the VPN and the rules that apply to the communications. Examples of IPSec security policies are relationships between networks, hosts, or services to the levels of encryption, security protocol, message authentication, and the termination point of the SAs.

A simple policy in a SPD might be:

10.23.7.0 255.255.255.0:80, AH_MD5, ESP_3DES, IKE_AUTO, PRE_SHARE
"thePASSWORD", DES, HASH_SHA-1

In this simplified example, HTTP protocol access to the network 10.23.7.0 is provided AH and ESP security protocols using MD5 and 3DES, respectively. IKE automatic key management will be invoked, the authentication will use a shared secret for origination authentication, and the key operations will use DES encryption with SHA message authentication.

A policy is a combination of management and process. Management is the interface and the ability to acquire administrative directives and process them into a deliverable package that can be used to populate the SPD and, ultimately, the entire solution. As mentioned, there are literally dozens of examples that are currently being deployed in VPN solutions; every vendor has its own way of doing things. This is the result of the lack of standards and because the IETF does not mandate a particular representation of policies. This is a natural position for the IETF, due to a standards board that is not designed to instruct policy management, however, it may standardize on various foundations, such as protocols and implementation techniques.

A policy implementation is cognizant of security implications as well as traffic flows. It is easy to say that all HTTP traffic from A to B will be encrypted for security reasons, but the policy must be aware of the traffic and have the ability to identify it properly, given the vast options provided by selectors.

There are several requirements placed on IPSec policies to be efficient, functional, and effective. The policy must be flexible and encompassing without affecting the integrity of the protocols that it is guiding. A policy implementation should not weaken an IKE or IPSec implementation, but rather support the protocol and all of its options. A policy will have to accommodate several environmental constraints, ranging from policy storage types and size limitations to processing formats. For example, a firewall may have a hard drive and use Solaris as the operating system, which provides various opportunities to the developers; whereas, a VPN device may not have a hard drive — only NVRAM — and use a proprietary operating system. If a policy is in the form of a file, the size of that file could impact the storage on the VPN device. In addition, the transmittal of a policy can consume bandwidth, take time, and be prone to errors. The ability to properly share, protect, and verify policy data can be directly associated with the platform, which could change from implementation to implementation. One can only begin to imagine the complexities.

Because IPSec was designed to be transparent and based on TCP/IP, the goal was to have true interoperability — as found in today's TCP/IP implementations. Regardless of the platform, if TCP/IP is implemented correctly and according to the standards, there is no solid reason why it could not talk to any other device using an equally compliant protocol stack. Granted, the policy required to support TCP/IP is simple when compared to IPSec, but existent nevertheless. The IP address, subnet mask, gateway, multicast domains, etc. are required for TCP/IP operations. For IPSec interoperability, the task of policy management is far more complicated. Imagine a router establishing an IPSec VPN with a VPNet VPN gateway, several other routers, a Check Point firewall, and a couple of remote user clients. Each solution has different system attributes that can affect the policy interpretation, protection, management — everything.

Policies must support all the capabilities maintained within IPSec and IKE, and therefore reflect the functions provided by the underlying protocols. The policy must be able to configure multiple policies for a single VPN system. For example, a host may need a policy for communications for a specific destination, and another set of policies for a specific remote network.

Note: Multiple policies that represent different aspects of communication from a single VPN endpoint are sometimes referred to as subpolicies and represent the working hand of the IPSec policy solution. The IPSec policy solution merely collects, controls, and manages subpolicies. However, in normal discussion, the entire process, whether multiple individual policies on a single system or a policy management system, the term "policy" is all-encompassing.

The ability of a policy to be defined for a network is required. Given this is available as a selector, the granularity must be able to reach up to include an entire subnet. At the other end of the granularity spectrum; the policy must be able to control application-level implementations. The TCP service ports used for the communications can typically identify applications that use TCP/IP. The ability to combine application-level controls with network and host policies is a fundamental requirement of the policy, as is the ability to implement policy with respect to the security protocols that are being implemented. Whereas previous requirements focused on what was required to identify the traffic, this aspect of IPSec policies also concerns how to handle the traffic. The application of multiple security protocols, AH and ESP, must be supported by the policy to afford the communication the highest security provided by IPSec. This is an example of one of the fundamental requirements of a policy — it must not weaken the supported protocols. These three options — network, application, and security protocol — are necessary to be combined to form a comprehensive policy to meet the minimum requirements set forth by th available selectors of IPSec. Another basic requirement of the policy is to provide basic filtering and control over traffic based on the three primary requirements of IPSec: drop, forward, or apply IPSec. This requirement is also related to the policy that enables support of multiple SAs and IKE SAs.

Each of these stated requirements are intimately related parts that make up the whole. Each section that needs to be supported must be provided to allow functionality of the other requirements. Therefore, any weakness in one area will affect many — if not all — of the others. This is an excellent opportunity to discuss limitations of existing implementations. Briefly introduced earlier, some vendor implementations do not necessarily follow the standards, nor do they implement all the features provided by IPSec; nesting VPNs is a good example. Nearly every solution this author has worked with, implemented, or tested has intense variations in functionality that can be immediately identified by the policy structure. In some cases, the policy implementation technique actually limited the entire implementation. This can be realized when the primary requirement of an IPSec policy is not to limit the underling protocol's functionality. An example is a VPN device that allows the ability to identify interesting traffic based on IP source and destination, but not on the transport layer application service ports. This could be expected if the system simply does not inspect the TCP header, which would be an understandable reason behind the limitation. However, the implementation did allow for the blocking of traffic based on application port on the interfaces. This means that TCP is being inspected and a more robust solution would provide access to this capability for standard IPSec operations and policy control. Another example is interface restrictions. On several occasions, it was impossible to establish a VPN with certain attributes, due to the lack of layering of rules, or the simple inability to do so. In other words, the policy would not allow the administrator to configure a VPN in a manner that would normally be allowable by the standards.

Above are examples where the policy configuration limits the ability of the solution. It is obvious that the system can perform the desired functions, but not in the combination needed within the IPSec VPN. In contrast, there are solutions where the policy will allow an administrator to configure a communication policy, but the VPN will not function. An example is the use of ESP and AH combined to provide encryption and total packet authentication. This implementation is supported by IPSec and is well-defined in the RFCs. Unfortunately, when configured to do so on a system, the VPN could not be established. Nearly every variation was tested, but until one of the security protocols was eliminated, the VPN remained lifeless. This is an example of something that the author often sees: a VPN solution that does not function as expected or operates under certain seemingly unrelated limitations. An example is, "Yes, you can use filters to control traffic flow but they only work when AH is not configured." When reviewing a VPN solution, it is imperative that options within the solution to be implemented are tested in combination to determine if (1) it is possible, and (2) if it works as expected. The policy module or application provided by the vendor may present limitations that only appear in a specific scenario. When found, this will expose a fundamental weakness in the IPSec or IKE implementation. As each policy requirement is reduced in functionality, the resulting implementation is weakened. The reverse holds true as well; if the IPSec solution is not well-constructed or designed, the policy will reflect it in configuration limitations.

It is amazing that some vendors implement a solution to a point where it meets the basic, expected functionality but is only one or two steps from having a great solution. This is very interesting because getting the basics of IPSec and IKE is the difficult part. All the same, policies can be complicated to implement to take advantage of all the possibilities. As will be seen in the next few chapter sections, when a policy attempts to support every possible configuration options (which it is supposed to), it can become very complicated and difficult to present.

Microsoft IPSec VPN

Microsoft's integration of Active Directory into its operating system provides an excellent platform for the distribution and management of enterprise IPSec policies. This section introduces Microsoft's implementation of IPSec through the use of the policy management tools and the control that they provide. Using Microsoft's solution as an example offers a good opportunity to illustrate how IPSec policies, when properly configured and implemented, can become a powerful solution. A quick example: when compared to other solutions that require manual or proprietary policy distribution techniques, Microsoft's solution allows an administrator to implement an IPSec policy throughout the entire domain if desired. The policy is automatically absorbed by the client systems and implemented. In only a few commands, an entire IPSec communication policy is defined, distributed, and employed.

In March 1998, Microsoft had the first Rapid Deployment Program (RDP) conference in Seattle, Washington, which this author attended for three days. Nearly all of the developers, project managers, and product directors for Windows NT 5.0 were there to detail the operations of NT 5.0. There were approximately 200 representatives from the Fortune 500 and professional services groups throughout the nation in attendance. It was Microsoft's opportunity to introduce NT 5.0 to the group that was more than likely going to be upgrading to it very soon, or the individuals implementing it. There were several labs where each attendee had two or three servers to perform exercises to see the operation of various options within NT 5.0. At that time, NT 5.0 looked and acted like NT 4.0 and Active Directory was nearly nonexistent. There was a lecture on the security features of NT 5.0 that included information about Microsoft's VPN solution; it was unimpressive and appeared to lack any operational value and it was completely based on L2TP and PPTP — with little mention of IPSec. At that time, IPSec was still experiencing developmental issues and adoption by vendors was in the early stages, so it was expected to see more IPSec operability; however, it appeared that Microsoft was not considering IPSec as a front-runner for its solution.

After working on many VPN engagements over the past several years, including many different vendor products, Microsoft has provided more and more information about the available options within its new product, now Windows 2000. As beta versions were deployed, the integration of IPSec increased — as did the options. Finally, at the release of Windows 2000, this author was very curious as to how the integration of IPSec was finalized into the system, as well as being very skeptical, based personal working history with Microsoft products (specifically, Windows 2000 over the past two years).

The final result was surprising. The astonishment, in some part, was due to the lowered expectations and the confidence that Microsoft could not put that many well-developed options into a single operating system. Nonetheless, the Windows 2000 implementation is a well-thought-out implementation that has numerous options to administrators that were hoped for, but not expected. The inclusion of Active Directory in the policy deployment and management was critical, and Microsoft integrated it beyond expectations. It is necessary to note that proper directory design and implementation is crucial to every aspect of Windows 2000 operations, IPSec notwithstanding. There are several points of interest in Active Directory (e.g., the Global Catalog and DNS) that when not properly designed can wreak havoc on a network. Thus, IPSec implementations are no different, and are susceptible to poor design. When properly designed and implemented in a homogeneous network, the IPSec policy management aspect of Windows 2000 is leaps and bounds ahead of the competition.

Configuration of MS VPN. The implementation of Microsoft's VPN can be difficult to manage due to the dozens of dialogs and access points throughout the solution. However, once the basic rules of the IPSec policy and communications have been applied, the interface and options begin to come together. What soon becomes complicated is finding a way to properly present the dialogs for explanation, without losing cohesiveness.

This section introduces the configuration process to display the options Microsoft has implemented at the IPSec level and its integration into AD. The examples shown were created using Windows 2000 Professional that was not part of a domain, and therefore the local AD was used to show these options. The advantage is that IPSec policies can be implemented on the local level all the way to enterprise implementations; therefore, the examples herein directly map to large implementations.

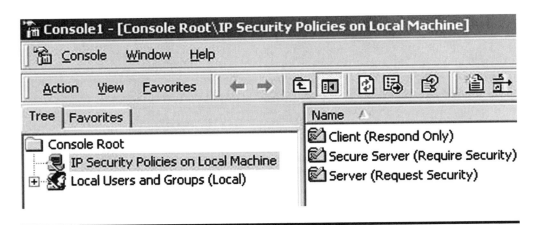

Exhibit 13-3.   MMC and the IP security snap-in.

The Microsoft Management Console (MMC) is the access point to AD and is used as an interface for administration of systems, local and remote. The MMC employs snap-ins, small management units that can be collected into a single interface for customized administration. In Exhibit 13-3, the MMC is used and the IP Security snap-in is installed pointing at the local machine's AD; therefore, all configurations will be available to the local system only.

In the right-hand pane of Exhibit 13-3 are the available policies. The ones listed are defaults that are available for general IPSec protection given common environments. In the event an administrator has implemented enterprise IPSec policies, they too would be available in the list to end users.

After opening the MMC, select (right clicked) the snap-in and pick "New" from the menu that starts a New Policy Wizard. Win2K highly leverages Wizards for the creation of many optional services. However, unlike some of the other services, IPSec policies allow one to bypass the Wizard on an interface-by-interface basis, which is a nice feature when one already knows exactly what one wants to accomplish.

Once the Wizard is complete, one has a generic policy called IPSEC POLICY in the right-hand window of the MMC. Exhibit 13-4 shows the initial dialog available once policy is created and edited.

There are several pieces of information available in this dialog. In this we see a list of filters that the policy is configured with. Each filter can be selected or deselected depending on the traffic you would like associated with the VPN. These filters are provided for identifying "interesting traffic" for the IPSec stack. This is exactly what the ACL in Cisco is providing. A list of traffic identifying filters that allows IPSec to isolate traffic that should, or should not have IPSec applied. The filters also control the three states: Pass without IPSec, Apply IPSec and transmit, and Drop packet. By collecting a list of filters, the exact traffic that is to have IPSec applied is dropped through the filter from the top down, until the traffic is matched or it reaches the end of the list where it is finally dropped or passed normally.

Note: The list contains a filter named Citrix Traffic that is explained in detail below.

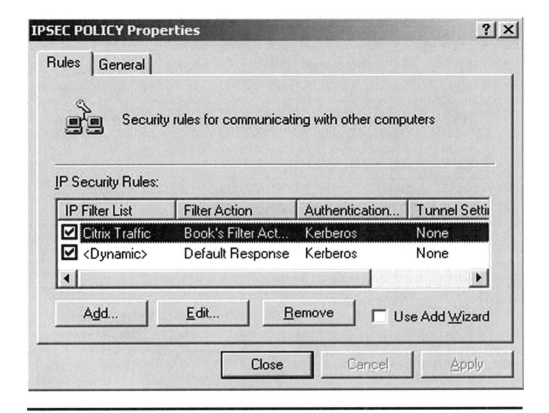

Exhibit 13-4. New policy "IPSEC POLICY" rules interface.

The added flexibility of adding and removing filters, and the ability to activate or deactivate those filters within a policy, allow the administrator to test and troubleshoot the VPN while providing robust policy management.

Before investigating the filters individually, the Edit button on the IPSEC POLICY Properties dialog box contains the specific rules about the IPSec implementation itself according to the default Dynamic filter.

As shown in Exhibit 13-5, there is a list of IPSec transform sets available to the VPN. This is nothing more than a collection of applied security suites that can be presented for use in a VPN. During the Quick Mode negotiation, these will appear in the SA payload for any original traffic that matches the assigned filters. The new traffic will be identified by the filter and initiate the IKE negotiations, ultimately leading to a Quick Mode exchange for the creation of an IPSec SA. The list contains the defaults provided by Microsoft, and is much too long to be managed or properly deployed. In many cases, the list of transforms will not exceed three options. Once again, Microsoft is attempting to accommodate everyone and many scenarios — a valiant attempt. Notice the PFS option at the bottom. This defines the relationship to key material within and between IPSec SAs. If this is selected, a new Quick Mode exchange ensues that includes Diffie-Hellman public values for the generation of completely new key material prior to the creation, or re-creation, of expired IPSec SAs.

If one of the IPSec transforms is selected, you are presented with a simple dialog that has two preconfigured transform sets and a custom button. Exhibit 13-6 shows

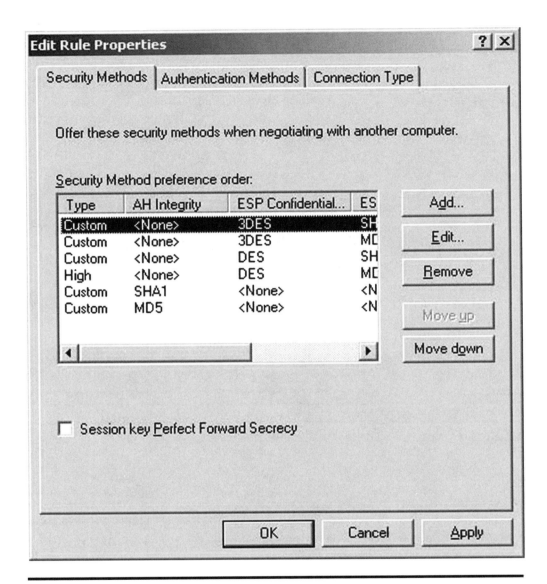

Exhibit 13-5. IPSec transform sets.

the dialog that appears for the custom button transform set configuration. There are several interesting details in this dialog. There is the option to employ AH or ESP, or both, and select the appropriate encryption of authentication algorithm. At the bottom is the SA Life Type and Duration configuration options that define how long the IPSec SA will last. One thing to remember is that each configuration affects two SAs and the options available appear to be for a single security association; however, remain aware that two SAs are being created for IPSec operations. It is necessary to maintain an approximate knowledge of the number of SAs being created to provide preliminary performance considerations for system and network designs and constraints.

For every IPSec operation, there must be key management, and Microsoft is no exception. Unfortunately, Microsoft presents the IPSec property dialogs *before* any IKE configuration. This is not catastrophic because much of IKE is simple and the

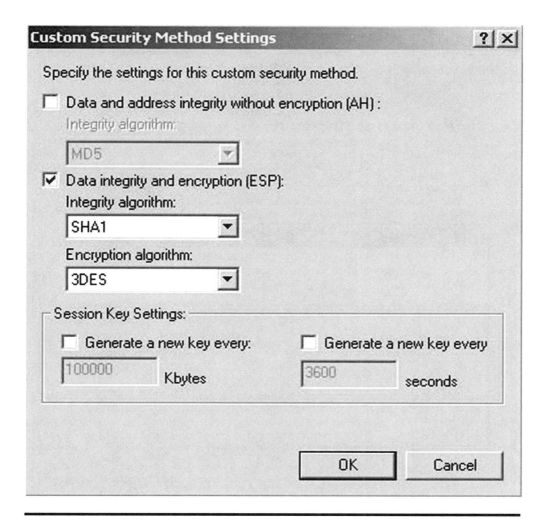

Exhibit 13-6. IPSec transform set custom configuration.

defaults integrated will suffice for the majority of the implementations. However, creating the IKE policy first and assigning IPSec policies to them would be a proper progression but, unfortunately, not a natural one. When most people think of IPSec VPNs, they do not immediately think about IKE, and therefore presenting them with IPSec transforms first is the most obvious answer, albeit slightly backward.

The General tab on the IPSEC POLICY Properties dialog, as shown in Exhibit 13-7, contains the name and description that can be assigned to the policy. The time option at the bottom is to inform the system to poll AD on a regular basis in the event of a change. This option applies mostly to policies stored in AD provided by domain controllers; whereas in this example, using the local AD, this would only affect new traffic in the event the policy is changed. Finally, inconspicuously hiding at the bottom of the dialog is a hint to the key management configuration.

As shown in Exhibit 13-8, there are a few very meaningful settings in this dialog. The master PFS setting affects the PFS from Phase I to Phase II operations. Ironically, the PFS was more available to IPSec where someone can easily select it, causing a great deal of processing overhead; whereas PFS for IKE could be considered much

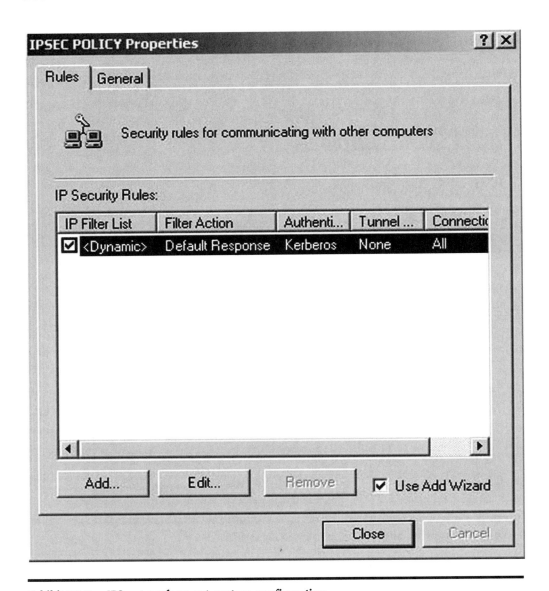

Exhibit 13-7.   IPSec transform set custom configuration.

more important to security and use a fraction of the processor. In short, use IKE PFS and unless moving very private data across a highly vulnerable network; and do not use PFS within IPSec. Also, to accommodate increased security and only spikes of performance derogation, implement PFS in IKE and not in IPSec, as suggested, and reduce the lifetime of IKE to force a shorter cycle on all the IPSec keys.

Once again, there is a tiny button at the bottom, Methods, that contains IKE-specific configuration properties that can have not only a security impact but a performance one as well. Exhibit 13-9 provides the acceptable list of IKE transforms.

The list defines the acceptable IKE security parameters for VPN negotiation communications, Phase I and II. Notice that the list starts with the most secure configuration, 3DES, SHA, and Diffie-Hellman group 2, and ends with the least secure, DES, MD5, and Diffie-Hellman group 1. By leaving the defaults in place, the system is

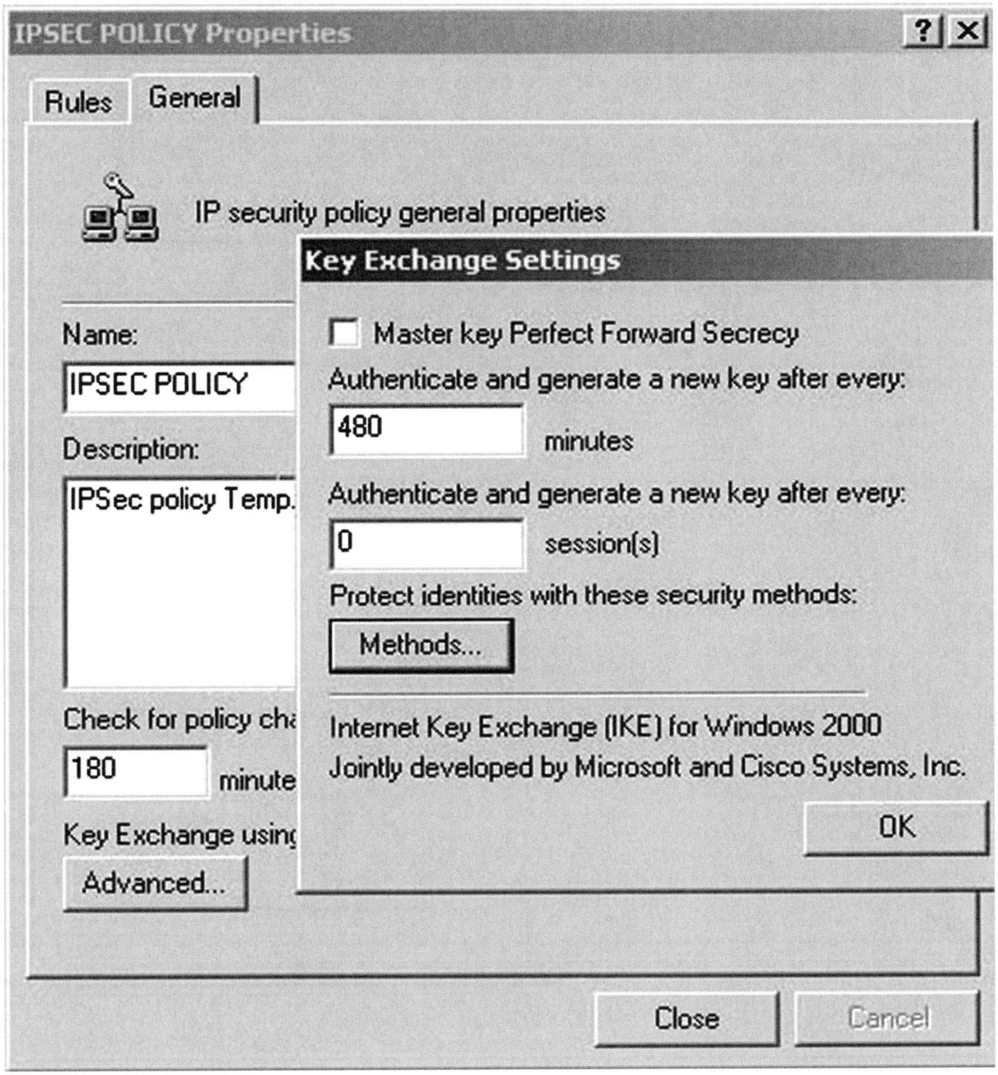

Exhibit 13-8. IKE settings.

configured to accept or negotiate communications all the way down to DES and MD5, and Diffie-Hellman group 1. Therefore, if a higher level of security is what is really desired, then remove the remaining three policies. By default, Microsoft employs an IKE policy that will accept nearly any communication. As with any policy or interesting traffic filter list, the order is paramount, and to accommodate this there is a Move up or down button to align the policies. An interesting aspect worth noting: Why should Microsoft not just automatically place the policies in the order from strongest to weakest and let IKE negotiate down with its peer from a secure beginning? The default list is just exactly that; it will negotiate an IKE SA presenting the most secure protocol suite listed with the others following in an IKE exchange. However, there may be times when a weaker suite may be preferred for performance reasons and increased security should only be made to those who specifically request it. Therefore, a limited

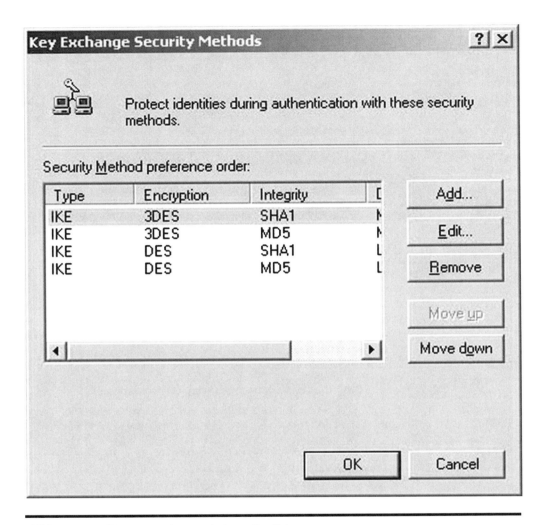

xhibit 13-9. IKE security suite negotiation policy list.

policy defining DES, MD5, and Diffie-Hellman group 1 may appear first, while a more secure policy will follow.

Exhibit 13-10 shows the dialog presented when the attribute of an IKE transform wishes to be modified. As with most IPSec-based VPN solutions, only groups 1 and 2 are supported.

Advanced Configuration of MS VPN. Thus far in the explanation, the policy created contains two filters in the list (from the Rules tab in the policy properties). The General tab provides access to the IKE settings for the entire policy, and the Generic filter provides access to the default IPSec configurations and transform sets introduced and detailed above. This chapter section delves into the next level of the policy: the filters.

When the Citrix filter is selected for editing, a filter configuration dialog is presented, as shown in Exhibit 13-11. From this dialog, one can edit or create a new filter. Exhibit 13-12 depicts the edit dialog, which allows one to modify the name, description, and most importantly, the extended filter list.

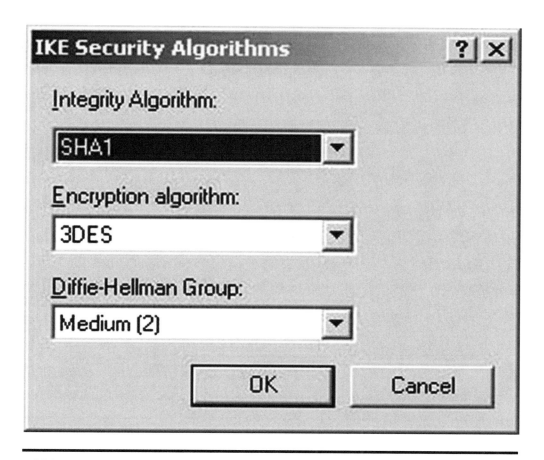

Exhibit 13-10.   IKE security transform set modification.

If one edits the filter shown in the list, one has the opportunity to define the exact traffic one wants to be identified by IPSec, shown in Exhibit 13-13, under the Addressing tab. In the example shown, my system is acting as if a Citrix server that wants all Citrix traffic from network 10.12.32.0/24 to my system (10.12.43.5) on a separate network, to be protected by IPSec. The option at the bottom to mirror connections is typically not used.

Under the Protocol tab (Exhibit 13-14), one can extend the IP filter to include application-specific protocol services ports. In the example, the protocol of interest within this filter is TCP, protocol number 6. If the protocol required is not listed, one can specify "Other" and enter the IANA protocol ID on the edit box. If the protocol defined supports ports, such as TCP and UDP, they can be defined in the filter.

Having defined a filter, other than using the Dynamic one provided by Microsoft, one must now define the IPSec transform sets to be used in the event the custom filter identifies traffic. At this point, it is necessary to understand that the IPSec information discussed earlier was access and associated with the default Dynamic filter included in the policy filter list. After defining the filter group to be included in the policy, one must provide the necessary transform information. Another point worth mentioning again is that the IKE transforms are associated with the policy itself and do not need further definition.

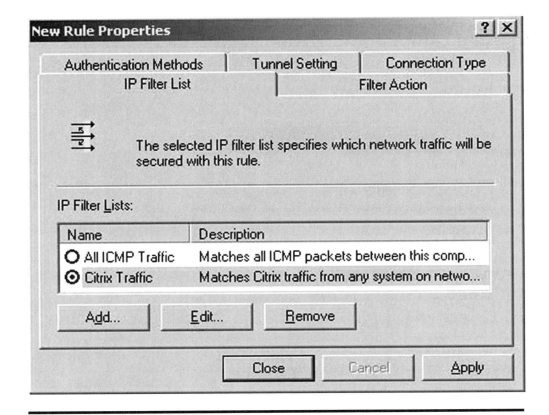

Exhibit 13-11.   Filter configuration dialog.

As illustrated in Exhibit 13-15, the IPSec transforms are referred to as filter actions that can be collected and assigned to different filters throughout the policy. The action can be to drop, permit, or apply the defined IPSec policy (Exhibit 13-16). As one can see, the transform set list is identical to those found in earlier dialog systems. Therefore, the same editing rules and options apply within the IPSec configuration.

The defined filter, Citrix, has several property tabs other than Filter Lists and Filter Actions. Exhibit 13-17 shows, the authentication types permitted for the filter, which in turn affects the authentication IKE uses. Microsoft Win2K's native authentication is Kerberos and therefore it can be aligned with VPN authentication. By configuring Kerberos as the authentication for IPSec, the user's normal credentials and Ticket will be passed as authenticating material.

Other forms of authentication can be configured. Certificates can be identified for use in VPN authentication. A pre-shared secret passphrase can be defined to establish a VPN based on a static secret known by all parties.

Exhibit 13-18 illustrates the ability to determine the tunnel endpoint of the VPN.

Finally, Exhibit 13-19 shows the dialog that is used to associate a network type to the policy.

Having defined an IKE policy, interesting traffic filter, and associated actions and IPSec transforms, one now needs to apply it to an interface, as shown in Exhibit 13-20. This is the equivalent of the Map command in Cisco at the interface level. The ability

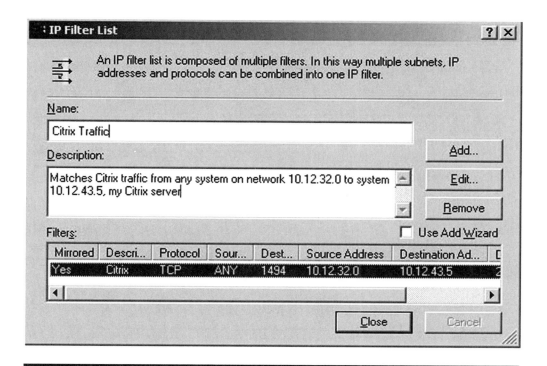

Exhibit 13-12. Detailed filters of the Citrix filter test filter.

to collect all the necessary information into a single point and associate it with an interface is the final step in nearly all IPSec solutions.

Policies and Performance. When defining policies, whether for IPSec transform sets or IKE security suites, if the system is ever the initiator of an IPSec VPN, each method defined in the entire policy will be presented in an SA payload with multiple proposals and transforms, resulting in a huge initial packet subject. For the setup of a single VPN, this does not produce much of an issue; however, if you are a server and 500 network systems attempt to establish a VPN, offering tons pf proposals, there are system and network performance issues that must be considered. Therefore, given Microsoft's default configuration, one can calculate the overhead, assuming an acceptable configuration of a single IKE and IPSec proposal.

There are a total of six IPSec transforms and four within the IKE policy; subtract one from each to obtain the overhead. It is also worth noting that AH is only configured for use alone and not in concert with ESP by default, reducing the possible number of payloads. This is the only good attribute of Microsoft's default structure; if ESP and AH are combined, the number of proposals skyrockets, as do the associated transforms.

As depicted in Exhibit 13-21, the IPSec proposals can add up. Not including the elements that would normally appear, the overhead payload size for the SA payload would be 88 bytes. The overhead calculated only includes the AH proposal, the new proposal header for it, and the three transforms detailed in proposal number 1. If

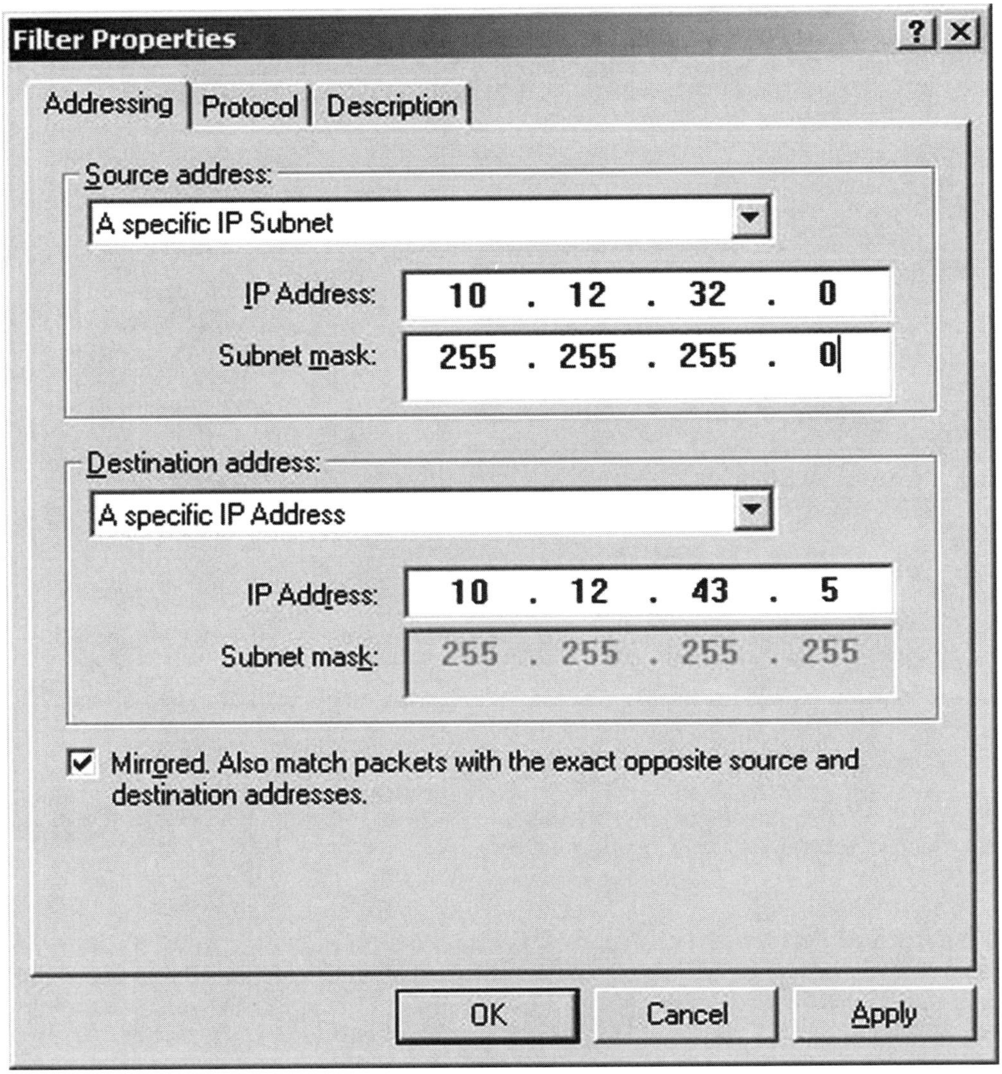

Filter Properties   **?** **X**

Addressing | Protocol | Description

Source address:

A specific IP Subnet   ▼

    IP Address: **10** . **12** . **32** . **0**

    Subnet mask: **255** . **255** . **255** . **0**

Destination address:

A specific IP Address   ▼

    IP Address: **10** . **12** . **43** . **5**

    Subnet mask: 255 . 255 . 255 . 255

☑ Mirrored. Also match packets with the exact opposite source and
destination addresses.

                             OK   Cancel   Apply

Exhibit 13-13.   Specific IP address filter properties.

there were a single addition to the IPSec methods list in the policy that simply included
AH with ESP, that number would increase by 56 bytes, nearly half the size of the original.

The default proposals for IKE (Exhibit 13-22) must be presented as well. The result
is 96 bytes of overhead just in defaults.

The policies that define how IPSec and IKE are to base a relationship must be
presented to the responder, who in turn must process each of them, compare against
its policy, and respond with the selected, unchanged proposal. Combining the overhead of the first Phase I message from the initiator to the responder and the first
Quick Mode message results in 184 bytes of unnecessary overhead if the defaults
remain in the policy and are not used.

Once again, this does not represent a great deal of traffic, but when combined
with other processing, such as the SA payload, the package can ecome excessive.

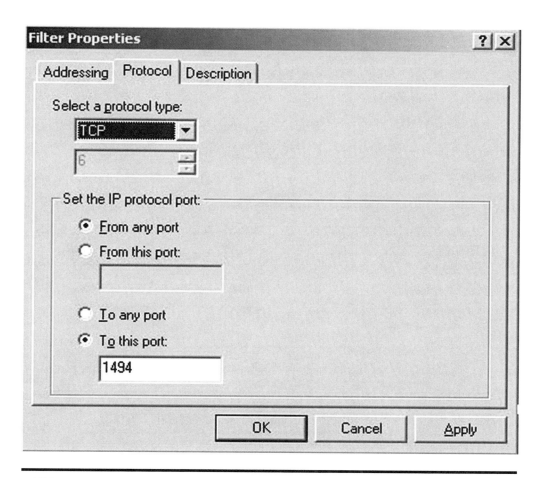

Exhibit 13-14. Specific application filter properties.

Given these additional circumstances, the seemingly limited traffic turns out to be the very thing that brings the system to its knees.

Routing within VPNs

Routing in a standard Frame Relay network can become very complicated. As networks are added, especially those that are acquired through business evolution, the address space begins to become complicated and the various routing protocols must be aligned. Open Shortest Path First (OSPF), Routing Information Protocol (RIP), Interior Gateway Routing Protocol (IGRP), and Extended Interior Gateway Routing Protocol (EIGRP) are some of the more popular routing protocols used in enterprise networks. Each of these routing protocols has different attributes and metrics that are used to determine routes across networks to get to the desired destination. Most common routing protocols operate based on connection status or connection distance, while some are a combination of both. There are other configurable attributes that can be leveraged by an administrator, such as cost configuration and static routes, that can enhance the routing decision-making process. As an example, two lines from a single router may have similar bandwidth, but one is much longer to the destination than

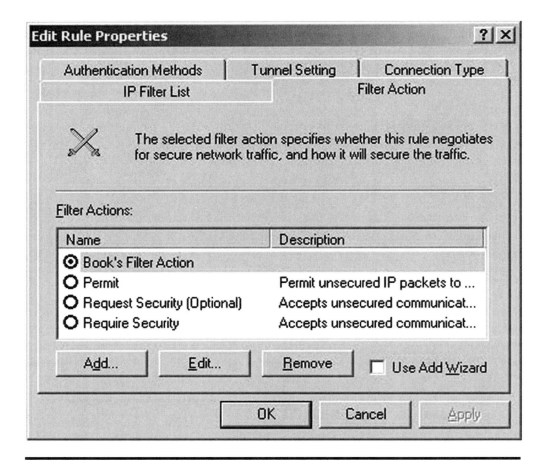

Exhibit 13-15.   Determining actions (IPSec rules) to associate with filter.

the other but much less expensive. Traditional routing may take the shortest path; however, an administrator can set costs associated with the connections to force the data down the less expensive path, ultimately saving communication expenses.

Routing protocols are aware of the communication environment; basically, that is the definition of their existence. Routing protocols transmit over the same network as the data. The fundamental difference is that the data is unaware of the network, whereas the routing protocol is concerned with the network it is traversing. As it travels over the network and is received at a routed point on the network, the protocol is used to make determinations based on the experiences of the transmission (i.e., bandwidth, latency, distance, etc.). Different types of interfaces support different topologies and therefore affect how the routing protocol will interact and make determinations. In other words, a router with several serial interfaces and several Ethernet interfaces may have issues when determining routes based solely on bandwidth. As more and more routers participate and share the routing tables, they can operate as a group. As changes occur in the communications, the routers converge and collectively make new determinations to accommodate the change.

As VPNs are introduced into this mix, the interactivity of routing protocols with the VPN can have an impact on the global routing infrastructure.

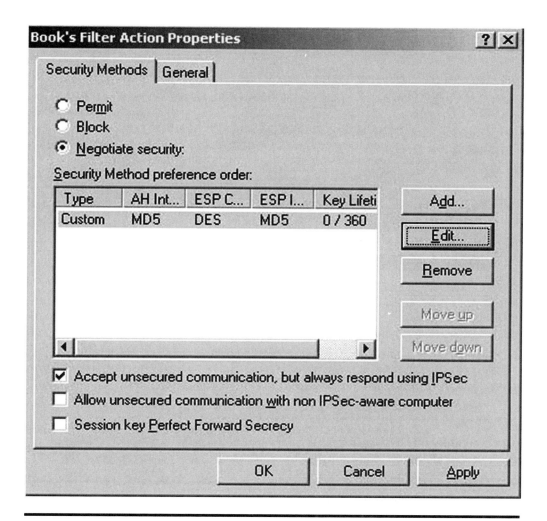

Exhibit 13-16. Configuring actions to associate with filter.

Finally, beyond routing protocols are simple routing determinations. For example, hosts on one network (network A), can communicate with others on a different network (network B) that is on the other side of a WAN connection provided by two routers. However, on network A, there is a VPN gateway connected to the Internet. In some solutions, the hosts will have a default gateway pointing to the core router that connects A to B. However, the core router on A must be aware of VPN networks that are available to properly forward traffic to the VPN device when appropriate.

On the surface, this appears quite simple. A static route or a summarization can be configured on the core router to properly send VPN requests to the VPN device. Unfortunately, this pristine situation of shear simplicity rarely exists. In reality, there are several exceptions and, typically, the number of remote networks is so great that the option of entering static routes is simply not applicable.

In one situation, all the remote sites, over a 1000, were connected by a global WAN that provided enterprise connectivity. The client wanted to have Internet connectivity

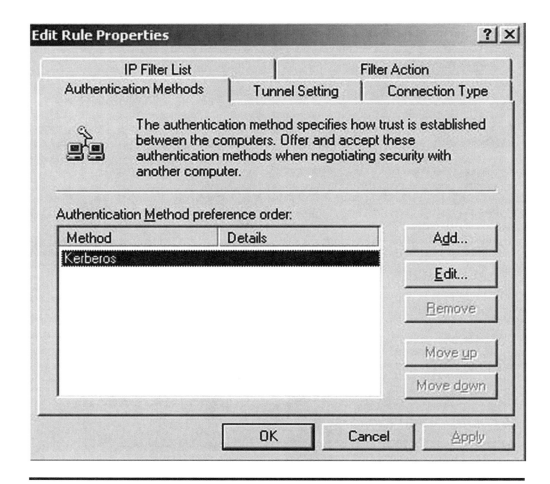

Exhibit 13-17. Configuring authentication for the policy.

at many of the locations to provide E-commerce activities relative to the region. As Internet connections were provisioned and configured with firewalls that supported IPSec, it came clear very early that the VPN could be leveraged in other ways. The final design was to route all internal e-mail through the VPN, releasing the internal WAN from heavy data flow that is not necessarily time sensitive. Therefore, e-mail was processing well within an exceptional time frame, and the more expensive internal WAN bandwidth was recovered. An example is shown in Exhibit 13-23, the internal WAN is used to connect all the internal sites. At the same time, each site has an Internet connection that can be leveraged for VPNs. The result is two backbones that can be leveraged for different traffic and communications.

In the simplified example, the options are not obvious. In the event that there are several layers of sites prior to reaching the core backbone, a site can connect to the Internet and easily bypass the WAN connection that may take several expensive hops.

As one can see, the final result, for lack of a better term or description, is two backbone networks. Therefore, routing determinations for traffic can become complicated and the support for routing protocols in the VPN solution can become very important.

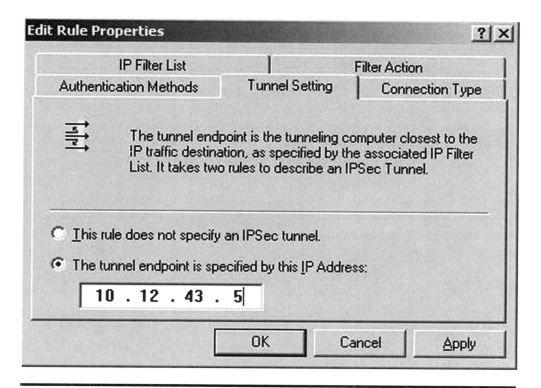

Exhibit 13-18. Configuring tunnel attributes for the policy.

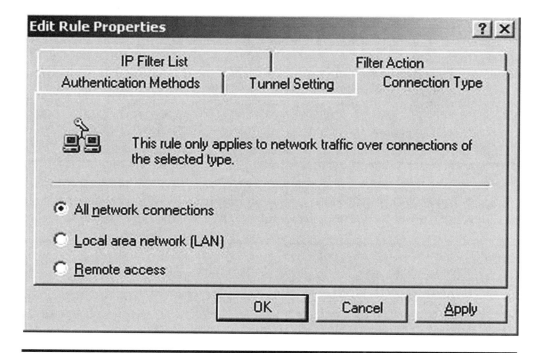

Exhibit 13-19. Configuring which connections (network types) to apply the IPSec policy.

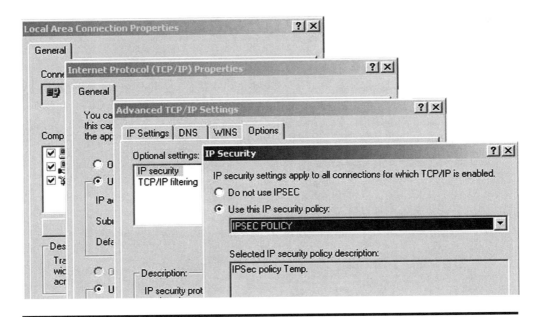

Exhibit 13-20.   Apply the IPSec policy to a specific interface.

Standard Example

With a standard network topology, routers typically provide the physical access to the WAN as well as the logical access. This position allows the router to accommodate several configuration scenarios that includes providing alternate data routes in the event of a Layer 1, 2, or 3 failure. In many large organizations, there are usually one or more primary offices that house the bulk of the connection terminations. Within these offices there are backbone routers that provide the gateway services to all the connected networks. This is evident in networks that not only employ large Frame Relay networks, but VLANs as well. To provide access to the Internet, there is usually a firewall between the internal network and the Internet router. As a request for an Internet destination is processed, it will reach one of the backbone routers, which will not have an internal entry in the routing tables for the Internet resource.

Note: This is another example of proper IP address assignment for internal use. By using RFC1918 and not Internet-routable IP addresses that are not owned by the organization, routing problems can be avoided.

In these circumstances, a final route configured in the routers will forward all requests to foreign systems to the firewall, which in turn will forward the request to the Internet router to be injected onto the Internet. For many companies, this example reflects what is currently taking place. As a request for an internal network is made, it gets appropriately routed to the remote resource supported by routing protocols that provide the direction for the data. If the destination is unknown, the default gateway finally forwards the data to the Internet via the firewall or other protection system.

Exhibit 13-21. Proposals can add up.

Microsoft Default Proposals

Proposal 1: (8-bytes — not counted)
   ESP
      DES and MD5 (TS header = 8-bytes)
                     (attribute payload = 16-bytes)
                     (not counted)
      DES and SHA (TS header = 8-bytes)
                     (attribute payload = 16-bytes)
      3DES and MD5 (TS header = 8-bytes)
                     (attribute payload = 16-bytes)
      3DES and SHA (TS header = 8-bytes)
                     (attribute payload = 16-bytes)

Proposal 2: (8-bytes — counted)
   AH
      SHA (TS header = 8-bytes)
           (attribute payload = 8-bytes)
      MD5 (TS header = 8-bytes)
           (attribute payload = 8-bytes)

Proposal 3: (8-bytes)
   ESP
      DES and MD5 (TS header = 8-bytes)
                     (attribute payload = 16-bytes)
Proposal 3:
   AH
      SHA (TS header = 8-bytes)
           (attribute payload = 8-bytes)

Exhibit 13-22. Proposals can also add up for IKE.

Microsoft Default Proposals
Proposal 1: (8-bytes — not counted)
   IKE
      DES, MD5, G1 (TS header = 8-bytes)
                     (attribute payload = 24-bytes)
                     (not counted)
      DES, SHA, G1 (TS header = 8-bytes)
                     (attribute payload = 24-bytes)
      3DES, MD5, G2 (TS header = 8-bytes)
                     (attribute payload = 24-bytes)
      3DES, SHA, G3 (TS header = 8-bytes)
                     (attribute payload = 24-bytes)

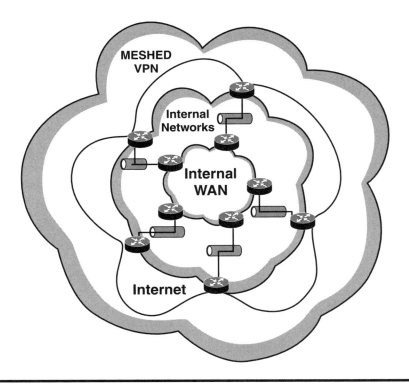

Exhibit 13-23.   WAN backbone augmented by Internet-based VPN mesh.

In the event a portion of the Frame Relay goes down, or a router failure or remote network outage occurs, alternate routes are engaged to maintain connectivity. In many conditions, secondary physical access is provided in the event a primary network connection fails.

VPN Network

As VPN products became available, they were typically a device that had either two or more Ethernet interfaces or were a server, such as a Microsoft PPTP server or Novell's BorderManager server with two or more interfaces. These systems were installed in parallel or behind a firewall to provide connectivity to the Internet with one interface, and used the other to connect to the internal network.

As remote VPNs were established, their network numbers could be added to the routing table of the backbone routers. This allowed requests for the remote VPN to be properly forwarded to the VPN device. As the sophistication of VPN devices grew, routing protocol support was enabled and enhanced to accommodate the automatic updating of internal routing tables. With the VPN devices interacting with the backbone routers, they could learn the necessary information to forward a request they received to the appropriate internal router. In contrast, the internal router could be constantly updated on any changes to the remote VPNs.

As discussed earlier, there are several methodologies for defining network IP addressing schemes for VPNs. Nearly all of these situations surround the remote access solutions. For VPN solutions that are for network-to-network connectivity, there typically is no virtual pool or address allocation to be concerned with. The far network on the other side of the VPN is simply the network that needs to be included in the routing protocol for enterprise distribution. An example is a network IP address of 192.168.1.0 and another foreign network with an IP address of 192.168.36.0. If there is a VPN device connecting the two networks over the Internet, the core router, or backbone router on the networks that provide access to other networks via the WAN, must have a route for the VPN network. The core router on 192.168.1.0 will need a route that states: to get to 192.168.36.0 go to the VPN device. Therefore, if the VPN device supports routing protocols, the administration will be greatly reduced.

The Difference

There are two fundamental differences when routing protocols are concerned. In the first discussion, routing protocols participate in the network as enablers. The protocols provide information about the network between the devices to accommodate changes and traffic management. On the other hand, routing protocols are aware of the transmission process and therefore when communicated over a VPN interesting things can arise.

The difference between the two may not be readily apparent or obvious. In the first example of a standard network, the connection between the routers, provided by the Frame Relay in this example, was used to transport the routing protocol information along with the normal data. The act of being transmitted over the same network as the data is used as one of the metrics in determining if the route is desirable for the situation. Another example is a remote site that is accessible from another site either directly, or indirectly by way of an alternate site. As shown in Exhibit 13-24, for site A to connect to site C, it can use site B or simply connect to it directly.

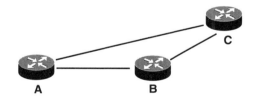

Exhibit 13-24.   Basic network with multiple routes.

The routing protocol can be configured to use a metric that has a preference for speed over cost or number of hops to the destination. In this example, the link from A to B and B to C are a 1.44 MB T1s, while the link from A to C is a 56K CIR with a port speed of 128K. The routing protocol can learn this information from the interaction with all the routers of the network, and by participating in the communication. Given our configuration preference, the data stream will take the route through site B. Certain decisions can be determined automatically by the routing protocol collaborating with the routers over the same connection the data is using. The connection itself becomes an attribute in the determination of a route. The various attributes used from the communication medium are determined by the routing protocol being implemented. There are two primary types of routing protocols:

- link-state
- distance-vector

OSPF is an example of link-state where the routers do not exchange distance information but rather the status of the link that may include the associated costs, speed, and utilization. RIP is an example of distance-vector where the routers share hop count information. In Exhibit 13-24, router B tells router A that site C is two hops away. Therefore, the routing table in router A will see site B one hop away and site C two hops away. However, because A is connected to C, it will also see a single hop to site C. This is where metrics are formulated and configuration preferences are applied to direct traffic accordingly.

For VPNs, this is not as simple in theory or practice and requires some re-thinking of the concept of routing within the network and not simply supporting the route. Imagine the same three sites connected to the Internet to provide data connectivity via a VPN. The routing protocol, at first glance, becomes irrelevant. There is no need for a routing protocol when there is only one direction. As far as the internal networks and routers are concerned, there is only one hop to the remote networks. As shown in Exhibit 13-25, a VPN can be established directly to the remote network to accommodate a request. If site A needs to connect to site C, a VPN is created and a point-to-point connection is established. If a connection from site A to site B is required, another point-to-point VPN is provided. Each site now has a single connection that can accommodate nearly any configuration.

However, there is still a situation where routing protocols can provide assistance to the VPN. In the event that each site has subordinate sites, the routing protocol should be shared for the other subordinate site to be aware of their existence. As detailed in Exhibit 13-26, if each site had three subordinate sites (i.e., site A had a1, a2, and a3), these sites would need to know that the others existed to make routing determinations in the event of multiple options.

In the event that site a1 needs to get to site c2, it would have to know the router that provided the access; in this example, router A maintains an SA to router C. Not only does the origination router need the information on where to forward the request and that the network exists, but the intermediate routers must have an understanding of the remote networks as well. This allows the routers to be aware, on some level, of the topology that can affect routing decisions.

In the example provided, this requirement is difficult to justify. The example is quite simple and there are very few alternate routes. However, as the network grows and more subordinate sites get removed from standard Frame Relay for VPN connectivity,

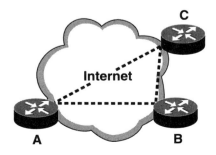

Exhibit 13-25.   Basic VPN network with no routes.

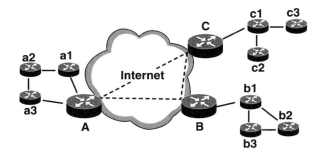

Exhibit 13-26.   Basic VPN network with subordinate networks and routes.

the issues become compounded. Imagine 50 or more countries that encompass 8000 sites, each with subordinate sites that may or may not use the Internet. Combine the internetworking complexities with partnering and customer VPN access and the associated controls and routing concerns they involve. The inclusion of sophisticated routing techniques becomes evident.

Solution Models

To accommodate the remote networks and the need for the routers to be aware of the peers on the other side of the VPN, routing protocols must be encapsulated and forwarded to the other networks. The process of encapsulating the protocol in the VPN is not to allow the routing protocol to make various decisions based on the VPN connection. The VPN can be much too dynamic and all the connections will appear point-to-point. The routing information is forwarded to convey information about routing between the remote networks. This is apparent in OSPF networks and the application of areas. OSPF works on a concept of routing areas that represent a domain of common routing environments. These can be logical, associated with IP addressing, or geographical. The concept is to provide a hierarchical approach to routing. All OSPF networks must have an Area 0, with other areas as subsidiaries that provide summarized routing information to Area 0 routers. These tables are then shared with other areas, allowing the enterprise to be aware of routing events in remote locations that are not directly connected or associated.

The complexity occurs when an internal router attempts to communicate with another router over a VPN. These issues are directly related to the type of routing protocol implemented. RIP uses a broadcast every 30 seconds to communicate routing table information. RIP data is contained within a UDP header assigned to port 520, and an IP header is added to provide connectivity through a network. If the interface associated with the routing protocol is a point-to-point configuration, such as a Frame Relay PVC defined on a serial interface, the packet is just sent to the communication peer. If the interface is connected to a broadcast support medium, such as Ethernet, the IP datagram is broadcast.

With OSPF, the situation is more complicated. OSPF does not employ UDP or TCP; it has its own protocol identification to be defined in the IP header. OSPF does not typically operate well with broadcast mediums and uses unicast and multicast for efficient communications. The use of multicast and unicast are also needed to determine link-state attributes; a broadcast could defeat the data contained within the OSPF packet.

Interestingly, each of these situations is supported by the IPSec standards but not entirely by the available VPN products. For example, as detailed later, Cisco network-to-network VPNs require the use of tunnel interfaces to assign OSPF areas to allow the IP addresses to coincide with the appropriate IP networks of that OSPF area. The interface providing connectivity to the Internet will almost surely not have an IP address that is associated with internal routing structures. Therefore, a tunnel interface must be constructed with a valid internal IP address and assigned the appropriate OSPF area and crypto map. To ensure that the OSPF area and data are properly routed through the tunnel, the tunnel interface is assigned to the physical interface providing access to the Internet. There are three primary reasons for associating OSPF with a tunnel interface that has IPSec applied to it.

1. The IP address of the interface will become part of the assigned area. In the event that a single area is defined for route summarization, the introduction of an Internet IP address could be problematic.
2. The tunnel interface can be configured as an OSPF point-to-point network, eliminating the need for multicasts.
3. By encapsulating the OSPF, along with the data, in generic tunnel (GRE) it is not affected by the link and, therefore, will not produce routing tables based on link-state information gained from the VPN. Of course, all this is provided IPSec security, much like the L2TP description in Chapter 3.

In summary, OSPF is associated with a virtual interface, in this example a tunnel interface, that has an IP address assigned to it that is part of the internal network. Imagine a WAN with three routers using point-to-point Frame Relay and the IP address network 172.18.32.0/24. That address will populate the routing tables. However, in this example, the IP address that would normally populate a standard WAN interface is assigned to a benign GRE tunnel interface. The physical interface is assigned the appropriate IP address provided by the ISP. It is crucial to understand that this does not have to be an Internet routable address. The ISP may provide a Frame Relay connection to its Internet routers to provide simple connectivity. The author has, in many cases, configured unnumbered interfaces or IP networks with extremely high subnet masks. An example might be 192.168.12.1/30, which only allows two devices on 62 networks — not to mention the private address space. This is perfect for an ISP — one address space that handles all the devices required and spreads across many networks. To identify the router with the IP address provided by the ISP for Internet connectivity, a loopback interface is assigned one of the IP addresses that would normally be assigned to the internal interface. In most cases, an Internet router will have a serial interface facing the ISP, with some IP address that simply provides connectivity to the ISP's network. The ISP will provide a block of Internet routable IP addresses for the Internet, and one is assigned to the internal interface of the router. Typically, a firewall is placed behind the router with an Internet routable IP address on the external interface and the internal interface is configured with an IP address of the internal network. From that point, NAT is typically implemented to provide connectivity. This is all being done in one route. Finally, the internal interface of the router is assigned an internal IP address of the network for internal communications.

The configuration would look something like the following:

Internal interface:	10.1.1.0/24 (connected to the internal network, Area 1)
Serial interface:	Unnumbered (Connection to the ISP)
Loopback:	Internet routable IP address from ISP
Tunnel:	IP address that would normally be WAN facing. Part of Area 0 (in this example, 172.18.32.0/24)

With this configuration, one has the physical connections defined for basic connectivity. The serial interface and internal interface are appropriately configured. Unfortunately, the serial interface's IP address (if even necessary) is completely worthless to this network — totally worthless. Here is where the VPN starts to separate from the norm. One now has a critical interface that would normally have a very specific IP address configured for foreign connectivity. Thus, one needs to associate the Internet routable IP address to actually route to the Internet and get data from the Internet. The loopback interface gives the router an identity it will answer to. Therefore, when the ISP routes data to the router from the Internet, it will accept it. The final attribute is the tunnel interface. Here is the virtual interface — somewhat like the loopback, but functional — which represents what would normally be facing the WAN and participating in Area 0, the core area.

One might be wondering where IPSec comes into play. In the remainder of the configuration are all the IPSec configurations that have been detailed in earlier sections. Finally, a map is associated to the physical interface; in this example, the serial interface is assigned a map. Next, the tunnel is associated with the serial interface. The map provides the link to IPSec, and the link between the tunnel and the serial interface provides the connection between the IP addresses and the areas. The result is a system that provides VPN connectivity and correctly participates in routing protocols over the VPN by encapsulating them in GRE and then applying IPSec.

If one needs to provide Internet access from the internal network, in this case 10.1.1.0/24, several NAT statements can be added to accommodate basic Internet access beyond the confines of the VPN. Finally, access control lists can be implemented to provide basic firewalling capabilities.

This is a difficult process to convey, but the goal is to show that by employing a combination of technologies and known router methodologies, a very comprehensive VPN can be established that very closely reflects a WAN environment.

Current Status of Routing and VPNs

Because most VPN devices act as a router, RIP broadcast and OSPF multicasts will not typically be forwarded to all the other VPN locations. Furthermore, if the VPN device does absorb the routing information, most solutions do not encapsulate it and send it through to the other sites to be processed, but rather collect the information to use in their own routing table.

There are five primary obstacles with regard to routing protocols and network-to-network VPNs:

1. Routing protocol interaction with link information would render the routing tables useless.
2. The point-to-point configuration of VPNs does not require the use of routing protocols directly.

3. Various routing protocols interact differently with broadcast mediums. Many VPN solutions use multiple Ethernet interfaces, complicating the use of OSPF.
4. Many VPN products absorb the routing information for use within their own routing tables and not forwarding it to their peers.
5. Support for routing protocols must be complete and VPN devices must operate as standard routers.

In the event that VPN devices are providing VPN connectivity with routers on the internal networks, the devices would have to be aware of the protocol state to ensure that the updates are properly forwarded. This would require that the VPN device operate fully as a router and implement the routing protocol to the fullest degree for interoperability (i.e., area support, cost configurations, standard metric support). Examples are VPN devices that provide all the services necessary to interoperate with internal routers, but only support OSPF within Area 0.

While Cisco is currently struggling with various aspects of VPN product development, their network-to-network solution is in a prime position to take advantage of IPSec VPN configurations. They already have the full support for nearly any type of routing protocol, and the existing configuration options available for standard networking application can easily be leveraged for IPSec VPN construction. However, many other products also provide robust network-to-network solutions that easily provide routing protocol features and interoperability. Xedia, now owned by Lucent Technologies, is a highly sophisticated router that support advanced features and implements a new approach to IPSec VPNs. As the demand for more refined VPN solutions surfaces, routing protocols will be incorporated deeper into VPN operations.

Client Character

In a remote access VPN solution, there are requirements for client software to be loaded on the remote system to make a VPN possible. The character and traits of the client can have an impact on the overall solution and the success of the project in the eyes of the remote user population. A solution must be selected not only for its capabilities but its client interface and operability provided to the user community. A solution might have perfect functionality and provide all the necessary functions for the business requirements, but if the client is difficult to use, troubleshoot, operate, or integrate, the overall impressions of the service will be poor.

System Interaction

Most VPN client packages are quiet and simply provide connectivity, while others tend to be more vocal about the connection and status. An example is when a client starts as a Windows NT service and resides quietly in the taskbar, only interacting with the user during specific points within the communication. On the other hand, some packages will provide extensive configuration tools, logging tools, and troubleshooting utilities to assist the user in establishing or troubleshooting a VPN connection. The extra tools and utilities allow advanced users and administrators to become more aware of the status of their communication. This is also true for an attacker. In the event that a laptop is stolen, an attacker could use error information contained within the logs to assist in obtaining access. As an example, the user name is correct but the password is not. An error message stating, "You have entered an incorrect password," will allow the attacker to make certain deductions. A more vague message, such as, "Improper credentials," or "Connection denied," will leave much more to question. Troubleshooting utilities and logging facilities also pose a concern for administrators of large remote user groups. Some organizations might not want to enable the user to troubleshoot and possibly reconfigure the client, possibly resulting in more problems.

Some products have taken centralized administration support to the point where only one item can be configured in the client and, in the event of an error, only one message is displayed, informing the user that no connection is established.

Helpdesk Opportunity

The advantage of providing a client that contains several tools and logging capabilities can be to assist the helpdesk in tackling technical problems that may arise. Many helpdesks do not have access to or control over the configuration of centralized equipment. In the event of failure, the user can be instructed to exercise the provided tools to assist the helpdesk in identifying or rectifying the problem. Of course, the disadvantage is made clear when the helpdesk finds that the user has inadvertently changed a crucial setting. Once again, this is related to the culture and technical knowledge of the remote user population and the company as a whole.

Centralized Control

For many solutions and organizations, the use of tools and utilities provided by the client software is not a concern. As the VPN solutions mature, we are seeing more client packages that have very few options and small system footprints. These small but functional clients obtain all the communication information from the security gateway (SGW). Some of these clients can be preconfigured with the vital information, such as SGW's IP address and a backup system's IP address if available, and placed into distribution packages. Users can collect the packages and install them at their leisure. At the time a remote session is required, the client has the primary data to get to the SGW. As the connection is initialized, information is fed to the client that allows the user to advance the interface to a VPN.

For example, VPNet's current client leverages SSL to provide an encrypted session from the client to the SGW. It ingeniously uses the encrypted session to feed centrally administered information on the SGW to the client software running on the remote system. Usually, authentication will take place using SSL for protection; then data is passed to the remote client that will allow it to drop the SSL connection and create an IPSec VPN.

By allowing the client to collect configuration and session information from the SGW, it releases the client from several administrative tasks, ultimately reducing its size and complexity. This process also reduces the administration of the remote systems. As an example, if the configuration must be set on each client to allow remote access VPNs, those client systems must be returned in the event of a change. Of course, in various cases, users can be informed of the change or to call the helpdesk for assistance. Nonetheless, each change option available to distributed configuration solutions will result in some form of interruption.

The advantages of centrally managed client implementations are numerous and many solutions are attempting to provide a middle ground to take advantage of the positive aspects of each type of client. Good examples are clients that require command-line switches that force the package to make several options and utilities available. This allows the client to provide a simple interface for nontechnical users, but an avenue for detailed configuration when necessary when directed by a helpdesk or administrator. In any case, the client information is populated by the SGW and is adjustable by the user if the client is executed with the command-line option.

Interoperability with Standard Applications

As with any new software being introduced into a production environment, it must be tested to verify its functionality — but also its interoperability with existing applications.

It is at this point in the selection process that client package operation choices come into focus. If a client runs as a service, there may be less opportunity to impact other necessary applications. To detail further, early remote access VPN clients operated by use of a virtual adapter in Windows 95 systems. Unfortunately, the virtual adapter conflicted with the AOL virtual adapter required to connect to the Internet using AOL as the ISP. Some organizations that used AOL for a remote user community ISP found themselves with a VPN that could not be utilized. Granted, this example does not include a necessary application, unless one was working for AOL, but simply represents a situation that is very realistic for many.

Client Deployment

Several client issues focusing on operations and implementation have been discussed thusfar in this chapter. Now, consider the hurdles that await when putting this technology to work. Deploying remote access VPN clients can be directly affected by several factors, ranging from the vendor product chosen to the number of users that require connectivity. IPSec is an evolving standard that is open to interpretation by developers. Consequently, there are many different types of obstacles that are the result of standards interpretation. The need to categorize and check the product options against the proposed solution design will assist in determining the best course of action for client deployment. It is not necessarily a common practice, nor is it typical to determine rollout procedures based on available products. But there can be so many options to each product, and each one is very unique.

Vendor-specific Considerations

It will be necessary to qualify all areas of the product that are open to influence and align them with the solution requirements and goals. An example of this is an implementation that must support 1500 simultaneous users. All the users are not computer-savvy; and to avoid a complicated learning curve or to simplify training endeavors, a concise, unobtrusive client package might be preferred. To accomplish this simple aspect, much of the configuration must be pushed to the client for each connection. The type and amount of information and the delivery process can have an impact on other areas of the solution, such as the extended authentication system required to provide the authentication data or a directory service used to store client configurations.

Product Interoperability Considerations

After selecting a client based on its user interaction, the next hurdle for client software is interoperability with other VPN solutions. Interoperability was one of the original goals of IPSec. However, developers have created solutions that do not follow the standards completely, but simply the spirit contained within. It must be said that this is not by design or on purpose. The IPSec RFCs can be vague in crucial areas, leaving the developers to determine the best course of action based on the currently available information. An excellent example of interoperability is the use of the commit bit. If a remote system uses a certain option, such as the commit bit, and the other system does not, error can arise and the VPN establishment can fail.

The complexity of interoperability is most prevalent in client-to-network VPNs. Client software interaction with VPN gateways typically requires more information processing in fewer steps. The increased complexity is the result of having to authenticate the user and the system with which the VPN is being incorporated. Communication controls are typically implemented and associated with the user after the VPN has been created with the system. These controls are shared with the client to accommodate customization of the SA for that particular authenticated user and is typically entrenched in the vendor's solution.

In contrast, interoperability between different products using network-to-network VPNs is typically successful due to the relative simplicity of the communication requirements. The establishment of a network-to-network VPN does not require extended information or data that may be associated with a user or group. Communication control is typically based on access controls and interesting data identifiers that would be implemented for normal network-to-network routing scenarios.

The interesting part of client support and integration is that some early developers used to provide much of the client software for other companies. A good example is IRE, which created an IPSec client package that could be used with several different products. IRE began writing a generic IPSec-compliant client package that would work with many vendor solutions early in IPSec history. Therefore, many vendors repackaged the client as their own to provide a complete product offering. In contrast to that example, some companies have developed such strong and flexible clients for their solution that other vendors licensed it from the original developer. As an example, TimeStep's client is now used for other vendor product solutions.

As the client interaction evolved, vendors began to include their own proprietary options. The result: enhanced, customized client packages that typically only operate with a particular vendor's product. Some vendors changed the previously licensed client — such as Altiga using IRE's client — to something completely different and added increased functionality to their solution. Unfortunately, the recent direction of client production typically renders client packages useless when attempting to connect to foreign products.

The capability of a client package to communicate with a VPN gateway that is a product from a different vendor must be investigated for growth capabilities. This aspect of client support does not typically concern small to medium implementations. It is usually associated with larger companies that might have several partnering organizations that have their own VPN solution. As VPN access becomes more accepted, the scenario of client interoperability will become increasingly more common. The goal is to determine the growth path and scheduled lifetime of the solution, compared to the foreseeable organizational requirements. The point is to address operational capabilities of the product if there is a possibility that a design-altering change is on the horizon.

Deployment Options

Deployment can be affected by many variables that are available to the administrators implementing the solution. There may exist an application delivery mechanism that can be leveraged to remotely install packages. For many organizations, the creation of a package to be delivered will be the most common.

Many solutions provide the ability to create preconfigured packages that can be placed on a Web server and accessed via the Internet. Some vendors provide applications for creating preconfigured installation packages for distribution. For example, some provide a utility to create a configuration profile and combine it with the client package into a single executable file. Other vendors allow one to simply add a group of critical files to the normal installation package and run the install normally. Both implementations result in a client configured to communicate based on options defined by the administrators.

Whatever the options or added support features, the process of getting a client installed on many remote systems is typically limited only by the tools available. Most, if not all, client packages are small and do not have complicated install procedures. Therefore, many methods exist for getting the file or files to the client. Because the packages are usually small, methods for distribution include e-mail attachments, a downloadable file from a server, creation of a floppy or CD-ROM that can be mailed to the user, a logon script to be used to push the client to the remote system, or a network management system that can be utilized to deliver and install the client. With any of these concepts, directions can be included to assist the user in the installation process and begin the learning process. Most clients are very basic, in that after they are properly installed and started, they simply work with little or no configuration. Users might need to be instructed on how to enter a username and password or be advised that they are part of a particular VPN group.

Key Implementation

IPSec is based on trusts, and many forms of client packages must be configured with a shared secret or certificate. These two types and how the vendor approaches them can have an impact on any preconfigured package delivery mechanism. An example is when a package is preconfigured with connection information that includes the shared secret. If that package were to be intercepted, it could be used for unauthorized purposes. If the stolen package is used for an attack, only the extended authentication process will provide the last line of defense.

In the case with shared secret, clients may require group identification to determine which key or password is used later in the creation of the VPN. This type of implementation is typically associated with access control capabilities of the VPN device. Groups are normally aligned with rules or filters that are applied to the SAs that a particular set of users can employ. It is necessary to properly plan the creation of groups and assign users to those groups to realize the security set forth in the security policy. After the groups are properly defined, the creation of different packages that represent group identification can be delivered to the appropriate end user.

Cost Issues

The cost of client support can emanate from many directions, and each can become very expensive. Several aspects of client costs are not readily apparent and require some detailed planning when designing and performing cost analysis for a VPN solution.

Cost per connection is typically associated with the solution's maximum number of users supported at any one time. The maximum number of simultaneous users, divided by the cost of the solution, will give an overall initial cost. However, the system is not typically implemented to the maximum number of users; and when that time comes, the system will need to be upgraded or replaced, ultimately negating the financial reasoning. Therefore, when pricing solutions, base the investment on 75 percent to 85 percent capacity. The remainder of the system's capacity will simply buy time until an upgrade or scale project can be initiated.

The cost for licensing client software can become a hidden cost. It is not uncommon to spend $50,000 on a site license for a solution that may support 5000 simultaneous connections. That calculates to $10 per client package. On the other hand, some solutions base their cost structure on a base system cost and charge for each client license used. Choosing which strategy is directly dependent on the ultimate goal of the VPN solution and the expected use trend. For example, if 1000 users are expected to use the solution at implementation and that number is expected to grow to 5000 users over two years, a solution that supports 7500 users with a one-time cost may not be the best path to take. However, a one-time cost may have its tax advantages — but this author is not a taxman.

Costs for support issues come in the form of technical support plans and upgrade plans. Both of these may be required if experience with the VPN solution is limited. Support programs provided by vendors vary in cost and typically are worth the investment. The most valuable type of plan is system replacement within 24 hours. In the event of a catastrophic failure, the vendor will deliver a new system. The success of the secondary implementation to restore operations is directly related to the administration of the previous system. Configuration files and critical options must be recorded so they can be implemented into the new system.

Chapter 14

Product Evaluation

Knowing IPSec and IKE inside and out can make one feel very confident when designing and implementing a VPN solution. As the design requirements and business requirements are addressed, a final design will tend to surface. However, the more one knows about IPSec, the more confusing the process can become when products are aligned with design requirements and business directives. While it is necessary to understand the idiosyncrasies of IPSec to determine a proper course of action for an organization, it is equally necessary to understand the available solutions, as well as their advantages and shortcomings.

Having discussed the details of IPSec and the concepts of VPN technology, it is necessary to understand the application of such knowledge in the real world with systems that do not necessarily follow the technology as expected.

The simple truth is that the IPSec standard is complicated, not entirely complete, and open to interpretation by vendors and developers. Knowing the standard is a requirement for designing a comprehensive solution that functions efficiently and operates according to the requirements set forth in the initial phases and discovery processes — but knowing the standard is half the battle. Think of the IPSec standard as a topographical map of a remote island in the South Pacific. The map is used to plot a course from one side of the island to the other, based on information on the map. The map was created with collected information at some point in the past, but until one sets foot on the beach and begins the trek across the island, one has only a guide and cannot make definitive assumptions until arrival. The IPSec standard is the map that is available to everyone, and the island is a landscape of products that will bend and twist the planned route to a final solution. One will show up on the other side of the island eventually, but one might be late and a few hundred feet from the mark.

To properly navigate to a solution, it is imperative that the business requirements are clearly defined and understood by all. While the first point is obvious, the latter is sometimes overlooked. As a consultant or designer, one must ensure that the client (or boss) is fully aware of the goals that one has interpreted from them and that the expectations are continuously verified. A simple comment can be made that is understood by the client as option "A," but not fully aware of the technological limitations or caveats with that stated requirement. It is up to the consultant to investigate all the feasible options that can meet that defined goal; therefore, the need to have very clear directives is essential. Of course, obtaining a clear directive may be impossible in the beginning; but as options are investigated and detailed, the path to a design will emerge. Once a clear directive is obtained, or enough to at least begin the process, products can be reviewed for consideration. By reflecting the stated requirements back to the client, the interpretation is verified. However, it is not enough to simply just repeat what was said, but the intention of the communication must be expounded upon. In other words, someone may say they need to route traffic according to service; this can be interpreted in many ways when all the variations are known.

This chapter is dedicated to describing the process for obtaining information about an organization and the requirements to fully understand the current and future needs and provide a design that best meets those needs.

Business Drivers

The business drivers are areas of interest defined by a company that are not necessarily considered definitive requirements but represent what the company would prefer as an acceptable solution.

There are several business drivers that have varying degrees of importance. To meet every business driver would be a perfect scenario, and to meet only a few with a limited degree of success would be considered a failure. Business drivers are points of interest in typical VPN solutions that must be evaluated to determine the degree of support required for the driver by the VPN solution. Business drivers can be categorized into several areas that represent common concerns with any new technology, including:

- functionality
- authentication process
- vendor integration
- manageability
- client system support

Each of these areas can have varying levels of importance, depending on the organization, and various levels of support, depending on the vendor product chosen.

Functionality

Functionality is the ability of the communication equipment and software to execute the desired minimum communication standard. It can also be used to determine the various vendor options available and their alignment with the design requirements. Functionality is a crucial element for a company to define. Typically, this is associated with three areas of focus.

1. application support
2. network environment
3. operational matters

Functionality compares the organizational requirements to a product's capabilities to determine the robustness of the proposed solution. Defining the general functionality areas of concern will assist in creating a comprehensive design and reduce the number of products that can support the design.

Application Support. This area can include the ability to maintain a consistent encrypted signal to support the applications the company will utilize. Some VPN solutions only encrypt certain communications or certain portions of the data. The ability of the solution to support the application's communication requirements may be affected by how the solution handles the data. In addition to the possible limitations, sensitive application-specific data or characteristics can be revealed.

The ability to coexist with other existing and planned software and hardware cannot be overstated. A VPN solution that is to provide communication to the network must be cognizant of all the hardware and software it will be used to access or interact with. Imagine implementing a perfect design that could potentially save the company huge amounts of money, but the primary time and billing application is not accessible from the VPN. The value of the solution will certainly plummet and the design engineers will be responsible for answering questions about why it is not functioning.

Application support is nearly always the first thing that is questioned of any remote access solution. If a VPN system is to provide access to services but has difficulty in extending those services to the client, it will certainly have functionality issues and scalability problems. The concern for application support is one of the main drivers of IPSec. Because IPSec operates at the network layer, there is no need for any upper layer protocols or functions to be concerned with the communications provided. However, there are custom applications with interesting communication requirements that may have difficulty; while rare, they must be searched out and tested.

Infrastructure Interactions. Supporting applications is a powerful aspect of IPSec and many concerns are put to rest. However, applications are one part of the many functionality issues that need to be investigated. Other network hardware and software that provide network communications must be examined to determine interoperability and overall coexistence. Good examples are routing protocol support and network management protocol support.

As learned above, a VPN gateway operates much like a router that provides access to remote IP networks. In large environments, routing protocols are used to reduce the administration of supporting the infrastructure and provide for alternate route calculation in the event of an outage. A VPN solution that can participate in routing protocols can greatly enhance its ability to seamlessly interact with network changes and modifications with limited administration. Also, routing protocols can be used to take advantage of certain network attributes to enhance performance, save money, or simply provide increased efficiency. Whichever the case, routing protocol support is typically desired and represents a product's overall strength as a well-rounded solution.

Network management is a concern for even the smallest of networks. In many scenarios, Simple Network Management Protocol (SNMP) is used to gather information about systems and provide a common protocol to administer a collage of network systems. A VPN gateway, for many solutions, is an appliance that not only operates much like a router, but also reflects many of the characteristics of a router. Some of these are command-line interface (CLI), console support, no hard drive, and other aspects commonly associated with network devices. For many organizations, the ability to manage the VPN device with the existing network management solution is a requirement very high on the list to obtain. In the event an organization is using SNMP for network management and analysis, the product's support for SNMP can be a very important requirement.

General Functionality Areas. For many companies, routing protocols and network management support are simply not of any interest. Combine this with standard applications that represent very little concern, and functionality seems complete. However, there are some aspects — considered common but a necessity — that must be discussed.

The ability to operate for extended periods of time while under duress must be evaluated. Also, to operate uninterrupted is a core requirement for many organizations. This does not necessarily reflect a system's stability, but rather its ability to remain operational during administration or process errors. As an example, the addition of a user or group in the system's database should not force the administrator to reboot the system before the changes take effect. If an IP pool of addresses is being utilized, it should be acceptable to add or modify the pool — within reason — without disturbing the operation of the system or the users attached. Determining the organization's expectations of the day-to-day operations is crucial.

Authentication Process

The authentication process covers many aspects. The ultimate goal is to reduce the amount of work required to add, modify, or eliminate communication support for users or vendor networks. It must also be a relatively simple process for creating access controls for applications and systems based on centralized user databases.

Many organizations have a central repository of user information. There are several examples, ranging from Novell Directory Services (NDS), Microsoft Active Directory (AD), Microsoft Domain, to RADIUS and Banyan Vines. In some cases, an organization might have several variations on one theme or a combination of the above to accomplish business requirements. The ability to authenticate users who are using the VPN for access is obviously very important. Therefore, the ability of the system to participate in an existing authentication system can be a significant point of interest.

Existing Projects. There are several interesting aspects to authentication in VPN environments. Integration with PKI, Directory, or RADIUS services can become a requirement if the company is in the process of implementing any of them before VPNs were considered. The utilization of existing projects will be extremely beneficial to the overall success of the project.

Authentication Collateral. Options and general operations of a product that appear to meet the requirements of an organization may have unforeseen dependencies that can cancel out the original advantage or just simply be too clumsy. User authentication requirements on the authenticating device and the authenticated device must be investigated to determine operational limitations or undesirable support requirements.

For example, an application must be loaded on the client, above and beyond the normal IPSec VPN client, to provide certain functionality that is desired from the solution. Early in VPN's existence, a vendor provided a product that appeared to meet the requirements. However, even after the client was installed, to provide one of the desired services, another application had to be installed. As users authenticated, the client was not able to cache credentials in a manner that supported continuous access. Therefore, another program was loaded that acted as middleware to avoid having the user be presented with an authentication prompt each time a service was requested.

Another example, which was still in existence at the time this book was written, is a single service-based authentication through the use of HTTP. A user would establish a VPN to the gateway and would have access capability based on default permissions. However, if the user used some application other than a browser for the first access, there would be no extended authentication and access would be denied to more restricted services. So, if privileged users needed Telnet access to a specific system only they had access to, they would have to open a browser, authenticate to the VPN gateway, and then continue as normal.

These types of limitations and caveats do not appear until proper lab and pilot programs are executed. Unfortunately, if the product is not properly tested, certain undesirable aspects are not discovered until implementation. Fortunately, a well-constructed testing process should reveal any issues early in the implementation.

Level, type, and granularity of control of the communication process defined by the authentication mechanism are either a high priority or not considered. It must be determined early in the process if the business requirements include access control and the granularity of that control. It is also necessary to understand that the type of authentication provided can have a direct impact on those capabilities.

An example of when access control is not considered a necessary aspect of remote access is when the VPN is implemented to emulate internal network activities. For many organizations, the act of limiting the user once connected seems counterproductive. Security experts cringe when faced with this train of thought because the security is completely focused at the host level. Many small organizations may not feel this is necessary, and large organizations may simply segment the networks with firewalls or physical isolation to reduce administration. To accommodate the disparity, there are several products that do not provide access controls while others combine firewalling capabilities and remote VPN access.

On the other hand, many implementations are geared toward extranet access and the combination of services through a single device. Many firewall implementations operate in this way by the implementation of Demilitarized Zones (DMZ), authenticated extranet access networks or EDMZ, and finally the protected internal network. Access to each network is based on various forms of authentication properties that can range from originating IP address to application to two-factor authentication.

The interesting aspect of authentication is that some capabilities are deeply related to the authentication medium. For example, one wants to filter access to a certain server based on user authentication and TCP/IP port. If using a remote RADIUS server for authentication, the application of access control lists (ACL) might only go to the group level. In these scenarios, a user provides a group ID or password at the time of the connection. Once Phase 1 has begun, RADIUS authentication can take place to authenticate the user. The user information is obtained from the RADIUS server, while the group information is maintained in the VPN device's memory. Thus, as ACLs are built, the VPN device is only aware of group IDs and is oblivious to the user database on the remote RADIUS server.

Vendor Integration

Vendors, partners, or affiliates of an organization that utilize VPN connectivity to access the organization's data may be required to implement what the organization has chosen for the VPN solution for the partner community. This is contrary to the IPSec standard — a common operating environment for true interoperability — but represents a real concern when creating VPNs with different equipment. Currently, VPN implementations are limited and most companies that have VPN solutions are not overlapping into business relationships with others that are using VPN as well. Occasionally, overlap occurs; but for the most part in today's landscape, it is still rare. As VPN solutions become more commonplace, the ability for product interoperability will become the center of concern. Unfortunately, this is nearly a moot issue because the interoperability needed in the future is typically unknown and only applies when it an identified necessity. In the latter case, the product selected is typically the same as the existing solution.

Nonetheless, there are organizations that have the ability to direct the partner community in what direction their VPN must conform to.

Several issues encompass the community, including the:

- *Cost of equipment to be implemented at the remote site:* The cost can have an impact on the relationship if the remote partner must purchase the equipment. For small vendors interacting with a larger organization, the cost to continue the business relationship over the VPN may be cost-prohibitive.
- *Support issues for the remote company in the event of a system failure or configuration modification:* VPN implementations can be complicated enough for a company that has complete control over the implementation. However, support for mandatory equipment at a remote site that is not part of the origination organization can represent some technical and political issues.

■ *Perceived security of the VPN equipment that the company has chosen for the partnering organization:* It is necessary to ensure the partner that connecting their network to the Internet using the company defined equipment will be secure. In other words, the solution's ability to apply security to the communications while protecting the internal network

Manageability

As briefly mentioned above, the ability to manage the VPN product installed can have an enormous impact on the assimilation of the VPN into existing infrastructures. If manageability is a concern for the organization, or it is in the process of defining a network management, any solution must fit into the scheme.

Some of the manageability issues, including:

■ the ability to control and manipulate the VPN devices from a central location, such as a Network Operations Center (NOC)
■ central management of users and groups and their associations with established rules and policies
■ type and security of the management application or protocol

Management is typically handled by a station with a software packaged loaded that can be used to communicate with one or more VPN systems. There are four major types of management types; each one can be supported with varying degrees of functionality. That is, from the console, one may have complete control of the system; but from browser-based access, certain options may be unavailable. It is necessary to explain each type to an organization to determine which process best fits into the network management design at the organization:

■ console
■ browser (Java, ActiveX, etc.)
■ SNMP
■ proprietary

Out-of-Band Management. The ability to obtain console-based, command-line interface can be crucial to management, configuration, and troubleshooting. While this option is common, it is also strongly recommended for any solution — specifically, appliance-based gateways. However, the manageability of the system from the console may be limited compared to a more preferred management process using a proprietary application.

Browser. The utilization of a common browser that supports Java, ActiveX, or CGI scripts is becoming increasingly prevalent. Browsers are a popular management platform for distributed environments. When considering a solution that utilizes browser management, the solution's ability to provide SSL, or some form of encryption, is recommend. However, this is not typical. In some scenarios, the product simply listens on a non-standard port for HTTP access. Typically, passwords are used to manage a system; and for an attacker to discover the port at which HTTP management is being processed is trivial.

SNMP. As discussed above, SNMP is a flexible and robust management protocol that can become the lowest common denominator for a product-diverse network. SNMP is anything but simple and, if not properly implemented, could expose the network to security vulnerabilities.

Many solutions will allow SNMP Puts and Gets, to gain information from the device and provide administration to the system. On the other hand, some solutions might only allow information to be gleaned from the product. Examples are system load, number of concurrent connections, who is attached, the IP addresses in use, etc. Systems that provide SNMP usually provide the necessary components to allow full management of the system from existing management solutions.

Proprietary. It is necessary to be aware that some solutions have specific software that is used to access their product. This can be seen as a limitation in many large implementations. It limits in-house program augmentations and the company may be limited by developmental constraints of the vendor. Furthermore, as with available client packages, Microsoft platforms are typically focused on management software. Many vendors provide a custom management application in concert with another type of management (detailed above). It will be necessary to weigh the advantages and disadvantages of each type of management to determine what is best for the organization.

Security of the Management Application. As mentioned, access to the VPN device from a management system needs to take security into consideration — especially in the case of browser based administration, because everyone has a browser.

The communication protocol between the management system and the VPN device can come in two basic flavors:

1. existing protocols
2. proprietary protocols

Existing protocols include Telnet, HTTP, FTP, and PPP for communicating with the VPN device. SSL (Secure Sockets Layer) is typically used for secure Internet browsing traffic where the server's and client's identity are established and the session is encrypted. SSH (Secure Shell) is typically associated with UNIX secure communications, but can be used to provide secure management protocol communications. And IPSec; it may seem obvious to use IPSec for an IPSec solution, but its use is limited. In some cases, one can configure an IPSec tunnel with the VPN device and then run the necessary management protocol within the IPSec tunnel.

Proprietary protocols are communication methods developed and maintained by the vendor. This type of management is typically associated with a proprietary management system. Therefore, the same possible limitations can be applied that exist with any proprietary solution.

Multiple Device Support. The solution's ability to support multiple devices from a single management station can be a valuable — sometimes mandatory — asset of a VPN product.

Network-to-network VPNs require that each system participating in a group of devices know certain information about the others: IP address, type of key management to use, and various aspects about the security association (SA) for that particular peer (such as a shared secret). The ability to manage several systems at once during a modification will allow the administrator to provide the updated configuration to all systems involved. A management system might allow the administrator to access the systems that require updated information and build a new configurations file. Then the management software will download the new file to the systems. However, some solutions do not have the ability to manage more than one system. It is strongly recommended to avoid such products, considering the environment and future plans for a company.

Client System Support

Client system support can become an enormous issue for administrative departments. There are several issues confronting the realm of client support, each one with a varying degree of impact. Of the many issues, two primary areas rise to the surface:

- The operating system that is installed on the clients participating on the VPN will have an impact on the product selection. Even the version of the operating system and the latest service pack or patch applied can have an impact on the product selection process.
- Application coexistence with the required VPN application is a possible barrier. The installation of the VPN client may have an effect on other system requirements.

Operating System Support. Few organizations can say they have the same operating system and versions on client systems throughout the entire organization. Obviously, the smaller the company, the less complicated having a common platform for all clients. In large organizations, especially in today's very diverse climate, a common platform may be impossible. Partnering organizations, affiliates, and departments with specific requirements represent areas where the client system software could be diverse and unchangeable. There are several situations that might affect the selection and control of the client operating system in large, diversified environments:

1. The Information Systems (IS) department of one organization may have little impact on a partnering organization, although they interact very closely and the delineation is blurred.
2. Specialized systems for engineering, development, or advanced applications (e.g., laboratories and graphic creation) may use operating systems such as Solaris, AIX, Macintosh, Linux, and HP-UX.
3. Custom applications may have requirements that dictate certain system operations that are not supported by a common or new version of the platform.
4. Cost is a huge factor. To save money, a company may want to replace its outdated remote access solution with a more cost-effective VPN solution. However, if the VPN requires the updating of hundreds of systems throughout the organization, the costs may be prohibitive.

In addition to the various operating systems available, there are the versions and available patches for each install base. UNIX systems represent the greater administration in patches as compared to Microsoft platforms. Microsoft tends to provide services packs that do not have to be applied sequentially and modify several portions of the operating system. Some UNIX systems, on the other hand, can have several patches, depending on the services installed, or simply one patch for each service.

Operating system support from the vendor community, for the most part, has been focused on Microsoft platforms. This is obviously due to the market share that Microsoft has in the PC market. Any organization that has non-Microsoft operating systems for use in the VPN will have a limited choice of products.

As discussed later in detail, a lab should be performed on the client software packages. The client software must be tested to ascertain the functionality of the client, the extent of the installation, and configuration requirements. Also, the client should be tested for rollout procedures and package deployment planning. The client system issues include:

- *Installation process:* determine the systems modifications, compatibility issues, and remote installation capabilities.
- *Performance of client package:* this includes system performance and communication performance as well as user interface and ease of use.

The installation process, installation options, and the resulting system operation should all be verified. Included in the lab must be continuous attention to testing the system's overall performance. This detail is overlooked in some scenarios. Although performance is a key issue for VPNs, most client packages operate unnoticeably on newer, faster systems. Nonetheless, lab tests should be cognizant of performance impacts on lab systems.

Grading Methodology

Once the business drivers are identified and categorized by priority level, it is necessary to compile a list of products that meet the needs of the design and business drivers. A grading methodology is the process of reducing the number of candidates to two or three for rigorous lab testing.

Once the final two or three solutions are identified, it will be necessary to obtain demo equipment for lab testing. This process can range from an easy process to nearly impossible and may require an agreement designed for testing the vendor equipment. The process depends on the vendor, product availability, willingness of the organization to provide the product — which may have a financial attachment, and the size of the purchase from the vendor. Money is the foundation of business, and I have had several experiences where demo equipment was out of the question because the organization seemed too small to allocate resources for developing a sale. In any case, be prepared for anything when attempting to obtain equipment for lab testing. At minimum, have the lab processes and tests detailed in a document for their inspection.

This chapter section outlines the important aspects used in grading the proposed vendor solutions. Using a grading methodology will give the company attempting to determine a VPN product a tool to quickly differentiate the VPN solutions. The grading methodology will provide a means to measure the various vendor solutions against each other and the system requirements to prepare for the lab.

There are several sections that will be defined for grading the solution's abilities. The sections are in no particular order and the level of importance may vary. Nonetheless, every VPN solution will have some level of compliance and, in turn, a resulting score. In these sections, one will see remnants of the previously defined business drivers and other VPN-specific characteristics.

- number of connections
- routing protocol support
- authentication mechanisms
- client functionality
- access control
- scalability
- cost considerations
- extra effort

An extra-effort section is also detailed that attempts to score vendors that display strong points where the products have exceeded the basic requirements. The scoring system will be from 1 to 10: 1 being the lowest and 10 being the highest score possible. The total score at the end of the process is the addition of each attribute value and the addition of the extra-effort score to the final tally.

Connections

This aspect is based on the product's capability of supporting multiple concurrent connections. If the vendor cannot support the necessary number of concurrent connections planned from a single platform, it will be identified and addressed in grading of scalability. The total number of users that can be supported rely on whether or not the product is able to interact with LDAP, RADIUS, TACACS, or some form of remote authentication service.

For many solutions, the number of concurrent connections is related to using authentication services provided by a separate facility. For some large solutions, an authentication support infrastructure must be established to support the VPN solution. If no authentication system is supplied, the internal user database of the VPN device must be employed, which is typically very limited. There have been examples of systems supportomg 10,000 users but only handling 100 users internally.

Routing Protocol Support

This aspect of grading identifies whether or not the vendor's solution will participate in routing protocols. This is not the same as allowing the protocol information to pass, as in the case with network-to-network VPNs. The solution should be able to participate in the common routing protocols, such as OSPF and RIP (v1 and 2). This would directly affect scalability, and the grade should reflect the number of supported protocols and the percentage of interfaces they are supported on.

In addition, the grading process must take into consideration the quality of the routing protocols. Various services and configurations are desirable in the area of routing support. Redistribution of routing information from one protocol to another is very desirable in distributed systems. The ability to specify the order in which routers are parsed can enhance both performance and efficiency. As an example, there are static routes that will provide a route to a particular network, but routing protocols can be employed to implement costing methods to reduce WAN utilization charges. In the event the routing protocol information is unavailable, the process should look to the static routes for final information. The security of the routing table is paramount. If an attacker modifies the routing table, he or she could direct traffic to unwanted destinations. Hashing and password support in the routing protocol can become a strong deterrent for attackers attempting to poison the enterprise's routing tables through the VPN gateway.

Authentication Mechanisms

This grade addresses the vendor's interaction with authentication mechanisms. The aspects of the solution that will receive the highest grade are the vendor's ability to interact with RADIUS, LDAP (i.e., Active Directory and NDS), and certificates. This is another area that influences scalability. Interaction with RADIUS is good, but could be a limiting factor if that is all the solution can interact with.

Typically, certificate support is the most complicated due to the client intelligence in handling the certificates. Most products support RADIUS because it has been a standard remote access authentication method and the install base is expansive. RADIUS is also utilized for the small packet information and the limited resources in handling the authentication process.

Client Functionality

This aspect of grading rates the vendor's VPN client. Key functionality of the client will be judged on how the client is installed on workstations, how the client establishes the session, and how the client can be managed. Other areas of functionality include the ability to lock down the client configuration, centrally administer client configuration, and enhance security during the session establishment.

Access Control

Probably one of the most important aspects of grading is the solution's ability to provide granular control of access to networks or groups of devices. Some vendors will separate themselves by offering the most robust filtering possible. Access control is vendor specific and is enhanced by including interaction with RADIUS for group information and rule passing. However, many products do not provide for filtering capabilities, due to the resource utilization of the processing and implementation overhead. Nonetheless, the more granularity of the filter capabilities, the higher the grade.

Scalability

All vendor solutions scale in some form or fashion. This aspect of grading focuses on how the vendors provide scalability compared to best practices and current techniques within the organization. Vendors provide scalability by adding other devices or adding components within the current device, such as an expansion card. If another device must be added to scale the solution, the management of multiple systems becomes an issue. Some vendors manage multiple devices very well, while others increase the administrative burden. Scalability in the form of additional components is limited to the capacity of the chassis.

If an organization is accustomed to adding separate devices to accomplish the scale of the solution, then multiple devices may be acceptable. A key issue with multiple devices is rack space. Typically overlooked, computer room real estate is becoming very expensive. Therefore, saving money in the solution and scaling by just adding more systems may cost more than immediately apparent.

As mentioned above, the other areas of scalability are interaction with the authentication mechanisms, routing protocol support, and simultaneous connections.

Cost Information

Cost is the primary driver, in some form or another, for implementing a VPN. Either to reduce tangible costs of phone lines and support equipment, reduce administration, or reduce the cost of expansion when more remote system support increases.

Several aspects of costs come into play and each is governed by the scope of the final solution. However, there are several areas in which cost issues tend to gain the attention of management. Several examples can be explained by discussing two different companies and directives:

- Company S is small and only needs 500 simultaneous user support for a 5000-user base.
- Company B is large and requires 9000 simultaneous user support for a 15,000-user base.

If the VPN system costs $70,000 but the clients are free, company S will pay $14 for each of the 5000 remote users but the effective cost is $140 for each of the 500 users. Company B will pay $4.65 for each of the 15,000 remote users, but an effective cost of $7.75 for each of the 9000 users.

However, for some solutions, the initial cost is low, but the clients have a licensing fee. If the VPN system costs $10,000 and the clients are $35 each, company S will pay $27,500 for the 500 users. Company B will pay $325,000 for the 9000 users.

To properly grade the solution's cost, the grade is based on cost per user when total solution cost is calculated against maximum user support. One must calculate against the maximum simultaneous user support to base the cost on the capability of the solution. If one buys a product that supports 5000 simultaneous connections, but only needs 300 for the foreseeable future, one may have the wrong solution — as it pertains to cost.

Extra Effort

Each of the vendors has focused on various aspects that will set them apart. Many examples exist, from unique hardware, to robust client management, to filtering capabilities, to performance capabilities. This grade recognizes the aspects in each of the vendor's solutions that indicate the extra effort. This grade is based on the total number of aspects in which the vendor displays greater functionality. That is, if a product has great support for routing protocols and access filters, it gets two points. However, the maximum points in this category cannot exceed the number of categories; in this example, 7 is the highest extra effort number.

Lab Testing

Once the grading is complete and a small, manageable list of products is compiled, a lab must be performed to ensure that the research performed is verified and not assumed. Unfortunately, not all information is made available by the vendors during the investigation process. This in no way reflects the vendor's performance or ethics, but details that are tested in a lab cannot be completely predicted by a vendor. Also, in several situations, customer labs have provided product insight and assisted in the development of the product or the creation of a patch or fix.

It is necessary to understand that time in the lab is not a waste of money and effort. Rather, the information collected will be used to implement the solution more efficiently and with greater understanding of the product. Performing a lab may take time and money, but the savings of time, money, frustration, and the possibility of purchasing a product that does not meet the organizations needs may be avoided at a later date.

Lab Setup

Portions of the network design that rely on connectivity issues through security devices and Internet connectivity issues must be duplicated as closely as possible in a limited environment. The lab should use several pieces of equipment and communication technology to emulate connections, networks, software, and environmental situations that allow the organization's engineers to test various VPN concepts and general functionality. The lab will allow the organization to find weaknesses in products or to fully utilize features that were not previously discovered. It will provide an opportunity to put vendor software and hardware into the network and security designs that best fit the company's business requirements.

Prior to actually performing the tests, a test plan, or lab goals, should be created to expedite the lab and testing processes. Also, providing lab goals will provide vendors with the ability to participate in a lab to which they feel comfortable providing equipment. If no lab goals are defined and the tests are not detailed, the vendor is completely unaware of the processes and could spend more time defending the product against an invalid test or result than assisting in the completion of the test. Defining a set of lab goals also proves that the organization has selected the right individuals for the VPN project and that creating comprehensive goals is not effortless.

Chapter 15

Report on IPSec

In February 1999, Niels Ferguson and Bruce Schneier, of Counterpane Internet Security, Inc., produced a document detailing the results of a report on the state of the security provided by IPSec requested by the NSA. The report is anything but flattering and represents Ferguson and Schneier's disenchantment with the resulting protocol. In the introduction, it stated, "IPSec was a great disappointment to us," which sets the tone for the remainder of the report. Shortly after the report was made available to the community, there was a great deal of discussion in the IETF IPSec workgroup. Everything ranging from anger to agreement was shared among the group's participants. During the process, Stephen Kent, one of the authors of RFC 2401, 2402, and 2406, and a well-established expert in the field, provided a rebuttal to the comments made by the Counterpane report.

Ferguson and Schneier are two highly respected individuals in the cryptographic community and the network security community as a whole, and are two of the authors of TwoFish, an AES candidate. Given their expertise in cryptography, their report carried a great deal of weight. Stephen Kent is one of a few, along with Randall Atkinson, Dan Harkins, Dave Carrel, IPSec experts and knows the internals of the protocol suite intimately — they wrote the RFCs!

In the IPSec workgroup, it was argued by some that Counterpane did not approach the workgroup prior to releasing the report, allowing the opportunity to provide reasoning behind some of the problems outlined. It was also argued that Ferguson and Schneier did not learn some of the reasoning behind the protocol, which may have shed light on areas of great contention.

On the other hand, many argued that some points introduced in the report were valid and should be addressed by the group, adding that by simply knowing the reason behind an option or functionality does not necessarily validate it. In the world of IPSec, there seems to be a constant undercurrent of finger pointing between vendors, developers, implementers, testers, and just about anyone that deals with IPSec on a regular basis. Conversations on the state of the protocol and the completeness of the protocol are constant reminders that high security is not easily obtained.

The final result of this adventure was a report on the state of IPSec and comments from Stephen Kent included in a document provided to the IETF IPSec workgroup. This hybrid document provides very interesting insight into various positions and opinions about issues regarding security, protocols, and operability. This author contacted Stephen Kent and Bruce Schneier and asked their permission to reprint the report with the comments included. They both graciously agreed and, therefore, the report and comments are included here.

Note: In no way was verbiage changed or modified from the version that was supplied to the workgroup. For the full report, go to www.counterpane.com/ipsec.pdf. The author would like to thank Bruce Schneier and Stephen Kent for permission to include this in the book.

(Stephen Kent's comments are in **bold** and the remainder is verbiage directly from the Counterpane report on IPSec.)

The Hybrid Report

"This evaluation is based on RFCs 2401–2411 and RFC 2451 {RFC2401,RFC2402,RFC2403, RFC2404,RFC2405,RFC2406,RFC2407,RFC2408,RFC2409,RFC2410,RFC2411,RFC2451}."

"IPSec is a set of protocols that provides communication security for computers using IP-based communication networks. It provides authentication and confidentiality services on a packet level. To support the IPSec security, a key management protocol called ISAKMP is used. ISAKMP uses public key cryptographic techniques to set up keys between the different parties to be used with IPSec."

"Both IPSec and ISAKMP are too complex. **[a protocol is too complex only relative to a specified set of requirements that are satisfied by a simpler protocol. To substantiate this observation, one ought to define the requirements that one believes the protocol is trying to satisfy, and then offer a simpler protocol.]** This high complexity leads to errors. We have found security flaws in both IPSec and ISAKMP, and expect that there are many more. We expect any actual implementation to contain many more errors, some of which will cause security weaknesses. These protocols give the impression of having been designed by a committee: they try to be everything for everybody at the cost of complexity. For normal standards, that is bad enough; for security systems, it is catastrophic. In our opinion, the complexity of both IPSec and ISAKMP can be reduced by a large factor without a significant loss of functionality."

"IPSec is in better shape than ISAKMP. The description and definitions are reasonably clear. A careful implementation of IPSec can achieve a good level of security. Unfortunately, IPSec by itself is not a very useful protocol. Use on a large scale requires the key management functions of ISAKMP. **[while I would tend to agree with this observation, I should note that a non-trivial number of IPSec implementations, used in constrained contexts, are manually keyed.]**"

"IPSec and ISAKMP are highly complex systems. Unfortunately, we cannot give a sufficiently detailed description of these systems in this document to allow the reader to understand our comments without being familiar with IPSec and ISAKMP. Our comments frequently refer to specific places in the RFC documents for ease of reference."

"Complexity is the biggest enemy of security. This might seem an odd statement in the light of the many fielded systems that exhibit critical security failures for very simple reasons. It is true nonetheless. The simple failures are simple to avoid, and often simple to fix. The problem is not that we do not know how to solve them; it is that this knowledge is often not applied. Complexity, however, is a different beast because we do not really know how to handle it."

"This process of making fairly complex systems and implementing them with a try-and-fix methodology has a devastating effect on the security. The central reason is that you cannot test for security. Therefore, security bugs are not detected during the development process in the same way that functional bugs are. Suppose a reasonably sized program is developed without any testing at all during development and quality control. We feel confident in stating that the result will be a completely useless program; most likely it will not perform any of the desired functions correctly. Yet this is exactly what we get from the try-and-fix methodology when we look at security."

"The only reasonable way to "test" the security of a security product is to perform security reviews on it. {A cracking contest can be seen as a cheap way of getting other people to do a security analysis. The big problem is interpreting the results. If the prize is not claimed, it does not imply that any competent analysis was done and came up empty.} A security review is a manual process; it is relatively expensive in terms of time and effort and it will never be able to show that the product is in fact secure. **[this seems to ignore the approaches usually employed for high assurance system design and implementation , i.e., careful design and review coupled with rigid development procedures, all prior to testing.]**"

"The IPSec and ISAKMP protocols do not specify clearly which security properties they claim to achieve. **[RFCs 2401, 2402, and 2406 clearly state the security services offered by the AH and ESP protocols.]** The same holds for the modules and functions. **[modules are not specified by these standards; they are implementation artifacts.]** We recommend that each function, module, and protocol be extended to include clear specifications regarding the security-related functionality they achieve. We feel that unless this is done, it will not be possible to perform an adequate security evaluation on a system of this complexity."

"IPSec is capable of providing authentication and confidentiality services on a packet level. The security configuration of an IPSec implementation is done centrally, presumably by the system administrator. **[In some environments, a single administrator might control the configuration of each IPSec implementation, or each user might have some control over it. The latter would tend to be characterized as a distributed management paradigm, not a central one. Also, two IPSec peers communicate ONLY if both agree on the security parameters for the SA, i.e., there is suitable overlap in the SPDs. In that sense too, security configuration is distributed.]**"

"IPSec is very suitable for creating a VPN over the Internet, improved security for dial-in connections to portables, restricting access to parts of a network, etc. These are very much network-level functions. IPSec by itself does not supply application-level security. Authentication links the packet to the security gateway of the originating network, the originating host, or possibly the originating user, but not to the application in question or the data the application was handling when it sent the packet. **[true, but for many applications, application layer security is not needed, and its**

implementation might well be accorded less assurance than the network layer security provided by IPSec. This paragraph seems to suggest that there is some important benefit to linking data to an application, through an application-specific security mechanism. There are good examples of where this is true, e.g., e-mail and directories. However, unless there are application-specific security semantics that cannot be captured by use of an application security protocol, your own arguments about simplicity, as well as a number of arguments re assurance, argue against proliferation of application security protocols.]"

"The IPSec functionality can significantly increase the security of the network. It is not a panacea for all security problems, and applications that require security services will typically have to use other security systems in addition to IPSec. **[I might disagree with the term "typically" here. A lot depends on the application, where IPSec is implemented, etc.]"**

"Our biggest criticism is that IPSec is too complex. There are too many options that achieve the same or similar properties. **[if they were completely equivalent this would be a good basis for simplifying IPSec. However, there are subtle differences that have resulted in the proliferation of options you address below.]"**

"IPSec suffers from an abundance of options. For example, two hosts that want to authenticate IP packets can use four different modes: transport/AH, tunnel/AH, transport/ESP with NULL encryption, and tunnel/ESP with NULL encryption. The differences between these options, both in functionality and performance, are minor."

"In particular, the following options seem to create a great deal of needless complexity: There are two modes that can be used: transport mode and tunnel mode. In transport mode, the IP header of the packet is left untouched. AH authenticates both the IP header and the packet payload. ESP encrypts and authenticates the payload, but not the header. The lack of header authentication in transport/ESP is a real weakness, as it allows various manipulations to be performed. In tunnel mode, the full original IP packet (including headers) is used as the payload in a new IP packet with new headers. The same AH or ESP functions are used. As the original header is now included in the ESP authentication, the transport/ESP authentication weakness no longer exists."

"Transport mode provides a subset of the functionality of tunnel mode. The only advantage that we can see to transport mode is that it uses a somewhat smaller bandwidth. However, the tunnel mode could be extended in a straightforward way with a specialized header-compression scheme that we will explain shortly. This would achieve virtually the same performance as transport mode without introducing an entirely new mode. We therefore recommend that the transport mode be eliminated. **[transport mode and tunnel mode address fundamentally different requirements, from a networking point of view. When security gateways are involved, the use of tunnel mode is an absolute requirement, whereas it is a minor (and rarely used) feature for communications between end systems. A proposal to make all traffic tunnel mode, and to try to offset the added overhead through compression, seems to ignore the IPCOMP facility that is already available to IPSec implementations. Today, transport mode is used primarily to carry L2TP traffic, although this is primarily an efficiency issue.]"**

"There are two protocols: AH and ESP. AH provides authentication, and ESP provides encryption, authentication, or both. In transport mode, AH provides a stronger authentication than ESP can provide, as it also authenticates the IP header. One of the standard modes of operation would seem to be to use both AH and ESP in transport mode. **[although this mode is required to be supported, it seems to be rarely used today. A plausible, near-term use for AH is to provide integrity and authenticity for IPSec traffic between an end system and a first-hop interme- diary. For example, AH can be used between a host inside an enclave and a security gateway at the perimeter, to allow the SG to control what traffic leaves the enclave, without granting the SG access to plaintext traffic. This, and similar concatenated SA examples, motivate retention of AH. One could achieve a similar effect with (authentication-only) ESP tunnels, but with increased bandwidth and processing overhead.]** In tunnel mode, the authentication that ESP provides is good enough (it includes the IP header), and AH is typically not combined with ESP {RFC2401}. **[the example above shows why one might wish to use AH for the outer header, but most likely with ESP in transport mode.]** (Implemen- tations are not required to support nested tunnels that would allow ESP and AH to both be used.)"

"The AH protocol {RFC2402} authenticates the IP headers of the lower layers. **[AH authenticates the IP header at the SAME layer, in many respects. AH was originally described as an IP (v4) option. In IPv6, AH is viewed as part of the AH header, and may appear before other header extensions (see section 4.1 of RFC 2401). I agree that AH represents ugly layering, but it's not as bad as you suggest here.]** This creates all kind of problems, as some header fields change in transit. As a result, the AH protocol needs to be aware of all data formats used at lower layers so that these mutable fields can be avoided. **[this is an inaccurate characterization, especially given the status of AH re IPv6. Don't think of AH as a transport protocol. It isn't.]** This is a very ugly construction, and one that will create more problems when future extensions to the IP protocol are made that create new fields that the AH protocol is not aware of. **[RFC 2402 explains how to deal with new IP header fields in v6 (see section 3.3.3.1.2.2). The existence of a mutability flag in such extensions makes processing relatively straightfor- ward.]** Also, as some header fields are not authenticated, the receiving application still cannot rely on the entire packet. To fully understand the authentication provided by AH, an application needs to take into account the same complex IP header parsing rules that AH uses. The complex definition of the functionality that AH provides can easily lead to security-relevant errors."

"The tunnel/ESP authentication avoids this problem, but uses more bandwidth. **[but it does not provide exactly the same features, as noted above, so the alternative is not quite equivalent.]** The extra bandwidth requirement can be reduced by a simple specialized compression scheme: for some suitably chosen set of IP header fields X, a single bit in the ESP header indicates whether the X fields in the inner IP header are identical to the corresponding fields in the outer header.\footnote{A trivial generalization is to have several flag bits, each controlling a set of IP header fields.} The fields in question are then removed to reduce the payload size. This compression should be applied after computing the authentication but before any encryption. The authentication is thus still computed on the entire original packet. The receiver reconstitutes the original packet using the outer header fields, and verifies the authentication. A suitable choice of the set of header fields X allows tunnel/ESP to achieve virtually the same low message expansion as transport/AH."

"We conclude that eliminating transport mode allows the elimination of the AH protocol as well, without loss of functionality. **[counter examples provided above suggest that this claim is a bit overstated.]**"

"The standard defines two categories of machines: hosts and security gateways. Hosts can use transport mode, but security gateways must always use tunnel mode. Eliminating transport mode would also allow this distinction to be eliminated. Various computers could of course still function as hosts or security gateways, but these different uses would no longer affect the protocol."

"The ESP protocol allows the payload to be encrypted without being authenticated. In virtually all cases, encryption without authentication is not useful. The only situation in which it makes sense not to use authentication in the ESP protocol is when the authentication is provided by a subsequent application of the AH protocol (as is done in transport mode because ESP authentication in transport mode is not strong enough). **[this is one example of when one might not need authentication with ESP, but it is not the only one. In general, if there is a higher layer integrity and/or authentication function in place, providing integrity/authentication in IPSec is redundant, both in terms of space and processing. The authentication field for ESP or AH is 12 bytes. For applications where packet sizes are quite small, and for some environments where packet size is of critical importance, e.g., packet voice in a wireless environment, ESP w/o authentication may be appropriate. This is especially true if the application protocol embodies an authentication mechanism. This might happen if the application protocol wants to offer uniform protection irrespective of the lower layers. Admittedly, this might also cause the application to offer confidentiality as well, but depending on the application, the choices of what security services are being offered may vary.]** Without the transport mode to worry about, ESP should always provide its own authentication. We recommend that ESP authentication always be used, and only encryption be made optional. **[the question of authentication as an intrinsic part of ESP is independent of mode, i.e., whether one choose to provide authentication as a part of ESP is not determined by the choice of transport vs. tunnel mode.]**"

"We can thus remove three of the four operational modes without any significant loss of functionality. **[sorry, can't agree, given the counter examples above.]**"

"There are existing combinations of options that are undesirable. These pose a problem when non-experts have to configure an IPSec installation. Given the fact that experts are rare and usually have better things to do, most IPSec installations will be configured by non-experts. **[yes, we were aware of this concern. However, there is always a trade-off between adopting the "we know what's best for you" approach, vs. the "you can screw it up if you want to approach." We opted for a point somewhere along this spectrum, but not at either end.]**"

"In transport mode, use of ESP provides authentication of the payload only. The authentication excludes the IP headers of the packet. The result is a data stream that is advertised as "authenticated" for which critical pieces of information (such as the source and destination IP number) are not authenticated. Unless the system administrator is intimately familiar with the different forms of authentication used by IPSec, it is quite likely that the administrator will assume that the authentication protects the entire packet. The combination of transport mode and the ESP protocol (without the AH protocol) should therefore not be allowed. **[The IP source and destination**

address are covered by the TCP checksum, which is covered by the ESP integrity check, so this does limit (a tiny bit) the ability to change these values without detection. A more significant observation is that transport mode IPSec SAs will probably always use source and/or destination IP addresses as part of the selector set. In such cases, tampering with either address will result in a failed authentication check.]"

"The standard allows ESP to be used with the NULL encryption, such that it provides only authentication. The authentication provided by ESP in transport mode is less functional than the authentication provided by AH, at a similar cost. If transport mode is retained, either the ESP authentication should be extended or the use of ESP with only authentication should be forbidden and replaced by the use of AH. **[ESP authentication is more efficient to compute than AH, because of the selective IP header coverage provided by AH. Thus there is good reason to allow authentication-only ESP as an alternative to AH. This point was debated by the group and, with implementation experience, vendors came to agree that this is true.]"**

"The ESP protocol can provide encryption without authentication. This does not make much sense in an application. It protects the application against passive eavesdroppers, but provides no protection against active attacks that are often far more devastating. Again, this mode can lure non-expert users into using an unsafe configuration that they think is secure. Encryption without authentication should be forbidden. **[as noted above, there are examples where this feature set for ESP is attractive.]"**

"IPSec also suffers from a lack of orthogonality. The AH and ESP protocols can be used together, but should only be used in one particular order. In transport mode, ESP by itself provides only partial authentication of the IP packet, and using AH too is advisable. **[not in most cases, as noted above.]** In tunnel mode the ESP protocol authenticates the inner headers, so use of AH is no longer required. These interdependencies between the choices demonstrate that these options are not independent of each other. **[true, but who says that this is a critical criteria? TCP and IP are not orthogonal either, e.g., note the TCP checksum covering parts of the IP header.]"**

"The IPSec protocols are also hampered by the compatibility requirements. A simple problem is the TOS field in the IP header {RFC2402}. Although this is supposed to be unchanged during the transmission of a packet (according to the IP specifications), some routers are known to change this field. IPSec chose to exclude the TOS field from the authentication provided by the AH protocol to avoid errors introduced by such rogue routers. The result is that, in transport/AH packets that have an authenticated header, the TOS field is not authenticated. This is clearly unexpected from the application point of view, which might want to rely on the correct value of the TOS field. This problem does not occur in tunnel mode. **[it is unfortunate that cisco chose to not follow the specs here, and in several other places. I agree that an unenlightened system administrator might be surprised in this case. But, in practice, the effect is minimal. Your example cites transport mode, which means that the TOS bits are being acted upon by the end system. If end systems really paid attention to these bits in the first place, cisco would not have been able to corrupt them with impunity! The reason that these bits are being reused by the ECN folks is because hosts have never made use of them. Still, going forward, one should pay attention to this vulnerability.]"**

"A more complex compatibility problem is the interaction between fragmentation and IPSec {RFC2401}. This is a complex area, but a typical IPSec implementation has to perform specialized processing to facilitate the proper behavior of higher-level protocols in relation to fragmentation. Strictly speaking, fragmentation is part of the communication layer below the IPSec layer, and in an ideal world it would be transparent to IPSec. Compatibility requirements with existing protocols (such as TCP) force IPSec to explicitly handle fragmentation issues, which adds significantly to the overall complexity. Unfortunately, there does not seem to be an elegant solution to this problem. **[The requirement here is the same that arises whenever an intermediate system adds info to a packet, or when a smaller MTU intermediate system is traversed. IPSec in an SG is doing what a router along a path would do if the "other side" network were smaller. IPSec in a host is doing what the NIC would do if the LAN MTU changed. The real complexity arises when we wish to do this optimally, at a security gateway or a BITS or BITW implementation, in cases where different SAs use different combinations of AH and ESP, or different algorithms, etc.]**"

"The overall result is that IPSec bulk data handing is overly complex. In our opinion it is possible to define an equivalent system that is far less complex."

"When both encryption and authentication are provided, IPSec performs the encryption first, and authenticates the ciphertext. In our opinion, this is the wrong order. Going by the "Horton principle" {WS:SSL30}, the protocol should authenticate what was meant, not what was said. The "meaning" of the ciphertext still depends on the decryption key used. Authentication should thus be applied to the plaintext (as it is in SSL {SSLv3Nov96}), and not to the ciphertext. **[The order of processing is intentional. It is explicitly designed to allow a receiver to discard a packet as quickly as possible, in the event of DoS attacks, as you acknowledge below. The suggestion that this concern be addressed by the addition of a secondary MAC seems to violate the spirit of simplicity that this document espouses so strongly, and the specific proposed fix is not strong enough to warrant its incorporation. Moreover, this ordering allows parallel processing at a receiver, as a means of increasing throughput and reducing delay.]**"

"This does not always lead to a direct security problem. In the case of the ESP protocol, the encryption key and authentication key are part of a single ESP key in the SA. A successful authentication shows that the packet was sent by someone who knew the authentication key. The recipient trusts the sender to encrypt that packet with the other half of the ESP key, so that the decrypted data is in fact the same as the original data that was sent. The exact argument why this is secure gets to be very complicated, and requires special assumptions about the key agreement protocol. For example, suppose an attacker can manipulate the key agreement protocol used to set up the SA in such a way that the two parties get an agreement on the authentication key but a disagreement on the encryption key. When this is done, the data transmitted will be authenticated successfully, but decryption takes place with a different key than encryption, and all the plaintext data is still garbled. **[The fundamental assumption is that an ESP SA that employs both encryption and an HMAC will have the keys bound together, irrespective of the means by which they are generated. This assumption probably could be better stated in the RFCs.]**"

"In other situations, the wrong order does lead to direct security weaknesses."

"Suppose two hosts have a manually keyed transport-mode AH-protocol SA, which we will call SAah. Due to the manual keying, the AH protocol does not provide any replay protection. These two hosts now negotiate a transport-mode encryption-only ESP SA (which we will call SAesp1) and use this to send information using both SAesp1 and SAah. The application can expect to get confidentiality and authentication on this channel, but no replay protection. When the immediate interaction is finished, SAesp1 is deleted. A few hours later, the two hosts again negotiate a transport-mode encryption-only ESP SA (SAesp2), and the receiver chooses the same SPI value for SAesp2 as was used for SAesp1. Again, data is transmitted using both SAesp2 and SAah. The attacker now introduces one of the packets from the first exchange. This packet was encrypted using SAesp1 and authenticated using SAah. The receiver checks the authentication and finds it valid. (As replay protection is not enabled, the sequence number field is ignored.) The receiver then proceeds to decrypt the packet using SAesp2, which presumably has a different decryption key than SAesp1. The end result is that the receiver accepts the packet as valid, decrypts it with the wrong key, and presents the garbled data to the application. Clearly, the authentication property has been violated. **[this attack is not a criticism of the choice of ESP operation ordering, but rather the notion of applying AH and ESP (encryption only) in a particular order, as allowed by RFC 2401. The specific combination of keying operations described here, though not prohibited by 2401, does not seem likely to occur in practice. Specifically, if an IPSec implementation supports automated key management, as described above for the ESP SAs, then it is highly unlikely that the AH SA would be manually keyed. The push to retain manual keying as a base facility for IPSec is waning, and most implementations have IKE available. Under these circumstances, this vulnerability is unlikely to be realized.]**"

"Doing the encryption first and authentication later allows the recipient to discard packets with erroneous authentication faster, without the overhead of the decryption. This helps the computer cope with denial-of-service attacks in which a large number of fake packets eat up a lot of CPU time. We question whether this would be the preferred mode of attack against a TCP/IP-enabled computer. If this property is really important, a 1- or 2-byte MAC (Message Authentication Code) on the ciphertext could be added. The MAC code allows the recipient to rapidly discard virtually all bogus packets at the cost of an additional MAC computation per packet. **[a one or two byte MAC provides so little protection that this does not seem to be an attractive counter-proposal. Also, as noted above, it adds complexity ...]**"

"The ordering of encryption and authentication in IPSec is wrong. Authentication should be applied to the plaintext of the payload, and encryption should be applied after that."

"Most of our aforementioned comments also affect the SA system; the use of two modes and two protocols make the SA system more complex than necessary."

"There are very few (if any) situations in which a computer sends an IP packet to a host, but no reply is ever sent. **[we have a growing number of apps where this functionality may be appropriate. For example, broadcast packet video feeds and secure time feeds are unidirectional.]** There are also very few situations in which the traffic in one direction needs to be secured, but the traffic in the other direction does not need to be secured. It therefore seems that in virtually all practical situations, SAs occur in pairs to allow bi-directional secured communications. In fact, the IKE protocol negotiates SAs in pairs. **[IKE has not always been well coordinated with IPSec, unfortunately. This is why we have to have null encryption and null authentication algorithms. So, I don't think one should cite IKE behavior as a basis for making SAs bi-directional. I agree that the vast majority of examples that we see now are full duplex, but we have examples where this may not apply, as noted above.]"**

"This would suggest that it is more logical to make an SA a bi-directional "connection" between two machines. This would halve the number of SAs in the overall system. It would also avoid asymmetric security configurations, which we think are undesirable. **[The SPI that is used as a primary de-multiplexing value, must be chosen locally, by the receiver, so having bi-directional SAs probably won't change the size of the SAD substantially. Specifically, how do you envision that a switch to bi-directionality would simplify implementations?]"**

"The security policies are stored in the SPD (Security Policy Database). For every packet that is to be sent out, the SPD is checked to find how the packet is to be processed. The SPD can specify three actions: discard the packet, let the packet bypass IPSec processing, or apply IPSec processing. In the last case, the SPD also specifies which SAs should be used (if suitable SAs have already been set up) or specifies with what parameters new SAs should be set up to be used."

"The SPD seems to be a very flexible control mechanism that allows a very fine-grained control over the security processing of each packet. Packets are classified according to a large number of selectors, and the SPD can match some or all selectors to determine the appropriate action. Depending on the SPD, this can result in either all traffic between two computers being carried on a single SA, or a separate SA being used for each application, or even each TCP connection. Such a very fine granularity has disadvantages. There is a significantly increased overhead in setting up the required SAs, and more traffic analysis information is made available to the attacker. At the same time we do not see any need for such a fine-grained control. **[a lot of customers for IPSec products disagree!]** The SPD should specify whether a packet should be discarded, should bypass any IPSec processing, requires authentication, or requires authentication and encryption. Whether several packets are combined on the same SA is not important. **[yes it is. By allowing an administrator the ability to select the granularity of protection, one can control the level of partial traffic flow confidentiality offered between security gateways. Also, fine-grained access control allows an admin to allow some forms of connections through the gateway, while rejecting others. Access control is often the primary, underlying motivation for using IPSec. A number of attacks become possible if one cannot tightly bind the authentication provided by IPSec to the access control decision. Also, given the computational costs of SA establishment via IKE, it is important to allow an administrator to select the granularity of SAs.]** The same holds for the exact choice of cryptographic algorithm: any good algorithm will do. There are two reasons for this. First of all, nobody ever attacks a system by cryptanalysis. Instead, attacks are made on the users, implementation, management, etc. Any reasonable cryptographic algorithm will provide adequate protection. The second reason is that there are very efficient and secure algorithms available. Two machines should negotiate the strongest algorithm that they are allowed. There is no reason to select individual algorithms on an application-by-application basis. **[if one were to employ ESP**

without authentication, because a specific higher layer protocol provided its own authentication, and maybe because the application employed FEC, then one might well imagine using different encryption algorithms, or different modes (e.g., block vs. stream) for different SAs. While I agree that the focus on algorithm agility may be overstated, it does allow communicating parties to select a higher quality algorithm, relative to the mandated default, if they both support that algorithm.]"

"In our opinion, management of the IPSec protocols can be simplified by letting the SPD contain policies formulated at such a higher level. As we argued, simplification will strengthen the actual system. **[examples provided above illustrate why fine-grained access control is important.]"**

"It would be nice if the same high-level approach could be done in relation to the choice of SA end-points. As there currently does not seem to be a reliable automatic method of detecting IPSec-enabled security gateways, we do not see a practical alternative to manual configuration of these parameters. It is questionable whether automatic detection of IPSec-enabled gateways is possible at all. Without some initial knowledge of the other side, any detection and negotiation algorithm can be subverted by an active attacker. **[the authors identify a good problem, but it is hardly an unsolvable one. A proposal was put forth (by Bob Moscowtiz, over a year ago) to include records in the DNS analogous to MX records. When one tried to establish an SA to a host "behind" an SG, fetching this record would direct the initiator to an appropriate SG. This solves the SG discovery problem. Other approaches have been put forth in the more recent BBN work on security policy management, which forms the basis for a new IETF WG, chaired by Luis Sanchez. The fact that none of the approaches has been deployed says more about the priorities of IPSec vendors and early adopters than about the intractability of the problem. The other part of the problem is verifying that an SG is authorized to represent the SA target. Here too, various approaches have been described on the IPSec mailing list.]"**

"In {RFC2401}, several fields in the SAD are required for all implementations, but only used in some of them. It does not make sense to require the presence of fields within an implementation. Only the external behavior of the system should be standardized. **[the SAD defined in 2401 is nominal, as the text explains. An implementation is not required to implement these fields, but must exhibit behavior consistent with the presence of these fields. We were unable to specify external behavior without reference to a construct of this sort. The SPD has the same property.]"**

"According to [p.\ 23]{RFC2401}, an SA can be either for transport mode, tunnel mode, or "wildcard," in which case the sending application can choose the mode on a packet-by-packet basis. Much of the rest of the text does not seem to take this possibility into account. It also appears to us to be needless complexity that will hardly every be used, and is never a necessity. We have already argued that transport mode should be eliminated, which implies that this option is removed too. If transport mode is to be retained, we would certainly get rid of this option. **[I agree, but at least one knowledgeable WG member was quite adamant about this. So, chalk it up to the committee process!]"**

"IPSec does not allow replay protection on an SA that was established using manual key management techniques. This is a strange requirement. We realize that the replay protection limits the number of packets that can be transmitted with the SA to $2^{32}-1$. Still, there are applications that have a low data rate where replay protection is important and manual keying is the easiest solution. **[elsewhere this critique argues for not presenting options in a standard that can be misconfigured. Yet here, the authors make an argument for just such an option! The WG decided that there was too great a chance that a manually keyed SA would fail to maintain counter state across key lifetime and thus made a value judgment to ban anti-replay in this context.]**"

"RFC2401 suggests that an implementation can find the matching SPD entry for a packet using back-pointers from the SAD entries. In general this will not work correctly. Suppose the SPD contains two rules: the first one outlaws all packets to port X, and the second one allows all incoming packets that have been authenticated. An SA is set up for this second rule. The sender now sends a packet on this SA addressed to port X. This packet should be refused as it matches the first SPD rule. However, the back-pointer from the SA points to the second rule in the SPD, which allows the packet. This shows that back-pointers from the SA do not always point to the appropriate rule, and that this is not a proper method of finding the relevant SPD entry. **[this is point #3 and is applied only after points #1 and #2. Since point #1 calls for a liner search of the SPD, the packet would be rejected, as required. Thus point #3 is not in error.]**"

"The handling of ICMP messages as described in RFC2401 is unclear to us. It states that an ICMP message generated by a router must not be forwarded over a transport-mode SA, but transport-mode SAs can only occur in hosts. By definition, hosts do not forward packets, and a router never has access to a transport-mode SA. **[the text in the beginning of section 6 is emphasizing that an SA from a router to a host or security gateway, must be a tunnel mode SA, vs. a transport mode SA. If we didn't make this clear, someone might choose to establish a transport mode SA from an intermediate system, and this would cause the source address checks to fail under certain circumstances, as noted by the text.]**"

"The text further suggests that unauthenticated ICMP messages should be disregarded. This creates problems. Let us envision two machines that are geographically far apart and have a tunnel-mode SA set up. There are probably a dozen routers between these two machines that forward the packets. None of these routers knows about the existence of the SA. Any ICMP messages relating to the packets that are sent will be unauthenticated and unencrypted. Simply discarding these ICMP messages results in a loss of IP functionality. This problem is mentioned, but the text claims this is due to the routers not implementing IPSec. Even if the routers implement IPSec, they still cannot send authenticated ICMP messages about the tunnel unless they themselves set up an SA with the tunnel end-point for the purpose of sending the ICMP packet. The tunnel end-point in turn wants to be sure the source is a real router. This requires a generic public-key infrastructure, which does not exist. **[RFC 2401 clearly states the dangers associated with blindly accepting unauthenticated ICMP messages, and the functionality problems associated with discarding such messages. System administrators are provided with the ability to make this trade-off locally. The first step to addressing this problem is the addition of IPSec into routers, as stated in the RFC. Only then does one face the need to have a PKI that identifies routers. Yes, this second PKI does not exist, but a subset of it (at BGP routers) might be established if the S-BGP technology is deployed. These are the routers most likely to issue ICMP PMTU messages. So, the answer**

here is that the specifications allow site administrators to make security/functionality trade-offs, locally. The longer term solution described would require routers to implement IPSec, so that they can send authenticated ICMP messages. Yes, this would require a PKI, but such a PKI may arise for other reasons.]"

"As far as we understand this problem, this is a fundamental compatibility problem with the existing IP protocol that does not have a good solution."

RFC2401 lists a number of possible ways of handling ICMP PMTU messages. An option that is not mentioned is to keep a limited history of packets that were sent, and to match the header inside the PMTU packet to the history list. This can identify the host where the packet that was too large originated. **[the approach suggested by the authors was rejected as imposing too much of a burden on an SG. Section 6.1.2.1 offers options (not suggestions) for an SG to respond to ICMP PMTU messages, including heuristics to employ when not enough information is present in the returned header. These options may not be as responsive as a strategy that caches traffic on each SA, but they are modest in the overhead imposed. Also, an SA that carries a wide range of traffic (not fine-grained) might not benefit from a limited traffic history, as the traffic that caused the ICMP might well be from a host whose traffic has been flushed from the "limited history."]"**

"RFC2401 mentions that each auditable event in the AH and ESP specifications lists a minimum set of information that should be included in the audit-log entry. Not all auditable events defined in RFC2406 include that information. **[you're right. Exactly one auditable event in 2406 does not specify the list of data that SHOULD be audited. We'll fix that in the next pass.]** Furthermore, auditable events in RFC2401 do not specify such a minimum list of information. **[there are exactly 3 events defined as auditable in 2401, one of which overlaps with 2406. So, to be more precise, the other 2 auditable events defined in 2401 ought to have the minimum data requirements defined. Another good point that we will fix in the next pass.]** The documentation should be reviewed to ensure that a minimum list of audit-log information is specified with each auditable event."

"Various algorithm specifications require the implementation to reject known weak keys. For example, the DES-CBC encryption algorithm specifications {RFC2405} requires that DES weak keys are rejected. It is questionable whether this actually increases security. It might very well be that the extra code that this requires creates more security problems due to bugs than are solved by rejecting weak keys."

"Weak keys are not really a problem in most situations. For DES, it is far less work for an attacker to do an exhaustive search over all possible keys than to wait for an SA that happens to use a weak key. After all, the easiest way for the attacker to detect the weak keys is to try them all. Weak-key rejection is only required for algorithms where detecting the weak key class by the weak cipher properties is significantly less work than trying all the weak keys in question."

"We recommend that the weak-key elimination requirement be removed. Encryption algorithms that have large classes of weak keys that introduce security weaknesses should simply not be used. **[I tend to agree with this analysis. The argument for weak key checking was made by folks who don't understand the cryptographic issues involved, but who are persistent and loud, e.g., Bill Simpson. Ted T'so**

(co-chair of the WG) and I discussed this problem, and tried to explain it to the list, [IETF Workgroup E-mail List] but were unsuccessful. Another flaw in the committee process.]"

"The only mandatory encryption algorithm in ESP is DES-CBC. Due to the very limited key length of DES, this cannot be considered to be very secure. We strongly urge that this algorithm not be standardized but be replaced by a stronger alternative. The most obvious candidate is triple-DES. Blowfish could be used as an interim high-speed solution.\footnote{On a Pentium CPU, Blowfish is about six to seven times faster than triple-DES.} The upcoming AES standard will presumably gain quick acceptance and probably become the default encryption method for most systems. **[DES as a default was mandated because of pressure from vendors who, at the time, could not get export permission for 3DES. Triple DES or AES will certainly augment DES as additional, mandatory defaults, and may replace it in the future.]"**

"The insistence on randomly selected IV values in RFC2405 seems to be overkill. It is true that a counter would provide known low Hamming-weight input differentials to the block cipher. All reasonable block ciphers are secure enough against this type of attack. Use of a random generator results in an increased risk of an implementation error that will lead to low-entropy or constant IV values; such an error would typically not be found during testing. **[In practice the IV is usually acquired from previous ciphertext output, as suggested in the text for CBC mode ciphers, which is easy to acquire and not likely to result in significant complexity. In hardware assisted environments an RNG is usually available anyway. In a high assurance hardware implementation, the crypto chip would generate the IV.]"**

"Use of a block cipher with a 64-bit block size should in general be limited to at most 2^{32} block encryptions per key. This is due to the birthday paradox. After 2^{32} blocks we can expect one collision.\footnote{To get a 10^{-6} probability of a collision it should be limited to about 2^{22} blocks.} In CBC mode, two equal ciphertexts give the attacker the XOR of two blocks of the plaintext. The specifications for the DES-CBC encryption algorithm \cite{RFC2405} should mention this, and require that any SA using such an algorithm limit the total amount of data encrypted by a single key to a suitable value."

"The preferred mode for using a block cipher in ESP seems to be CBC mode {RFC2451}. This is probably the most widely used cipher mode, but it has some disadvantages. As mentioned earlier, a collision gives direct information about the relation of two plaintext blocks. Furthermore, in hardware implementations each of the encryptions has to be done in turn. This gives a limited parallelism, which hinders high-speed hardware implementations. **[first, this is not an intrinsic part of the architecture; one can define different modes for use with existing or different algorithms if the WG is so motivated. Second, current hardware is available at speeds higher than the associated packet processing capability of current IPSec devices, so this does not appear to be a problem for the near term. Transition to AES will decrease the processing burden (relative to 3DES), which may render this concern less serious.]"**

"Although not used very often, the counter mode seems to be preferable. The ciphertext of block i is formed as $C_i = P_i \oplus E_K(i)$, where i is the block number that needs to be sent at the start of the packet.\footnote{If replay protection is always in use, then the starting i-value could be formed as 2^{32} times the sequence number. This saves eight bytes per packet.} After more than 2^{32} blocks counter mode also reveals some information about the plaintext, but this is less than what occurs in CBC. The big advantage of counter mode is that hardware implementations can parallelize the encryption and decryption process, thus achieving a much higher throughput. **[earlier the authors criticize IPSec for a lack of orthogonality, but introducing interdependence between the anti-replay counter and encryption would certainly violate the spirit of the earlier criticism! Counter mode versions of algorithms can be added to the list easily if there is sufficient vendor support.]"**

"RFC2451 states that Blowfish has weak keys, but that the likelihood of generating one is very small. We disagree with these statements. The likelihood of getting two equal 32-bit values in any one 256-entry S-box is about ${256 \choose 2} \cdot 2^{-32} \approx 2^{-17}$. This is an event that will certainly occur in practice. However, the Blowfish weak keys only lead to detectable weaknesses in reduced-round versions of the cipher. There are no known weak keys for the full Blowfish cipher."

"In RFC2451, it is suggested to negotiate the number of rounds of a cipher. We consider this to be a very bad idea. The number of rounds is integral to the cipher specifications and should not be changed at will. Even for ciphers that are specified with a variable number of rounds, the determination of the number of rounds should not be left up to the individual system administrators. The IPSec standard should specify the number of rounds for those ciphers. **[I agree that this algorithm spec ought not encourage negotiation of the number of rounds, without specifying a minimum for each cipher, although this gets us into the crypto strength value judgment arena again. Also, the inclusion of 3DES in this table is inappropriate as it is a 48 round algorithm, period. So, yes, there is definite room for improvement in this RFC.]"**

"RFC2451 proposes the use of RC5. We urge caution in the use of this cipher. It uses some new ideas that have not been fully analyzed or understood by the cryptographic community. The original RC5 as proposed (with 12 rounds) was broken, and in response to that the recommended number of rounds was increased to 16. We feel that further research into the use of data-dependent rotations is required before RC5 is used in fielded systems. **[RC5 is not required by IPSec implementations. In the IETF spirit of flexible parameterization of implementations, vendors are free to offer any additional algorithms in addition to the required default. In general, the IETF is not prepared to make value judgments about these algorithms and so one may see RFCs that specify a variety of additional algorithms.]"**

"RFC2406 specifies that the ESP padding should pad the plaintext to a length so that the overall ciphertext length is both a multiple of the block size and a multiple of 4. If a block cipher of unusual block size is used (e.g., 15 bytes), then this can require up to 59 bytes of padding. This padding rule works best for block sizes that are a multiple of 4, which fortunately is the case for most block ciphers. **[this padding rule is based primarily on IP packet alignment considerations, not on common block cipher sizes! This is stated in the text.]"**

"RFC2406 states that the padding computations of the ESP payload with regard to the block size of the cipher apply to the payload data, excluding the IV (if present), Pad Length, and Next Header fields. This would imply that the Pad Length and Next

Header fields are not being encrypted. Yet the rest of the specification is clear that the Pad Length and Next Header fields are to be encrypted, which is what should happen. The text of point a should be made consistent with the rest of the text. **[The text says "...the padding computation applies to the Payload Data exclusive of the IV, the Pad Length, and Next Header fields." The comma after "IV" is meant to terminate the scope of the word "exclusive," and thus the intent is to include the pad length and next header fields. The term "payload" in ESP applies to a set of data not including the latter two fields, so the sentence is, technically, unambiguous, and it is consistent with the terms employed in the Exhibit in section 2. But, I admit the wording could be improved.]"**

"The NULL cipher specifies an IV length of zero {RFC2410}. This would seem to imply that the NULL cipher is used in CBC mode, which is clearly not the case. The NULL cipher is in fact used in ECB mode, which does not require an IV. Therefore, no IV length should be specified. **[use of the NULL cipher in ECB mode would be inconsistent with the guidance in FIPS 82, and thus CBC mode is intended, to preserve the confidentiality characteristics inherent in this cipher :-).]"**

"The IPSec system should be simplified significantly. This can be done without loss of functionality or performance. There are also some security weaknesses that should be fixed. **[the extensive comments above illustrate that the proposed changes to IPSec would change the functionality, contrary to the claim made here. One might argue about the importance of some of this functionality, but several examples have been provided to illustrate application contexts that the authors of this report did not consider in their analysis. Several misunderstandings of some RFCs also were noted.]"**

Due to its high complexity, we have not been able to analyze IPSec as thoroughly as we would have liked. After simplification, a new security analysis should be performed."

Appendix

Etherpeek IKE Decode

IPSEC.TXT

```
DCod Src ISAKMP;
   DWRD 0 1 90 c2 Destination Port:;
   CST# ffffffff 1 0 14 UDP/TCP Port Names;
   TNXT 0 0 0 0 ISAKMP UDP;

DCod ISAKMP UDP;
   DWRD 0 f 90 c2 Length:;
   HWRD 0 0 90 c2 Checksum:;
   CKSM 3 0 24 14 Checksum invalid. Should be:;
   LABL 0 0 0 b1 ISAKMP Header;
   HEX# 8 0 90 c2 Initiator cookie:;
   HEX# 8 0 90 c2 Responder cookie:;
* store the next payload in 'd'
   DBYT 0 d 90 c2 Next Payload:;
   CST# ffffffff d 0 14 ISAKMP Payloads;
   HBYT 0 0 90 c2 Version:;
   DBYT 0 c 90 c2 Exchange Type:;
   CST# ffffffff c 0 14 ISAKMP Exch Type;
   BBIT 5 0 90 c2 Other Flags:;
   BBIT 1 0 90 c2 Authentication Only Flag:;
   BBIT 1 0 90 c2 Commit Flag:;
   BBIT 1 2 90 c2 Encryption Flag:;
   DLNG 0 0 90 c2 Message ID:;
* Length of total message (header + payloads)
   DLNG 0 e 90 c2 Total Length:;
* if encypt is set then rest can't be decoded
   CBIT 0 2 0 b1 Encrypted:;
   SKIP 1 0 0 0;
* Branch based on the value of next payload 'd'
   TNXT 0 0 0 0 ISAKMP Payload branch;
```

```
DCod ISAKMP SA;
   LABL 0 0 0 b1 Security Assocation Payload;
*  store next payload in 'd'
   DBYT 0 d 90 c2 Next Payload:;
   CST# ffffffff d 0 14 ISAKMP Payloads;
   DBYT 0 0 90 c0 Reserved:;
   DWRD 0 a 90 c2 Payload Length:;
   DLNG 0 8 90 c2 Domain of Interpretation:;
   CST# ffffffff 8 0 14 ISAKMP DOI;
*  subtract previous field from the length
   SUBG 8 a 0 0;
   HEX# 0 a 90 c2 Situation:;
*  Branch based on the value of next payload 'd'
   TNXT 0 0 0 0 ISAKMP Payload branch;


*  Proposal Payload
DCod ISAKMP P;
   LABL 0 0 0 b1 Proposal Payload;
*  store next payload in 'd'
   DBYT 0 d 90 c2 Next Payload:;
   CST# ffffffff d 0 14 ISAKMP Payloads;
   DBYT 0 0 90 c0 Reserved:;
   DWRD 0 a 90 c2 Payload Length:;
   DBYT 0 0 90 c2 Proposal #;
   DBYT 0 0 90 c2 Protocol ID;
   DBYT 0 0 90 c2 SPI size;
   DBYT 0 0 90 c2 # of Transfroms;
*  subtract previous field from the length
   SUBG 4 a 0 0;
   HEX# 0 a 90 c2 SPI:;
*  SUB goes to next payload 'd'
   TNXT 0 0 0 0 ISAKMP Payload branch;


*  Transform Payload;
DCod ISAKMP T;
   LABL 0 0 0 b1 Transform Payload;
*  store next payload in 'd'
   DBYT 0 d 90 c2 Next Payload:;
   CST# ffffffff d 0 14 ISAKMP Payloads;
   DBYT 0 0 90 c0 Reserved:;
   DWRD 0 a 90 c2 Payload Length:;
   DBYT 0 0 90 c2 Transform #:;
   DBYT 0 0 90 c2 Transform-Id:;
   DWRD 0 0 90 c2 Reserved:;
*  subtract previous field from the length
   SUBG 8 a 0 0;
   HEX# 0 a 90 c2 SA Attribates:;
*  SUB goes to next payload 'd'
   TNXT 0 0 0 0 ISAKMP Payload branch;


*  Key Exchange Payload;
DCod ISAKMP KE;
   LABL 0 0 0 b1 Key Exchange Payload;
*  store next payload in 'd'
   DBYT 0 d 90 c2 Next Payload:;
```

```
   CST# ffffffff d 0 14 ISAKMP Payloads;
   DBYT 0 0 90 c0 Reserved:;
   DWRD 0 a 90 c2 Payload Length:;
* subtract previous field from the length
   SUBG 4 a 0 0;
   HEX# 0 a 90 c2 Key Exchange:;
* SUB goes to next payload 'd'
   TNXT 0 0 0 0 ISAKMP Payload branch;

* ID Payload;
DCod ISAKMP ID;
   LABL 0 0 0 b1 Identification Payload;
* store next payload in 'd'
   DBYT 0 d 90 c2 Next Payload:;
   CST# ffffffff d 0 14 ISAKMP Payloads;
   DBYT 0 0 90 c0 Reserved:;
   DWRD 0 a 90 c2 Payload Length:;
   DBYT 0 0 90 c2 ID Type:;
   HBIT 18 0 90 c2 DOI Specific Id data:;
* subtract previous field from the length
   SUBG 8 a 0 0;
   HEX# 0 a 90 c2 Identification Data:;
* SUB goes to next payload 'd'
   TNXT 0 0 0 0 ISAKMP Payload branch;

* CERT Payload;
DCod ISAKMP CERT;
   LABL 0 0 0 b1 Certificate Payload;
* store next payload in 'd'
   DBYT 0 d 90 c2 Next Payload:;
   CST# ffffffff d 0 14 ISAKMP Payloads;
   DBYT 0 0 90 c0 Reserved:;
   DWRD 0 a 90 c2 Payload Length:;
   DBYT 0 b 90 c2 Cert Encoding:;
   CST# ffffffff b 0 14 ISAKMP Cert Type;
* subtract previous field from the length
   SUBG 5 a 0 0;
   HEX# 0 a 90 c2 Certificate Data:;
* SUB goes to next payload 'd'
   TNXT 0 0 0 0 ISAKMP Payload branch;

* Certificate Request Payload;
DCod ISAKMP CR;
   LABL 0 0 0 b1 Certificate Request Payload;
* store next payload in 'd'
   DBYT 0 d 90 c2 Next Payload:;
   CST# ffffffff d 0 14 ISAKMP Payloads;
   DBYT 0 0 90 c0 Reserved:;
   DWRD 0 a 90 c2 Payload Length:;
   DBYT 0 b 90 c2 Cert Encoding:;
   CST# ffffffff b 0 14 ISAKMP Cert Type;
* subtract previous field from the length
   SUBG 5 a 0 0;
   HEX# 0 a 90 c2 Certificate Authority:;
* SUB goes to next payload 'd'
   TNXT 0 0 0 0 ISAKMP Payload branch;
```

```
*  Hash Payload;
DCod ISAKMP HASH;
   LABL 0 0 0 b1 Hash Payload;
*  store next payload in 'd'
   DBYT 0 d 90 c2 Next Payload:;
   CST# ffffffff d 0 14 ISAKMP Payloads;
   DBYT 0 0 90 c0 Reserved:;
   DWRD 0 a 90 c2 Payload Length:;
   SUBG 4 a 0 0;
   HEX# 0 a 90 c2 Hash Data:;
*  SUB goes to next payload 'd'
*  TNXT 0 0 0 0 ISAKMP Payload branch;

*  Signature Payload;
DCod ISAKMP SIG;
   LABL 0 0 0 b1 Signature Payload;
*  store next payload in 'd'
   DBYT 0 d 90 c2 Next Payload:;
   CST# ffffffff d 0 14 ISAKMP Payloads;
   DBYT 0 0 90 c0 Reserved:;
   DWRD 0 a 90 c2 Payload Length:;
   SUBG 4 a 0 0;
   HEX# 0 a 90 c2 Signature Data:;
*  SUB goes to next payload 'd'
   TNXT 0 0 0 0 ISAKMP Payload branch;

*  Nonce Payload;
DCod ISAKMP NONCE;
   LABL 0 0 0 b1 NONCE Payload;
*  store next payload in 'd'
   DBYT 0 d 90 c2 Next Payload:;
   CST# ffffffff d 0 14 ISAKMP Payloads;
   DBYT 0 0 90 c0 Reserved:;
   DWRD 0 a 90 c2 Payload Length:;
   SUBG 4 a 0 0;
   HEX# 0 a 90 c2 Nonce Data:;
*  SUB goes to next payload 'd'
   TNXT 0 0 0 0 ISAKMP Payload branch;

DCod ISAKMP N;
   LABL 0 0 0 b1 Notification Payload;
*  store next payload in 'd'
   DBYT 0 d 90 c2 Next Payload:;
   CST# ffffffff d 0 14 ISAKMP Payloads;
   DBYT 0 0 90 c0 Reserved:;
   DWRD 0 a 90 c2 Payload Length:;
   DLNG 0 8 90 c2 DOI:;
   CST# ffffffff 8 0 14 ISAKMP DOI;
   DBYT 0 0 90 c2 Protocol-Id:;
   DBYT 0 4 90 c2 SPI Size:;
   DWRD 0 7 90 c2 Notify Message Type:;
*  Notify type string is for values 1-16383
   CST# 0 7 0 14 ISAKMP Notify Type;
*  Notify type status is for values 16385-65535
*  subtract 16384
```

```
   CST# ffffc001 7 0 14 ISAKMP Notify Status;
   HEX# 0 4 90 c2 SPI:;
   SUBG 18 a 0 0;
   HEX# 0 a 90 c2 Notification Data:;
*  SUB goes to next payload 'd'
   TNXT 0 0 0 0 ISAKMP Payload branch;

DCod ISAKMP D;
   LABL 0 0 0 b1 Delete Payload;
*  store next payload in 'd'
   DBYT 0 d 90 c2 Next Payload:;
   CST# ffffc001 d 0 14 ISAKMP Payloads;
   DBYT 0 0 90 c0 Reserved:;
   DWRD 0 a 90 c2 Payload Length:;
   DLNG 0 8 90 c2 DOI:;
   CST# ffffffff 8 0 14 ISAKMP DOI;
   DBYT 0 0 90 c2 Protocol-Id:;
   DBYT 0 4 90 c2 SPI Size:;
   DWRD 0 7 90 c2 # of SPIs:;
   TNXT 0 0 0 0 ISAKMP SPI;
DCod ISAKMP SPI;
*  goto next payload if # of SPIs (g7) is zero
   TEQU 0 7 0 0 ISAKMP Payload branch;
*  For each SPI print (g4) bytes
   HEX# 0 4 90 c2 SPI:;
   SUBG 1 7 0 0;
*  loop for all SPIs
   TNXT 0 0 0 0 ISAKMP SPI;

*  VID Payload;
DCod ISAKMP VID;
   LABL 0 0 0 b1 Vendor ID Payload;
*  store next payload in 'd'
   DBYT 0 d 90 c2 Next Payload:;
   CST# ffffffff d 0 14 ISAKMP Payloads;
   DBYT 0 0 90 c0 Reserved:;
   DWRD 0 a 90 c2 Payload Length:;
   SUBG 4 a 0 0;
   HEX# 0 a 90 c2 Vendor ID:;
*  SUB goes to next payload 'd'
   TNXT 0 0 0 0 ISAKMP Payload branch;

*  Unknown Payload;
DCod ISAKMP Unknown;
   LABL 0 0 0 b1 Unknown Payload;
*  store next payload in 'd'
   DBYT 0 d 90 c2 Next Payload:;
   CST# ffffffff d 0 14 ISAKMP Payloads;
   DBYT 0 0 90 c0 Reserved:;
   DWRD 0 a 90 c2 Payload Length:;
   SUBG 4 a 0 0;
   HEX# 0 a 90 c2 Unknown:;
*  SUB goes to next payload 'd'
   TNXT 0 0 0 0 ISAKMP Payload branch;
```

```
* Sub to branch based on the value of next payload 'd'
DCod ISAKMP Payload branch;
   TEQU 1 d 0 0 ISAKMP SA;
   TEQU 2 d 0 0 ISAKMP P;
   TEQU 3 d 0 0 ISAKMP T;
   TEQU 4 d 0 0 ISAKMP KE;
   TEQU 5 d 0 0 ISAKMP ID;
   TEQU 6 d 0 0 ISAKMP CERT;
   TEQU 7 d 0 0 ISAKMP CR;
   TEQU 8 d 0 0 ISAKMP HASH;
   TEQU 9 d 0 0 ISAKMP SIG;
   TEQU a d 0 0 ISAKMP NONCE;
   TEQU b d 0 0 ISAKMP N;
   TEQU c d 0 0 ISAKMP D;
   TEQU d d 0 0 ISAKMP VID;
   TNEQ 0 d 0 0 ISAKMP Unknown;

STR# ISAKMP Payloads;
   NONE;
   Secuity Association (SA);
   Proposal (P);
   Transform (T);
   Key Exchange (KE);
   Identification (ID);
   Certification (CERT);
   Certificare Request (CR);
   Hash (HASH);
   Signature (SIG);
   Nonce (NONCE);
   Notification (N);
   Delete (D);
   Vendor ID (VID);

STR# ISAKMP Exch Type;
   NONE;
   Base;
   Identity Protection;
   Authentication Only;
   Aggressive;
   Informational;

STR# ISAKMP Cert Type;
   NONE;
   PKCS #7 wrapped X.509;
   PGP;
   DNS Signed Key;
   X.509 Certificate - Signature;
   X.509 Certificate - Key Exchange;
   Kerberos Tokens;
   Certificate Revocation List;
   Authority Revocation List;
   SPKI Certificate;
   X.509 Certificate - Attribute;
```

```
STR# ISAKMP Notify Type;
   invalid payload type;
   DOI not supported;
   situation not supported;
   invalid cookie;
   invalid major version;
   invalid minor version;
   invalid exchange type;
   invalid flags;
   invalid message id;
   invalid protocol id;
   invalid SPI;
   invalid-transform-id;
   attributes-not-supported;
   no-proposal-chosen;
   bad-proposal-syntax;
   payload-malformed;
   invalid-key-information;
   invalid-id-information;
   invalid-cert-encoding;
   invalid-certificate;
   cert-type-unsupported;
   invalid-cert-authority;
   invalid-hash-information;
   authentication-failed;
   invalid-signature;
   address-notification;
   notify-sa-lifetime;
   certificate-unavailable;
   unsupported-exchange-type;
   unequal-payload-lengths;
STR# ISAKMP Notify Status;
   connected;

STR# ISAKMP DOI;
   Generic;
   IPsec;
```

Protocol Numbers

Assigned Internet Protocol Numbers

Decimal	Keyword	Protocol	References
0	HOPOPT	IPv6 Hop-by-Hop Option	[RFC1883]
1	**ICMP**	**Internet Control Message**	**RFC792]**
2	**IGMP**	**Internet Group Management**	**[RFC1112]**
3	GGP	Gateway-to-Gateway	[RFC823]
4	**IP**	**IP in IP (encapsulation)**	**[RFC2003]**
5	ST	Stream	[RFC1190,IEN119]
6	**TCP**	**Transmission Control**	**[RFC793]**
7	CBT	CBT	[Ballardie]
8	EGP	Exterior Gateway Protocol	[RFC888,DLM1]
9	IGP	Any private interior gateway (used by Cisco for their IGRP)	[IANA]
10	BBN-RCC-MON	BBN RCC Monitoring	[SGC]
11	NVP-II	Network Voice Protocol	[RFC741,SC3]
12	PUP	PUP	[PUP,XEROX]
13	ARGUS	ARGUS	[RWS4]
14	EMCON	EMCON	[BN7]
15	XNET	Cross Net Debugger	[IEN158,JFH2]
16	CHAOS	Chaos	[NC3]
17	**UDP**	**User Datagram**	**[RFC768,JBP]**
18	MUX	Multiplexing	[IEN90,JBP]
19	DCN-MEAS	DCN Measurement Subsystems	[DLM1]
20	HMP	Host Monitoring	[RFC869,RH6]
21	PRM	Packet Radio Measurement	[ZSU]
22	XNS-IDP	XEROX NS IDP	[ETHERNET,XEROX]
23	TRUNK-1	Trunk-1	[BWB6]
24	TRUNK-2	Trunk-2	[BWB6]
25	LEAF-1	Leaf-1	[BWB6]
26	LEAF-2	Leaf-2	[BWB6]
27	RDP	Reliable Data Protocol	[RFC908,RH6]
28	IRTP	Internet Reliable Transaction	[RFC938,TXM]
29	ISO-TP4	ISO Transport Protocol Class 4	[RFC905,RC77]
30	NETBLT	Bulk Data Transfer Protocol	[RFC969,DDC1]
31	MFE-NSP	MFE Network Services Protocol	[MFENET,BCH2]
32	MERIT-INP	MERIT Internodal Protocol	[HWB]
33	SEP	Sequential Exchange Protocol	[JC120]
34	3PC	Third Party Connect Protocol	[SAF3]
35	IDPR	Inter-Domain Policy Routing Protocol	[MXS1]
36	XTP	XTP	[GXC]
37	DDP	Datagram Delivery Protocol	[WXC]
38	IDPR-CMTP	IDPR Control Message Transport Proto	[MXS1]
39	TP++	TP++ Transport Protocol	[DXF]
40	IL	IL Transport Protocol	[Presotto]
41	IPv6	IPv6	[Deering]
42	SDRP	Source Demand Routing Protocol	[DXE1]
43	IPv6-Route	Routing Header for IPv6	[Deering]
44	IPv6-Frag	Fragment Header for IPv6	[Deering]
45	IDRP	Inter-Domain Routing Protocol	[Sue Hares]
46	RSVP	Reservation Protocol	[Bob Braden]
47	GRE	General Routing Encapsulation	[Tony Li]
48	MHRP	Mobile Host Routing Protocol	[David Johnson]

Assigned Internet Protocol Numbers (continued)

Decimal	Keyword	Protocol	References
49	BNA	BNA	[Gary Salamon]
50	ESP	Encap Security Payload for IPv6	[RFC1827]
51	AH	Authentication Header for IPv6	[RFC1826]
52	I-NLSP	Integrated Net Layer Security TUBA	[GLENN]
53	SWIPE	IP with Encryption	[JI6]
54	NARP	NBMA Address Resolution Protocol	[RFC1735]
55	MOBILE	IP Mobility	[Perkins]
56	TLSP	Transport Layer Security Protocol using Kryptonet key management	[Oberg]
57	SKIP	SKIP	[Markson]
58	IPv6-ICMP	ICMP for IPv6	[RFC1883]
59	IPv6-NoNxt	No Next Header for IPv6	[RFC1883]
60	IPv6-Opts	Destination Options for IPv6	[RFC1883]
61		Any host internal protocol	[IANA]
62	CFTP	CFTP	[CFTP,HCF2]
63		Any local network	[IANA]
64	SAT-EXPAK	SATNET and Backroom EXPAK	[SHB]
65	KRYPTOLAN	Kryptolan	[PXL1]
66	RVD	MIT Remote Virtual Disk Protocol	[MBG]
67	IPPC	Internet Pluribus Packet Core	[SHB]
68		Any distributed file system	[IANA]
69	SAT-MON	SATNET Monitoring	[SHB]
70	VISA	VISA Protocol	[GXT1]
71	IPCV	Internet Packet Core Utility	[SHB]
72	CPNX	Computer Protocol Network Executive	[DXM2]
73	CPHB	Computer Protocol Heart Beat	[DXM2]
74	WSN	Wang Span Network	[VXD]
75	PVP	Packet Video Protocol	[SC3]
76	BR-SAT-MON	Backroom SATNET Monitoring	[SHB]
77	SUN-ND	SUN ND PROTOCOL-Temporary	[WM3]
78	WB-MON	WIDEBAND Monitoring	[SHB]
79	WB-EXPAK	WIDEBAND EXPAK	[SHB]
80	ISO-IP	ISO Internet Protocol	[MTR]
81	VMTP	VMTP	[DRC3]
82	SECURE-VMTP	SECURE-VMTP	[DRC3]
83	VINES	VINES	[BXH]
84	TTP	TTP	[JXS]
85	NSFNET-IGP	NSFNET-IGP	[HWB]
86	DGP	Dissimilar Gateway Protocol	[DGP,ML109]
87	TCF	TCF	[GAL5]
88	EIGRP	EIGRP	[CISCO,GXS]
89	OSPFIGP	OSPFIGP	[RFC1583,JTM4]
90	Sprite-RPC	Sprite RPC Protocol	[SPRITE,BXW]
91	LARP	Locus Address Resolution Protocol	[BXH]
92	MTP	Multicast Transport Protocol	[SXA]
93	AX.25	AX.25 Frames	[BK29]
94	IPIP	IP-within-IP Encapsulation Protocol	[JI6]
95	MICP	Mobile Internetworking Control Pro.	[JI6]
96	SCC-SP	Semaphore Communications Sec. Pro.	[HXH]
97	ETHERIP	Ethernet-within-IP Encapsulation	[RXH1]

Assigned Internet Protocol Numbers (continued)

Decimal	Keyword	Protocol	References
98	ENCAP	Encapsulation Header	[RFC1241,RXB3]
99		Any private encryption scheme	[IANA]
100	GMTP	GMTP	[RXB5]
101	IFMP	Ipsilon Flow Management Protocol	[Hinden]
102	PNNI	PNNI over IP	[Callon]
103	PIM	Protocol Independent Multicast	[Farinacci]
104	ARIS	ARIS	[Feldman]
105	SCPS	SCPS	[Durst]
106	QNX	QNX	[Hunter]
107	A/N	Active Networks	[Braden]
108	IPComp	IP Payload Compression Protocol	[RFC2393]
109	SNP	Sitara Networks Protocol	[Sridhar]
110	Compaq-Peer	Compaq Peer Protocol	[Volpe]
111	IPX-in-IP	IPX in IP	[Lee]
112	VRRP	Virtual Router Redundancy Protocol	[Hinden]
113	PGM	PGM Reliable Transport Protocol	[Speakman]
114		Any 0-hop protocol	[IANA]
115	L2TP	Layer 2 Tunneling Protocol	[Aboba]
116	DDX	D-II Data Exchange (DDX)	[Worley]
117	IATP	Interactive Agent Transfer Protocol	[Murphy]
118	STP	Schedule Transfer Protocol	[JMP]
119	SRP	SpectraLink Radio Protocol	[Hamilton]
120	UTI	UTI	[Lothberg]
121	SMP	Simple Message Protocol	[Ekblad]
122	SM	SM	[Crowcroft]
123	PTP	Performance Transparency Protocol	[Welzl]
124		ISIS over IPv4	[Przygienda]
125	FIRE		[Partridge]
126	CRTP	Combat Radio Transport Protocol	[Sautter]
127	CRUDP	Combat Radio User Datagram	[Sautter]
128	SSCOPMCE		[Waber]
129–254	Unassigned	[IANA]	
255		Reserved	[IANA]

References

1. [CFTP] Forsdick, H., *CFTP*, Network Message, Bolt Beranek and Newman, January 1982.
2. [CISCO] Cisco Systems, *Gateway Server Reference Manual*, Manual Revision B, January 10, 1988.
3. [DDN] Feinler, E., Ed., *DDN Protocol Handbook*, Network Information Center, SRI International, December 1985.
4. [DGP] M/A-COM Government Systems, Dissimilar Gateway Protocol Specification, Draft Version, Contract no. CS901145, November 16, 1987.
5. [ETHERNET] The Ethernet, A Local Area Network: Data Link Layer and Physical Layer Specification, AA-K759B-TK, Digital Equipment Corporation, Maynard, MA. Also as: The Ethernet — A Local Area Network, Version 1.0, Digital Equipment Corporation, Intel Corporation, Xerox Corporation, September 1980. And: The Ethernet, A Local Area Network: Data Link Layer and Physical Layer Specifications, Digital, Intel and Xerox, November 1982. And: XEROX, The Ethernet, A Local Area Network: Data Link Layer and Physical Layer Specification, X3T51/80-50, Xerox Corporation, Stamford, CT, October 1980.
6. [IEN90] Cohen, D. and J. Postel, Multiplexing Protocol, IEN 90, USC/Information Sciences Institute, May 1979.
7. [IEN119] Forgie, J., ST — A Proposed Internet Stream Protocol, IEN 119, MIT Lincoln Laboratory, September 1979.
8. [IEN158] Haverty, J., XNET Formats for Internet Protocol Version 4, IEN 158, October 1980.
9. [MFENET] Shuttleworth, B., A Documentary of MFENet, a National Computer Network, UCRL-52317, Lawrence Livermore Labs, Livermore, CA, June 1977.
10. [PUP] Boggs, D., J. Shoch, E. Taft, and R. Metcalfe, PUP: An Internetwork Architecture, XEROX Palo Alto Research Center, CSL-79-10, July 1979; also in *IEEE Transactions on Communication*, Volume COM-28, Number 4, April 1980.
11. [SPRITE] Welch, B., The Sprite Remote Procedure Call System, Technical Report, UCB/Computer Science Dept., 86/302, University of California at Berkeley, June 1986.
12. [RFC741] Cohen, D., Specifications for the Network Voice Protocol, RFC 741, ISI/RR 7539, USC/Information Sciences Institute, March 1976.
13. [RFC768] Postel, J., User Datagram Protocol, STD 6, RFC 768, USC/Information Sciences Institute, August 1980.
14. [RFC791] Postel, J., Internet Protocol — DARPA Internet Program Protocol Specification, STD 5, RFC 791, DARPA, September 1981.
15. [RFC792] Postel, J., Internet Control Message Protocol — DARPA Internet Program Protocol Specification, STD 5, RFC 792, USC/Information Sciences Institute, September 1981.
16. [RFC793] Postel, J., Transmission Control Protocol — DARPA Internet Program Protocol Specification, STD 7, RFC 793, USC/Information Sciences Institute, September 1981.
17. [RFC823] Hinden, R., and A. Sheltzer, The DARPA Internet Gateway, RFC 823, BBN, September 1982.
18. [RFC869] Hinden, R., A Host Monitoring Protocol, RFC 869, Bolt Beranek and Newman, December 1983.
19. [RFC888] Seamonson, L. and E. Rosen, STUB Exterior Gateway Protocol, RFC 888, BBN Communications Corporation, January 1984.
20. [RFC905] International Standards Organization, ISO Transport Protocol Specification — ISO DP 8073, RFC 905, April 1984.
21. [RFC908] Velten, D., R. Hinden, and J. Sax, Reliable Data Protocol, RFC 908, BBN Communications Corporation, July 1984.
22. [RFC938] Miller, T., Internet Reliable Transaction Protocol, RFC 938, ACC, February 1985.
23. [RFC969] Clark, D., M. Lambert, and L. Zhang, NETBLT: A Bulk Data Transfer Protocol, RFC 969, MIT Laboratory for Computer Science, December 1985.
24. [RFC1112] Deering, S., Host Extensions for IP Multicasting, STD 5, RFC 1112, Stanford University, August 1989.

25. [RFC1190] Topolcic, C., Ed., Experimental Internet Stream Protocol, Version 2 (ST-II), RFC 1190, CIP Working Group, October 1990.
26. [RFC1241] Woodburn, W. and D. Mills, A Scheme for an Internet Encapsulation Protocol: Version 1, RFC 1241, SAIC, University of Delaware, July 1991.
27. [RFC1583] Moy, J., The OSPF Specification, RFC 1583, Proteon, March 1994.
28. [RFC1735] Heinanen, J. and R. Govindan, NBMA Address Resolution Protocol (NARP), RFC 1735, Telecom Finland and USC/ISI, December 1994.
29. [RFC1826] Atkinson, R., IP Authentication Header, RFC 1826, Naval Research Laboratory, August 1995.
30. [RFC1827] Atkinson, R., IP Encapsulating Security Payload (ESP), RFC 1827, Naval Research Laboratory, August 1995.
31. [RFC1883] Deering, S. and R. Hinden, Internet Protocol, Version 6 (IPv6) Specification, RFC 1883, Xerox PARC, Ipsilon Networks, December 1995.
32. [RFC2003] Perkins, C., IP Encapsulation within IP, RFC 2003, IBM, September 1996.
33. [RFC2393] Shacham, A., R. Monsour, R. Pereira, and M. Thomas, IP Payload Compression Protocol (IPComp), RFC 2393, Cisco, Hi/fn, TimeStep, AltaVista Internet, December 1998.

Index